RICH THANKS TO RACISM

RICH THANKS TO RACISM

How the Ultra-Wealthy Profit
from Racial Injustice

Jim Freeman

ILR PRESS

AN IMPRINT OF CORNELL UNIVERSITY PRESS ITHACA AND LONDON

First published 2021 by Cornell University Press
Printed in the United States of America

Library of Congress Cataloging-in-Publication Data

Names: Freeman, Jim, 1976– author.
Title: Rich thanks to racism : how the ultra-wealthy profit from racial injustice / Jim Freeman.
Description: Ithaca, [New York] : ILR Press, an imprint of Cornell University Press, 2021. | Includes bibliographical references and index.
Identifiers: LCCN 2020033574 (print) | LCCN 2020033575 (ebook) | ISBN 9781501755132 (hardcover) | ISBN 9781501755156 (pdf) | ISBN 9781501755149 (epub)
Subjects: LCSH: Race discrimination—Economic aspects—United States. | Racism—Economic aspects—United States. | Minorities—United States—Economic conditions. | United States—Race relations—Economic aspects.
Classification: LCC E184.A1 F7347 2021 (print) | LCC E184.A1 (ebook) | DDC 330.9730089—dc23
LC record available at https://lccn.loc.gov/2020033574
LC ebook record available at https://lccn.loc.gov/2020033575

*To all those who are willing to fight
for a better and more just world*

Contents

Preface

In the summer of 2020, there were two significant developments in US race relations, the first of which was unprecedented and the second of which has been repeated countless times across our history.

First, following the killing of George Floyd on May 25th, for the first time ever in the United States, there was widespread public recognition of the existence of systemic racism. Proclaiming one's support for ending racial injustice became so trendy that seemingly every corporation and policy maker in the United States issued a public statement in support of the Black Lives Matter movement.

Second, by July, as has happened over and over again, our collective attention to systemic racism had quickly and substantially waned. The mainstream media had largely moved on from covering this issue. Most of those newly "woke" corporations were back to business as usual once the protests were over and the process of actually eliminating the racist policies and practices being protested had begun. And the vast majority of policy makers were doing what they nearly always do in the face of protest: figuring out the bare minimum amount of change needed to quell the uprising and get things back to "normal."

When faced with such widespread loyalty to a profoundly unjust status quo, it is unclear how much progress those who remain committed to racial justice will be able to make in the coming months and years. As of the time of this writing (August 2020), I am optimistic that the uprising being led by the communities most impacted by systemic racism will be able to create the waves of transformative change that are so obviously necessary and overdue. I am, however, also realistic about the need for many more people—of all races and ethnicities—to become active members and supporters of the racial justice movement before we will truly be able to eradicate systemic racism from US society.

This book is for all those who think they might want to become part of that effort. Make no mistake: in the coming years, we have a chance to institute the most significant social change in US history. Of all the things we could accomplish as a country, of all the milestones we could achieve, of all the injustices we could remedy, none would be more significant than dismantling the centuries-old systemic racism that continues to devastate and marginalize tens of millions of people of color across the United States. It is the foremost challenge of our lifetimes to not merely be content in saying "black lives matter," but to collectively step up and truly actualize those words. I sincerely hope that you will find a way to contribute whatever you can to this movement and that this book can be helpful to you along the way.

RICH THANKS TO RACISM

STRATEGIC RACISM

I can only hope that other people are not as resistant to the conclusions reached in this book as I would have been if I had read them ten years ago.

Back then, I wouldn't have wanted to believe them. The implications would have been too much for me to handle. While I certainly wish I could say that, as a longtime civil rights lawyer, I have always had a clear understanding of the causes of racial inequality, that would be a lie. I now know that, for much of my career, I didn't fully appreciate what people of color were up against. I was working alongside predominantly black and brown communities all across the United States, helping to fight the injustices they faced as best I could, but in truth I didn't really have a clear grasp of who and what we were fighting.[1] At the time, I thought that the biggest obstacle to justice was ignorance. That is what I believed to be our greatest enemy. It was only much later in my career that I realized that what we were really fighting against was much, much worse than that.

How do we explain our racial divide in the United States? Where does it come from? Why does it persist? For me, the answers to those questions used to be found in grainy news footage of Bull Connor turning his fire hoses and attack dogs against children in Birmingham, or of state troopers and civilians brutally beating marchers on "Bloody Sunday" in Selma. I could find more than enough explanation in the videos of the Arkansas National Guard being used to prevent the integration of Little Rock schools, and of Governor George Wallace of Alabama proudly proclaiming his support for "segregation now, segregation tomorrow, and segregation forever."[2] I thought that our lingering racial inequities could all be traced back to the most unenlightened aspects, and individuals, of my parents' and grandparents' generations, and that the ideology upholding these injustices would inevitably be phased into obsolescence by my more progressive-minded generation. In other words, our current inequities were, in my estimation, merely the toxic residue of a tragic yet distant era that would soon be swept into the dustbin of history. And I, for one, was eager to work that particular broom. In my mind, all that we had to do was point out the lingering injustice in our society, and surely the American public and policy makers would spring into action to achieve true racial equality. Surely the moral arc of the universe would, as Dr. King said, bend toward justice.[3]

Over time, though, I came to realize that justice wasn't quite so forthcoming, and that the moral arc wasn't bending in the ways I anticipated. However, this realization didn't come from losing the struggle for equality. It came from winning, or at least from what we typically think of as winning.

For many years, my work has been devoted to supporting grassroots movements to eliminate systemic racism and create positive social change. At the center of those efforts have been advocacy campaigns to advance the most critical priorities of communities of color, such as achieving education equity, ending mass incarceration, protecting immigrants' rights, dismantling the "school-to-prison pipeline," and creating a more inclusive and participatory democracy. The leaders of these campaigns have been youth and adults from some of the most politically and economically marginalized communities in the country. These are the neighborhoods that American society typically does its very best to ignore, such as the predominantly black and brown sections of Chicago, New York, Miami, Los Angeles, Denver, Philadelphia, Oakland, Jackson, New Orleans, Phoenix, Newark, and Baltimore, among many other places. Yet because of these community leaders' remarkable perseverance and fierce devotion to their people, they have won many, many significant and even groundbreaking victories. They have notched so many wins that one would naturally assume that the racial inequities they face would have substantially diminished or even disappeared by now. However, even after all these years, and staggering sacrifices by the individuals who led those efforts, it is difficult to make the case that those communities are better off than when we started.

That is not to say that those victories didn't represent significant steps forward, or that they haven't produced many undeniably positive effects. They did, and they have. It's just that for every two steps forward these communities have been able to make, there are other forces at work that are quick to push them two steps back, if not more.

At first you don't see it. All your attention is focused on winning the campaign in front of you. Initially you also think that doing so should be quite straightforward, as these efforts were all intended to address what should have been seen as clear-cut, no-brainer issues. All we were doing was pointing out obvious injustices that were deeply harmful to large segments of the population: the rampant overuse of out-of-school suspensions and expulsions in K–12 schools, far too many people being pushed into the criminal justice system, the inhumane treatment of immigrants by Immigration and Customs Enforcement (ICE), transparent attempts to limit people's voting rights, the decimation of the public school system, etc. In every instance, there were easy, vastly superior alternatives available to the government agency that was responsible for the injustice. Yet every fight was a slog. We met extreme resistance at every turn. And even when we won, the opposition never stopped fighting against racial equality.

We would strike down a discriminatory policy, but then another one that may have looked a little different but had the exact same effects would soon follow. We would successfully pass a policy that we had written ourselves—one that was designed to address an obvious injustice and institute a superior and more equitable set of practices—but it would never be fully implemented. Plus, while we were fighting on one set of issues, several other horrific policies would be passed around other sets of issues. It was as if we were in a big game of Racism Whack-a-Mole. For every injustice we thought we were solving, an equally nasty one would pop up to replace it. No matter how hard we fought, and how many victories we accumulated, we rarely felt like we were really moving the needle.

It was then that I began to detect some patterns to what I was seeing. While of course each individual campaign and community has had its own unique set of stakeholders and decision makers, I started to notice that the opposition we faced in each site was rather consistent. Regardless of which state or region of the country I was working in, the bad policies we were up against were usually being supported by the same set of advocacy organizations, think tanks, and media outlets. All across the country, when communities of color would attempt to address the most significant barriers they faced in their day-to-day lives, they would often run squarely into the same people, from the same organizations, pushing the same set of opposing policy ideas. Even if the opposition didn't have a physical presence in each location, they were quite effective in ensuring that their preferred policies got into the right hands to advance their agenda. Thus, over and over, I would encounter policy makers in various states who would all seem to have the exact same ideas for new policy initiatives at almost the exact same time. It was eerie. Legislators in Tallahassee, Florida, would suddenly come up with the same "innovative" reform proposal as the legislators in Denver, Colorado, and Springfield, Illinois. Local school districts and police departments in Maryland, Arizona, Mississippi, California, and New York would somehow all implement virtually identical policies at the same time. While these policy initiatives cut across a variety of issue areas, they would all have one thing in common, which is that they would all have a crushing effect on communities of color.

That's when I got curious. I started to research these policies and where they came from. I looked more deeply into the organizations that were supporting them. Then I began to research who was providing the funding for this network of organizations. I was shocked to discover that my research kept leading to the same small group of names. Most of the policies that were causing massive human suffering on a daily basis could all be traced back to a relatively small group of billionaires and multimillionaires.* In other words, every day the communities I was working with were fighting back against racial inequities—in many cases, they were fighting for their very lives—and at the same time a group of ultra-wealthy Corporate America and Wall Street executives was investing in organizations that were actively opposing those communities' efforts.† They were, in effect, *promoting* the perpetuation of racial injustice.

Not only were these organizations standing in the way of racial progress, they were typically doing so with exponentially more resources at their disposal than the communities of color they were opposing. That, I was startled to learn, was because of how heavily invested the ultra-wealthy were in these efforts. These weren't rich people donating their version of spare change to organizations they found appealing for one reason or another so that they could get a tax deduction. This was billions of dollars being pooled together and invested strategically around a particular agenda that was ravaging low-income communities of color. This was a massive investment that was propping up an entire industry of organizations peddling racial inequality at the national and even international levels. Yet because of how effectively these efforts had been hidden or at least disguised, virtually no one seemed to know what they were up to.

---

*Obviously not all wealthy individuals are using their money and influence in this way, and there are many who are responsible corporate citizens and humanitarians. However, as will be shown in the chapters that follow, there are many more billionaires and multimillionaires who are aggressively advancing this agenda than you might think. In fairness, it is also true that most of these individuals also allocate some of their wealth toward other, more noble, purposes, such as supporting the arts, museums, public health initiatives, etc. Unlike most of the investments described in this book, those donations typically receive a lot of publicity (much of which is sought out by the ultra-wealthy donors). I leave it to the reader to judge how best to weigh the benefits of such initiatives against the harms created by the largely under-the-radar efforts discussed in this book.

†Throughout this book, I use the term "ultra-wealthy" to refer to this group of billionaires and multimillionaires who have put their wealth and power to use in ways that are highly advantageous to their interests and deeply harmful to low-income, working-class, and middle-class people of all races and ethnicities, and particularly people of color.

The Intention behind the Devastation

At the time I stumbled upon these findings, it wasn't as if I was some wide-eyed novice. My entire career has been devoted to addressing systemic racism. I had learned long ago that while many of us think of racism primarily, or even exclusively, in terms of biased person-to-person encounters, the reality is that the overwhelming majority of harm from modern-day racism comes not from individual bigots, but from the policies and systems that shape our lives. This form of racism isn't as obviously repugnant as calling someone the n-word, but it can be just as damaging, if not more so, while affecting far more people—tens of millions of people, in fact, just in the United States.

For example, youth of color are routinely undereducated in the United States compared to their white peers. Every year, the racial inequities reflected in the "achievement gap," high school graduation rates, college attendance rates, and countless other indicators make that apparent, and every year the grim consequences they produce are felt deeply and painfully in countless families across the country. Yet no more than a tiny fraction of those inequities can be attributed to any explicit racial biases held by individual adults within the education system. The much larger problem is how, collectively, we have simply failed to create a level playing field for youth of color.

Similarly, the enormous racial disparities within our criminal justice system are far more attributable to a series of major policy decisions than they are to the actions of any prejudiced police officers, prosecutors, or judges. Thus, even if we could somehow purge the criminal justice system of whatever "bad apples" there might be, our existing mass incarceration system would still reliably produce profoundly harmful and racially inequitable outcomes.

In other words, we know for a fact that entire communities of people will be severely harmed by these and other systems every year—that these inequitable outcomes will inevitably occur based on how these systems have been set up—and yet we demonstrate no collective urgency to fix them. That, in a nutshell, is the most pervasive form of modern-day racism. We have simply become far too willing to implement public policies that inflict needless harm on large groups of people of color, and far too unwilling to address that harm appropriately when it becomes apparent.

After dedicating twenty years of my life to these dynamics, I thought I was fairly well-versed in how they worked. I thought I knew how cruel the United States could be at times to its people, and particularly to people of color. What I didn't know was that there were higher forms of cruelty than the ones I assumed I had been fighting.

Because I had been under the impression that the driving force of systemic racism was ignorance, I believed that all but the most hateful of individuals could be persuaded to address deeply rooted racial inequities. I was clinging to the idea that my opponents were people who, because of a lack of knowledge about the conditions within communities of color, simply had a different viewpoint about how to address equity concerns. However, as I researched how the ultra-wealthy were using their resources to defend and advance racial injustice, I realized that the problem wasn't that they were unaware of the devastating harm being caused by systemic racism. The problem was that, for the ultra-wealthy, the harm being caused by systemic racism wasn't a bug; it was a feature.

As will be described in chapter 1 and throughout this book, I began to learn how powerful a tool racial injustice has been for the ultra-wealthy in advancing their economic and political interests. I discovered that while such sordid realities are rarely mentioned in our public discourse, it was nevertheless true that there was a lot of money being made off of this type of large-scale cruelty. Indeed, for anyone who has ever wondered why deep racial inequities persist more than fifty years after the civil rights movement, the biggest reason is as simple as it disturbing: systemic racism is, for a small number of people, enormously profitable.

I also realized that this horrific form of modern-day racism wasn't adequately captured by the term "systemic racism." That descriptor is too impersonal and abstract to fully convey what the ultra-wealthy were up to. It suggests that persistent racial inequities are merely the accidental byproducts of our economic and political systems. In reality, what the ultra-wealthy have been doing was worse than that, because behind all of the billions of dollars in investments they were making in opposition to communities of color, there was intentionality. There was strategy.

My eyes were opened to the fact that many of the policies that plague communities of color aren't doing so incidentally; they are doing so purposefully. And the devastation I was witnessing being caused to families across the country wasn't the side effect or unintended consequence of some well-meaning set of policies; it was the direct result of their communities being sabotaged. Once I recognized that, it became clear that this particular brand of injustice—what the ultra-wealthy had been doing for decades, and were still doing today—went far beyond what I had understood to be systemic racism. This was different. This was *strategic racism.*

Thus, I finally realized the truth—one that is intuitively obvious to most people of color but took me an embarrassingly long time to recognize. My generation hadn't merely inherited a race relations mess that we were responsible for cleaning up. We had inherited a living, breathing monster that had never stopped promoting racial injustice; it had simply changed its tactics. In short, my long-held beliefs about racism were dead wrong. Our current racial divide wasn't the residual effect of a backward era in American history; it was part of an unending tradition as American as apple pie.

In other words, I finally came to see that the moral arc of our universe wouldn't naturally be bending toward anything resembling justice. On the contrary, it was being forcibly bent toward injustice.

I must admit that I initially didn't want to believe any of this. It was so deeply unsettling that I found a dozen different ways to rationalize what I was seeing, to explain why it was that these individuals were using their extraordinary wealth this way. I think I just wanted to give them the benefit of the doubt. I tried to convince myself that they, like many of us, were simply misguided on these matters, only their errors were magnified because of the number of zeroes that they could comfortably write on a donation check.

Additionally, while it is easy for most of us to condemn people who say or do blatantly racist things, it is much harder to get one's mind around the dynamics of strategic racism and the notion that some people have powerful economic incentives to support those dynamics. I know it was for me. But as will be shown in the following chapters, the impact of those incentives, and the damage that has resulted from them, are undeniable. (Note that saying that these individuals contribute to, and profit from, racism isn't to say that they are, as individuals, racists. They very well may be, as former President Trump has said of himself, the "least racist" people in America.[4] Or they may not be. What is clear is that they have chosen to capitalize upon the dynamics of systemic racism in ways that have been profoundly beneficial for themselves.)

Dear White People

The purpose of this book is to shed some light on strategic racism and identify who is doing it, and why. These are essential questions for everyone who is committed to eliminating America's racial divide because it is impossible to win a fight when you don't know who and what it is that you are fighting.

This book is particularly directed at my fellow white Americans.[5] As a whole, what I have observed over the years is that we have developed an elaborate system of defense mechanisms and avoidance strategies around issues of race. We have become remarkably skilled at being able to avoid confronting the stark inequities that surround us. As a result, we, as a whole, continue to demonstrate a shocking lack of awareness about the realities of racial inequality in this country. In the chapters ahead, I attempt to unpack why and how so many white

Americans—myself included—accumulate such deep wells of ignorance on these issues. In other words, why do we have such a hard time diagnosing and fixing these glaring problems? And within those racial blind spots, how have the ultra-wealthy been able to successfully convince so many of us that to fix our education system we have to destroy it (chapter 2), to maintain our freedom we must incarcerate more people than any other country in the world (chapter 3), and to remain the "land of opportunity" we need to oppress the immigrants that come to it (chapter 4)? (Spoiler alert: the same people who invest so heavily in racial injustice are also committed to our being uninformed and/or misinformed on these issues.)

Additionally, this book is intended to demonstrate that while the problems we face are severe, they are also eminently fixable, particularly if more people recognize that the injustice being engineered by this group of billionaires and multimillionaires hasn't been limited to people of color. Their portfolio is far more diversified than that. Never was this more apparent to me than when I was investigating how they were contributing to the preservation of racial injustice. As I learned more about where they direct their money and the ideology that guides those decisions, I realized how heavily invested the ultra-wealthy are in pushing a political agenda that has been deeply harmful to most white Americans as well.

Thus, the living, breathing monster responsible for racial injustice actually has two heads: one focused on people of color, the other with its gaze fixed on the vast majority of white people. In other words, if white people examine the reasons their lives are far more difficult than they need to be, they will likely eventually run into the same set of organizations and individuals who are leading the opposition against racial equality. I, for one, was astonished to discover just how enormous an influence the ultra-wealthy have on my life and that of every white person I know. This book is intended to demonstrate why that is so, and how broader recognition of the fact that the struggles of people of color are deeply interconnected with those of white people would open up entirely new possibilities for creating an America that works for all its residents.

That is ultimately what we all want, isn't it? Regardless of our race or ethnicity, we all just want to live in a country that supports us in living good, happy, fulfilling lives. Yet while there may not be much that unites Americans of diverse backgrounds and political ideologies, we can all see quite clearly that America falls short in this regard. We all recognize that our country could simply be better than it is. It could be stronger. It could be *more*. And as will be shown in the pages to come, the key to unlocking America's full potential is for more people of all races and ethnicities to stand up for racial justice. That is how we build a stronger democracy. That is how we build a brighter future and make America a more truly free country. And that is how we move beyond our ugly legacy of racial injustice and find reconciliation and redemption.

This path *is* available to us. While actually walking it may not be easy, it almost certainly won't be as difficult as continuing to walk the path we are on now. And though there are many steps that we will need to take together to find our way along this unfamiliar route, none may be more important than this: we need many more people to listen far more closely to what people of color are telling us about the America that they have come to know.

THE RACISM PROFITEERS

Anna Jones wasn't sure what to expect. When the Chicago Public Schools closed fifty schools in 2013, she was certainly concerned about the effects of displacing so many children and families. She was particularly worried because so many of the school closures were concentrated in black and brown neighborhoods that had long been neglected by the city's power structure and were thus struggling with issues of poverty and violence. But she also believed Mayor Rahm Emanuel when he said that the closures were necessary because those schools were "under-utilized."[1] She was willing to accept him at his word that the result would be better educational experiences for the tens of thousands of students who would be affected, including her four young children. So, the following fall, she entered the new school year with an open mind.

Her attitude shifted immediately once she saw the actual impact of the closures on her children's schools. When she dropped her daughter off for her first day of kindergarten and saw that her class had fifty-four students and just one teacher, she cried. Then she saw how her children's teachers didn't even have enough books and paper to go around for every child. The elementary school was so overcrowded that her son's pre-K class had to eat lunch on the floor of the school gym. To make matters worse, her already severely underresourced local schools had faced multiple rounds of budget cuts in recent years, forcing them to eliminate staff, valuable student programs, extracurricular activities, and por-tions of the curriculum, such as art, music, and world language classes. Those effects, combined with the impact of the closures, meant that in many schools there simply weren't nearly enough educators, support staff, and educational resources to create a healthy learning environment and meet the diversity of children's needs. "What I saw was nothing short of a catastrophe," she says.

As a result, day after day, month after month, Anna was tormented by the knowledge that her children were not receiving the education they needed. She didn't blame their teachers. Anna knew them well, and she recognized that they were quality educators who loved the kids that they taught. She also knew that those teachers' skill and devotion were not enough to overcome the horrendous conditions under which they were forced to work. Anna tried her best to help out and even volunteered extensively at her children's schools, but still it wasn't enough. It was painfully obvious to her that her children, along with countless others in their schools, were being failed by their policy makers. She was also acutely aware of how inequitable the education system had been and continued to be, and how her kids' chances at a good life were diminishing by the day because of it. "They don't have to deal with this in privileged neighborhoods where white folks are," she says. "They just don't. And I'm happy for those children. They should be educated—*properly*. Those families should have access to everything they need to meet the needs of their children. But so should we on the South Side of Chicago."

The last straw for Anna came when the Chicago Public Schools announced that they would be closing Walter H. Dyett School in 2015. Dyett was a treasured community institution and the last traditional, open-enrollment high school in the area. Anna had desperately wanted her children to attend Dyett, so when the closure was announced, she was heartbroken. "My kids had already lost so much," she says, "I couldn't stand to see them lose this as well." So she decided to join together with the many other concerned parents and community members to try to persuade the mayor and the school system to reconsider.

Their large community coalition attempted to arrange meetings with the mayor and the CEO of the Chicago Public Schools, but they were ignored. They tried writing letters, but got no results. They engaged in multiple protests—still nothing. They even worked with education policy experts to create their own research-based plan for improving Dyett. For months, they did everything they could think of to show their public officials how beloved Dyett was and how important it was to the community, but were repeatedly brushed aside. "No one listened to us," Anna says. "When we saw how the mayor and other political people disrespected our community, we knew we had to take drastic action."[2]

That action came in the form of a hunger strike. Anna and eleven other community members decided that they wouldn't eat until Mayor Emanuel agreed to keep Dyett open and adopt the community's school improvement plan. For thirty-four days, Anna and others went without food. Many of the hunger strikers suffered serious health complications and lost dangerous amounts of weight.

Several became so ill that they were forced to drop out. Anna herself had to be hospitalized at one point, but she insisted on continuing. Meanwhile, the mayor was hosting ribbon cuttings on shiny new charter schools in more affluent neighborhoods across town. The protest only ended because the remaining hunger strikers realized, Anna says, that "the mayor would leave us out there to die."

Why would someone endanger themselves by taking such an extreme measure as going without food for over a month? Because, Anna says, "seeing my children being starved of education was killing me more than not eating would."

All of us face obstacles and threats to our well-being at some points during our lives. Fortunately, for most of us the obstacles are usually rather small, the threats are minimal, and we don't have to face either very often.

However, many US residents aren't so lucky. For these individuals, every day can feel like walking through a minefield where one small misstep could end your life as you know it.

Carlil Pittman's minefield starts bright and early in the morning. Every day, when he gets in his car to drive to work or to take his kids to school, he does so with the understanding that there is a high likelihood he will be pulled over by the police. (He typically gets pulled over several times a week, and sometimes it's several times a day.) When he is at home, a patrol car drives down his street and past his house at least every hour, and sometimes every fifteen minutes. Even when he was in high school, it seemed that there was always a school resource officer (SRO) nearby, patrolling the hallways. Carlil is twenty-six years old, and while he doesn't have a criminal record, he has never known a world in which the police weren't a nearly constant presence in his life.

He has been stopped, questioned, searched, and asked if he is a gang member more times than he can count. Sometimes these incidents have been deeply humiliating, such as when an SRO pulled Carlil's pants down to his ankles in the middle of a crowded school hallway during a search. Other times they have been frightening, such as the numerous times that officers have drawn their guns on him during routine traffic stops, or when he has been pulled over and officers have been aggressive with him while his kids were in the car. "People try to say this is about 'public safety,'" he says. "But my question is, are they really trying to keep me safe, or do they think they're keeping other people safe *from* me? Because having cops around all the time doesn't make me feel safe. It makes me feel like a target."

"Tough on crime" has been a popular slogan for many politicians over the years, but Carlil has observed up close what that actually looks like in practice. He has seen the pain that it has caused. He has watched as far too many families have been torn apart by it, including his own. He has witnessed many times over how easily the overwhelming and hyperaggressive police presence in his community has led to the needless incarceration of his loved ones and neighbors. Even as a teenager, he repeatedly saw how, in his heavily policed high school, what would normally be considered minor school disciplinary issues led to his friends and peers being put in handcuffs, arrested, and taken to jail. He tries not to blame the individual officers who are policing him, because he knows that they are, for the most part, just doing the job that they have been told to do. Nevertheless, he has seen enough over the years to know that he has to treat all officers as a threat. "They don't live in our community, and they don't understand our community, but they're very quick to come in and label the people of our community as criminals, or criminals-to-be," he says.

What really bothers Carlil, though, is the lack of investment in his community for anything other than the police and the criminal justice system. Because while there has been an enormous dedication of resources to ensure that individuals who are empowered to arrest and shoot him are never far away, there seems to be no such urgency to address the severe employment, health, housing, and education needs of people in his community. "They don't invest in the schools or in making sure that people have good-paying jobs and health care," he says, "so of course there are lots of people who struggle to feed their families, who have mental health issues, and who have drug and alcohol issues. But instead of providing social workers or counselors or other people who can give them the help they need, here they send in the cops. And those people wind up behind bars, or worse."

Carlil knows that nobody in his community is immune from that particular fate, including himself. He also cannot escape the realization that the world has been, for most of his life, openly hostile to his very existence: "It often seems like society has been patiently waiting for me to make a mistake and give it a reason to get rid of me just like it's gotten rid of so many other members of my family and community."

Imagine what it would be like to leave your house every morning without knowing whether you would ever be able to see your family again. You would say goodbye to your parents, siblings, children, or other loved ones, and you wouldn't know if you were doing so for the last time. You wouldn't know whether they would be there when you returned at the end of the day, or if you would even be able to make it home to see them again.

For most people, that sounds like it could be the plot of a horror movie. For Mónica Acosta, it has been her daily life for decades.

Mónica was born in Mexico and moved to Colorado with her family when she was three. She is now thirty-four years old, and for most of her life, she has lived with the constant, paralyzing fear that she, her family members, and her friends would be deported; that one day she would be snatched up by ICE and sent to a place entirely foreign to her, or that suddenly her family and friends would be gone. Disappeared. "I'm always worried about my safety and that of my loved ones," she says. "It never stops. So even if I call someone and they don't answer, I immediately assume the worst." Her concern hasn't been unwarranted, either. She has had many of her loved ones taken from her life by the immigration system, including her mother when Mónica was just a teenager. It was ten years before they would be able to see each other again. Because her mom was pregnant at the time, Mónica didn't even get to meet her youngest sister in person until she was ten years old.

All throughout her life, Mónica has been reluctant to leave the house for anything other than school or work out of fear that she wouldn't make it home. While she has lived in the United States for over thirty years, was a stellar student, and has been an exemplary employee and community member as an adult, she has to take anxiety medication every day because her living situation—indeed her very existence—has always been so precarious. She has almost always had to hide aspects of herself, to be extra careful every minute of every day, to make sure that she never lets her guard down. "I've never really felt like I could trust anyone," she says. "There's a level of paranoia that becomes a part of you. And along with it there's so much day-to-day stress, anxiety, depression, and illness. Hiding yourself like that—it literally makes you sick, both mentally and physically."

Even now, after being able to acquire temporary legal status as a "Dreamer" through the federal Deferred Action for Childhood Arrivals program (DACA), she is afraid to put down too many roots. "How can I do the things my friends are doing, like buying a house and having children," she wonders, "when there would be a chance that I could be forced to leave? A chance that I could be separated from my child, like my mother was from me?"

The experiences of Anna, Carlil, and Mónica are certainly not unique to them. On the contrary, there are millions of people who have to endure the same type of daily burdens that they do. Millions of people who cannot escape these constant, unwelcome reminders of their inferior status within US society. An unavoidable side effect of that is a type of persistent emotional and psychological torture that comes from the knowledge that their lives, or the lives of their children, are not valued as much as others. They have to live with the fact that all available indications have made it abundantly clear that our society simply doesn't care as much about their well-being as it does about other people. They have to somehow stomach the undeniable reality that it is far more acceptable to inflict harm on them than it is to do so on others.

Even worse is that this devaluation of their lives comes not from the actions of private citizens, but rather from our government institutions. It is government action (or inaction) that has them living in fear that their children won't be able to escape the burdens of inequality; that has them terrified that they might wind up as the next George Floyd or be added to what is already the largest incarcerated population in the world; that has them uncertain of whether they will even be able to wake up in their home tomorrow and see their loved ones again. There are many types of injustices that our government has inflicted, and continues to inflict, on people of all races and ethnicities. However, this particular brand of injustice is very nearly the worst sort of horror that can be inflicted on a person by their home government. And not to minimize the inequities faced by other marginalized people, but in the United States, our most atrocious treatment is almost exclusively reserved for the residents of black and brown communities.*

The best way to learn about how these dynamics affect communities of color across the United States is to, of course, hear directly from those who live in those communities. Thus, I must confess that I was quite reluctant to even write this book. I have dedicated my entire career to supporting the leadership of the people most affected by systemic racism, to creating spaces in which they can tell their own stories and then assisting them as they work through the democratic process to have those stories heard and responded to appropriately. So the last thing I would want is to undercut their leadership by offering *my* version of *their* experiences.

However, what I have also learned over the years is that, as a society, we systematically ignore the lived experiences of people of color to a shocking degree. That is especially true for people of color from low-income and working-class communities. There are just very few platforms for the residents of these communities to share their perspectives. (Consider this: When was the last time you saw a news story on a prominent TV network or an article in a mainstream publication that included more than a short sound bite or quote from a person directly affected by systemic racial injustice? It almost never happens. These are horrific, ongoing crises, and yet the people suffering their effects are virtually invisible in the public conversation about them.) So this book is intended to be one such— albeit limited—platform to share a set of perspectives that too often go ignored. The goal isn't for readers of this book to adopt my views on racial justice, but

---

*To be clear, many of the dynamics faced by other communities of color, people of color living in predominantly white communities, low-income and working-class white people, women of all races, LGBTQIA+ individuals, persons with disabilities, and other marginalized communities are similar or even identical in some cases. The intent here isn't to minimize those experiences, but rather to focus on a particularly egregious form of injustice to hopefully raise awareness of the need to address all such inequities in a comprehensive and intersectional way.

rather to persuade more people to listen to what people of color are saying about the challenges they face and how they should be addressed. Indeed, that is how I have learned virtually every worthwhile thing I know about these subjects.

Of course, it is also true that I bring my own perspective on the American racial divide. That comes from having had an uncommon set of opportunities to see what both sides of that divide look like up close. In fact, while the first half of my life was spent growing up on one side of it, the second half has been devoted to working closely with communities that are firmly on the other side of it. Through those experiences, I have seen both the best and the worst that America has to offer its people. In fact, the gap between those experiences is so large that it would probably be more accurate to describe what I have observed as two entirely distinct Americas.

In the first America that I came to know, I lived in predominantly white, midwestern communities, attended predominantly white schools and churches, and worked alongside predominantly white coworkers. During this period, I had what could fairly be described as a typical white middle-class American experience. It was spent mostly in suburbs, on university campuses, and in sections of cities that were populated with mostly college-educated white professionals. If you could imagine a composite of the environments depicted by *The Wonder Years*, *Saved by the Bell*, *The Breakfast Club*, *Animal House*, *Friends*, and *Legally Blonde*, you wouldn't be too far off.

The other America with which I have become familiar consists of a broad group of primarily low-income and working-class African American and Latinx communities across the country. I certainly wouldn't suggest that the experiences of their residents are representative of all people of color in the United States. Many families—of all socioeconomic levels—have undoubtedly lived very different lives. I also cannot claim to understand anywhere near the full depth of the injustices these communities face; nor do I purport to be a spokesperson for them. However, I have spent most of the past twenty years learning as much as I could about those communities from their residents while being immersed in the policies that shape them.

At the risk of overgeneralizing, I have observed that the residents of these communities of color share a set of common experiences, some of which are similar to what I experienced in the predominantly white communities I grew up in, and some of which are remarkably different.

Let's start with the similarities between those two Americas. The one that stands out the most is this: each was filled with people who, on a daily basis, would make significant, and frequently heroic, sacrifices to ensure the health, safety, and well-being of their family and their community. The numerous people I met like that during the first half of my life were responsible for putting me on the path that led to the second half of my life. And the multitudes of people I have met like that during the second half of my life are my constant source of inspiration.

Now for the differences. The most significant is this: across those two Americas, residents' lived experiences with their government have been so divergent that it can be difficult to fathom how we have been able to claim that they are both part of the same society.

For example, in the white communities that I was a part of, it was largely taken for granted that residents would have access to quality public schools, health care, housing, parks, and community centers. In the communities of color, however, residents are continually told—usually by white policy makers—that there are insufficient resources for such things. Nevertheless, policy makers always seem to be able to locate enough resources to fund additional police, jails, prisons, prosecutors, and ICE officers in these communities.

In those white communities, law enforcement had virtually no presence in people's day-to-day lives beyond routine traffic stops, despite the fact that many of the people I knew as a teenager regularly engaged in what is considered elsewhere to be criminal behavior. When our lawlessness was so extreme that the police did feel compelled to intervene, we usually encountered a genial "Officer Friendly" type. These officers treated us as if they were our mentors, and typically the most severe consequences any of us received from them were a stern look and a verbal warning. When I describe this to residents of communities of color— particularly those under the age of thirty-five—they think I am making it up.

Where I grew up, we were repeatedly told that we could achieve whatever we wanted, and the opportunities and assistance available to us made us believe that to be true. It was obvious to us that the society around us had prioritized our healthy development. In the communities of color, however, the pervasive lack of resources and developmental support provides many young people with daily reminders that the society they live in isn't invested in their success. It is heartbreaking to see how clearly young people perceive and internalize that they are not being properly cared for, and it is tragic how many of them become alienated from their families, schools, and other community institutions as a result.

In the white communities, it was taken for granted that virtually everyone who wanted to work would have access to a good job. In the black and brown communities that I have become familiar with, such quality, living-wage jobs are frequently rare to virtually nonexistent. The jobs that are available often barely pay well enough to survive on, and sometimes they don't even reach that level. People who work so extraordinarily hard—often at multiple jobs—that they are left with little to no time with their children and other loved ones are nevertheless often just one slip-up, just one illness, just one missed paycheck from calamity for their families.

When I was young, we never had to worry that we were being poisoned by our drinking water or that our schools and homes were located on land that was unsafe for our health. In the communities of color, residents have no such luxury, and are typically the ones harmed first and most severely by environmental degradation.

In the communities I grew up in, when white people made mistakes, typically they were simply not allowed to fall through society's cracks. Missteps were met with compassion, soft landings, and as many "second chances" as were needed. (If not for this feature, the many poor choices made by this particular author during his youth could have produced some *very* different life outcomes.) Within black and brown communities, however, people who make mistakes—even small children—often find that their government institutions have "zero tolerance" for them, and they are punished severely and oftentimes discarded accordingly.

In the white communities, residents were typically encouraged to participate in civic life, and when a problem arose with regard to some government function, residents were usually able to hold their policy makers accountable and address it through their democratic institutions. In the communities of color, residents are almost never allowed to play any sort of meaningful role in shaping the policies that affect them. Instead, people who are usually largely unfamiliar with those communities are nevertheless allowed to impose their own views on what is best for the residents, and then when the inevitable problems arise, they typically ignore community input and pushback.

None of this is to suggest that there aren't plenty of people who have struggled in those white communities for a variety of reasons, and plenty of others who have been able to flourish in the communities of color. Of course there have. But it is undeniable that government action and inaction have forced the residents of those black and brown communities to live exponentially more difficult lives than the residents of those white communities I grew up in years ago. Simply put, within those white communities, it was made far easier for us to succeed in reaching our goals, and far more difficult for us to fail. In contrast, within the communities of color, it often takes nearly superhuman efforts by families to get ahead.

What is even worse is how hard communities of color have had to fight just to attain such obviously inequitable opportunities. It typically requires massive, long-term collective efforts merely to achieve the subpar conditions described earlier. Community leaders have to be constantly vigilant and beat back an endless series of public policies that threaten the well-being of their people. They have to assume this immense responsibility just to give the residents of their communities a chance at a better life. In many cases, they have to do so just to raise the odds that their people can avoid being killed by the same dynamics that have taken so many other lives around them. Meanwhile, there is no such imperative within white communities. I have lived in many, all across the country, and while each faced challenges, at no time did those communities have to fight for their basic survival. That particular distinction may just represent the most fundamental form of white privilege that there is.

Who Benefits?

How can it be that we have allowed so many of our people to suffer needlessly? After all these years, how can we still have such profoundly inequitable schools? How can we still have a mass criminalization and incarceration system that has devastated communities across the country? Why are we still forcing millions of immigrants to live in perpetual fear of deportation? How do we have a health care system that doesn't address all people's needs? Why do we allow people to be paid poverty wages? Why haven't we taken decisive action to protect our environment? How can we allow so many of our people to be effectively shut out of our democracy? These are obvious, catastrophic, and long-standing policy failures affecting huge portions of the US population, and particularly communities of color, so why haven't we been able to address them? It isn't because we aren't capable of fixing them—we absolutely are. And it isn't because there are good and valid justifications for them. On the contrary, each one of them is morally indefensible. There is no "other side of the story" that justifies the immense harm they cause. There is no pros-and-cons list that you can make where the value of the pros come close to reaching the severity of the cons. So why have these problems persisted and even grown over time?

In short, it is because they have supporters. In particular, they have extraordinarily wealthy and powerful supporters who benefit from these problems *not* being fixed.

By this point, most Americans are aware of the shocking, and rapidly expanding, wealth inequality in our country. To give just one example, the four hundred richest American individuals now have far more wealth than the combined total of *all sixteen million black households* in the United States.[3] Most people also have some sense of how that concentration of wealth translates into an outsize influence for certain wealthy Corporate America and Wall Street executives in shaping policy. What most do not fully grasp is how much economic and political gain these individuals have realized as a result of racial injustice. For these racism profiteers, the enduring racial divide creates both lucrative moneymaking opportunities and the social, economic, and political inequality that fuels their extreme wealth and power. In other words, the unjust education, criminal justice, and immigration policies that have been so thoroughly devastating for millions of individuals like Anna Jones, Carlil Pittman, and Mónica Acosta are, for the ultra-wealthy, desirable.

The following chapters describe how, and why, ultra-wealthy leaders from Corporate America and Wall Street are the driving force behind many of the public policies that uphold systemic racism and cause severe harm to communities of color across the country. For example, you will learn how the Koch family, Bill Gates, the Walton family, Mark Zuckerberg, and a handful of others have spent billions of dollars in aligned efforts that are dismantling the public school system and directly causing the suffering of Anna Jones and countless others. You will come to understand how the nation's mass criminalization and incarceration system, which forces Carlil Pittman and many more people like him to navigate a gauntlet of police officers and other law enforcement officials every single day, can be traced back to the leaders of many of the largest and best-known corporations in the United States, Wall Street banks, private prison companies, and the Kochs' network of ultra-wealthy allies. You will also discover how many of the same individuals and organizations have played a significant role in the creation of the extreme anti-immigrant policies that have plagued Mónica Acosta and millions of other migrants for decades.

If there is one thread that ties all these dynamics together, it has been the American Legislative Exchange Council (ALEC). ALEC is the primary vehicle through which the ultra-wealthy have organized themselves politically. It has a reported three hundred–plus corporate members and two thousand legislative members who work together—usually secretively—on legislation that advances those corporations' common agenda.[4] ALEC is incredibly prolific; over one thousand of its "model bills" are introduced every year in state legislatures across the country, with one in five of them being passed into law.[5] While that legislation covers a broad range of issues, a large percentage of it has been directed at protecting, expanding, and benefiting from systemic racism. In other words, perhaps the most powerful force advancing strategic racism in the United States is an organization whose current and recent members represent a "Who's Who" of US corporations, including Walmart, Google, Home Depot, AT&T, General Electric, Coca-Cola, Ford, ExxonMobil, Johnson & Johnson, Kraft Foods, Verizon, Pfizer, Chevron, Bank of America, Microsoft, Visa, Coors, General Motors, American Express, Koch Industries, Facebook, UPS, Eli Lilly, Time Warner Cable, Comcast News Corporation, Dell, Amway, IBM, FedEx, Anheuser-Busch, Dow Chemical, McDonald's, State Farm, Northrop Grumman, Procter & Gamble, and Wells Fargo, along with hundreds of others.[6]

As ALEC's activities have been brought to light in recent years, some of these corporations and the high-profile individuals who run them have tried to disassociate themselves from the harm being caused by their political activity and affiliations.[7] However, that hasn't meant that they have stopped promoting systemic racism; they have simply changed their tactics. Overall, most ultra-wealthy racism profiteers have made it clear that they have no interest in ever truly changing course. Strategic racism is far too valuable to them for that. On the contrary, they are escalating their efforts. As just one example, chapter 5 describes how ALEC and others are leading efforts to rewrite the US Constitution so that it is more aligned with their agenda.

Looking in the Mirror

It must be said that while the ultra-wealthy are the primary beneficiaries of racial injustice, they are not the only ones. It may be uncomfortable for many to think about, but if we examine our collection of public policies carefully and honestly, we soon learn that many, many millions of other working-class, middle-class, and wealthy white Americans have reaped, and continue to reap, significant benefits from the injustice heaped upon people of color. Some of the most obvious examples include the major role that slavery, the seizure or annexation of tribal and Mexican land, and Jim Crow–era legalized segregation have all played in establishing the foundation of inequities that continue to persist today.[8] However, it would be a grave mistake to limit our thinking to those examples that occurred before many of us were even born.

For example, most American adults attended public schools that were funded in significant part by local property tax revenues. Such systems frequently result in profoundly inequitable funding structures, the impact of which has been particularly devastating for communities of color.[9] That injustice has received considerable attention over the years. What is almost never discussed is the flip side of that issue: how children from other communities benefit from that inequity. For example, let's assume a white student in a relatively affluent community has an additional $3,000 in taxpayer dollars dedicated to her education every year, compared to a student of color in a nearby community.[10] In a classroom of thirty students, that amounts to an additional annual investment of $90,000 that could be used to hire a teacher's aide, buy classroom computers, and otherwise enrich the educational experiences of those children. Now let's say there are five thousand students in each of these two districts. The more affluent district would receive an additional $15 million per year. Over the course of that one white child's K–12 journey, that would mean an additional $195 million in taxpayer dollars was invested in her education system, compared to the neighboring system with the student of color.

Similarly, most American adults have, at some point, worked within a company that pays some of its employees poverty or near-poverty wages, and among those workers there was likely a heavy concentration of people of color.[11] If at any point you were receiving higher wages than they were, then it must be acknowledged that the failure to pay adequate wages to your coworkers probably resulted in an increase to your own income.

Along the same lines, if you, like almost everyone, pay for goods and services that are priced more cheaply because some of the employees of the companies providing them aren't paid a living wage, then you are receiving a sizable economic benefit while the low-wage workforce that is disproportionately black and brown struggles to survive.

If you own a home in a predominantly white community, it is likely that its value is higher as a result of a combination of policies, practices, and racial biases that depress home values in communities of color. For example, very similar or even identical homes in two adjacent communities can be separated in economic value by tens of thousands or even hundreds of thousands of dollars as a result of these dynamics.

When social services are underfunded in communities of color and the tax bills of white communities' residents are lower as a result, if you reside in one of those white communities, it is likely that you profited from harm being done to others.

We could go on and on about the myriad ways in which white people have been able to utilize their political, economic, and social power to advance their interests at the expense of people of color. Moreover, there is much to be said about the profound advantages associated with not having to face the various slights, indignities, and outright discrimination that many people of color regularly encounter. But even if we put those things aside and just focus on the few factors mentioned here, the fact is that by the time most white people reach middle age, they have accumulated hundreds of thousands of dollars in benefits as a result of this type of systemic racism. When those benefits accrue across generations, even middle-class individuals can essentially inherit millions of dollars in educational and economic benefits from racial injustice. Again, this isn't to say that every white person has benefited from all of these factors, or that there aren't also people of color who benefit from these dynamics. The point is that for a great many white people in particular, even those of us who may not feel like we were born with a silver spoon in our mouths often benefit from an enormous, but sometimes difficult-to-perceive, head start in life. And even the poorest and most marginalized white people in the United States still benefit from privileges they are afforded that similarly situated people of color are not.

Complicity

The uncomfortable truth is that white Americans—yes, all white Americans—have allowed ourselves to become accomplices to racial injustice on a massive scale. Whether we choose to admit it or not, we all share responsibility for allowing systemic racism to persist and grow deeper and deeper roots over time. We all have to own up to the fact that our collective response to these long-standing, widespread inequities has most often been to exhibit apathy or neglect. We have simply failed to see what was going on under our noses, and when we did see it, we have collectively failed to do enough to stop it. That is an absolute tragedy, and we shouldn't sugarcoat it.

Of course, our contributions to racial injustice go beyond our general myopia and passivity. For systemic racism to survive, it needs people to actively defend and promote it. The ultra-wealthy have certainly taken on much of that responsibility, but they cannot preserve the system alone. They need foot soldiers. They need legislators who will support their preferred policies. They need voters to elect those legislators. They need people to help shape a public dialogue that advances their priorities. They need the public to resist social change efforts. Without these troops on the ground, the ultra-wealthy would be grossly outnumbered, and the entire system of racial injustice would fall apart.

Thus far, however, there has been no shortage of recruits, the vast majority of whom have been white. So who are these people? You might know someone who you think belongs to this ignominious group. Maybe it's a racist uncle or neighbor. Or maybe you don't have anyone in particular in mind and you just think of this group as a collection of nameless, faceless bigots. Maybe you pin it on those who call themselves the "alt right" (as if they were these cool, alternative thinkers—the Kurt Cobains of conservative politics—rather than just being a sewing circle for pathetic racists). Or perhaps you primarily think of them, as I once did, as out-of-touch dinosaurs.

The one thing that all of these definitions share in common is that they imagine the defenders of systemic racism as societal outliers. We all have this tendency to try and put some psychological distance between ourselves and those we believe to be culpable. We tell ourselves, "*They* are the racist ones, not *us*." What we fail to see is that systemic racism is like the most contagious of diseases; if you are anywhere in the vicinity of it, you are going to get infected.

Indeed, the sad reality is that almost all of us have spent time as foot soldiers for the ultra-wealthy. Almost all of us have supported elected officials who defended or advanced the policies underlying systemic racism. (This isn't an exclusive club. It includes perhaps every US president, most members of Congress and state legislatures, and nearly all locally elected officials.) Almost all of us have expressed support, at one time or another, for the ideology at the root of racial injustice. Almost all of us have, on occasion, been hesitant to support social change efforts because we thought they were unnecessary or went too far in addressing racial inequities. Of course, people of color aren't immune to these dynamics either. Yet there may not be a single white person in America who hasn't made a contribution to systemic racism at some point.

I was blind to these realities for a very long time. During my youth, while I was certainly aware that I had family members, coworkers, and neighbors who held what I thought to be backward views on issues of race or who supported the politicians responsible for racial injustice, I attributed it to a generational gap. Later on, when I became a lawyer and started spending my days confronting the individuals responsible for doing the day-to-day dirty work of defending systemic racism, it was still quite easy to draw distinctions between myself and them. When I looked at them sitting on the other side of the negotiating table, or casting their votes in the legislature, or going on TV to rally support for their position, I didn't see peers. I saw historical relics clinging to the vestiges of white supremacy.

However, now, as I have aged, when I hear people in my life express troubling views on race or support politicians who defend the status quo, or I look across the negotiating table at the people defending racist policies, I am startled to discover how similar we are. Most of them are products of the same generation as me. We were raised with the same values. Many of us went to the same type of schools, or attended the same types of churches, or enjoy the same TV shows, movies, and hobbies. Thus I finally came to realize that it isn't old, ignorant white men who are upholding racial injustice. I couldn't pin it on people I assumed to be fundamentally dissimilar from me. On the contrary, I had to acknowledge that we were alike in far more ways than we were different—and how at earlier points in my life we wouldn't have been different at all. I also had to recognize that systemic racism had now become my generation's badge of dishonor to wear. And just as it was passed down to us, soon we will pass it along to the next generation, unless we find a way to withhold this cultural inheritance from them.

Racial Miseducation

These experiences allowed me to finally understand how the US racial divide is preserved year after year, generation after generation. It's because those who defend that divide are reproduced with remarkable efficiency. A large part of that comes from the values and beliefs handed down to us. Rugged individualism. Pulling oneself up by one's bootstraps. A firm belief that America is a meritocracy. All of that contributes to the creation of a culture that discourages us from acknowledging and addressing systemic racism.

Of course, that doesn't absolve us of our responsibility for allowing racial inequities to fester, but it is nevertheless true that the vast majority of us haven't been provided anywhere close to the whole story on these issues. On the contrary, and as will be discussed in the following chapters, systemic racism is effectively hidden from our view. Then we are further dissuaded from helping to address it by the persistent myth that we are a "colorblind" or "post-racial" society. This fallacy tells us that racial injustice is a thing of the past, that any lingering issues aren't that severe, that those that do persist are mostly the result of individuals' moral failings, and thus there is nothing to be done at the systemic level to fix them. (To put it another way, the colorblind approach is based on the sophisticated "I'm Gonna Close My Eyes and Pretend the Bad Things Aren't Happening" theory and its elegant companion, the "When the Bad Things Keep Happening, It's Your F–ing Problem" corollary.) As a result, when it comes to issues of race, while most of us think of ourselves as being conscientious and good-hearted, in reality we are largely clueless and confused. That is why so many white people believe that they are the ones most victimized by discrimination, and why the mere assertion that "black lives matter" causes so many white people to lose their minds.[12]

Our miseducation doesn't end there. On the more unsavory side, we have all been inundated since birth with both subtly and overtly racist messages. That people of color were different from "us" and didn't share "our" values. That "they" were inherently lazy, irresponsible, prone to criminality, and less intelligent.[13] Our highest level of scorn was supposed to be reserved for low-income people of color who supposedly drag down the rest of us because of the many "handouts" and "special privileges" they receive. These beliefs have resulted in some truly troubling views and theories around people of color and issues of race (which, for whatever reason, countless other white people have felt comfortable sharing with me over the years, as if I were their own personal race psychiatrist). Yet even if we didn't consciously subscribe to those vile and ignorant beliefs, decades of exposure to them in various forms surely had some effect on how we viewed the world. How could they not?

For my part, while my family ensured that I would avoid accumulating the most egregious versions of these biases, I must admit that the values and beliefs that filtered down to me through other influences made me self-centered and egotistical. They convinced me that because of my educational and professional achievements, I was more worthy of a good life than others. And that those who received worse grades, got lower SAT scores, attended less-esteemed universities, or had less-prestigious jobs were less deserving. These were all key elements of the culture that shaped much of my development and that of so many others like me.

Ultimately, I had to reexamine my own education. I had to recognize that the stories middle-class and wealthy white folks tell ourselves about how we were self-made men and women who succeeded because of our greater merit and superior work ethic were pure fantasies. They were either patently false or omitted essential elements of the story. (For example, yes, I worked hard to get to where I am, but lots of people who weren't given the types of opportunities that I was given work just as hard or harder. Plus, it's easy to work hard when the institutions charged with your development have made a clear investment in your success.) Additionally, I had to unpack the many ways in which the culture I was raised in had effectively dehumanized people of color in my eyes and the eyes of my peers; how the effect had been for us to actually value their lives less than those of others.

That was Step One. Step Two was coming to realize that my life and the lives of other white people like me are also far more difficult than they need to be. However, it isn't because of the people of color whom we have been encouraged to disregard, look down upon, and resent. It's because we have the same people inflicting needless harm on us and our families that they do.

Colorblind Profiteering

People all across the United States, of all races and ethnicities, face a wide variety of day-to-day challenges. However, the most serious may be this: *Most of us go from our births to our deaths without our lives being appropriately valued and without having a meaningful role in shaping the decisions that most affect our lives.*

What does that mean? That the systems we all encounter day to day aren't centered on what we all need to lead a good, fulfilling life, and our opportunities to exercise some control over our lives through the democratic process have been, or are being, stripped away. It means that the country we love, or at least want to love, too often doesn't love us back.

This was made painfully apparent during the COVID-19 pandemic when our government—spurred on by the large corporate members of ALEC—displayed an extraordinarily callous indifference to people's health and safety in the rush to send adults back to work and children back to school.[14] However, these dynamics have long manifested themselves within many aspects of our lives and plague both white people and people of color—though of course, overall, not in anything approaching equal fashion. For example,

1. In the United States, most adults with children send them to public schools to learn what they need to help them grow into healthy, successful adults who can achieve their dreams. However, those schools are increasingly deprived of the resources required to meet our children's needs. In far too many schools, the curriculum is narrowing, class sizes are growing, teachers are undermined, and young people aren't receiving an education that engages them and speaks to their interests and their lives.[15] Rather than education being about the well-rounded development of our children and valuing them for who they are as individuals, our policy makers typically prefer one-size-fits-all initiatives and pay far too much attention to standardized test scores and whether our children are being educated to, as is often said, "compete in the global economy." (To my knowledge, no parent has ever walked out of a hospital with a new baby dreaming about the day when their child would become more economically valuable than someone else's child in Asia, Africa, or South America.) These dynamics push countless young people out of school and away from their educational path. Even those young people who are able to make it through to college find that our government has drastically reduced its investment in higher education, thus shifting the costs to students and families and leaving them saddled with massive amounts of debt.[16]

2. To make a living, most of us are more than willing to work hard. However, we increasingly have to work much harder for much less income and fewer benefits.[17] Many of us are at constant risk of losing our jobs to someone—whether in the United States or another country—who is willing to do it for less money. We are told that our compensation is determined by "the market," which is another way of saying that many of us are paid the lowest amount our employers can get away with, regardless of whether it is sufficient to support an adequate standard of living. Meanwhile, the executives and investors in the companies most of us work for have accumulated extreme wealth while the rest of us are left with far too little economic security and time to enjoy life with family and friends.

3. In the United States, we treat health care as a privilege and not as a right. Among other things, that means that if we can't afford the exorbitant cost of private insurance and then suffer or die from a preventable illness, or go bankrupt in paying for medical costs, then it is treated as our own fault. (Shouldn't we all be deeply embarrassed that hundreds of thousands of Americans per year have to resort to GoFundMe campaigns to pay for their medical care?)[18] It also means that our health care system

has become far too focused on the profitability of insurance companies and other corporations at the expense of supporting health care professionals in meeting the full array of physical, mental, and behavioral health needs of the people and communities they serve.

4. There is nothing more important to our collective future than the health of our planet—our very survival as a species depends upon it. Yet many of our policy makers and business leaders continue to endanger us all by neglecting or opposing efforts to address climate change and provide all people with a clean and healthy environment, purely because it is in their individual economic and political interests to do so.

5. Over the past forty-plus years we have spent a huge percentage of our national wealth to create perhaps the largest system of mass incarceration, criminalization, and surveillance that the world has ever seen.[19] We have also built the most expansive (and expensive) military and national security system of all time.[20] Aside from being ineffective at creating truly safe and healthy communities, all of these systems have diminished the humanity of tens of millions of people, including those who have been needlessly degraded by the criminal justice and immigration enforcement systems, had their privacy violated, been harmed as a result of unnecessary military aggression, have had to enforce unjust policies, and—like many US troops—had their lives put at risk without sufficient cause. In short, we have made astounding investments in systems that have been deeply harmful to our own people, and to people around the world, instead of putting our money into systems that meet our most pressing education, employment, health, housing, and environmental needs.

6. In recent years there has been a determined effort to dismantle the social safety net, such as Social Security, Medicare, Medicaid, and other social welfare programs. As a result, many people who are experiencing challenging periods in their lives—including those who have lost their jobs, lost their homes, are experiencing health issues, are attempting to escape unhealthy or abusive relationships, have to care for their children or an aging family member, or are aging themselves—are finding it increasingly difficult to have their basic needs met and live with dignity.

7. The United States is a pluralistic society with a population that comprises a marvelous tapestry of differences. However, too often our laws, policies, and political rhetoric lead not to the celebration of our diversity, but rather to attacks and discrimination against those identified as being different from an artificial set of norms. In the process, they impede our ability to recognize our common humanity and obscure the fact that all of our lives have equal value. Additionally, our policy makers

cynically exploit the differences between us around hot-button social issues—such as abortion, gun control, and immigration—to build a base of support that allows them to advance other political agenda items that are much higher priority for them, but far less popular with voters. To make matters worse, when people do face widespread injustice on the basis of their differences, or circumstances clearly indicate the need for policy change on one of the hot-button social issues, our policy makers consistently fail to respond with meaningful efforts that address the root causes of the problem.

8. Currently, in our country, because of the Supreme Court decision in *Citizens United*, restrictions on our voting rights, attacks on labor unions, and other efforts to allow our politics to be dominated by the ultra-wealthy, our democratic processes have deteriorated to the point that Corporate America and Wall Street executives have far more control over most of the policy decisions described in this list, and thus our lives, than all the rest of us have combined.[21]

While these certainly aren't the only systemic issues facing our people, they do constitute a large percentage of the most pressing, day-to-day issues faced by the vast majority of US residents. What they all have in common is that regardless of your race or ethnicity, when you examine the factors that devalue your life and make it harder than it has to be, virtually all roads lead back to the same place. The individuals who benefit most from racial injustice are the same individuals who benefit most from the challenges facing white people.

When the relentless pursuit of profits is allowed to take priority over people and the planet, the ultra-wealthy benefit. When the public embraces the perversity of an education system that pushes more of its students out and a criminal justice system that pulls more people in, the ultra-wealthy benefit. When tax breaks for the rich are prioritized over vital services to low-income, working-class, and middle-class families, they benefit. When education becomes less about what our children need and more about what Corporate America needs, the ultra-wealthy benefit. When we permit "public safety" to be used as a justification for repressive law enforcement and military strategies, they benefit. When the underfunding of our public institutions paves the way for the functions of those institutions to be privatized, they benefit. When our democratic structures are allowed to deteriorate, and communities lose their right to self-determination, the ultra-wealthy benefit. When we create competitive systems that aren't designed to meet everyone's needs but rather to help only a select few "winners" while the "losers" are made to believe that they deserve less, they benefit. When people become convinced that resources are scarce and that one community's gain is another's loss, they benefit. When people and communities are pitted against each other and are convinced to resent each other for their differences, they benefit.

As will be discussed, not only do the ultra-wealthy benefit, but they have been at the forefront of all these efforts to ensure that our public policies are aligned with their interests and not those of the vast majority of US residents. As a result, a very small number of people have become absurdly wealthy and powerful on the backs of the rest of us. This isn't an entirely new problem, of course, but it is an escalating one. Unfortunately, too many of us, and especially white people, have been conditioned to acquiesce to these realities. However, there is nothing inevitable about underresourced schools, widespread public health deficiencies, high unemployment rates, poverty wages, environmental degradation, mass criminalization, perpetual war, plutocracy, and widespread discrimination. These aren't unavoidable aspects of American life. On the contrary, these are problems that we have created for ourselves. And they can be changed.

There is no good reason why our government cannot be set up in a way that honors the life of every person, that allows all people to have a voice in shaping the decisions that affect their lives, and that creates a just and equitable society. There is no reason why we cannot truly have a government that is "of the people, by the people, and for the people." As will be described in chapter 5, there is no reason why the resources currently being used to severely harm people of all races and ethnicities couldn't be repurposed to address our most pressing social problems and meet all people's basic needs. This type of transformative change is within our grasp. But to get there, we need white people to recognize that racial justice isn't somebody else's fight. It has to be our fight too.

Divided and Conquered

> The future of the negro in this country is precisely as bright or as dark as the future of the country. . . . It is entirely up to the American people whether or not they're going to face and deal with and embrace the stranger who they've maligned for so long. What white people have to do is try to find out in their own hearts why it was necessary to have a n****r in the first place. I am not a n****r. I am a man. But if you think I'm a n****r, it means you need it. . . . You, the white people, invented him, and you have to find out why. And the future of the country depends on that. Whether or not it is able to ask that question.

—James Baldwin, *The Negro and the American Promise*[22]

Imagine that there are a series of races pitting two teams against each other: Team A and Team B. They are grueling and perilous races, so much so that many members of each team won't survive, and all participants get bruised and bloodied along the course. In each race, Team A is given a huge head start—though many of its members somehow fail to notice it—and in most races, they win as a result. Team A's members exult in each victory, overjoyed with their dominance and all too willing to share their theories about how the individual and collective failings of Team B explain their defeats. Their gloating, flaunting of their success, and general shortsightedness understandably irk Team B, and over time hostilities grow between the teams. Meanwhile, the organizers of the races are desperately hoping that the disadvantages given to Team B, Team A's pride in its victories, and the hostilities between the teams accomplish two things. First, that they prevent anyone from noticing that the organizers have taken most of the races' prize money for themselves. Second, that the teams never stop to ask themselves, "Wait, why are we even competing against each other in the first place?"

The principle of divide and conquer (or divide and rule) is almost as old as government itself. It's far older than the United States of America, though we may have perfected it with our racial divisions. Our wealthiest citizens have been expertly stirring up conflict between white communities and communities of color pretty much since the first white US inhabitants got off of their boats from Europe and saw that there were multitudes of brown faces staring back at them.[23] For white people, that has often meant directing our anger at our own lot in life toward people of color. They are the convenient scapegoats and the group that fulfills our apparent need to feel superior to someone, both of which serve to distract us from what the ultra-wealthy are doing. It's an old trick that seemingly never stops working.[24] We get thrown a few crumbs and guard them as if our lives depended on it, never bothering to think about what would be possible if we all were able to share the whole pie.

As will be discussed later on, there is much more pie to be had, but it will remain uneaten unless white people join the fight for racial justice and find their common interests with people of color. Of course, white people shouldn't need self-serving reasons to address systemic racism. We should do it because our government is causing human suffering on a massive scale. Millions of our neighbors are being devastated by systems that are benefiting the rest of us, and nobody should be okay with that. While there have been many periods during US history—such as during the post–Civil War Reconstruction and the 1960s civil rights movement—in which we have taken steps forward on issues of race, we have always stopped far short of creating true equity. Instead, we have been content with "making progress." But as James Baldwin asked decades ago, how much longer are people of color supposed to wait for this "progress" to actually produce a racially just nation?[25] How many more people, or generations of people, have to face the devastation of systemic racism before enough of us become compelled to act? For nearly the entire history of our country, people of color have been told to wait, to be patient, and that eventually their time would come. Yet generation after generation has passed without us honoring our stated commitment to equality and without doing what is necessary to ensure that all our people are able to enjoy the full benefits of living in the United States. Removing that noxious stain from our collective morality should be more than enough justification to make a commitment to advancing racial justice.

Beyond that, we must all understand that combating racial injustice is an essential element to all Americans' well-being. While it is true that the lives and voices of low-income, working-class, and middle-class people of all races are undervalued, it is especially true for people of color. Systemic racism is the rotten core at the center of the injustice that plagues us all, and there is no substantially better world that can be created on top of such a deeply flawed foundation. Thus we all need to analyze why we, as a collective whole, have developed such a high level of tolerance for racial inequities. And if we are serious about building a society that works for all people, then we need to be honest about the ways in which our current society fails to do so. Systemic racism is a huge, and unavoidable, part of that equation.

Additionally, and as a purely pragmatic matter, when a group of people has consolidated as much wealth and power as these ultra-wealthy Corporate America and Wall Street executives have, a divided resistance will inevitably fail. Those individuals have far too much influence over the media and political, economic, and legal systems to have their power threatened by a public that is split along racial lines. Thus, it is going to take all of us working together to build a just, equitable, and truly democratic society.

Unfortunately, our house is on fire, and white people are acting like the smoke is coming from a barbecue to which we weren't invited. People of color continue to fight back against systemic racism in large numbers; in fact, they have never stopped. Their efforts have often been the only thing standing in the way of even worse policies being implemented. They have also been the driving force behind the racial justice advances we have made, demonstrating over and over the power of organized and strategic mass movements. Yet while there is an abundance of white people who are strong advocates around issues of poverty and virtually every other righteous—and often unrighteous—cause, white people who will publicly stand up for racial justice consistently, over time, are alarmingly rare. To be sure, there are many white folks who will show up at an occasional rally or give to charities supporting low-income communities of color. However, there are very few who put in sustained work or resources toward truly addressing the root causes of racial injustice. Instead of fighting for real solutions to systemic racism, white people have a long history of limiting our support to superficial, symbolic, or "race-neutral" reforms that tend to be far more effective at making us feel better about race relations than they are at actually addressing the inequities faced by people of color.

Even those self-described liberals and progressives who do advocate for policies that explicitly address issues of race rarely prioritize the issues facing communities of color. Time and time again, in political and advocacy circles, racial justice priorities are the first things to be compromised.[26] In determining how to present issues for public discussion, racial justice topics are the first to be deemphasized or cut altogether. The justification is almost always that it must be done to more successfully appeal to white constituents. In practice, what this usually looks like is white people telling other (mostly) white people not to talk about race for fear of alienating all the other white people. It's not a good look.

Given that history, one cannot blame people of color for feeling pessimistic about whether white people will ever step up around racial justice issues. Many have become discouraged to the point that they have resigned themselves to the idea that white people will never get this right. When taking a long view of US history, who can blame them? For far too long, they have been largely isolated around these issues, creating a thoroughly unhealthy us-versus-them dynamic.

However, there is still hope. I do not believe that there is a shortage of compassion or capacity within white communities; it's just that our better angels aren't directed at racial justice efforts often enough, or they are misdirected altogether.[27] Nevertheless, white people can, and have, played meaningful roles in advancing racial justice when they are given the facts and are willing and able to receive them. I also believe that there are millions more out there who are primed to join the fight for racial justice. These are the multitudes of white people who continually find themselves frustrated over, and even pained by, racial inequities, but aren't quite sure what to do about it, as though they had a splinter in their mind. Folks who feel compelled to pitch in and help those from underresourced communities. People who realize that their well-being is inextricably linked to that of people of color. And those who just want to bring a little more justice into the world.

This goes well beyond party politics, Democrats and Republicans, progressives and conservatives. Those are categories and affiliations that should always be secondary to the larger moral questions of how we are going to engage with and support each other as human beings. Moreover, none of our mainstream political groupings have done nearly enough to advance racial justice. Thus, we need to move beyond provincial politics in order to assemble the latent army of conscientious white people out there who can help to create a stronger and more unified America by working together in solidarity with communities of color and other marginalized communities. That is what the following chapters are about: identifying how we can work together to undo the damage that has been done and build something better in its place.

To be clear, no one is asking for "white saviors" to swoop in and save the day. However, we do need white folks to start stepping up more often and in more meaningful ways with their time, energy, and resources to support the racial justice movement alongside any other justice movements (gender, economic, LGBTQIA+, climate, etc.) with which they identify. Because while we are the key ingredient in continuing to prop up the strategic racism that mostly benefits the ultra-wealthy, that also means that we are uniquely well-positioned to help tear it down in ways that benefit people of all races and ethnicities.

That doesn't mean that every white person has to become a racial justice advocate overnight. Fortunately, just ten individuals coming together within a community can have a major impact. If one hundred white people from each state devoted themselves to racial justice advocacy and joined the people of color already in the fight, the results would be profound. If one thousand white folks came together from every state, it would create a major sea change. If ten thousand from each state got organized and devoted themselves to supporting the efforts of communities of color and advancing their mutual interests, it would be revolutionary. This may seem pie-in-the-sky to some, but these folks are out there, and this is all eminently feasible.[28]

This also happens to represent the worst nightmare of the ultra-wealthy: that masses of white people and people of color come together to imagine the world we can build together once we stop to ask, "Wait, why are we even competing against each other in the first place?"

THE SQUANDERED BRILLIANCE
OF OUR DISPOSABLE YOUTH

Many young people across the United States are able to take for granted that their schools will provide them with a healthy, supportive learning environment in which they can thrive. It is simply assumed that they are being set up for success. When these students walk into their school buildings every morning, they know that their education is valued. They know that *they* are valued.

In other communities, however, the day-to-day reality for many young people is quite different.

Many of these children and youth wake up and go to dilapidated school buildings, with leaky roofs, broken heating and cooling systems, and no drinkable water. When they pass through the doors of their schools in the morning, they are greeted not by the smiling faces of trusted adults but rather by police officers, security guards, metal detectors, and surveillance cameras. Their schools and classrooms are so overcrowded that they can't even maneuver down the hallway or find a desk at which to sit. They go to class only to find that their teachers aren't given nearly enough resources and support to meet their needs. Young people across the country are routinely subjected to a mind-numbingly tedious curriculum that is largely irrelevant to their lives and dominated by filling in bubble sheets. In many schools, the few parts of the day that make such conditions bearable for students—such as art, music, and drama classes, PE, recess, and extracurricular activities—have been cut back or even eliminated. And far too often, when students' lives outside of school make things difficult for them in school, or they have a bad day, or they simply make the same type of mistakes that young people have always made, there are no counselors, social workers, school psychologists, or other supportive adults to help them through it. Instead, they are often suspended, expelled, or taken out of school in handcuffs and brought to jail.

While there are children of all races and ethnicities who encounter some of these obstacles, the millions of young people who encounter many or even all of them on a daily basis are overwhelmingly youth of color. Rather than being set up for success, these young people have, quite simply, been set up to fail. Rather than being able to attend schools in which every student is valued, these young people are treated as if they were disposable.

There is a sad reality that all Americans have to own up to, which is that perhaps *the* defining feature of our education system is it has never been equitable. At no time in US history have we been willing to put children of color on equal footing with white children. There is simply no "golden age" of education equity that we can point to, no moment in time in which you could go into schools within communities of color and expect to find the same level of educational opportunities that you would find in schools within predominantly white communities.[1] For literally hundreds of years, people of color have been fighting for the same opportunities to learn that white Americans have enjoyed, and they have been met with massive resistance at every turn. This long and shameful legacy has been created and sustained through numerous policies and practices over the years. Modern-day policies such as school funding inequities, the school-to-prison pipeline, and the overuse and misuse of high-stakes standardized testing are direct descendants of policies such as the legalized segregation of schools during the Jim Crow era and the extreme opposition to school desegregation following *Brown v. Board of Education.* The end result is a long-standing, largely separate and thoroughly unequal system that has left deep wounds in students, parents, and other community members across the country.

For nearly twenty years, I have been working with black and brown communities across the country to address education inequities. Over that time, I have spoken with countless students, parents, and other community members and asked them about their schools, the challenges they face within them, and how they think they should be improved. We have talked at length and in great detail about major deficiencies they experience with regard to their schools' facilities, class sizes, curriculum, learning materials, instructional practices, professional development, support for English learners, disciplinary practices, wraparound supports, special education programs, assessments, accountability systems, school climate, family and community involvement, funding, and numerous other factors. However, at no time in any one of those conversations did any of the students and parents point their fingers at the public administration of their schools as the culprit for inadequate education. None of these people ever suggested that privatizing their public school—such as by turning it into a charter school or providing its students with vouchers to attend private schools—would address their needs. Instead, perhaps the most common and urgent concern in recent years has been about what happened to their school systems *after* they were privatized.

Tatanisha Jackson's top priority in buying a new house in her home city of New Orleans was finding one with good local schools. Like many parents, she shopped around until she finally found the right one in the right neighborhood. Not only was the local elementary school very well regarded, it was just half a block away from the house. Tatanisha was thrilled about what this move would mean for her two young daughters. Being able to spend their early years in a good school within walking distance of their house—that was the type of solid foundation she wanted for them. It would put them on a good trajectory. So immediately after closing on the house, Tatanisha went directly to the school, eager to enroll her older daughter, Janelle, in kindergarten.[2] That is when she learned about the system of "school choice" in New Orleans.

What Tatanisha hadn't known was that the New Orleans school system was the subject of an ongoing "experiment." While there had long been some individuals on the fringes of education policy discussions pushing for the privatization of public schools, they had made very little progress in putting their theories into practice. That all changed after Hurricane Katrina decimated New Orleans in 2005. Shortly after the storm, the famed right-wing economist Milton Friedman, who initiated the idea of school vouchers back in the 1950s, wrote an op-ed in the *Wall Street Journal* that argued against rebuilding the New Orleans public schools. He proposed that the devastation caused by the storm presented "an opportunity to radically reform the educational system."[3] Before long, school privatization advocates had descended on New Orleans, eager to use the city as their laboratory for the types of reform that they favored. While there were already charter schools and voucher programs scattered across the country, this was their opportunity to take their ideas to scale. Eventually every public school in the city was closed, and New Orleans became the first 100 percent charter school district in the country. It also became the poster child for the school privatization movement, and the "New Orleans miracle" was touted nationally and internationally, paving the way for many more districts nationwide to replace traditional public schools with charter schools.

What that meant for Tatanisha was that when she went down the block to enroll her daughter in the local elementary school, she was told that all the schools operated on a lottery system, and families weren't guaranteed slots in their local schools. She was surprised and disappointed by the news, but she went ahead and entered the lottery, hopeful that it would all work out. However, when she got the lottery results, she saw that Janelle didn't get into her school of choice.

So she entered the second round of the lottery, which was for those who didn't get into any of their top choices in the first round. Still she wasn't able to get into the school down the street.

There was one final round of the process, in which parents could try to secure a slot in one of the few schools that still had openings. It was scheduled to start one summer day at 8:00 a.m., and it was done on a first-come, first-served basis. Tatanisha is a tough-minded and thoroughly practical woman, and she wasn't going to leave anything to chance. She was standing outside the office, first in line, at 4:00 in the morning. Once the doors opened, though, she learned that none of the remaining schools were close to her house. Without any other options left, she went ahead and enrolled Janelle in the best and most convenient of the remaining schools. "I wanted to trust the system," she says. "I wanted to trust that they were looking out for my child's interests."

However, her faith was tested immediately. To get to her new school, six-year-old Janelle had to wake up by 5:30 a.m. to leave the house—in the dark—and catch a 6:00 bus for an hour-long ride across town. After school was even worse. Once school got out at 3:30, it took a two-hour or even a two-and-half-hour bus ride for her to get home. Thus, this kindergartner's school day was essentially 6:00 a.m. to 6:00 p.m. Tatanisha was in disbelief that the school system would place such extreme demands on their students. "That's longer than an adult's day, and you want to put that kind of strain and stress on a child?"

That wasn't the end of it, however. Because New Orleans schools were under extraordinary pressure to raise student performance and validate the "experiment" they were conducting, many schools substantially ratcheted up the workload of educators, students, and their parents. For Janelle, what that meant was that even though she was only in kindergarten, she typically had several hours of homework every night. Thus, by the time her homework was done and she had eaten dinner, taken a bath, and gotten ready for bed, it was often between 11:00 p.m. and midnight. That left her with precious little time to sleep before she had to be up and start over at 5:30 the next day. "Most adults can't even function on that little sleep," Tatanisha says. "How can you expect a small child to work up to their full potential and be able to give their full attention on that little rest, day in and day out?"

Aside from the grueling demands on such a young child, this arrangement posed a number of other challenges for the family. For example, because the school was so far away from home and Tatanisha's workplace, if Janelle missed the bus or had to come home early, it was a multiple-hour process to shuttle back and forth to the school. "I don't have a huge support system," Tatanisha says, "so if my child gets sick, how am I going to get to her?" Plus, it was impossible for Tatanisha to be as involved in her daughter's education as she wanted to be. If she

had to meet with Janelle's teacher or wanted to attend a parent-teacher organization meeting, she would have to take almost a half day off of work to get to the
school in time. "You can't communicate and have the proper relationship with
your child's teacher when they're all the way across town," she says.

However, by far the biggest complication concerned Janelle's health, and in
particular, her sickle cell disease. For her, the combination of long bus rides and
lack of sleep was toxic. They triggered numerous agonizingly painful sickle cell
crises. Thus, while her classmates were learning their ABCs and how to add and
subtract, Janelle was often in the emergency room or forced to stay in the hospital
for multiple days until her pain subsided. The New Orleans system of "school
choice" was literally making her sick.

To relieve some of Janelle's symptoms, her pediatrician suggested to Tatanisha
that she enroll her in a school closer to home and recommended to the school
district that they show the family some leniency. So Tatanisha immediately got
to work. She met with every school district staff member who was willing to
talk with her about her options. She attended numerous school board meetings
to plead for assistance. Finally, after months of advocacy for her increasingly ill
daughter, she was provided with an alternative: a school that was ten to fifteen
minutes away from her house. That was the upside. The downside was that the
slot was available only because the school was rated as failing within the district's
ranking system. So Tatanisha had to decide: Should she prioritize academics by
keeping Janelle at the higher-rated school that was compromising her health, or
should she prioritize Janelle's health by switching schools and compromising her
academic progress? "What do you do as a parent in that situation?" Tatanisha
asks. "And how can this be the only choice that we're given? It's damned if you
do and damned if you don't." She sighs wearily. "It just leaves you feeling . . .
hopeless."

She's right, of course. The choice she was given was an impossible one. It is
also one that no one should ever have to make.

School privatization and the fight over charter schools and voucher programs
have dominated the broader education policy discourse for most of the past two
decades.* "School choice" has been the magic bullet that has been put forward
by Republicans and, increasingly, by Democrats as a solution to the despicable

---

*Throughout this chapter, I will distinguish between "public schools" and "charter schools."
Though I recognize that this is itself controversial, and charter schools have taken to referring themselves as public schools, for the sake of clarity it is important to be able to distinguish between the
two. Additionally, the facts remain that charter schools have chosen to differentiate themselves from
the public system and have sought to exempt themselves from many of the characteristics we expect
of public institutions.

history of undereducation of youth of color. What is particularly notable here is what hasn't been part of that conversation. There has been virtually no serious attention given to *what* the ingredients of a high-quality, equitable education system would be, or *how* we can create schools and communities that can better meet the developmental needs of youth of color. Instead, an education holy war has erupted around *who* should be managing the education of our children: public officials or private operators.

I realize that there is considerable public support for charter schools and some support for vouchers. I also realize that, as with all wars, the proponents for each side have very deep and heartfelt beliefs about the righteousness of their cause, and often refuse to engage with any information that might conflict with their beliefs. Thus, there are many diehard supporters of charters and vouchers who may be inclined to shut this book right now because they can sense that they are behind enemy lines. Please don't. What follows in this chapter doesn't come from a rigid ideological perspective. While I think there is plenty to be said about the relative merits of the private and public sectors as they relate to education, that isn't the primary focus here. My main priority is the same as that of the parents and students I work with: to simply ensure that the young people in their communities are able to have the same high-quality educational opportunities that exist in so many predominantly white communities. I, for one, don't believe that there is only one way to make that happen.

Additionally, what follows doesn't come without empathy for views on both sides of this holy war. Thus, if you are a parent or student who has had a positive experience with a charter school or voucher program, or who is considering such a program, you won't find any judgment here. I know how difficult it can be to make these choices for your kids, how limited the options that have been provided for many parents and youth are, and how that can make anyone desperate for any hopeful possibility. I also know from personal experience that the overriding concern has to be what is best for the child, not how that decision factors into a political debate.

If you are an educator or community member who has become personally invested in a charter school or voucher program and are proud of the work you have done, please know that the intent here isn't to criticize your efforts. There is no dispute that many charter schools—like many public schools—do an excellent job, and it is not difficult to understand the many reasons one might have to pursue nontraditional routes for meeting the needs of children and youth.

If you are a policy maker who has supported charter schools or voucher programs because you wanted to help students of color, then please don't mistake the following for an attack on your work. I understand how artificially limited the options for addressing education inequities have become, as well as the impulse to want to do something different, to want to disrupt the status quo.

If you fall into one of these categories, or any other that makes you predisposed to reject what follows out of hand, I would ask that you suspend your judgment for a bit. I would also ask that you be open to the idea that the reforms proposed by school privatization advocates, even if implemented to perfection, are nowhere close to being responsive to the challenges presented by deep-seated education inequities. Additionally, I would request that you consider how, alongside whatever benefits you have witnessed from school privatization, this set of reforms has also brought widespread devastation to students, families, and communities of color across the country. Indeed, those who have been harmed the most are the young people who were supposed to be the primary beneficiaries of school choice.

Finally, I would ask that you be open to the idea that your benevolent intentions in supporting charter school and voucher expansion may not align with the aspirations of those who are most responsible for pushing this agenda forward. School privatization is unquestionably a billionaire-led effort, and for many of these individuals, the primary motivation isn't to raise overall educational quality or remedy education inequities. Instead, charter schools and voucher programs are being used as a Trojan horse. They have been weaponized in order to advance a massive money grab that threatens the educational opportunities of almost every child in America. And rather than being a solution to systemic racism, as is often claimed, school privatization has instead been a quintessential example of strategic racism in action.

As will be discussed, there *are* strategies available to us that would truly address the massive education debt we owe to our nation's youth of color and ensure a high-quality education for every child in the United States.[4] We can eliminate these disgraceful obstacles to learning and opportunity that far too many children and youth have to confront. However, we will never get there unless we all put down our swords for a bit and investigate the real motives behind school privatization efforts, the risks they pose, the harms and benefits that they have produced, and how they have enabled a small group of billionaires to exploit many well-intentioned people along the way.

A National Epidemic

A useful place to start in examining school privatization is with the impact it has had on public school systems. All across the country, public schools are being closed in huge numbers and essentially replaced with charter schools and voucher programs. Sometimes public schools are simply converted to charters. Other times, charters schools and voucher programs are brought in and put in direct competition with public schools. Regardless, it has produced a national epidemic of mass public school closures. For example,

- Chicago—at least 126 school closures since 2009
- Detroit—more than 200 public schools closed since 2000
- Saint Louis—at least 44 schools closed since 2003
- Kansas City—28 schools closed in 2010
- Cleveland—at least 22 schools closed since 2010
- Philadelphia—at least 29 schools closed since 2013
- District of Columbia—at least 39 schools closed since 2008
- Flint—more than 20 schools closed since 2003
- Oakland—24 schools closing beginning in 2019[5]

While these public school systems are being decimated, the charter systems within these and many other communities of color are expanding rapidly. For example, in addition to New Orleans, which is 100 percent charter, the school systems in Detroit, Kansas City, and Washington, DC, now have over 40 percent of their students in charter schools. Both Los Angeles and New York City now have more than one hundred thousand students in charters, while Miami, Philadelphia, Chicago, and Houston all have at least fifty thousand. As can be seen in table 1, the charter sector is rapidly swallowing up school systems in cities nationwide. In fact, as of 2017–18, there were 214 districts with at least 10 percent of their students in charter schools, compared to just 64 districts in 2007–8.[6]

Charter schools also continue to spread to new states across the country.[7] In particular there has been a remarkable increase in the number of students attending virtual charter schools, or "cyber-charters," despite the notoriously poor quality of many of these schools.[8] Additionally, state legislatures and governors continue to push for more charter schools and expand the exemptions that charter schools enjoy from the regulations that public schools must follow.[9] A number of states have also created, or are considering creating, state-run school districts that take over schools deemed to be low performing.[10] Typically, these initiatives have resulted in states converting large numbers of public schools within communities of color into charter schools.[11]

As for vouchers, there are currently twenty-five such programs operating in fourteen states and the District of Columbia.[12] Voucher-like programs that redirect public money to private schools (such as "education savings accounts," "scholarship tax credits," and "tuition tax credits") are also proliferating.[13] The political push for voucher or voucher-like programs was particularly aggressive after the 2016 elections. The Trump administration and Republican-controlled Congress made the expansion of these programs a priority, and numerous other states attempted to create or expand voucher programs.[14]

TABLE 1 Our disappearing public schools

DISTRICT	% STUDENTS OF COLOR	REDUCTION IN PUBLIC SCHOOL ENROLLMENT—2005–6 TO 2017–18	INCREASE IN CHARTER SCHOOL ENROLLMENT—2005–6 TO 2017–18	CHARTERS' SHARE OF TOTAL ENROLLMENT—2017–18
Gary (IN) Community School Corporation	99%	↓69%	↑207%	49%
Detroit Public Schools	98%	↓66%	↑50%	46%
Camden (NJ) City Public Schools	99%	↓50%	↑144%	37%
Kansas City (MO) School District	91%	↓41%	↑77%	43%
Saint Louis Public Schools	88%	↓34%	↑146%	32%
Cleveland Metropolitan School District	85%	↓34%	↑86%	30%
Los Angeles Unified	90%	↓33%	↑363%	26%
Indianapolis Public Schools	80%	↓32%	↑403%	36%
The School District of Philadelphia	86%	↓29%	↑140%	33%
San Antonio Independent School District	98%	↓23%	↑610%	30%
Chicago Public Schools	90%	↓23%	↑282%	16%
Baltimore City Public Schools	92%	↓18%	↑413%	18%
Miami-Dade County Public Schools	93%	↓16%	↑289%	18%
Newark Public Schools	92%	↓15%	↑458%	33%
District of Columbia Public Schools	87%	↓12%	↑148%	47%
Atlanta Public Schools	85%	↓11%	↑341%	19%
Oakland Unified School District	89%	↓11%	↑138%	30%

Sources: Kevin Hesla, Jamison White, and Adam Gerstenfeld, *A Growing Movement: America's Largest Public Charter School Communities,* 13th annual ed., National Alliance for Public Charter Schools, March 2019; National Alliance for Public Charter Schools, "Charter School Data Dashboard"; US Department of Education Office of Civil Rights, "Civil Rights Data Collection."

It is important to remember that school privatization efforts were initially billed as seeking to provide a few "laboratories of innovation" that would better meet the needs of a small number of students of color forced to attend "chronically failing schools." However, the goal of that sector is now quite clearly to simply take over large chunks, if not the entirety, of public school systems. That has been made apparent in post-Katrina New Orleans and elsewhere. For example, in 2015, the superintendent of the Palm Beach County (Florida) Public Schools, home to over 180,000 students, sought permission from state lawmakers to turn the entire school district over to charter schools.[15] Additionally, in 2015 the *Los Angeles Times* uncovered a secret plan being developed that sought to place half of all students within the Los Angeles Unified School District (the second-largest district in the country) into charter schools over the following eight years.[16]

Within school privatization circles, the replacement of public schools with charter schools or voucher programs is seen as a positive development. It is even celebrated, and there is a seemingly never-ending torrent of news stories and advocacy reports that highlight the successes of charter schools and voucher programs, most of which focus on reportedly higher standardized test scores and graduation rates. These results are often attributed to the introduction of "market dynamics" to the education system, which, it is said, spur greater innovation, competition, and performance. To be fair, there are some studies that support their claims around test score improvements (though there are significant concerns with the validity and significance of these findings, which will be discussed later). There are many other studies that don't support their claims. Taken as a whole, the overall body of research is inconclusive as to how being in a charter school or voucher program affects test score or graduation outcomes.[17] And there have been some deeply concerning findings, such as the study showing that one-quarter of all charter schools graduate fewer than half their students.[18] Nevertheless, those facts are almost never acknowledged in the public narrative around school privatization, and the fact that charter schools and voucher programs are being used to replace public schools is virtually ignored altogether.

Additionally, as someone who has spent many years working closely with the residents of numerous cities that have been heavily affected by school privatization, witnessing the public discussion around the shift away from public schools has been difficult to process and tough to swallow. The glowing media reports and even outright glee within policy circles simply didn't match up to the lived experience on the ground in Los Angeles, Philadelphia, New Orleans, Chicago, Washington, DC, and other cities. Over the past decade, I have attended dozens of community meetings, surveyed thousands of parents, students, and community members, and interviewed scores of residents in the communities most affected by these dynamics. The disconnect between what they describe and what is typically reported publicly is striking.

While there are undoubtedly students within those communities who have benefited from being able to attend some of the new charter schools or receive vouchers, the impact of such an enormous change to the education system goes well beyond those individual students. It also goes well beyond charter schools' or voucher recipients' overall academic outcomes, though unfortunately that is all that most commentators and even researchers typically explore. Focusing just on test scores or graduation rates when examining the consequences of mass school closures and radical shifts in school systems is like dumping a vat of chemicals into a stream and then measuring the impact by merely counting the number of fish that are still alive. Sure, that matters, but the implications go well beyond that one metric.

If we take a more holistic view, what can be observed is a catastrophic impact on many low-income communities of color due to the expansion of charter schools and vouchers.[19] (To illustrate the impact of school privatization, the text boxes that follow include excerpts from interviews or surveys that I have done with community members from some of the cities most affected by school privatization.)

Harm to Community Health and Well-Being

> "I have seen my neighborhood lose an eighty-five-year-old institution that signified its very identity. I have seen the kids from my neighborhood bused twice as far to be herded into what was already an overcrowded building. I have seen my neighborhood lose teachers and staff that were dedicated to our community and intended to work within it for their entire careers. I have seen my neighborhood endure a catastrophic loss to its character and place in the city."—Pittsburgh resident

Public schools are typically the backbones of communities. More than any other institution, they connect people around shared goals and interests. They anchor our communities and knit our families and neighborhoods together. They are also often the hubs of community activity and resources, and the source of considerable local pride. When they are closed down, it can be extremely destabilizing for the entire community, triggering a whole series of harmful effects. People lose their jobs, community bonds are severed, families are strained, people and businesses often leave the area, property values are often reduced, community violence often increases, and those neighborhoods become less desirable places to live. Overall, there are very few things that are more traumatic to communities than closing their schools.

> "We were put out of our neighborhood school, Anthony Overton. . . . Anthony Overton wasn't just a school; it was the heart of the community. I can't tell you how many family and friends we had connected there. Some of the teachers were like mothers to me. They helped me raise my children. So to see the same people who raised my children raise my grandchildren, that's a blessing. . . . Until [then-mayor of Chicago] Rahm Emanuel came into our community and it was like a bomb exploded."—Irene Robinson, grandparent, Chicago

Harm to Remaining Public Schools

When schools are closed, the remaining public schools often have to assume a substantial additional burden. They have to absorb many of the students displaced by the closures, creating overcrowded schools and larger class sizes. They typically become even more underresourced as funds are siphoned off to charter schools and voucher programs.[20]

> "[Because of school closures] the classes are very overcrowded. There's like forty kids in each class. Some students have to stand up, sit on tables, or sit on the heating vents to write their notes."—Eric Wright, high school student, Philadelphia

Plus, as the student population becomes split across charter schools, private schools, and public schools, it is the public schools that often wind up with a heavy concentration of the highest-need students. The combination of these effects almost inevitably results in diminished teaching and learning in those public schools. When these dynamics are coupled with persistent public criticism of public schools and educators, the frequent result is the loss of many high-quality teachers and staff members. Even very good schools, and schools that are taking the necessary steps to improve their performance, are harmed by these dynamics.

> "Teachers are overwhelmed with the class size; therefore they cannot plan lessons properly to cater to the needs of each student."—Pittsburgh teacher

Harm to Students

Closing schools can have a devastating impact on the children and youth who are displaced as a result. All at once, some of the most important relationships in their lives—with friends, teachers, and mentors—can be severed. For many young people, the loss of their school also represents the loss of a reliably safe and stable place in their lives. For some, it means losing the only such place they have.

> "With the recent school changes, I have seen many students shut down. In the high school environment many students have expressed to me that they feel abandoned by their home school and teachers who they have grown to trust."—Pittsburgh teacher

In other words, while school closures are often treated as a simple bookkeeping matter of shifting bodies from one building to another, in reality they are a form of trauma being inflicted on—typically—youth of color from low-income and working-class neighborhoods.

> "They go into this neighborhood high school that they don't even fund, and they want to take that away from you as well? They want to close down your school? They're putting a message on you that you're not going to be anything in life."—Nathan Quiles, high school student, Philadelphia

Plus, when public schools are closed, many students find that there aren't even any charter schools nearby that will serve them, particularly if those students have disabilities, are English learners, have had behavioral challenges, or aren't perceived to be academically inclined.[21] The problem is often even worse for private schools, which have virtually unfettered discretion to deny admission to or push out students for almost any reason. Students with disabilities, in particular, are frequently excluded from voucher programs.

"When we took our son with multiple disabilities to New Orleans schools to enroll, we quickly discovered that by having a disjointed school system there was no accountability. No one school felt an obligation to serve all kids. . . . The message very quickly was that schools had the ability to pick and choose their students and how they'd serve them. . . . Our first year, we went to three different schools just to get the services already put into place on his IEP. . . . No one ever flat-out said 'don't come,' but they'd say that they weren't a good fit. . . . If your child doesn't fit into the traditional mold and can't be educated inexpensively or easily, he becomes a liability. The corporate model isn't inclined to educate him."—Kelly, parent, New Orleans

Furthermore, most voucher programs don't cover the entire cost of tuition at private schools, leaving many families to make up the difference out of pocket, which obviously affects low-income, working-class, and middle-class families the most, and oftentimes prevents them from participating at all. Thus, the students with the fewest educational opportunities are often effectively shut out of many voucher programs.

For those students affected by school privatization who are able to find a new school, they often find—as Tatanisha Jackson did—that they have to travel much farther to get there. Along with the obvious inconvenience, this frequently puts children and youth at significant risk. This isn't hypothetical, either; children and youth have died as a result of these dynamics, often because their new commute forced them across or into neighborhoods where they weren't safe.[22]

Because of all these dynamics, not surprisingly, there is frequently an alarming number of students who, when their schools are closed, fall through the cracks and never make it back into school.[23]

Harm to the Overall Education System

Across the overall education system, including public schools, charters, and vouchers, there has been clear, and very concerning, harm caused by increased privatization:

- Creating an entirely new system of charter schools—with fewer regulations in place that ensure a baseline level of performance—has unsurprisingly led to an extremely wide range of quality in the schools being created. Some are excellent, some are terrible, and most fall somewhere in between. However, while most of the public attention is focused on the top-performing schools, we must not lose sight of the fact that many parents have been lured into sending their children to new charter schools that have absolutely no business educating children, or that don't even fall within our broadest definitions of what schools are and should do.[24] One example: There is a charter school network called Learn4Life that operates fifteen schools in California. The schools, which claim to provide "personalized learning," are located in office buildings, strip malls, and former liquor stores. At one such school, Desert Sands Charter High School in Lancaster, California, there are no dedicated teachers or classrooms. The "school" is merely the place where students pick up and drop off their paper packets of work, take tests on those packets, and occasionally meet with tutors. The 2015 four-year graduation rate at Desert Sands was 11.5 percent.[25]

- While charter schools have certainly attracted good, new teachers to the profession, the mass closure of public schools has also resulted in the loss of many highly effective and experienced educators, and particularly black and Latinx teachers, within communities that can ill afford it. Overall there has been a noticeable deprofessionalization of the teaching profession, making it more difficult to attract and retain excellent teachers. As a result, within many of the communities most affected by school privatization, there are severe teacher shortages.[26]

- Because public schools and charters schools have been pitted against each other in a competition for scarce resources and their very survival, there has been even more emphasis put on standardized test performance, resulting in an increasingly narrow, unengaging, and test-driven curriculum in many schools, across both public and charter schools.

"The victims are first and foremost the children. They are going to school in a supercharged atmosphere where there is tension, where teachers who love children can't help but feel stressed out and angry toward the children who are not going to raise their scores, because they could be costing them their job."—Washington, DC, teacher

- More students have been pushed out of school and into the school-to-prison pipeline because of particularly harsh disciplinary practices in charter schools, overburdened public schools, and private schools.[27]

"When your child doesn't conform to the rigid punishment—that they call discipline—in charter schools, they are forced out. . . . They're given constant suspensions, constant detentions. . . . There are many children who just give up."—Yvonne Malone, parent, Newark, NJ

- Overall funding for both public schools and charter schools is, in many communities, being reduced, resulting in fewer resources for instruction, student support services, extracurricular activities, and other vital wraparound supports.[28]

"When I was in Detroit Public Schools, you had wood shop, you had singing, you had chess club, you had debate. You had all these activities, so a lot of my friends, you stayed in school or around school. Now [because of privatization and defunding of public schools] there are no other activities. So what happened to the young people that didn't have those activities? They ended up out in the streets."—Kamau Kheperu, parent, Detroit

- The creation of high-quality schools is fundamentally about building high-quality relationships between educators and families. For many schools that have been closed, important relationships that had been built across many years, and even generations, were ruptured almost instantly.

"By closing down schools, they're tearing apart relationships. A lot of these young people don't have role models at home, but they have strong relationships with teachers or principals in their schools. Ending those relationships can shatter those children."—Carmen Wallace, parent, Philadelphia

- Another predicable result of the Wild West landscape of charter school expansion has been the widespread waste, fraud, and abuse among many charter operators across the country, leading to hundreds of millions of misspent taxpayer dollars.[29]

- There has been a noticeable loss of transparency and democratic accountability in our school systems. First, privatization has often been achieved only after the implementation of antidemocratic measures, such as the mayor or the state taking control of the school system. Second, charter schools are often (though not always) less accountable to the public, and less open to community involvement, than public schools. And third, the private schools receiving public resources as a result of voucher and voucher-like programs are subjected to even less public scrutiny.

"When [parents] go into the [charter] schools, the attitude is 'Why are you here? What are you doing here?' It's almost as if they're trespassing. That's the reaction they get when they go into their kids' schools. They get no information, and they're made to feel immediately unwelcome on sight."—Donald Chopin, grandparent, New Orleans

Overall, school privatization frequently triggers a downward spiral from which many communities never recover.[30] There is now a familiar pattern to how these dynamics take place. The public schools are systematically under-resourced and overly maligned as "failing," which drives many families away. Desperate for better options, many of those families go to the shiny new charter schools or voucher programs that are being touted by policy makers and are receiving glowing media coverage. The remaining public schools are then further strained as a result of the dynamics described above, which often leads to their closure. However, that only deepens the spiral as the remaining public schools are increasingly overburdened, more families and educators are driven away, there is additional harm caused to the surrounding community, and thus more closures. As a result, one of the most likely outcomes from school closures is that additional closures will soon follow, with the collateral damage expanding exponentially.[31]

"H. D. Woodson is one of the schools of last resort. We receive students from schools that have been closed, we receive the students that charter schools have decided they no longer want to teach, and then we're asked to perform at the level of schools that have decided they can't teach these students. We're held to corporate standards like the [DC-CAS high-stakes standardized] test, and that's used to explain why our budget should be

> taken over by the central office. They constantly shuffle our administration
> and every year threaten to fire all of the staff, which then causes teachers
> to burn out and want to leave because how can you raise a family or do
> these things when your job is constantly being threatened? It's very hard
> for everyone to want to stay at the school—students, parent, teachers,
> and administrators—because we're being told how awful we are all of the
> time."—Washington, DC, teacher

When you add all that up, no matter how much weight is given to any inno-
vations or competition-related advances that may have occurred as a result of
school privatization, no one could reasonably suggest that the changes were
worth the enormous harm that has been caused. That in itself should be more
than sufficient to invalidate, and put an end to, this series of "reforms," particularly as the harm threatens to become increasingly severe as charter schools
and voucher programs proliferate further. Nevertheless, school privatization
efforts have dramatically intensified in recent years, and as a result we now spend
approximately $50 billion in local, state, and federal funds per year on charter
schools, vouchers, and voucher-like programs.[32] This is despite the fact that the
proponents of those efforts have, since the beginning of the school privatization
effort, been repeatedly warned about the risks involved and made aware of the
destruction they are causing.

Indeed, the severe harm caused by school privatization has led to a fierce
backlash from the communities most affected by it. For many years, there has
been an unmistakable public outcry from parents, students, and community
members. All across the country, they have been speaking at school board
meetings, city council meetings, town hall meetings, and every other venue
available to them to inform their elected officials of the irrevocable and often
catastrophic harm that would result, and has resulted, from school privatization. They have engaged in protests, picket lines, hunger strikes, sit-ins, walkouts, walk-ins, and boycotts.[33] At least a dozen cities filed complaints with the
US Department of Education Office of Civil Rights under Title VI of the Civil
Rights Act of 1964.[34] Prominent national organizations with membership in
the most affected communities, such as the Movement for Black Lives, the
NAACP, and the Journey for Justice Alliance / We Choose Campaign have all
called for a moratorium on school privatization because of the harm being
inflicted. The damage has been so severe that school privatization has pro-
voked the rise of two other national campaigns, the Alliance to Reclaim Our

Schools (AROS) and the Network for Public Education, to oppose these efforts and promote public schooling. School privatization and its effects were also invoked as one of the key reasons for the wave of teacher strikes and walkouts across the country in 2018 and 2019.[35]

Despite this resistance from the very communities that school privatization claims to benefit, and some promising victories in slowing down that agenda, advocates for charter schools and vouchers haven't been deterred.[36] Thus, there continues to be a legitimate concern that the public schools in many more communities of color across the country will soon be eliminated. Plus, if there is one thing that school privatization advocates have made clear over the years, it is that they are willing to be patient and play the long game. Indeed, while their efforts have been primarily directed at black and brown communities thus far, as will be discussed later in this chapter, it is clear that school privatizers have their ultimate targets set much more broadly than that.

From Gates to Koch: A Billionaire-Led Effort

Given the extensive harm caused by school privatization and the fervent opposition to it from the communities where it is being implemented, it is fair to ask how it continues to receive such broad bipartisan support, and what continues to drive the charter school and voucher agenda forward. The answer is simple. The school privatization agenda is being led and aggressively funded by a very small group of American billionaires.

Virtually all of the most prominent supporters for charter schools and voucher programs come from the Forbes 400 list of wealthiest Americans.[37] In fact, supporting school privatization has become almost a defining feature of US billionaires. Of the fifty wealthiest individuals listed by Forbes in 2017, at least forty-two of them have been directly connected to school privatization efforts.[38]

However, to fully understand the impact the ultra-wealthy have had on the education system, one must dig deeper into the extent of their investments, and the strategy behind them. (I recognize that most people's eyes glaze over once they start to see data and financial figures. Try as they might, once they see those little numbers on a page, they immediately feel compelled to find something—anything—else to do. If that applies to you, I would strongly urge you to fight that inclination and plow through the next several pages. Trust me—you will soon understand why I risked making almost every reader miserable to include it.)

The following individuals and foundations have been among the main drivers of the school privatization agenda (to give a sense of the extraordinary levels of wealth involved, I have included their Forbes ranking):

- The Walton family, whose wealth comes primarily from Walmart, is the richest family in America (net worth $130 billion) and has seven members of the family among the eighty-five wealthiest individuals. By 2016, the Walton Family Foundation had invested more than $1.3 billion in school privatization efforts, and individual family members have invested large sums on top of that.[39]
- Bill Gates (Forbes #2, net worth $106 billion), founder of Microsoft, is cochair of the Bill & Melinda Gates Foundation, which invests hundreds of millions of dollars a year on K–12 education issues, primarily to promote or support school privatization.[40]
- Eli Broad (#84, $6.8 billion) is the former head of home builder KB Homes and the annuities company SunAmerica. Through his Broad Foundation, he has donated hundreds of millions of dollars to a wide variety of organizations advancing a school privatization agenda.
- Charles Koch (#13, $41 billion) and his late brother David Koch, who formerly shared majority control of Koch Industries, have invested heavily in school privatization, particularly in the promotion of voucher programs. They also organized a network of "dark money" donors to support their agenda.[41] Leaked documents have indicated that it includes hedge fund manager Ken Griffin (#38, $12.7 billion); the former head of ABC Supply roofing company, Diane Hendricks (#79, $7 billion); the head of oil and gas company Continental Resources, Harold Hamm (#55, $8.8 billion); the president and CEO of Menard's home improvement stores, John Menard Jr. (#41, $11.5 billion); hedge fund manager Paul Singer (#239, $3.5 billion); and the head of the well-known discount brokerage firm, Charles Schwab (#63, $7.7 billion), among other multimillionaires and billionaires. Until his death in 2018, it also included the billionaire cofounder of Amway (and father of former US secretary of education Betsy DeVos) Rich DeVos.
- Facebook CEO Mark Zuckerberg (#4, $69.6 billion) and Netflix CEO Reed Hastings (#239, $3.5 billion) both invest heavily in school privatization through the Silicon Valley Community Foundation, which also pools investments from other wealthy Silicon Valley investors.
- Michael Dell (#18, $32.3 billion), the chairman and CEO of the computer company Dell, has invested hundreds of millions of dollars in a multifaceted school privatization strategy.

- Former hedge fund manager John Arnold (#261, $3.3 billion) has been investing heavily in school privatization only since 2012 but has made major investments in that agenda in recent years.
- Gap cofounder Doris Fisher (#355, $2.4 billion) and her late husband, Donald Fisher, were among the earliest and most dedicated investors in the expansion of charter schools.
- Former hedge fund manager Julian Robertson (#154, $4.4 billion) has been a major investor in national school privatization efforts through his Robertson Foundation. He also founded the Tiger Foundation, which focuses specifically on New York City–based efforts and is also supported by his former hedge fund colleagues.
- The Lynde and Harry Bradley Foundation (which was formed from wealth generated by Allen-Bradley, a manufacturer of factory automation equipment) has been a significant force in advancing various right-wing initiatives, including school privatization.

There are many other billionaires who have devoted millions, and even tens of millions of dollars, to school privatization efforts. However, to give a sense of the impact that just a very small number of individuals have had on public education, the tables in this chapter show the funds donated in recent years by the individuals and foundations listed above to fifty organizations of various sorts that are highly influential in the school privatization effort.[42] It is important to note that this represents just a small fraction of the organizations supported by these individuals. It also doesn't include the considerable resources they spend on political donations and lobbying in this area. Nevertheless, this sample serves to illustrate the incredible impact that even a very small number of ultra-wealthy individuals can have.

Table 2 shows the donations (listed in millions of dollars) from these ten sources to some of the more prominent school privatization advocacy organizations. These organizations represent some of the most influential voices in this field, owing in significant part to the fact that they have collectively received over $730 million from just these ten sources. For many of these organizations, the donations reflected in table 2 represented a substantial percentage, or even a majority, of their funding.

Similarly, table 3 lists the donations provided to certain think tanks—including those considered to be progressive and those considered to be conservative—that have been active in advancing school privatization. (Note that not all the donations listed are necessarily directed at school privatization–related projects. That wasn't possible to determine through tax filings. However, even if some of these grants weren't directly related to school privatization, the donation of such large

TABLE 2 Prominent school privatization advocacy groups

	GATES	WALTON	BROAD	DELL	ARNOLD	ROBERTSON	BRADLEY	FISHER	SILICON VALLEY COMMUNITY FOUNDATION	KOCH NETWORK	TOTALS
50Can / StudentsFirst	$2.8	$36.0	$5.5	–	$8.1	$1.3	$0.1	$0.3	$7.1	$0.0	**$61.1**
Alliance for School Choice / American Federation for Children	–	$31.6	$0.2	–	$0.8	$7.1	$0.4	–	$0.0	$0.1	**$40.2**
American Legislative Exchange Council (ALEC)	$0.2	–	–	–	–	–	$2.9	–	–	$4.4	**$7.6**
Americans for Prosperity	–	$0.6	–	–	–	–	$1.9	–	–	$217.6	**$220.1**
Bellwether Education Partners	$8.0	$4.4	$0.1	$0.0	$2.0	–	–	–	$1.3	–	**$15.8**
Black Alliance for Educational Options	$4.3	$18.1	$0.2	–	$4.1	$0.1	$2.7	$0.1	–	–	**$29.5**
Center for Education Reform	$1.3	$10.1	$0.1	–	–	–	$0.9	$0.2	–	$0.2	**$12.8**
Education Reform Now / Democrats for Education Reform	$1.1	$19.4	$6.2	–	$3.1	$0.3	–	$0.6	$1.7	–	**$32.3**
Education Trust	$75.6	$9.1	$2.0	–	$4.0	–	–	$0.0	$5.5	–	**$96.1**
Educators for Excellence	$12.0	$5.4	$2.4	–	$0.5	$2.0	–	–	$0.9	–	**$23.2**
Families for Excellent Schools	–	$14.9	$1.4	–	–	$3.0	–	–	$1.2	$0.1	**$20.6**
Foundation for Excellence in Education	$11.4	$16.6	$2.4	–	$1.0	$3.0	$0.5	$0.1	$0.8	–	**$35.7**
Libre Initiative	–	–	–	–	–	–	–	–	–	$27.0	**$27.0**
National Alliance for Public Charter Schools	$21.3	$19.9	$2.4	–	$1.2	$4.2	–	$3.0	$0.3	–	**$52.1**
Parent Revolution	–	$8.6	$1.4	–	$4.5	–	–	–	$1.5	–	**$16.1**
Stand for Children	$20.9	$4.1	$0.5	–	$6.6	$1.0	–	–	$2.5	–	**$35.6**

(donations in millions of dollars)

TABLE 3 Select think tanks promoting school privatization

	GATES	WALTON	BROAD	DELL	ARNOLD	ROBERTSON	BRADLEY	FISHER	SILICON VALLEY COMMUNITY FOUNDATION	KOCH NETWORK	TOTALS
American Enterprise Institute	$7.7	$1.9	$0.1	–	$0.2	–	$11.2	–	$1.4	$28.5	**$50.9**
Brookings Institution	$37.5	$4.1	–	–	$4.3	–	–	$0.0	$0.3	$3.5	**$49.6**
Cato Institute	–	$0.5	–	–	–	–	$2.5	–	$0.1	$13.2	**$16.3**
Center for American Progress	$14.0	$2.0	$2.0	–	$0.0	–	–	–	$6.0	$0.0	**$24.0**
Heritage Foundation	–	$0.7	–	–	–	–	$6.6	–	$0.0	$8.1	**$15.4**
State Policy Network	–	$0.5	–	–	–	–	$1.1	–	–	$30.0	**$31.7**
Thomas B. Fordham Institute	$9.6	$6.9	$0.6	$0.1	$0.3	$0.3	$0.9	$0.1	$0.4	$0.0	**$19.2**

(donations in millions of dollars)

sums can still be influential in shaping organizational positions on these issues and can also free up other organizational resources to be devoted to school privatization efforts.)

Many of the largest investments have been reserved for individual charter schools and charter school management organizations. They are often funneled through charter school investment organizations such as the Charter School Growth Fund or the NewSchools Venture Fund, which subsequently invest in what they determine to be the most promising charter school organizations. Note that over $761 million has been invested in these two organizations by these ten sources (see table 4).

In addition, the ultra-wealthy individuals driving the school privatization effort often invest directly in charter school networks. Table 5 shows their donations to ten prominent networks nationwide.

To get a more complete picture of some of the large-scale investments going toward these individual charter school networks, table 6 provides the same list of ten charter school networks with (a) their direct donations from these ten ultra-wealthy sources; (b) the donations they have received directly from the Charter School Growth Fund and the NewSchools Venture Fund (much of which comes indirectly from the same ten sources); and (c) the grants each received from the US Department of Education from 2010 through 2018 (which are, in significant part, the result of extensive lobbying and advocacy efforts by these ten sources or organizations funded by them).[43]

Note that these ten charter school networks have received over $1.4 billion in supplemental financial support beyond what they receive from their state and local governments to operate their schools. KIPP, by itself, has received almost $643 million from this small group of donors. (Let this be the end of any attempts by wealthy individuals to claim that school quality is unrelated to school funding.)[44]

In addition to funding charter school networks, these billionaires frequently invest heavily in state charter school associations to support lobbying, advocacy, and charter school operations within that state. Table 7 presents examples of three such organizations, from California, Colorado, and Illinois.

The ultra-wealthy have also recognized that in order for their strategy to work, they also need (a) low-cost teachers to replace those who are laid off or pushed out of the profession by school privatization efforts, and (b) public school administrators who will be supportive of school privatization. Thus, these ten sources have contributed over $443 million to Teach for America and $105 million to the Broad Center for the Management of School Systems (see table 8).

Some of the savvier school privatization investors have also recognized that they can expedite their reform efforts by investing directly in local school

TABLE 4 Charter school investors

	GATES	WALTON	BROAD	DELL	ARNOLD	ROBERTSON	BRADLEY	FISHER	SILICON VALLEY COMMUNITY FOUNDATION	KOCH NETWORK	TOTALS
Charter School Growth Fund	$60.5	$191.5	$0.6	$22.4	$32.4	$5.0	$25.5	$9.0	$111.6	–	$458.6
NewSchools Venture Fund	$100.2	$45.9	$15.6	$9.3	$3.1	$20.1	–	$0.2	$108.2	–	$302.6

(donations in millions of dollars)

TABLE 5 Select charter school networks

	GATES	WALTON	BROAD	DELL	ARNOLD	ROBERTSON	BRADLEY	FISHER	SILICON VALLEY COMMUNITY FOUNDATION	KOCH NETWORK	TOTALS
Achievement First (CT, NY, RI)	$7.9	$4.8	$3.2	$3.8	–	$9.3	–	–	$1.1	–	$30.0
Aspire Public Schools (CA, TN)	$22.6	$3.3	$6.6	$8.7	–	–	–	$0.3	$10.4	–	$51.9
Idea Public Schools (TX)	$6.6	$1.8	$0.4	$8.8	$0.1	–	–	–	–	–	$17.7
KIPP (20 states plus DC)	$43.7	$108.1	$30.1	$23.9	$11.3	$30.8	$0.1	$80.0	$37.3	–	$365.3
Mastery Charter Schools (PA, NJ)	$1.8	–	$0.2	$0.4	–	–	–	–	–	$1.5	$3.9
Noble Network (IL)	$1.8	$0.8	$0.1	$2.1	–	–	–	–	–	–	$4.8
Rocketship (CA, TN, WI, DC)	$1.2	$0.4	$2.0	$1.7	–	–	$0.6	–	$2.4	–	$8.4
Success Academy (NY)	$0.4	$12.3	$14.2	–	–	$24.3	–	–	$8.4	$0.2	$59.6
Uplift Education (TX)	$2.8	$1.7	–	$8.1	–	–	–	–	–	–	$12.6
YES Prep (TX)	$3.6	$1.0	$0.3	$8.2	$7.4	–	–	$0.0	–	$0.0	$20.5

(donations in millions of dollars)

TABLE 6 Select charter school networks

	DIRECT DONATIONS FROM 10 PROMINENT SOURCES	GRANTS FROM CHARTER SCHOOL GROWTH FUND AND NEWSCHOOLS VENTURE FUND	GRANTS FROM US DEPARTMENT OF EDUCATION	TOTALS
Achievement First (CT, NY, RI)	$30.0	$13.1	$24.2	**$67.3**
Aspire Public Schools (CA, TN)	$51.9	$21.3	$31.2	**$104.4**
Idea Public Schools (TX)	$17.7	$31.8	$225.8	**$275.3**
KIPP (20 states plus DC)	$365.3	$58.7	$218.8	**$642.9**
Mastery Charter Schools (PA, NJ)	$3.9	$13.0	$17.5	**$34.5**
Noble Network (IL)	$4.8	$13.8	$19.7	**$38.3**
Rocketship (CA, TN, WI, DC)	$8.4	$19.6	$18.8	**$46.8**
Success Academy (NY)	$59.6	$12.4	$54.2	**$126.2**
Uplift Education (TX)	$12.6	$9.5	$10.3	**$32.4**
YES Prep (TX)	$20.5	$7.0	$16.0	**$43.5**

(donations in millions of dollars)

districts—or organizations closely related to district leadership—that express openness to school privatization. These investments may not always go directly toward charter school expansion, but they do serve the purpose of creating relationships with what the billionaires view as "soft targets."[45] These ten sources have made such investments in a number of urban areas across the country. Table 9 shows three examples, from Chicago, Denver, and Philadelphia.

In addition to all these other types of organizations, the ultra-wealthy have invested significant resources in the education media to support coverage that is aligned with their agenda. Table 10 gives examples of five such media outlets. Note that there are many others. For example, Eli Broad has funded education coverage at the *Los Angeles Times*.[46] It is also worth noting that many of the wealthiest Americans own or are heavily invested in media outlets that have taken pro–school privatization positions, such as Michael Bloomberg (#8, $53.4 billion) and Bloomberg News; Rupert Murdoch (#24, $19.1 billion) and Fox News, the *Wall Street Journal*, and the *New York Post*; and the Koch family and Time Inc., which includes *Time* magazine, *People* magazine, *Fortune* magazine, and numerous other publications.

If you add up all these investments across all these tables, these ten sources have, by themselves, invested almost *$3.2 billion* in just these fifty organizations. Again, this represents just a small percentage of the entire field being funded by the ultra-wealthy to advance the school privatization agenda. Nevertheless, this

TABLE 7 Select state-level charter school associations

	GATES	WALTON	BROAD	DELL	ARNOLD	ROBERTSON	BRADLEY	FISHER	SILICON VALLEY COMMUNITY FOUNDATION	KOCH NETWORK	TOTALS
California Charter Schools Association	$8.4	$56.6	$7.3	$7.5	–	$0.5	–	$9.2	$27.0	–	**$116.5**
Colorado League of Charter Schools	$0.8	$10.1	–	–	–	–	–	–	$0.3	–	**$11.2**
Illinois Network of Charter Schools	$1.3	$10.5	–	–	–	–	–	–	–	–	**$11.8**

(donations in millions of dollars)

TABLE 8 Educator-focused organizations

	GATES	WALTON	BROAD	DELL	ARNOLD	ROBERTSON	BRADLEY	FISHER	SILICON VALLEY COMMUNITY FOUNDATION	KOCH NETWORK	TOTALS
Broad Center for the Management of School Systems	$5.2	–	$92.2	–	–	$7.5	–	–	–	–	**$105.0**
Teach for America	$14.8	$155.2	$44.4	$20.9	$25.8	$55.5	$0.9	$100.0	$25.7	–	**$443.2**

(donations in millions of dollars)

TABLE 9 Select investments in local school privatization efforts

	GATES	WALTON	BROAD	DELL	ARNOLD	ROBERTSON	BRADLEY	FISHER	SILICON VALLEY COMMUNITY FOUNDATION	KOCH NETWORK	TOTALS
Chicago Public Schools	$31.5	$0.5	$6.6	$17.1	–	–	–	–	$4.1	–	**$59.7**
Denver Public Schools	$39.0	$3.2	$4.1	$15.7	–	–	–	–	–	–	**$62.1**
Philadelphia Schools Partnership	$2.5	$5.4	–	$4.5	–	–	–	–	–	$1.5	**$13.9**
School District of Philadelphia	$3.8	–	$3.4	$1.0	–	–	–	–	–	–	**$8.2**

(donations in millions of dollars)

TABLE 10 Select education media outlets

	GATES	WALTON	BROAD	DELL	ARNOLD	ROBERTSON	BRADLEY	FISHER	SILICON VALLEY COMMUNITY FOUNDATION	KOCH NETWORK	TOTALS
Chalkbeat	$2.2	$1.3	–	–	–	–	–	–	$1.2	–	**$4.6**
Editorial Projects in Education / *Education Week*	$12.9	$1.5	$0.9	–	–	–	–	–	–	–	**$15.2**
Education Writers Association	$5.1	$1.8	$0.0	$0.8	–	–	–	–	$0.0	–	**$7.8**
National Public Radio	$17.5	$5.5	$0.2	–	–	–	–	–	$0.8	–	**$24.0**
The 74	$1.6	$1.6	$0.3	–	–	–	–	–	$0.1	–	**$3.5**

(donations in millions of dollars)

small sample can provide a sense of how these individuals use their wealth in ways that create an exponentially greater role for themselves in shaping education policies than the parents, students, and community members who are most affected by those policies.

There are several important features to note about the strategy reflected in these investments. First, when viewed as a whole, their approach has been remarkably comprehensive and strategic. These aren't billionaires mindlessly spreading their money around to a variety of unrelated or loosely connected organizations. In fact, this is as far removed from that model of philanthropy as can be imagined. In this sector, the ultra-wealthy are laser-focused on using their wealth to create the greatest possible systemic change. Their investments are designed quite intentionally to reshape the education system through the promotion of charter schools and school vouchers. Their goal is to create an echo chamber of supportive individuals and organizations at every level so that their vision of change becomes inevitable. Thus, they don't just fund organizations; they fund ecosystems of organizations. And because of their extraordinary wealth, they have been able to create and sustain an entirely new sector of organizations that didn't exist previously and wouldn't exist now without their support.

This strategy is particularly noticeable at the local level. The Gates Foundation, for example, has identified a number of large, urban districts that it deemed to be hospitable environments in which to implement its agenda. Within those communities, the foundation doesn't take the usual approach of philanthropic organizations and fund a small number of advocacy organizations working on a particular issue. The Gates Foundation funds *everyone* who has any influence on the school privatization debate, including school districts, charter schools, charter school associations, grassroots organizations, policy advocacy groups, research organizations, Teach for America and other educator-based organizations, local media outlets, etc. It has spread so much money around so broadly that it has been able to create dramatic shifts in policy within relatively short amounts of time. For example, in cities like Chicago, Denver, and Philadelphia, among others, the Gates Foundation has invested tens of millions of dollars in each to cultivate a network of organizations that have all advanced the school privatization agenda in recent years. Other billionaires have taken notice and employed similar strategies, including Mark Zuckerberg, who invested $100 million in a school privatization strategy in Newark and then another $120 million in Northern California's Bay Area schools.[47]

A second feature to notice about this school privatization strategy is that the individuals behind it have increasingly been using their staggering wealth to influence elections. For example, school board elections used to be low-key, low-budget affairs. Now, billionaires are pouring in hundreds of thousands or even millions of dollars into school board races that are strategically important to their agenda.[48] For example, in the 2017 Los Angeles Unified School Board elections, school privatization supporters spent nearly $10 million to win control of the board. Among the largest donors were members of the Walton family, Reed Hastings, Doris Fisher, Michael Bloomberg, and John Arnold, none of whom lives in Los Angeles.[49]

The level of wealth brought to bear on these issues is so extreme that it can be used to simply overwhelm any opponents. In Washington State, supporters of efforts to change state law and allow charter schools to be created within the state were continually defeated in the legislature and by voters through state ballot initiatives. Nevertheless, they kept raising more and more money until finally, on their fourth attempt to pass a ballot initiative, they eked out a victory after repeatedly, and soundly, outspending their opponents. The vast majority of the financing for that multiyear effort came from billionaires such as Gates, the Walton family, the Fisher family, Reed Hastings, Microsoft cofounder Paul Allen, and former Microsoft CEO Steve Ballmer (#9, $51.7 billion).[50]

Third, it is important to note that the Corporate America and Wall Street executives who are advancing the school privatization agenda are also often the same individuals who are impeding efforts to ensure that public schools have adequate resources to serve their students. Of course, where education dollars are finite, all of the efforts to push for investments in charter schools and voucher programs necessarily result in reductions in public school funding. Beyond that, though, many of these billionaires have directly opposed efforts to generate new revenue for public schools. For example, a 2010 ballot initiative in Washington State directed at raising taxes on those earning more than $200,000 in order to increase funding for schools and other priorities was opposed by Steve Ballmer and Paul Allen, each of whom made six-figure donations to the opposition effort.[51]

Another approach the ultra-wealthy have taken is to push for tax cuts that reduce revenue that can be used for schools and other priorities. For example, Kansas's extreme 2012 tax cuts were heavily influenced by the Koch brothers and have led to such severe financial straits and budget cuts that the Kansas Supreme Court ruled in 2017 that the state's public education funding is unconstitutionally low.[52]

Sometimes the undermining of public school funding can be more indirect. When corporations secure tax breaks from states and localities, that results in lost revenue for school systems. Similarly, when the ultra-wealthy avoid paying their fair share of taxes due to various loopholes or the use of offshore tax shelters, they deprive schools of much-needed resources.

A fourth feature to note about the billionaire-led school privatization strategy is that these individuals have exploited any available opportunity to advance their agenda. In the case of New Orleans, it was Hurricane Katrina that created the opportunity to close down the public schools and reopen them as charter schools. In Puerto Rico, it was Hurricane Maria.[53] In other cities, it has been budgetary challenges, declining enrollment, or public school performance that have been used to justify school privatization. Most recently, it has been the COVID-19 pandemic.[54] In virtually all instances, the "crises" that supposedly necessitate privatization have been largely manufactured and pretextual.[55]

Fifth, the school privatization strategy is remarkable for how it has brought together some strange bedfellows. Consider the dramatically different public reputations of Bill Gates and Charles Koch. Gates is viewed as politically progressive, receives very favorable press for his philanthropy, and is widely admired by the public.[56] Koch, on the other hand, is often portrayed as the arch-villain of conservative politics, the dark, sinister force behind an ambitious right-wing agenda. (Fun fact: the fortune inherited by the Koch brothers from their father, Fred Koch, was accumulated in part through lucrative business relationships with the regimes of Adolf Hitler and Joseph Stalin.)[57] Note, however, that as it relates to school privatization, Gates and Koch are quite aligned. They fund several of the same organizations, and beyond that direct overlap, the additional organizations they each fund work with each other as allies in promoting school privatization. As will be discussed later in the chapter, though their end goals may be different, there is very little space separating Gates and Koch on this issue.

Finally, it is important to recognize that there has been absolutely no sign of the ultra-wealthy changing course or relenting in their strategy. On the contrary, they are escalating their efforts. The Walton Family Foundation announced that it plans to spend $1 billion over the five-year period from 2017 through 2021 to create new charter schools.[58] The Koch network is wielding far more money and influence than it was a decade ago and is increasingly using that clout to advance school privatization.[59] And younger billionaires, such as Mark Zuckerberg and John Arnold, are aggressively expanding their influence.

Additionally, school privatization advocates have been increasingly successful in getting their allies into positions of power. For example, Betsy DeVos, the US secretary of education in the Trump administration, is not only the daughter of one of the Koch brothers' former allies, Rich DeVos; she is also the former board chair for the Alliance for School Choice and American Federation for Children, two of the prominent school privatization organizations that received over $40 million in donations from the ten sources highlighted earlier.

One of the primary vehicles for aggressively pushing this agenda has been ALEC, which is heavily tied to the individuals and organizations discussed previously. For example, as was already mentioned, Gates, Koch, and the Bradley Foundation have all donated directly to ALEC. Additionally, Microsoft, Walmart, the Walton Family

Foundation, Facebook, the Bradley Foundation, and Dell have all been members of ALEC, and some of the most prominent school privatization advocacy organizations, such as the Alliance for School Choice / American Federation for Children, the Center for Education Reform, and the Thomas B. Fordham Institute, have also been active within ALEC.[60] To give a sense of the impact of their collaboration, consider that just in 2015, at least 172 bills were introduced in forty-two state legislatures around the country that reflected ALEC's school privatization priorities.[61]

Make no mistake: School privatization efforts may have garnered support from various stakeholders over the years, but it is unmistakably a hostile takeover of public schools that is being led by a small group of billionaires. If not for the staggering financial investment of this small group of individuals, there is simply no way that charter schools and school vouchers would have caused such extensive harm in black and brown communities across the country.

Superficial Reform and the Illusion of Progress

Nevertheless, these billionaires and their grantees continually make lofty claims about how their efforts are improving education quality and addressing racial inequity. The obvious question to ask in response would be, "How?" If they are going to insist that school privatization is the magic bullet, they have to be able to provide an explanation for it. How does privatizing schools improve the quality of teaching and learning? How is it making the education system more equitable? What is the secret that would allow them to achieve such results? And what is it about public schools that doesn't allow for the same results?

If you strip away all the noise surrounding these issues, the premise advanced by school privatization advocates is this: if you shift from public to private management and eliminate some regulations that the schools have to follow, then education quality will improve dramatically, and the impact of generations of multifaceted racial inequities will be eliminated, or at least substantially reduced. The entire idea is ludicrous on its face. There is no way that any thoughtful observer could examine the challenges faced by the students, families, and educators within low-income communities of color and conclude that privatization would magically solve them. It simply doesn't compute. $A + B \neq C$.

This is the dirty little secret of school privatization advocates, that their "movement" is based on hype, not substance. This becomes obvious when you go to the websites of the most prominent school privatization advocacy organizations to learn about what they claim to be the value provided by charter schools and vouchers.

For example, here is the entire response of the National Association of Public Charter Schools to the question "What makes charter schools different than other schools?"

> Each of the more than 6,900 charter schools is unique—both inside and out. Some may focus on college prep, some follow a Montessori curriculum, and others integrate the arts into each subject. Most charter schools are located in urban areas, but there are charter schools in suburban and rural areas as well. Some charter schools require uniforms, others have longer school days, and some teach their entire curriculum in two languages. The possibilities are endless, but charter schools aim to provide a range of options so that parents can choose the school that best fits their child.[62]

There isn't a single characteristic in that paragraph that is unique to charter schools. Every one of them is also true of some public schools. Indeed, while we shouldn't be fooled into thinking that more variety necessarily produces better quality, it is nevertheless true that public schools have been adopting a variety of pedagogical methods and curricula for decades. While school privatization advocates frequently assert that charters represent choice, and public schools represent a monolith, it's just not supported by the facts. More broadly, everyone can agree that parents should have meaningful choices when it comes to their children's education. However, while many ingredients are necessary to make that happen, privatization isn't one of them.

Similarly, if you look at the websites for the Center for Education Reform and Jeb Bush's Foundation for Excellence in Education, the only identifiable explanation for school privatization improving overall education quality is that charter schools are supposedly superior because they face fewer regulations and are more accountable for results. The Center for Education Reform says that charters "are judged on how well they meet the student achievement goals," and if they cannot perform, they will be closed. It also says that being freed from "red tape" allows charters to focus more on "educational excellence."[63] The Foundation for Excellence in Education says that, in contrast to public schools, charter schools are provided more "operational autonomy" in exchange for being "held accountable for student success."[64]

Once again, the rhetoric doesn't match reality. Regarding their supposedly greater accountability, anyone who has monitored the education policy debates for the past twenty years should know that there is no basis for suggesting that public schools face less public accountability than charter schools. While there are serious concerns with regard to the methods by which we hold public schools accountable for their performance—see more in the following pages—there can be no denying that they face rigorous scrutiny.

Also, it is deeply concerning that this sector is so nonchalant about simply closing charter schools that don't "perform." The harms that often result from the closure of public schools can also be triggered by the closure of charter schools. These are schools after all, not pop-up businesses.

As for the claim that fewer regulations produces higher-quality education, that is also unfounded. Many of the regulatory areas from which charters seek exemptions often have no connection with education quality at all.[65] For example, many charters have sought to become exempt from various school disciplinary protections for students. However, making it easier for charter schools to exclude and push out students using suspensions and expulsions doesn't translate to educational improvement, though it can be useful in creating the *appearance* of educational improvement.

To be fair, there are regulations from which charter schools often receive exemptions that can have some impact on student learning. For example, having greater freedom to select the teachers for a school can be beneficial when there are excessive staffing barriers that have been put in place. Also, under certain circumstances, providing quality educators with greater autonomy can have merit. However, in the grand scheme of challenges facing our education system, and in particular facing low-income students of color, these are relatively minor issues. The idea that we would need to spend hundreds of billions of dollars and cause massive harm in creating a parallel, privatized school system to address these issues is absurd. That would be similar to commissioning the entire Seventh Fleet of the US Navy to kill a mosquito. Where there are real concerns around such issues, there are far more efficient and less damaging ways to address them than school privatization.

Ultimately, while there is no shortage of bluster surrounding charter schools and school vouchers, the reality is that they do virtually nothing to address the most significant issues facing our education system, and racial injustice within that system. Privatizing schools doesn't even represent a serious attempt at addressing the challenges faced by many youth of color.

Nevertheless, the school privatization effort continues to grow because its proponents continue to seek out, and highlight for the public, examples in which students in charter schools or voucher programs scored higher on standardized tests than students in public schools. That supposed test score superiority is the foundation on which the entire school privatization "movement" is built. However, as mentioned earlier, such claims are unfounded. But what if they were right, and charter schools and private schools were somehow inherently better at raising test scores than public schools? How would we use that information?

These are important questions to ask because of how central high-stakes standardized test scores have become in the public conversation around school privatization and the education system more generally. We put an enormous amount of weight on these metrics, so it is critically important that we all understand what they actually mean and the purposes for which they can reliably be used.

Brief personal confession: I love data. I have spent many a day with an Excel spreadsheet on my computer and a smile on my face. But after many years of analyzing standardized test scores in cities and states around the country, the conclusion I have reached is this: They tell us virtually nothing of value about education quality in a particular school or school district. We simply don't have any large-scale data systems that can reliably tell us where high-quality education is happening, where it isn't happening, and why it is or isn't happening. Even the best standardized tests can't be depended on to tell us whether students are receiving a well-rounded education. They can't tell us whether students have mastered content or simply mastered taking a test on that content. They can't tell us whether a school is overly focused on rote learning and "drill and kill" activities designed specifically to raise test scores at the expense of higher-order thinking. They can't tell us with any certainty what a school or a teacher has contributed to students' knowledge and ability versus what those students already knew or could do when they walked in the door. They can't tell us if students are being pushed out of school to boost results. They can't tell us if some schools are doing better than others because they are provided with more resources and institutional support than others. They can't tell us how many students have lost or gained a love of learning as a result of the education they received prior to the test. They can't tell us if the student body in a charter school is truly representative of the larger community. They simply can't tell us most of what parents want to know about how their child is being educated.

That is intuitively obvious to most adults. Life isn't like an episode of *Jeopardy*, or a game of Trivial Pursuit. Adulthood isn't a long series of multiple-choice and short-answer questions. Being a high-functioning adult means being able to think critically and creatively. It is being able to work collaboratively with people. To communicate effectively. To apply academic learning to real-world situations. To be a problem solver. To be able to build healthy relationships with others and be an engaged global citizen. The world doesn't need people who can provide the "right" answers to standardized test questions. We need people who can seek out multiple answers, who can identify the flaws in the questions they are being asked, and who can point us to new and different questions that we should be asking instead. We need people who are willing to pursue knowledge independently and are able to think deeply to find it. We need people who are conscientious and compassionate and can effectively navigate the world and put their education to use in serving their communities. Unfortunately, ever since the passage of the No Child Left Behind Act in 2001, anyone who has been paying attention knows all of the following to be true as a result of our national obsession with high-stakes testing. It has led to

- severe undervaluing of the many aptitudes, skills, and curricular areas that are untested;
- a great many young people doubting their own abilities and value, and becoming disengaged from school as a result;
- many other young people developing a false sense of superiority over their peers;
- educational opportunities being unjustifiably rationed out on the basis of test scores;
- many schools and educators being punished for the failure of policy makers to provide them with the resources necessary to meet their students' needs;
- degradation of the quality of education nationwide;
- the worst consequences falling on students, families, educators, and communities of color.

On the flip side, it is difficult to point to any significant systemic benefit that has resulted from the explosion of high-stakes testing. The most common justification for these tests is that they highlight inequities in educational outcomes. However, we already had many years of low-stakes data demonstrating the exact same thing. Plus, attaching high stakes to standardized tests hardly serves any function at all that isn't negative or punitive. Rarely are the results used for anything beyond shaming, punishing, or preventing the advancement of students, teachers, schools, and school systems.

To be clear, standardized tests can serve a limited purpose as a diagnostic or formative tool. However, it is a profound misuse and abuse of these instruments to make important decisions on the basis of them. School accountability is far too important to be based on such shoddy evidence. While we must of course ensure that schools are doing what the communities they serve need them to do, that accountability should be based on factors far more meaningful than the ones we use currently.

Ultimately, then, it comes down to this: virtually the entire justification for school privatization can be boiled down to the claim that it can raise test scores. But not only is that claim unsubstantiated, even if it were true, those gains are of such limited educational value that using them to make enormous policy decisions is both irresponsible and indefensible. Frankly, if small, inconsistent standardized test score differences are all that you have to point to as evidence of your value, then you don't really have anything. And even if you disagree with these assessments of the evidence and believe that school privatization does improve test scores in ways that are connected to actual improved school performance, then those marginal gains would still not even come close to overriding all the harm that has been created in the process.

This isn't the only fundamental flaw of school privatization efforts. In fact, the entire endeavor is riddled with hypocrisy. For example, school privatization advocates claim that shifting from public to private management and reducing bureaucracy are the keys to school success, yet they neglect to explain how all of the thousands of high-achieving public schools across the country are able to achieve their results despite those "challenges."

The hypocrisy certainly doesn't end there. School privatizers often blame public school "failures" on the existence of large bureaucracies, and thus for many years they have argued that the remedy is small, personalized, community-based charters.[66] Also, for many years, charter school advocates claimed that their intent was to create a small number of charter schools as a supplement to, not a replacement for, the public school system. However, the reality is that the school privatization sector has invested particularly heavily in creating massive corporate charter school franchises that are already larger than almost all the public school districts in the country and continue to grow dramatically.[67]

The original charter schools were intended to try out new, innovative instructional strategies that could be employed in the public school system more broadly. However, after thirty years of charter schools, advocates have shown no interest in taking whatever they have learned and applying it to public schools. They also haven't been able to identify a single education innovation that couldn't be easily implemented in public schools if those schools were provided the appropriate resources.[68] Plus, for all the talk about innovation, the school privatization sector really only has one idea. Whatever problem arises with a public school system, their proposed remedy is the same: privatization.

Additionally, school privatization advocates often claim that they are focused exclusively on the interests of children while their opponents are focused too much on the interests of educators.[69] Yet these individuals are typically silent when public school budgets get cut, when public schools get closed, and when students in public schools suffer as a result of the expansion of charters and vouchers.[70] Also, if young people really were the primary concern, why not just use all the billions of dollars invested in school privatization to improve existing schools and address students' other developmental needs rather than creating a parallel system of schools that competes for resources?

Moreover, if their primary interest really were children, then one would think that they would be laser focused on supporting those who have dedicated their careers to educating those children. However, a key tactic in advancing school privatization has been attacking and deprofessionalizing teachers and teacher unions, and using the expansion of charter schools as a union-busting tactic. While there are undoubtedly some local unions that have made some highly questionable decisions over the years, which can occasionally be *a* problem, teachers' unions as a whole have often been treated as if they were *the* problem.[71] In other words, school privatization advocates have located the epicenter of our education inequities squarely within the teaching profession, and not, for example, with the policy makers who repeatedly undermine and underfund public schools, or the ultra-wealthy who avoid paying taxes that would support education. Moreover, privatization advocates have yet to explain how they intend to attract and retain quality teachers after waging a long, sustained attack against the teaching profession that has led to cuts in teachers' wages and benefits, and deterioration in their working conditions. (Also, it is worth mentioning that teachers unions have played a central role, and perhaps the most significant role, in preventing school privatization advocates from causing even more harm to students, families, and communities than they already have.)

Another one of the key arguments made in support of privatized education is that it will use resources more efficiently and cut costs. Yet there is absolutely nothing efficient about creating a separate, deregulated system of schools in which waste, fraud, and abuse are prevalent and taxpayer dollars are being used to support fly-by-night charter school operators.[72] And with regard to cost cutting, school privatization advocates have dramatically changed their tune in recent years. Now, instead of arguing that they can educate children more affordably, they claim that it is unfair if they receive less funding than public schools and thus have been mounting advocacy campaigns aimed at receiving equal funding.[73]

Furthermore, if the goal is to ensure that every child has access to a high-quality education, as school privatizers claim, then how does it make sense to replace public schools that have been charged with serving all students—including students with many different types of disabilities and English learners from all over the world—with charter schools and private schools that haven't been so charged and that often aren't equipped to do so?[74]

The No-Excuses Trap

Perhaps the most damaging hypocrisy of school privatization advocates is that the most celebrated charter schools, the ones that are lifted up as models and used to justify expansion of the whole sector, are frequently the ones that are the least accommodating for the full range of student needs and learning styles. The networks that are proliferating the fastest are the "no excuses" charter schools such as KIPP, Success Academy, Aspire, Idea, Mastery, YES Prep, and Achievement First that often employ narrow, strictly regimented curricula and heavy-handed, deeply harmful disciplinary methods.

For example, remember Anna Jones from chapter 1, whose children were severely affected by school closures on the South Side of Chicago? Many of the public schools that were closed were essentially replaced by charter schools, and many of those new schools were Noble Network schools. In recent years, Noble has expanded from a single school to a network of eighteen schools on the South Side and West Side of Chicago. Noble's growth has been fueled by the enormous private donations it received, including more than $155 million it collected from 2006 to 2018.[75] As mentioned earlier, Noble has received $1.8 million from the Gates Foundation, $2.1 million from Michael Dell, almost $14 million from the Charter School Growth Fund and NewSchools Venture Fund, and almost $20 million in grants from the US Department of Education since 2010.

Noble has long been a darling of the school privatization community and has been heavily supported by both Republicans and Democrats. For example, former mayor of Chicago Rahm Emanuel (D) has been a longtime fan, claiming that Noble has found the "secret sauce" of school success and has "the most successful high schools he's seen."[76] Before he took office, former Illinois governor Bruce Rauner (R), a billionaire former private equity executive, donated $3.5 million to Noble.[77] The family of the current governor, J. B. Pritzker (D) (Forbes seventh-richest family in America, $29 billion), has also made sizable donations to Noble.[78] (Two of the Noble schools are even named after Rauner and the Pritzkers.) And in 2015, the Broad Foundation awarded Noble with the national Broad Prize for Public Charter Schools as the "best-performing large public charter school system in America."[79]

So what did all this support from Noble's wealthy and politically powerful benefactors go toward building? What was the model of education that they were so excited to replicate that they subjected residents like Anna Jones to tumultuous school closures?

Well, perhaps the most notable feature of Noble's model of education is how many of their students they choose *not* to educate. For example, according to data from the US Department of Education, Noble's expulsion rate in 2015–16 was over seven times higher than the national average.[80] That year, out of the 575 schools in Chicago, the eight schools with the highest number of expulsions across the city were all Noble schools.[81] Even Noble's own teachers have described their methods and high rates of student push-out as "dehumanizing."[82]

Additionally, Noble received national condemnation in 2012 for its extreme approach to school discipline that involved imposing monetary fines on students for even the most minor disciplinary infractions. Noble collected almost

$400,000 from its student body, which was overwhelmingly composed of black and Latinx youth from low-income families.[83] Even after it became a national news story, Noble refused to change its practices until state legislation outlawing disciplinary fines was introduced.

Moreover, Noble is known for devoting much of its curriculum to standardized-test preparation. In fact, teacher pay has been linked to test performance at Noble, creating even more incentives to use "drill and kill" methods that may produce more superficially impressive data but don't actually improve the quality of teaching or learning.[84]

Nevertheless, as a result of the largesse of their ultra-wealthy supporters, Noble schools and others like them have expanded dramatically in Chicago in recent years. Meanwhile, it is families like Anna Jones's that suffer the consequences from the city's unwillingness to build a system that provides a high-quality education for all children.

Similarly, at the national level, KIPP schools have been perhaps the most high-profile and most highly decorated charter schools in the country. KIPP schools are consistently cited as examples of charter school excellence, have been featured in hundreds of news stories lauding their academic performance, and their network has now grown to 242 schools serving over one hundred thousand students.[85] (Eight of those schools were among those that replaced the public school system in New Orleans, causing severe hardship for Tatanisha Jackson's family and so many others.)[86] As described earlier, they have received enormous financial support from both the ultra-wealthy and the federal government—almost $643 million just from the aforementioned ten billionaire sources, the Charter School Growth Fund, the NewSchools Venture Fund, and the US Department of Education. However, like Noble, they are well known for their extremely strict and punitive disciplinary approaches, along with a highly regimented, standardized-test-focused curriculum.

For example, despite serving a heavy concentration of elementary school students, according to the US Department of Education, in 2015–16 KIPP schools issued out-of-school suspensions at nearly twice the national average.[87] Examining individual schools can be even more illustrative. In Baltimore, the school with the most suspensions and expulsions in the entire city during the 2015–16 school year was a KIPP school.[88] In Boston, a KIPP school had the third-highest out-of-school suspension rate in the city during 2014–15.[89] In Washington, DC, where charter schools suspend students at higher rates than public schools, five of the ten highest-suspending charter schools in 2015–16 were KIPP schools.[90] And a KIPP school in Oklahoma had the third-highest suspension rate of black students of any charter school in the country.[91]

Beyond these high suspension rates, KIPP schools, like many "no excuses" charter schools, have cultivated ultra-strict learning environments. They have embraced the "broken windows" theory of cracking down on even what appear to be trivial rule violations. Many KIPP schools have also embraced methods such as requiring students to walk silently through the halls on one side of a painted line.[92]

When I first saw those lines, and watched a row of black children being marched down the hall of a KIPP school with their heads down and their hands behind their backs, I actually had flashbacks to a time in my career when I spent a lot of time working with, and representing, inmates within maximum security prisons. The method used by the prisons for moving inmates from one place to another was identical. The parallels didn't end there, however. KIPP's extreme focus on social control of its students and the strict enforcement of its rules was startlingly similar to how those prisons were run. It was also hard to miss the stark contrast between the predominantly white teachers and the predominantly black students at many KIPP schools, and how that compared to the racial makeup of the prison guards and the inmates. It was almost as if KIPP had modeled much of its educational approach after what were quite literally the worst places I have ever encountered. Considering that prison administration is, in practice, largely based on the fear of, and contempt toward, inmates, seeing elementary schools employing the same techniques was jarring.

More broadly, the aggressive expansion of charter schools like Noble and KIPP is troubling because they are not offering a model of education that is going to fit the needs of most students and families. They are essentially the modern-day equivalent of the old Catholic schools where the nuns would rap you across your knuckles with a ruler. Their no-excuses approach and "weeding out" of students who don't measure up may appeal to a small number of parents who haven't been provided with any better options for their kids. However, they are not going to be a desirable option for most parents and students, who may rightly question whether those methods are developmentally appropriate or healthy for their children.

This should be especially concerning because, unlike the old private Catholic schools, these "no excuses" charter schools are being funded by public dollars and should thus be serving public purposes. Instead, they are being used as models to expand the entire charter school sector and replace the public schools that are charged with educating all children.

This also demonstrates the ever-increasing problem with comparing the academic results between charter schools and public schools. KIPP operates like a network of private schools, and most parents now know what sending their children there entails, just as parents in the 1950s knew what sending their children to the nuns was going to entail. Thus, schools like KIPP are going to attract students who will thrive in schools like KIPP. If parents don't think that a school like KIPP will be appropriate for their children, they won't send them there—unless, of course, they are not provided with any other viable options. Public schools, on the other hand, have to serve students from across the entire spectrum of human diversity, representing an incredible array of interests, aptitudes, and needs. Comparing the test scores of those students to the test scores of KIPP students, and then using those comparisons to justify privatization, is supremely disingenuous.

Moreover, imagine that you assembled two teams of educators that are of equal quality. The first team is put in charge of a school that uses various methods to shape its student body in favorable ways, is given broad discretion to push out low-achieving or challenging students, is encouraged to focus its curriculum on the improvement of standardized test scores, and is given millions of dollars in private money to supplement its budget.[93] The second team is put in charge of the nearby neighborhood public school that is facing annual budget cuts and has to accept everyone that walks through the door throughout the year, including the students that leave or are pushed out of the first school. Under those conditions, the first team of educators wouldn't have to do anything extraordinary to achieve better results. In fact, it would be shocking if that team didn't post higher test scores, given the enormous advantages it had been provided.

That, in a nutshell, is why the battle between charter schools and public schools is a farce. Charter schools are starting off at third base and acting like they hit a triple. Public schools are being labeled as failing, but in reality, they are being sabotaged. If you really step back and analyze it honestly, the unavoidable conclusion is that the entire school privatization "movement" is a scam, a fraud perpetrated on the American public. Privatization has been presented as a solution to failing schools and education inequities, but it is clear that for many of the key individuals advancing this agenda, privatization isn't a means to an end; it is the end itself. Privatization itself is the goal. It doesn't matter that it is not based on sound research or reasoning. It doesn't matter that it is a house of cards that does nothing to address the root causes of education inequities while causing catastrophic harm in communities across the country. It doesn't matter that there is absolutely nothing to suggest that this is a school improvement strategy on which we, as a country, should be spending massive amounts of time and billions of dollars in public and private resources. All that matters to the leaders of the school privatization movement is that the agenda moves forward, even if that means millions of people are harmed along the way. Even if that means that what they have advertised as an effort to benefit communities of color is, at its roots, profoundly racist.

The Racism of School Privatization

Many readers are already probably recoiling at the use of the "r word." But consider the following:

1. The harms caused by school privatization have been overwhelmingly concentrated in communities of color.

2. While school privatization has been advertised as a racial justice effort, its actual impact has been to suck up much of the oxygen within education reform conversations over the past twenty years and divert attention from the most pressing issues facing students of color.

3. If, as school privatizers suggest, charter schools are inherently superior to public schools, then why have their most aggressive initial efforts been directed entirely at communities of color? If there were truly something intrinsically special about the charter school model, then don't predominantly white, affluent suburbs also deserve to benefit from it? If these schools are so effective, why didn't these billionaires fund privatization efforts in their own communities? And why aren't the residents of predominantly white, affluent communities in the offices of their school superintendents and elected representatives clamoring for more charter schools? The answer, of course, is that communities with well-resourced public schools aren't interested in those superficial and harmful reforms, and everyone who has been paying attention knows that black and brown communities were targeted for school privatization efforts because (a) they have been so thoroughly disempowered politically over the years that they wouldn't be able to provide as much resistance as other communities; (b) school privatizers wouldn't face as much public scrutiny for implementing their "reforms" in communities of color; and (c) after enduring decades of neglect and the undermining of the public schools within communities of color, many people in those communities would be desperate enough to try anything. Thus, these youth of color have been used as a proof-point so that charter schools and voucher programs could gain enough of a toehold to subsequently expand more broadly.

4. What school privatization efforts have demonstrated is that, rather than requiring that education reforms be based on sound, research-based practices, our policy makers are very comfortable in conducting education "experiments" on students of color. (If you analyze this situation and catch a faint whiff of a modern-day Tuskegee syphilis study, you are on the right track.)

5. While there are certainly many individual charter school operators that work with the communities they serve in a responsible, accountable fashion, at the broader, systemic level, school privatization efforts have been done *to*, and not *with*, black and brown communities.[94] In many instances, these communities were robbed of their democratic control over their schools in order to implement school privatization efforts.

6. Here is what the billionaires funding school privatization didn't do: They didn't go into communities of color and explain that they were interested in using their wealth to improve education quality and equity. They didn't engage in a participatory process in which community members could share their views and experiences with inadequate educational opportunities. They didn't create processes by which community members could help to develop and lead processes for school improvement. They didn't enable parents, students, and other community members to use their extensive local expertise to inform reform efforts. They didn't create an authentic, collaborative process by which the benefits associated with great wealth could be leveraged to greatest effect through thoughtful, responsible partnership with communities. Instead, they typically went into communities of color that they identified as low-hanging fruit with a predetermined set of reforms that they wanted to implement, and then used their extraordinary wealth to essentially bully communities into going along with their agenda.

7. This is a question that doesn't get asked enough: Why do communities of color not have the same rights to self-determination that other communities have? Why do Bill Gates, the Walton family, Charles Koch, Mark Zuckerberg, and other ultra-wealthy hedge fund managers and corporate executives get to decide what the school systems are going to look like in the Bronx, South LA, Chicago's South Side, West Philadelphia, New Orleans, Newark, and other communities of color across the country? No one elected them. The parents and students in those communities never consented to having them implement their vision for social change. They never agreed to "reforms" that would affect not only the so-called failing schools but also trigger massive ripple effects across entire education systems and communities. These billionaires typically aren't knowledgeable about the neighborhoods they are destabilizing, the schools they are closing, the teachers who are being fired as a result of their efforts, and the students who are being harmed in the process. What right do they have to

essentially do whatever they want to communities of color? Why is this assumed by so many to be an acceptable use of one's wealth and political influence? If you don't think the answers to those questions have a strong racial component, and instead believe that ultra-wealthy people should simply be trusted to do good things with their money, then ask yourself this: What would be the public reaction if it was divulged that Oprah Winfrey was targeting predominantly white communities across the country to work behind the scenes and transform their public school systems? (In a word, hysteria. And people *love* Oprah.)

8. When communities of color push back on school privatization, they have typically been ignored. However, on those rare occasions when school privatization advocates have felt compelled to respond, they have often replied to well-founded concerns with shameful attacks. For example, as the NAACP was considering its call for a moratorium on charter school expansion, the editorial board of the *Washington Post* wrote a piece that was shocking in its condescension. It began by suggesting that NAACP board members "might want to do a little homework," made the claim that charter schools have "reshaped education" in Washington, DC, and said that "hopefully" it is "not lost on an organization that is supposed to be looking out for the interests of minority people" that the beneficiaries of this "rich school choice" are children of color.[95] Similarly, while he was board chair for the Success Academy charter schools in New York (featured earlier), hedge fund manager Daniel Loeb (#306, $2.8 billion) attacked a black state senator for opposing school privatization efforts, referring to her as a "hypocrite" who "does more damage to people of color than anyone who has ever donned a hood."[96]

9. As described earlier, many of the charter school networks that are being pushed aggressively within communities of color aren't the types of schools that most parents truly want for their children. It is never a parent's first choice to send their child to a "no excuses" charter school that uses prison techniques to maintain order and aggressively pushes students out using harsh disciplinary methods. Those are decisions made out of necessity, when parents haven't been given a real choice of high-quality educational options for their kids. Unfortunately, many parents have been forced into this position, where they have to select the "least worst" option available to them. However, make no mistake: this is an authoritarian model of education that is focused on creating docile, obedient citizens, not critical thinkers. It's about achieving compliance, not liberation.

10. On one side of this equation, you have white billionaires bankrolling school privatization efforts, while individuals such as former US secretary of education Arne Duncan, John McCain, Mitt Romney, Jeb Bush, and now even President Trump defend their school privatization agenda by claiming that it addresses the "civil rights issue of our time."[97] On the other side, there is a massive resistance from people of color around the country who have made it abundantly clear that school privatization is harming their communities, and yet they are treated as if they were collateral damage in the quest to remake our education system.

11. No one can reasonably claim that the communities most affected by school privatization don't need substantial improvements to their education system. But as decidedly imperfect as these public schools are, they are still the product of decades of collective school improvement efforts by students, parents, and community members within black and brown communities. People have worked very hard for a very long time to create higher-quality schools in their neighborhoods, often while facing stiff resistance and major obstacles put in place by some of the same individuals who are now responsible for school privatization. Tragically, many of those hard-fought victories are being washed away as their public schools are closed and undermined by school privatization.

    For example, over the past twenty years, there has been a major, nationwide movement that has been built to dismantle the school-to-prison pipeline. Leading this effort have been students, parents, and community members from the black and brown communities most affected by zero-tolerance school discipline. Together, they achieved remarkable results, substantially shifting policies and practices in schools nationwide. However, charter schools and private schools promoted by voucher programs are largely exempt from, and resistant to, these advances. Also, as described already, the charter school sector stands in direct opposition to these changes by aggressively promoting schools that employ the same harmful, punitive approach that communities of color have been fighting against in public schools. Thus, the school privatization effort is a direct affront to the efforts of all the people of color who have been fighting for years to ensure that their schools are respecting each young person's right to an education.

12. Public school closures and the expansion of charter schools have led to many experienced teachers of color being replaced with inexperienced, nonunionized white teachers.[98] Among many other effects associated with these dynamics, this has meant that there has been a significant loss of unionized teaching jobs within communities of color, which

constituted one of the most stable, well-paying careers available within many communities. The ripple effects of this loss have been substantial, affecting not only these teachers, but also their children, families, and communities.

13. Sadly, one side effect of the school privatization effort is that it has divided communities by turning quality education into something that is generally understood to be scarce. In other words, people are forced to fight over limited spots at the "good schools" because the school privatization effort hasn't been directed at taking the necessary steps to ensure that every child has access to high-quality educational opportunities.

14. During the civil rights movement of the 1960s and throughout history, there were many critical moments in which local, state, and federal government officials stepped up on behalf of children and youth of color who were facing the threat of racist education policies and practices. Now, by aggressively pursuing the privatization of education for children of color, the government is essentially abdicating responsibility for their education.[99] Government officials are washing their hands of what was formerly their responsibility and handing off their duties to private actors without any legitimate reason to believe that it will lead to better results. This represents a painfully ironic twist in the struggle for racial justice because the origins of "school choice" lie in attempts by white communities to avoid integrating their schools after *Brown v. Board of Education*.[100] In other words, school privatization is being sold to the public as an attempt to achieve racial equity when it was initially conceived as an effort to resist racial equity, and our government is a willing partner.

15. Advocates for school privatization say that they want to provide parents with school choice, but what about the vast majority of parents whose choice is to have their children educated in high-quality neighborhood public schools? Why do so many parents in black and brown communities not get to make that choice when parents in predominantly white communities can take that as a given? In many communities of color, the "choice" is now between underresourced public schools and a profoundly harmful privatized system, which is no choice at all.

I am not suggesting here that the billionaires who are advancing the school privatization agenda are closeted racists who believe in the inherent inferiority of people of color. I am suggesting that if you target communities of color to implement an unsound, deeply harmful set of reforms in a nondemocratic way, ignore the harm you cause, fail to respond appropriately to community pushback, and use those communities as your guinea pigs to justify the further expansion of your agenda, all the while neglecting to address, and even exacerbating, the serious, long-standing inequities faced by those communities, then you simply haven't valued the lives of the residents of those communities appropriately, and you *have* contributed to systemic racism.

For too long, communities of color have been treated as speed bumps in the school privatization process. They have been continually exploited and treated as undeserving of the respect and even deference typically afforded predominantly white communities. Indeed, there has likely never been an example of a predominantly white community being treated the way school privatization advocates have routinely treated black and brown communities. The thought itself is practically unimaginable.

This is a different form of racism from what most people are accustomed to. However, modern-day systemic racism rarely involves anything like an angry white bus driver telling a black seamstress to get up from her seat. Instead, it often looks like this: While rolling out the No Child Left Behind Act, which set into motion or dramatically accelerated many of the school privatization dynamics we are facing today, President George W. Bush repeatedly spoke of the law as a racial justice effort, and famously decried the "soft bigotry of low expectations" that it would address.[101] Instead, what has resulted from school privatization has been, at best, the soft bigotry of destructive, paternalistic reforms. Quite often, it has been the hard bigotry of deliberate indifference.

To be clear, if a community comes together and legitimately decides that school privatization represents the best path forward for advancing its children's educational opportunities, then so be it. But that hasn't been how these dynamics have played out. The reality is that school privatization efforts have simply replaced one form of educational neglect in communities of color (underresourced and inequitable public schools) with another. Both can, and have, ruined the lives of many youth of color. And it should be indisputable that moving forward with either will inevitably lead to more children of color being tragically undereducated. Thus, both are unacceptable, meaning we are in dire need of a "third way." Unfortunately, our public debate around these issues has been so thoroughly distorted by school privatization advocates that even the most obvious truths can be difficult to see.

Manufacturing White Consent

Given the context around school privatization, how has it been able to receive so much public support? Specifically, how has it been able to generate so much support among white people, and particularly those who identify as being liberal or progressive, which has been the critical element in transforming school privatization from a right-wing and Republican priority into an issue that has received widespread bipartisan support over the past fifteen years?

The answer is marketing. School privatization's billionaire benefactors have funded a highly sophisticated, multifaceted, and hugely expensive public relations campaign to advance their efforts. This hasn't been, and couldn't have been, a communications campaign based on meaningful reforms and authentic progress. It's been Don Draper selling cigarettes by focusing consumers' attention on anything but the fact that they are poisonous. In short, the public has been misled—oftentimes deliberately—and their sympathies for children have been exploited.

The mechanisms that the ultra-wealthy have used to achieve this shift in public narrative include flooding the media with stories and ads that are favorable to their agenda, utilizing their control and influence over media outlets to shape public opinion, using popular culture to reinforce their messages, funding charter schools to implement advertising and direct marketing campaigns, capitalizing on the long-standing failure of mainstream media outlets to cover the issues and priorities of communities of color on equal footing with those of other communities, and ensuring that individuals favorable to their agenda—such as former US secretaries of education Arne Duncan and Betsy DeVos—are in positions of power where they can guide the public narrative around these issues.

Through these mechanisms, school privatization advocates have focused on a number of key messages, such as the following:

Message 1: Public Schools Are Failing

Central to the school privatization strategy was creating a perceived need for an alternative to public schools. Privatization advocates had to actually create a new market. They had to make people believe that they needed something new. That could only be achieved by convincing people that public schools are irretrievably broken, or at least fundamentally flawed. Thus, every school privatization advocate has made it a consistent habit to reference "failing public schools" or "the crisis within our public education system" at virtually every opportunity. Within just a two-year period in 2016–17, those (or closely related) terms appeared in US newspapers over five thousand times.[102]

Of course, while it is certainly true that public schools have failed many children, and especially youth of color, that doesn't mean that the entire institution is irredeemable. There are many flaws in the system, but they are not attributable to its being a public system. Nevertheless, as the saying goes, if you repeat a lie enough, it eventually becomes the truth. So the notion of "failing public schools" began to creep into the rhetoric of more and more people until it became nearly axiomatic that families need other choices beyond the public school system.

Message 2: Charter Schools and Vouchers Are Directed at Meeting the Needs of Poor Children of Color

Many of the savvier communicators among the ultra-wealthy class and the policy makers who support their agenda have learned that they can dramatically increase their chances of implementing their right-wing agenda if they claim that it is being done out of compassion for low-income and working-class families, even if that is patently false. That is, in short, how the "No Child Left Behind" Act got its name. It is why Arne Duncan largely insulated himself from criticism over his role in dramatically expanding school privatization by continually talking about it as a racial justice issue. It is also why former President Trump recycled Duncan's talking points to announce his plans to make unprecedented federal investments in vouchers.[103]

These are all just manipulative word games. Frank Luntz, who specializes in messaging that makes the policies supported by the ultra-wealthy more palatable for the public, years ago instructed school privatization advocates to say "equal opportunity in education" rather than "school choice," and "opportunity scholarships" instead of "vouchers" (similar to how he reframed the "estate tax" as the "death tax" and named a bill that allows more pollution the "Clear Skies Act," among many other examples).[104] Continuing on that path, school privatization advocates have skillfully exploited people's natural compassion and empathy by crafting compelling messages and marketing techniques centered on the need to promote education equality. Over and over, they reference the urgent need to help children of color "escape their failing public schools" and "close the achievement gap."[105] Most of the organizations pushing this agenda have sophisticated websites featuring an abundance of photos of what appear to be happy, studious, black and Latinx children. They also all operate off the same talking points. Consider the home pages and tag lines of several of the most prominent school privatization advocacy organizations:[106]

- National Alliance for Public Charter Schools: "Every Child Deserves a Great Education—We are working to grow the number of high-quality charter schools available to all families, especially those who do not have access to high-quality public schools."
- Families for Excellent Schools: "A movement to ensure all kids have great schools."
- American Federation for Children: "Every child deserves a world-class education. The American Federation for Children, the nation's voice for

educational choice, works across the country to ensure every child has equal opportunity to obtain a quality education."

- 50Can: "Hi there! We're 50Can! We're a nonprofit network of local leaders advocating for a high-quality education for all kids, regardless of their address."

These are persuasive messages that virtually no one with a beating heart can oppose. Which is precisely the point—to make the public believe that this is a social movement on behalf of needy children and not a billionaire-led privatization effort.

These techniques are evident in the policy debates happening across the country. For example, in Massachusetts, a ballot initiative called Question 2 that would have raised the state's cap on charter schools was brought to a vote in 2016. The effort was led by Great Schools Massachusetts, which ran numerous TV ads featuring almost exclusively black and Latinx families who, the ad claims, "need your help" because they are "trapped" in "failing" schools.[107] They are meant to tug at the viewer's heartstrings, and they do. In fact, they bear a certain, likely intentional, resemblance to those commercials that ask you to donate your coffee money to help starving children in Africa.

However, those pro–Question 2 ads weren't paid for by black and Latinx parents from Massachusetts who believed that additional charter schools would benefit their communities. In fact, much of that expensive ad campaign wasn't even paid for by Massachusetts residents. Great Schools Massachusetts collected $21.7 million in donations for their campaign, $15 million of which came from the New York–based Families for Excellent Schools, which collects money from Wall Street hedge fund managers and other ultra-wealthy donors to support school privatization.[108] (As described above, Families for Excellent Schools has received almost $15 million in donations from the Walton Family Foundation, as well as grants from Eli Broad, Julian Robertson, the Koch network, and the Silicon Valley Community Foundation.) Following the Question 2 campaign—which was defeated by voters—Families for Excellent Schools received the largest fine in state campaign history for hiding the identity of its donors to the Question 2 effort. As part of the settlement, the organization was forced to disclose its donor list, which revealed that among the largest benefactors behind the effort were Michael Bloomberg, former CEO of Continental Cablevision Amos Hostetter (#225, $3.6 billion), Walmart heiress Alice Walton (#11, $51.4 billion), Doris Fisher and her son John Fisher (#342, $2.5 billion), and billionaire hedge fund manager Seth Klarman, among many other multimillionaires and billionaires who gave hundreds of thousands or even millions of dollars to raise the cap on charter schools.[109]

The message that school privatization is fundamentally a racial justice effort has also been infused into popular media. For example, the 2010 movie *Waiting for Superman* brilliantly dramatized the desperation that many black and Latinx families feel about their children's education while identifying charter schools as the solution. The film—as well as the similarly themed 2012 movie *Won't Back Down*—was produced and distributed by Walden Media, which is owned by Philip Anschutz (#41, $11.5 billion). There was a massive public relations campaign surrounding its release, much of which was financed by Bill Gates, who gave $2 million to Participant Media—whose chairman is Jeff Skoll (#131, $5 billion)—to "execute a social action campaign that will complement the campaign of *Waiting for Superman*."[110] Gates also appeared in the film, along with many other grantees of the Gates Foundation.

Beyond the blatant manipulation of these efforts, what is also noteworthy about them is what they demonstrate about the potential for white people to step up on issues of racial equity. All across the country, there are white folks who are working passionately to build and expand charter schools because they truly believe it to be a racial justice fight. It's a shame, of course, that as a result of their being lied to or misled by the billionaires driving this agenda, their idealism has been channeled into a different form of racial injustice. Nevertheless, for anyone who doubts the willingness and capacity of white people to tackle issues of race in America, school privatization is, in many ways, Exhibit A in the case for hopefulness.

Message 3: Charter Schools and Voucher Programs Are Innovations That Produce Better Results Than Public Schools

People like new or innovative things. It is far more exciting to say that you have a fresh idea for meeting a need than talking about how you are going to work out the kinks in the old thing. In education, charter schools and vouchers have been treated as the shiny new thing for around twenty-five years, but especially in the past ten years. There has been an endless string of puff pieces with cherry-picked data and stories from high-achieving charter schools that are intended to give the impression that charter schools are inherently better than public schools. Some of the most popular are the "miracle schools" that send all or most of their graduates from communities of color to college.

What is particularly notable about this charter school media coverage is what isn't included. For example, what you will almost never see mentioned is how there were typically large numbers of students who were pushed out or weeded out of those "miracle schools" before graduation and thus don't factor into those impressive graduation and college attendance statistics.[111] Similarly, within this media coverage you will almost never see an article highlighting the many decidedly unsuccessful charter schools or the many public schools that are just as successful as, or even more successful than, the best charter schools.

Message 4: It Is Parents Who Are Demanding More Charter Schools and Vouchers

About the only thing Americans love more than fresh new products are fresh new products that are scarce. We might get excited about buying our kids the hot new toy for Christmas. However, if we are told that there is only a limited number of them, we will literally wake up in the middle of the night, stand outside in the dark waiting for Walmart to open, and then run faster than we have in decades across the store to make sure that we get one.

School privatization advocates have learned this lesson well and have thus taken to using the waiting lists at some charter schools to create the impression of exclusivity.[112] They also now cite the existence of such waiting lists as a reason to expand the charter school sector.[113] In other words, they exploit many families' short-term desperation—created by the failure to provide all children with high-quality public schools—to create radical, long-term change. Considering the central role of school privatization advocates in creating a system in which high-quality education is artificially scarce, this tactic is unseemly at best. It is also disingenuous, because there is no apples-to-apples comparison available. Public schools will never have waiting lists because they have to enroll any eligible young person who walks through the door. Plus, if we did have a system where students could shop around across all public schools, there would undoubtedly be many who would gladly line up to be admitted to public schools that aren't their home schools.

Moreover, while there are charter schools that have fewer open slots than applicants, the reality is that many charters are struggling to fill their classrooms. In fact, an entire public relations industry has been developed around supporting charter schools with direct marketing strategies that will increase enrollment by poaching students from public schools. (Go ahead: Google "charter school marketing" and see for yourself.) It has now reached the point where K–12 schools are being hawked like any other consumer product.

For example, a "Digital Marketing 101" presentation at the 2015 California Charter School Conference advised attendees that a "digital marketing strategy can help your charter school overcome obstacles such as fundraising, enrollment, and gaining necessary support from the community." Charters are given marketing tips for their websites and promotional materials, such as using words like "motivating," "challenging," "stimulating," "effective," "options," and "choice," but staying away from words like "competition" and "experimentation." They are encouraged to use the power of marketing to vanquish their adversaries—namely, public schools ("Don't let your competition win" exhorts one marketing company focused on charter schools). Some schools even give out gift cards to families that enroll in their school or refer other families to them.[114]

It is worth pointing out that it is often taxpayer dollars that are being used for these marketing campaigns. A study of cyber-charters found that just ten schools spent a total of $94.4 million in public funds on advertising over a five-year period.[115] Not only does this demonstrate that this sector is often seeking to create demand rather than responding to demand, but it also raises important questions about whether this is what public resources should be spent on, particularly when already underresourced public schools are having their budgets cut. (It also further exposes the hypocrisy of celebrating the "efficiency" of charter schools.)

Message 5: Charter Schools Are Public Schools

In recent years, there has been a decided shift in tactics among charter school advocates. It used to be the case that charter schools wanted to distinguish themselves from public schools. However, in recent years they have begun insisting vehemently that charter schools *are* public schools.[116] In the 2016 campaign around Question 2 in Massachusetts, one of the slogans used by school privatization advocates was "Yes on 2 for Stronger Public Schools."[117] Additionally, consider how many school privatization advocates describe themselves. Democrats for Education Reform identifies its mission as this: "We are Democrats leading a political reform organization that cultivates and supports leaders in our party who champion America's public school-children."[118] Similarly, Stand for Children's motto is "We work to improve public education."[119] Indeed, for many of the advocacy organizations in this sector, it can be difficult to even discern where they stand on school privatization issues from what they state on their websites and in other materials.

One has to question the integrity of these organizations when they are reluctant to even be transparent about the major social change they are trying to create. Nevertheless, this trend clearly demonstrates two things. First, that school privatizers have apparently recognized that the public actually likes public schools, and they are hoping to leverage that to their advantage. Second, it demonstrates quite clearly that, for all the talk from school privatization advocates about how the education sector needs the competition of market dynamics to improve, school privatizers aren't actually interested in competing. They don't want to be

Pepsi battling it out against Coke for market share. They want to change their name to New Coke to trick customers into buying their product instead of the product that they really want.

Message 6: Any Dissenting Voices Are Misguided Defenders of the Status Quo

One of the key strategies used by school privatization supporters to advance their agenda has been to marginalize their opposition. Thus, any dissenting voices are either ignored or dismissed as mere "defenders of the status quo."[120] Plus they use their resources to lift up the perspectives of their allies while there are precious few opportunities provided to their opponents to share their experiences with school privatization.

For example, consider how pro-privatization pieces like *Waiting for Superman* are covered compared to the coverage of dissenting views from organizations representing thousands of residents from the black and brown communities most affected by school privatization. *Waiting for Superman* was featured in hundreds of stories within major newspapers across the country, even years after it was released.[121] In contrast, when the Movement for Black Lives called for an end to school privatization in the policy platform it released, there were precisely zero stories in major newspapers around the country that mentioned it.[122]

Similarly, in 2014, the Journey for Justice Alliance, which represents parents and students from dozens of cities that have been affected by school privatization, released a report titled *Death by a Thousand Cuts: Racism, School Closures, and Public School Sabotage*. In it, they cataloged the extensive harms associated with school privatization and declared a state of emergency in communities of color around the country, yet it wasn't covered by a single major newspaper in the country.[123]

Even outside of major events like movie and report releases, the voices that are typically covered in the media around these issues skew heavily toward pro-privatization advocates and rarely feature anyone from the communities most affected by the expansion of charter schools and voucher programs. For example, the heads of prominent pro-privatization organizations like the Foundation for Excellence in Education, StudentsFirst, the National Alliance for Public Charter Schools, the Center for Education Reform, and the Success Academy (all of which have been heavily funded by the billionaires highlighted earlier) were all mentioned or quoted between 27 and 194 times in major newspapers during the three-year period of 2015–17. Meanwhile, Jitu Brown, the head of the Journey for Justice Alliance, was mentioned or quoted only seven times during the same time period (see table 11).[124]

Margaret Mead once said, "Never doubt that a small group of thoughtful, committed citizens can change the world; indeed, it's the only thing that ever

TABLE 11 The voices we hear on school privatization

NAME AND ORGANIZATION		MENTIONS IN MAJOR US NEWSPAPERS—2015–17
Pro-privatization	Eva Moskowitz, Success Academy	194
	Jeb Bush, Foundation for Excellence in Education	125
	Michelle Rhee, StudentsFirst	49
	Nina Rees, National Alliance for Public Charter Schools	34
	Jeanne Allen, Center for Education Reform	27
Anti-privatization	Jitu Brown, Journey for Justice Alliance	7

Source: Westlaw.

has." What she failed to mention was the devastation that could be caused by a small group of ultra-wealthy, committed citizens who seek to change the world and, in the process, ignore or marginalize the large group of people who are most affected by those changes.

Message 7: There Are Only Two Choices: School Privatization or the Status Quo

A critical element in the school privatization playbook is using the echo chamber proponents have engineered to create a false choice for the public: you either support failing public schools, or you support the innovation and equal opportunity created by charter schools and vouchers. Those are, typically, the only options that are presented. Thus, if the message around failing public schools sinks into the public narrative effectively, as it often has, then school privatization comes across as the only viable alternative. Indeed, it comes across as an almost evolutionary inevitability.

Message 8: The Billionaires Backing School Privatization Are Benevolent Philanthropists

The billionaires who are financing school privatization efforts have received an abundance of media coverage extolling their generosity and leadership in spearheading bold, social change efforts. Some of this coverage is undoubtedly fueled by the egos involved. However, it also serves a strategic purpose. The notion that they are advancing school privatization out of benevolence serves to divert attention from some of the other reasons they have for pushing this agenda. And those other reasons may not sit as well with the public.

Strategic Racism in Education: Who Benefits?

What all the previous messages have in common is that they mislead and confuse the public. As with all policy issues, and particularly issues of systemic racism—where advocates and policy makers have learned to talk a good game without backing it up with action—we have to train ourselves to focus far less on what these individuals are saying and far more on what they are doing.

We must also not allow our attention to be diverted from the most important questions that should be asked about any social policy: (1) Who benefits? and (2) Who is harmed? Question 2 has already been covered at great length, but there is more to say about Question 1.

As discussed earlier, there have been some individual students, parents, and educators who have realized (often very limited) benefits from school privatization. However, those gains are miniscule in comparison to the enormous benefits realized by the ultra-wealthy. School privatization has already dramatically expanded the wealth of corporate and Wall Street executives, and that is just the tip of the iceberg compared to how they intend to profit from the dismantling of public education in the coming years. Of course, the billionaires driving the school privatization agenda undoubtedly have a variety of motivations, and there are some critical differences among them. Some of them are more altruistic; some are more obviously self-interested. Some are motivated by radical, decades-old political ideas; others are grounded in short-term political expediency. Some limit their support to charter schools; others have their hearts set on vouchers. But one thing they all have in common is a profound economic interest in school privatization, and the overwhelming majority of their actions have been in alignment with that interest, not in opposition to it.

This might not seem all that relevant for many Americans. Predominantly white communities, in particular, have thus far been largely unaffected by school privatization, at least in terms of the most direct effects. However, the opportunity for these issues to be "out of sight, out of mind" for so many Americans is quickly coming to an end, as many of the most powerful school privatizers have made it clear that they have their sights set not just on the schools within low-income communities of color, but rather on *all* public schools. Getting their agenda adopted within black and brown communities was merely the ruse that allowed them to get through the door. They are now aggressively pursuing the real goal, which truly is colorblind in that it would affect all, or virtually all, children.[125]

In short, there is blood in the water, and the sharks are circling. While the threat of a dramatically expanded charter school sector is itself extremely serious, it is now apparent that many of the most prominent charter school supporters within the school privatization sector see charters merely as the gateway drug toward their even more radical goals.[126] Now that "school choice" has achieved considerable traction nationwide, they are beginning to show their true colors and advocating for universal voucher programs.[127]

Regardless of their preferred destination, school privatization advocates are rapidly accumulating the wealth and political power to spread their agenda far and wide, while their shock-doctrine tactics for implementing it continue to be effective.[128] And as bleak as the results from school privatization have already been in communities of color, the implications of expanding charter schools and vouchers further would be substantially more devastating.

The Doctrine of Corporate Greed

While it can be tempting to view school privatization solely as an education issue, it is actually part of a much larger ideology and strategy. To understand what is driving the privatization process and why it is such a threat, it is helpful to understand some of that broader context. In particular, it can be valuable to tease out how it fits within the primary Corporate America and Wall Street political agenda.

Within the swirling winds of politics, that agenda has been the one constant in recent decades. While it has been presented to the public in a number of different ways over the years, the actual content of it has been remarkably consistent and predictable. It has invariably focused very narrowly on the economic interests of large corporations and Wall Street. While its proponents often portray their efforts as part of some deeply principled ideology, ultimately what it amounts to is perhaps best characterized as the Doctrine of Corporate Greed. What that doctrine includes, and what is advocated by its proponents—including many (but certainly not all) top executives from the country's largest corporations, banks, and investment firms—is a series of policies whose common denominator is that they all allow Corporate America and Wall Street executives to expand their wealth, often at the expense of everyone else. This agenda has dominated Republican politics for decades, and elements of it now hold sway over segments of the Democratic Party as well.[129] It prioritizes the following types of policy positions:[130]

1. Lowering taxes on the wealthy and on corporations
2. Fighting increases to the minimum wage

3. Cutting public services that benefit low-income, working-class, and middle-class individuals

4. Promoting the creation of new profit-making opportunities (such as through privatizing public services and tapping into "new markets" in the United States or abroad)

5. Reducing business regulations (particularly those that impede wealth accumulation)

6. Opposing labor unions (thus facilitating wage cuts and reductions in worker protections)

7. Convincing the public to subsidize corporations (either directly, such as through tax breaks and bailouts, or indirectly, such as through publicly funded services that favor corporate interests)

The dominant forces that have been driving this agenda forward include ALEC; corporate lobby groups such as the US Chamber of Commerce; advocacy groups such as Americans for Prosperity, the Club for Growth, Americans for Tax Reform, and FreedomWorks; and right-wing think tanks such as the Cato Institute, the Heritage Foundation, the American Enterprise Institute, and the State Policy Network and its affiliates.[131] These organizations haven't always had the political majorities necessary to fully implement their vision of unfettered capitalism, but they have taken the long view, and through massive financial investments in their efforts they have successfully made the profitability of large corporations arguably the single most dominant consideration in contemporary American politics.

You will note that many of the organizations listed here have been very active in promoting school privatization, and the billionaires most responsible for school privatization have funded nearly all of these organizations quite heavily. So what do the priorities reflected in the Doctrine of Corporate Greed have to do with the education system?

The Education Cash Cow

To understand why school privatization is such a high priority for this sector, it is important to first understand how many Corporate America and Wall Street executives view public services such as the public education system. When the government uses tax dollars to provide a service for free, many within the billionaire class view that as wasting several opportunities to increase their own wealth: (1) the opportunity for businesses to provide the same services for profit; (2) the opportunity to restructure those services so that they better support corporate priorities and generate additional corporate wealth; and (3) the opportunity to lower their own tax bills—and potentially increase their own profits—by providing those services more "efficiently," such as by cutting wages, eliminating "non-essential" services, and having more people pay for those services. Thus, when these individuals look at the public education system, they don't see a public good or a vital hallmark of a democratic society. They see a massive, untapped market just waiting to be exploited.

For example, school privatization creates the possibility of transferring the assets and revenue of a $600+ billion industry from public to private hands, and of being able to realize corporate profits from activities that are currently performed by public employees. Here are just some of the myriad ways in which the ultra-wealthy have already profited from school privatization:

- Creating for-profit charter and private schools, including cyber-charters (note that one in five charter schools nationally are run by for-profit companies)[132]
- Developing curricula and other educational programming used by charter schools and private schools[133]
- Producing the standardized tests that drive the school privatization agenda[134]
- Providing cleaning, food preparation, student transportation, security, accounting, legal, and consulting services to charter and private schools[135]
- Investing in government-backed bonds from charter schools[136]
- Investing in real estate and leasing space to charter schools[137]
- Creating for-profit companies to manage charter school chains or conduct real estate deals (and often exploiting the intricacies of municipal bonds and complex real estate transactions to garner substantial private profits from the use of public resources)[138]
- Providing construction loans to charter schools[139]
- Claiming generous tax credits for investing in charter school construction[140]
- Using the tax credits for voucher programs to reduce their own tax bills and even turn a profit[141]
- Collecting taxpayer-funded interest payments from struggling public school districts that were forced to take out loans[142]
- Exploiting the gentrification that is often associated with school privatization[143]

It is little wonder that all the major investment banks have established special funds devoted to profiting from school privatization.[144]

Another way in which the ultra-wealthy benefit extensively from school privatization is through their successful effort to have the education system subsidize corporate operations. Throughout the privatization process, as the ultra-wealthy have gained more and more influence over education policy, they have used it to convince education policy makers throughout the country that K–12 curricula should be aligned with employer needs.[145] While most people would agree that the education system shouldn't be oblivious of the future job market of students, Corporate America has successfully convinced many Americans that such job training is the most important, or even the sole, purpose of our education system, at the expense of many other facets of education that are needed to create well-educated youth and adults. As just one example, consider the decreased emphasis in recent years on the arts, social sciences, and physical education alongside the surge in attention given to STEM (science, technology, engineering, and mathematics), such that there are now even day care centers and preschools that market themselves as STEM focused. These types of dynamics are immensely valuable to Corporate America because they essentially shift the cost associated with job training to the general public (which may just represent our country's largest social welfare program).

The ultra-wealthy also prioritize school privatization because it enables them to reduce the cost of the education system. For example, this sector has aggressively pursued both deregulation and deunionization in education because, from their perspective, it is expensive and inefficient to have to meet the full set of educational needs for all students and to pay experienced teachers appropriate wages. Thus, they are advancing a privatized, deregulated education model that is primarily nonunionized and has fewer protections for students' educational opportunities, particularly for students with special needs, immigrant students, and students who are considered to be challenging to teach.[146] Each one of these actions promises to reduce the cost of education, with the vast majority of benefits being enjoyed by the ultra-wealthy and virtually all of the extensive harm flowing to everyone else.

Similarly, the desire to cut education costs is why the ultra-wealthy are making such a strong push to expand voucher programs, home schooling, cyber-charters, and online education generally.[147] Widespread voucher programs would result in millions of families having to pay at least some of the cost of the education that they currently receive for free. From the perspective of the ultra-wealthy, that both creates new profit-making opportunities and reduces their tax liability. Additionally, the more students there are who are homeschooled, the fewer students there are who have to be budgeted for with public dollars. Similarly, widespread online education allows for the elimination of many of the costs associated with traditional schools, such as school buildings, teachers, and support services. Not only does this again translate to lower taxes, but it also creates vast profit-making opportunities. For example, the infamous "junk bond king" Michael Milken (#217, $3.7 billion) and other Wall Street investors founded the online education service K12, Inc., which takes in close to a billion dollars in revenue annually, produces dismal results, and nevertheless plays a leading role in expanding online education through ALEC.[148]

The Fast Food Model of Education

If you follow the Doctrine of Corporate Greed to its logical conclusion, there is every reason to believe that the continued expansion of charter schools and vouchers would result in a severe reduction in services for virtually all students. Ever since our public education system was created, our wealthiest and most politically powerful citizens have had every opportunity to support efforts to fund schools adequately and equitably, and they have consistently failed to do so. Instead, they have continually impeded those efforts. Does anyone truly believe that they would voluntarily advance education equity now that they have gained substantially more power over schools than they have ever had before? On the contrary, the ultra-wealthy will continue to do the same thing they do in every other area of policy, which is try to limit their tax bill by cutting government spending in areas that don't benefit them. And the private sector will do, and already is doing, what it always does when it enters a market, which is attempt to maximize its profits. In practice, what this means is that the ultra-wealthy will continue to look to cut education spending for the vast majority of students, secure as much of the available education revenue for themselves that they can, and find as many areas to cut costs as they can.

In fact, that is precisely what has happened where the school privatization agenda has taken hold, even though we are still just in the early stages of implementing a privatized system. To illustrate, note that immediately upon coming into office, the Trump administration prioritized the aggressive promotion of vouchers and charter schools, the slashing of education funding, and the rollback of important regulations that protect students' right to an education.[149] These efforts come on top of other federal cost-cutting measures that have been led by school privatization advocates in recent years, such as expanding the reliance on low-cost standardized tests and developing a standardized, "Common Core" curriculum. At the state and local levels, as described previously, policy makers have typically responded to school privatization by devoting less funding to schools overall, using narrower and more regimented school curricula—such as those based on Common Core—and cutting back on student services.[150]

What this looks like on the ground is that within the districts most affected by privatization, the public schools have often had to cut student services to the bone, and the charter schools have typically reduced labor costs by paying teachers less and using a higher percentage of inexperienced and uncertified teachers.[151] These local school systems are increasingly dominated by schools offering second-rate education, if not worse. It's a "fast food model" of education, where schools offer standardized, relatively low-quality products delivered by inexpensive, inexperienced workers.[152] There are still, of course, some higher-quality schools, but the vast majority of students in these districts are getting the McDonald's hamburger of education, not the prime rib.

To be sure, there are some charter schools that are able to offer some services and opportunities that other schools cannot, primarily because of the substantial private donations that they receive. However, one shouldn't make the mistake of assuming that those bells and whistles will be permanent features of those schools, or that all the schools within an expanded charter school sector would also have those traits. Those schools are funded the way they are in significant part because it is strategically beneficial to have schools that can be the poster children for the school privatization agenda. These schools are the "loss leaders" of this effort; they are the products sold at a loss to attract future customers and secure a larger share of the "education market." The vast majority of charter schools don't receive anywhere near the same level of private donations, and the amount of private donations the average charter school would receive in a dramatically expanded charter school sector would be even less. Thus, as the charter school sector expands, the best features of many charter schools are far more likely to disappear entirely than they are to be replicated widely. Plus, the idea that billionaires would permanently fund all schools the way they have funded schools like KIPP is simply unfathomable.

Ultimately, if you have any doubt about the direction that school privatization will take, all you have to do is examine the other priorities of most of the leaders of the effort. The members of the Koch network, members of ALEC, and Republican Party leaders have made it very clear where they stand with regard to services for low-income, working-class, and middle-class families. They have consistently advocated against the minimum wage, welfare benefits, environmental protections, and affordable health care coverage, among many other vital services and protections.[153] Thus, it would be foolish to think that the furtherance of the school privatization agenda will be the one exception to these well-established patterns.

These billionaires leading the school privatization effort have demonstrated no interest in creating a rising tide of education quality. Instead, they have recognized that it is far cheaper to cut an occasional check to a particular charter school or network of schools than it is to actually pay for high-quality, equitable educational services for all children. To illustrate, imagine that you make $100 million per year. If there was a proposed tax increase of 5 percent for individuals in your tax bracket to generate more money for local schools and other priorities, it would cost you $5 million more per year. If your priority is to maximize your wealth, it is far preferable for you to oppose the tax increase but make a $5 million donation to local charter schools. You can deduct it on your taxes, make use of the variety of mechanisms available to profit off the increasingly privatized system, and cut your tax liability further by facilitating the effort to undermine public schools. You come out way ahead financially, and you may even turn a profit. You also reduce the likelihood that the public will bother you about not paying your fair share of taxes. In fact, you will likely even receive some favorable publicity and maybe even win an award for your "humanitarianism." Of course, the only students who benefit are the ones in the individual schools you donate to, while lots of other students and the surrounding community will probably be harmed in the process. Plus, unless you plan on making the same type of donation on a recurring basis, whatever benefits you create are going to be short-lived.

In other words, it should be no surprise that members of the billionaire class are leveraging their resources to essentially buy our education system because doing so creates an enormous economic bonanza for themselves. They get to appear to be philanthropic heroes for funding charter schools and private schools without actually having to address the real, underlying challenges facing our education system, and they are able to get even wealthier in the process. In short, they have figured out how to make money off rearranging the deck chairs on the *Titanic* while they are the ones who are sinking it.

The Path to Lower Taxes . . . and "Happiness"

During a meeting of the Koch brothers' network in 2014, the Kochs' "master strategist," Richard Fink, gave a presentation in which he lamented that many American voters were uncomfortable with the Kochs' right-wing agenda. He acknowledged, "We want to decrease regulations. Why? It's because we can make more profit, okay? Yeah, and cut government spending so we don't have to pay so much taxes." To be successful in that pursuit, he suggested, they had to convince voters that they weren't motivated by greed, but rather that their intent was virtuous. "We've got to convince these people we mean well and that we're good people," said Fink. His proposal was to launch a "movement for well-being" in which they would sell the idea that free markets were the "path to happiness" and that government intervention would lead to dependency, tyranny, and fascism. Thus, he reasoned, they could convince the public that eliminating policies like the minimum wage weren't about maximizing their profits through cheap labor, but rather were about advancing "freedom."

Source: Jane Mayer, Dark Money: The Hidden History of the Billionaires behind the Rise of the Radical Right (New York: Anchor Books, 2016).

Reading the Tea Leaves

Where is this agenda ultimately headed, unless and until it is stopped? All indications are that it is somewhere between a virtually all-charter school system, like that of New Orleans, and a voucher-dominant system, such as the one implemented by Chile under the dictatorship of General Augusto Pinochet.[154] Some of the billionaire benefactors of school privatization, particularly those who identify as Democrats, are clearly more supportive of charter schools than they are of vouchers. Their preference is to continue expanding the charter school sector broadly, and even if they may not support a mostly or fully charterized system, that outcome is likely inevitable if current trends continue. Charter schools have such substantial built-in advantages over public schools that the "competition" between them is a profoundly unequal one, thus fueling charter expansion. Plus, most of the power and the wealth are on the side of those with an unquenchable appetite for growth, and so they would almost certainly overwhelm those with more measured aspirations.

On the other end of the spectrum are those who are very clearly pursuing a universal voucher system. This has been the goal of the far right for decades, and many highly influential figures in conservative politics—including the Koch family and Jeb Bush, among many others—are committed to this vision.[155] For example, when David Koch ran for vice president on the Libertarian ticket in 1980, not only did their platform oppose all personal and corporate taxation and the elimination of most of the government services provided to low-income, working-class, and middle-class families; it also called for an end to compulsory education laws and publicly funded education.[156] In other words, they didn't want any public money being used for education, not even for charter schools or voucher programs. While the campaign was an abject failure because of the public's thorough rejection of their ultraconservative ideas, the Koch brothers and their allies have nevertheless spent the years since then working largely behind the scenes to advance this very agenda.[157]

While the implementation of either a charter- or voucher-heavy system would have devastating consequences, it is important to distinguish their supporters, as the billionaires driving school privatization are certainly not monolithic. For

example, the ideologies motivating Charles Koch and Bill Gates are quite different. With regard to Koch, there is scant evidence that he is motivated to improve
the educational opportunities of youth of color and abundant evidence that he
is driven by an ideology that favors his own economic and political interests and
those of other ultra-wealthy individuals. With Gates, it is the opposite. There is
nothing to suggest that he is anything but sincere in his stated desire to improve
education quality and equity. Unfortunately, he has been severely misguided in
profoundly harmful ways. While he doesn't publicly express support for vouchers, and most of his investments have been connected to charter schools, he has
nevertheless provided tens of millions of dollars to organizations that are aligned
with the Koch voucher agenda, including Jeb Bush's Foundation for Excellence in
Education. Moreover, his support for charter schools has been critical in paving
the way for the more radical school privatization goals of those like Charles Koch,
the Waltons, and Betsy DeVos. Thus, while the intentions of Gates and others
like him may have been pure, he has contributed to "letting the monster out"
and advancing the agenda of those who want to tear down the entire system of
public education. In other words, he has been doing Charles Koch's work for him.

Playing the Long Game

Joseph Bast, president of the Heartland Institute, an ALEC affiliate and
major grantee of the Koch brothers' network, had this to say about their
strategy for education reform: "Elementary and secondary schooling in
the U.S. is the country's last remaining socialist enterprise. . . . The way
to privatize schooling is to give parents . . . vouchers, with which to pay
tuition at the K–12 schools of their choice. . . . Pilot voucher programs
for the urban poor will lead the way to statewide universal voucher plans.
Soon, most government schools will be converted into private schools or
simply close their doors. Eventually, middle- and upper-class families will
no longer expect or need tax-financed assistance to pay for the education
of their children, leading to further steps toward complete privatization."

Source: Gordon Lafer, *The One Percent Solution: How Corporations Are Remaking
America One State at a Time* (Ithaca, NY: Cornell University Press, 2017).

The Education Hunger Games

Unless we change course, the future of our education system looks terrifyingly
grim. To illustrate, consider that New Orleans has been the focus of the absolute
best the charter school sector has to offer, and even so, it has produced a system

of schools that evaluators have found to be highly stratified by race, class, and educational advantage and where rich educational experiences are reserved for the highest tier of students, where student push-out and exclusion are rampant, where the graduation rate is the lowest in the state of Louisiana, where severe logistical burdens have been placed on families, where mismanagement is severe and widespread, and where there has been extreme dissatisfaction from the families who were supposed to benefit from the "New Orleans miracle."[158]

Similarly, in Chile, after that country switched to a system that was 54 percent voucher schools or private schools, the remaining public schools mainly consisted of students from families that couldn't afford admission to the other schools even with the vouchers.[159] Public funding of education dropped dramatically, education inequality was exacerbated, and public schools declined substantially in quality.[160] Meanwhile, teachers' salaries in the country dropped by 70 percent, and there was an overall degradation in many aspects of the teaching profession.[161] As a result, indicators of education quality demonstrated relatively poor results for Chile, especially compared to countries that didn't embrace the privatization agenda.[162] Dissatisfaction with the stratified, voucher-based system was so severe that hundreds of thousands of Chileans organized a massive series of protests and boycotts in 2011–12 to demand the end of education profiteering.[163]

To understand the direction in which this agenda is headed, it can be instructive to consider the type of education system that best aligns with the Doctrine of Corporate Greed and the interests of its proponents. From that perspective, the goal for constructing an education system is to make it as "efficient" as possible in meeting the economic needs of corporations. The most "efficient" system would match people's education levels with what is needed by the jobs they will fill. Thus, for the limited number of high-skill jobs that are available, corporations need highly educated people to fill them. However, for the many lower-skilled jobs, they don't need highly educated individuals. If fact, those individuals are undesirable, because highly educated people expect to be paid well. It is far preferable, from this perspective, to have a large number of fungible, low-skill workers who can be paid low wages. In other words, the economic interests of the ultra-wealthy are to provide children with only as much education as is necessary to maximize corporate profits. (This isn't to say that other interests beyond the purely economic ones don't occasionally rise to the surface. They do, but far more often than not, they get overwhelmed by the interest in accumulating wealth.)

Thus, for these very wealthy and politically powerful individuals, providing a high-quality, equitable education for all children is inefficient. It is inefficient to invest in a rich, well-rounded curriculum for every child. It is inefficient to ensure that every child is able to access a high-quality teaching and learning environment staffed by well-trained professionals earning a living wage. It is inefficient to commit to meeting the particular needs of every child and ensuring that children with disabilities and English learners get what they need to maximize their potential.[164]

None of this should be surprising. These dynamics have been reflected in policy for a very long time.[165] While the private schools attended by many children of wealthy families often cost $30,000 to $50,000 or more per year, our wealthiest and most politically powerful citizens have never deemed it to be an efficient use of resources for the children from low-income, working-class, and middle-class families to receive a comparable level of educational investment. This is why the expensive education enjoyed by children from wealthy families has typically prepared them for prestigious jobs, why the children from low-income and working-class families have typically received relatively low-quality education and disproportionately wind up working in low-wage jobs, and why the children from middle-class families have typically received intermediate-level educational opportunities that prepare them for jobs comparable to those of their parents. Of course, there are plenty of exceptions to these generalizations, and there has been some allowance for upward mobility. But it has nevertheless largely been the reality that most US residents have experienced.

What would be different under a more privatized school system is that the stratification and inequities within our education system would be exacerbated, the overall quality would be diminished, and many fewer students would receive the type of high-quality education that all parents want for their children. In other words, there would be even less of a societal commitment to the education of all children, and even more rationing of educational opportunities, than there are currently. As privatization increases, education would increasingly become a *Hunger Games*–like competition in which students would vie for the opportunity to receive the scarce spots in the few schools providing the highest-level corporate job training, and the many "losers" would receive only the level of education that was necessary for their future as relatively low-skill, low-wage workers. In some instances, that could mean little to no formal education at all, particularly if Charles Koch and his allies get their way. Of course, this wouldn't apply to the children from wealthy families. They could continue to use their wealth to pay for the highest-quality educational opportunities at expensive private schools (or even use taxpayer dollars to subsidize their children's education through private school vouchers or charter schools that are designed to function like exclusive private schools). Everyone else, however, would face a future of even less upward social mobility and, in the case of the middle class, far more downward mobility. Only those children who demonstrated substantial talent, docility, and "grit" would be able to "rise above their station." In other words, non-wealthy children would increasingly be treated as most low-income children of color are treated; they would have to prove themselves to be truly exceptional in order to be provided with high-quality educational opportunities.

This is what privatization and efficiency look like in education. It is a race to the bottom in which the vast majority of children are consigned to a fate that is not of their choosing. It is an education system in which the brilliance of even more children will be squandered. It is an escalation of the tendency to treat young people as if they were disposable, with even larger cracks for students to fall through and even fewer protections and services for the students who are most resource-intensive and challenging to teach. It is the decimation of even more communities around the country. It is a future in which those who start off with the greatest disadvantages, such as the residents of low-income communities of color, would suffer the most, and become a virtually permanent underclass. It is the rejection of the idea that we should be enabling all children to reach their full potential in favor of the treatment of children as commodities, as mere cogs in the wheel of our economy.

Thus, the school privatization debate isn't just a fight to save public schools in communities of color, or even public schools overall. It is a fight to ensure that we even have a meaningful right to education in this country. Those rights are already being severely undercut, and once again there are highly powerful billionaires who are exerting enormous influence over education policy decisions across the country and *don't believe that the government should be making any investment in education at all.*[166] Thus, we have reached a critical tipping point in this education holy war because those individuals and a great many other allies of theirs are both winning and escalating their efforts to expand school privatization broadly. It is now clear that these individuals won't stop on their own; they will have to be defeated. And everyone whose family doesn't have sufficient money in the bank to pay for expensive private school education has a very direct interest in ensuring that they are defeated.

This fight is both necessary and, fortunately, highly winnable, because there are exponentially more people who stand to lose from expanded school privatization than there are who stand to gain from it. But winning will require the residents of the communities that are next on the school privatization chopping block—namely, predominantly white communities—to join the communities of color that have been on the front lines of this struggle.

The Path toward Excellence and Equity

The target of such a unified, multiracial struggle is obvious: the end of school privatization. What is less clear is the alternative vision that we should be advancing. In other words, if charter schools and vouchers aren't the answer to creating high-quality, equitable schools, then what is?

Based on our history with school privatization, it is clear that our best chance for providing all our children with the education that they deserve, that every parent hopes for, and that best serves the interests of society overall, is through our neighborhood public schools. This isn't to suggest that we need a cookie-cutter system of identical schools throughout the country. Far from it. We need to promote innovation and experimentation, and we should be flexible when necessary, but all of that is fully compatible with a school system centered on neighborhood public schools as its primary delivery mechanism.[167] Thus, there can and should continue to be public schools that explore different educational methods, adopt different areas of curricular emphasis, and focus on meeting particular sets of student needs. (And any high-quality charter schools that fulfill such functions should be absorbed into the public schools system.) Plus, children need not be locked into their home schools when other schools have programming that would be a better fit. All this can all be achieved within a public system that, as a baseline, guarantees all children a high-quality education at the public schools in their neighborhood.

Of course, while a robust public education system represents our best approach, the long-standing and grossly inequitable educational opportunities offered within that system continue to be unacceptable. The students and parents in low-income communities of color, and all communities, deserve much more than a school system in which children's educational opportunities and outcomes are largely determined by their race and the zip code in which they live. All parents in the United States should be able to expect that their children will receive a high-quality education. How could we possibly be willing to accept anything less than that? Shouldn't that be a fundamental guarantee that we, as a society, offer to every child? That no matter who you are or what your life circumstances are, you will receive an education that allows you to live just as good of a life as anyone else?

Unfortunately, while most constitutions in the world recognize an explicit right to an education, the US Constitution does not.[168] We all do have a right to an education under our state constitutions, but those rights are so weak that even the abominable conditions described earlier that exist in many schools have not, with rare exceptions, been found unconstitutional.

So how do we address these problems? Here are three very simple suggestions:

1. Let's create schools based on what parents and communities want for their children, not on what the ultra-wealthy want.
2. Let's design our education policies around students' developmental needs.[169]
3. Let's collectively repair the harm caused by racial inequities and address the education debt owed to communities of color across the country.

With regard to no. 2, for too long we have designed our schools as if students are mere empty vessels that we can just fill up with knowledge. But as every parent knows, the reality is that meaningful learning and academic growth can happen only if we pay attention to the whole child. As Ken Robinson says, children aren't just brains on legs. That means that all of their social, emotional, physical, psychological, moral, and intellectual needs must be addressed for them to thrive in school. Unfortunately, while most parents think of their public schools as youth development systems—as places devoted to supporting children in becoming healthy, successful human beings—that that has never really matched up with how the education system has been governed and resourced. Our schools have never truly been structured around comprehensive youth development.

Thus, when students come to school suffering from hunger, unmet health needs, or unstable living environments, our schools too often aren't equipped to help them. When young people are struggling with the impact of community violence, the mass incarceration system, or anti-immigrant policies and rhetoric, our schools typically aren't designed to meet their needs. And when students are experiencing anxiety, depression, or low self-worth, are having difficulty managing their emotions, or are struggling to develop healthy, positive relationships with their peers and their teachers, our schools frequently struggle to provide them with the assistance and support they need. Over and over, our education policies simply fail to account for students' developmental needs and the reality of what they are dealing with on a daily basis.

However, while the world outside of schools has undoubtedly created a great many challenges for educators within schools, that doesn't mean that we are doomed to see broader societal inequities re-created in the education system. On the contrary, there are a number of effective strategies that can used by schools and other youth-serving systems to effectively mitigate the thoroughly inequitable difficulties that students face. Unfortunately, there are also many other commonly used strategies that instead exacerbate students' challenges. All of these educational strategies, as well as the experiences that students bring with them to school, can be thought of as "developmental inputs."

Children are in large part a product of these inputs. Some of them are positive, meaning they are responsive to children's developmental needs. Many positive inputs are received outside of school, such as prenatal care, a stable living situation, quality health care, and enriching early childhood opportunities. Other positive inputs are often received within schools, such as well-rounded, engaging, and culturally responsive curricula, small class sizes, social-emotional learning supports, and quality afterschool enrichment opportunities.

On the flip side are negative developmental inputs, which are those that work in conflict with students' developmental needs and that inflict harm on them or otherwise compromise their learning and growth. Examples from outside of school include the effects of poverty, trauma, toxic stress, and systemic racism, such as those mentioned previously. Examples from within schools include overcrowding; the lack of student support personnel such as school psychologists, social workers, and nurses; narrow, ponderous, and standardized-test-driven curricula; unnecessary reliance on suspensions, expulsions, and the justice system for school disciplinary matters; and the instability created by the constant threat of school closure.

It is the allocation of those inputs that determines the size of our education inequities and how they either grow or shrink over time. For example, the children from relatively affluent communities already tend to come into school with an abundance of positive developmental inputs and very few negative inputs, and their school experiences typically replicate and reinforce those ratios. However, there are many young people who come into school with fewer positive inputs and more negative inputs. Their schools could help, and in some cases do help, to counteract those inequities by investing in an abundance of positive inputs that they need to essentially make up developmental ground. More common, however, is that students who enter school with a greater set of developmental needs receive fewer positive inputs and more negative inputs than their peers, thus exacerbating our education inequities and deepening our broader social inequities.

These are the dynamics that absolutely must be addressed. In other words, if we want our schools to serve all children well, then they have to be structured around the needs of *all* children. That is the one and only one surefire way to create a truly equitable education system: we have to start with an assessment of students' developmental needs and proceed from there. Everything else is a waste of time and resources. Indeed, if you are not using that as your starting point and making the appropriate investments in young people, you are simply not making a serious effort at addressing the real challenges and conditions they face, and you have absolutely no right to complain about the subpar academic outcomes that will inevitably result. Unfortunately, while we know from the experience of the many "sustainable community schools" around the country that taking this approach will succeed, as a society we have been unwilling to actually do it for all children.[170]

So to truly address the root causes of education injustice, we need all our schools to be resourced, staffed, structured, and managed in ways that can address the disparities in developmental inputs. For the young people who have been most harmed by social inequities, we should be dramatically pumping up the number of positive inputs they receive in schools. Plus, we should be eliminating all the negative inputs that they and all students receive from their schools. Then, when students make their developmental needs apparent, as they inevitably do, we must refuse to allow them to fall through the cracks of the system. Instead, our focus should be on addressing the root causes of those behaviors and ensuring that each and every child feels truly seen and cared for. And then we should get to work in eliminating those cracks entirely, so that never again will we allow children to fail because the adults charged with their education and development neglected their needs.

A Student Bill of Rights

One strategy that would allow us to prioritize the views of those who have the most invested in their schools, to center students' developmental needs, and to do so equitably would be to finally create and actualize a more meaningful definition for the right to an education. We could decide collectively: What should be included in a high-quality, equitable education system? What should students, their families, and their communities be entitled to expect? What should educators and education policy makers be expected to provide?

These are essential questions, and ultimately, they are ones that communities will need to answer together for us to address the challenges described earlier. As a model for what the product of such discussions can look like, the following text box shows a sample Student Bill of Rights that is based on similar documents I helped to create through participatory processes with students, parents, educators, and other community members in various cities across the country. I include it in the hope that it won't discourage readers from answering the above questions for themselves, but rather that it will serve as a starting point for conversation. It reflects the views of a great many stakeholders, as well as our best research on what we know works in creating excellent, equitable schools that meet the needs of all children.

Student Bill of Rights

All children and youth have the right to a free, equitable, high-quality pre-K–12 education in their neighborhood public schools. Such education shall be directed at meeting the full range of students' intellectual, social, emotional, physical, psychological, and moral development needs. The educational opportunities offered shall be culturally responsive, focused on nurturing each student's unique talents and enthusiasm for learning, and directed at remedying historical inequities and creating an egalitarian and participatory democracy. They shall prepare each student to be a critical and creative thinker, a conscientious and compassionate adult, and a responsible and engaged civic participant.

Every education policy decision made by local, state, and federal policy makers shall be guided by these values and ensure that every child and youth has a full opportunity to such an education, which shall include, at a minimum, the following:

1. Safe, clean, comfortable, and welcoming facilities that are conducive to learning and demonstrate respect for those who go to school and work there.
2. An affirming, inclusive, and supportive learning environment for every student, regardless of race, ethnicity, national origin, socioeconomic status, English language proficiency, sexual orientation, gender identity, gender expression, immigration status, disability, or religion.
3. Schools that are equipped to address students' physical, mental, and behavioral health needs, provide high-quality before-school, after-school, and year-round learning and enrichment opportunities for students who need them, and address any other significant barriers to learning through wraparound supports.
4. High-quality learning conditions in schools, including classes of a size that ensure individualized instruction, all necessary support staff, up-to-date classroom materials and school libraries, modern classroom technology, daily access to healthy food and exercise, school employees who are all paid a living wage and treated as professionals, and no school-based law enforcement officers, armed security guards, metal detectors, or surveillance cameras.
5. A curriculum that is enriched, engaging, community-based, culturally relevant, and well-rounded, including the arts, world languages, science, mathematics, literature, social studies, civic education, ethnic/cultural studies, physical education, social-emotional learning, and age-appropriate play for young children.
6. Effective instruction provided by qualified, well-trained, and well-supported staff who are given the time and resources necessary to plan their lessons, collaborate with colleagues, receive meaningful professional development, and address each student's particular developmental and academic needs.
7. A high-quality assessment system that is centered on authentic learning, is aligned with the curriculum, uses performance assessments and portfolio assessments to provide students with meaningful opportunities to demonstrate what they know and can do, is used diagnostically and formatively to improve the teaching and learning process, enables timely and effective intervention

if students experience academic difficulty, and does not attach
punitive consequences to the results of standardized tests.

8. Developmentally appropriate disciplinary methods that support
   student learning and positive school climates, use preventive
   and restorative approaches to disciplinary issues, do not use out-
   of-school suspensions or expulsions unless there are no other
   alternatives for protecting members of the school community
   from imminent threats of serious harm, and do not involve the
   criminal or juvenile justice systems.

9. Democratic control over the education process, including elected,
   representative school boards; meaningful opportunities for
   students, parents/guardians, and other community members to
   participate in school and district decision making around issues
   that affect them; and opportunities for students' parents and
   guardians to participate actively in the educational process.

10. A robust accountability system that provides community
    members with high-quality quantitative and qualitative data
    covering all elements of the Student Bill of Rights, uses a
    community-based approach to drive school improvement and
    enforce this Student Bill of Rights, and supplements those efforts
    with periodic, comprehensive school quality reviews performed by
    qualified teams of experts.

Implementing what is reflected in the Student Bill of Rights would benefit
every single public school student in the United States. Of course, the degree to
which students would benefit varies widely. Within many communities, what is
reflected in the Student Bill of Rights won't strike residents as particularly noteworthy or extravagant. Their schools already largely meet this standard. However,
for many others, and particularly the residents of low-income communities of
color, the type of education reflected in the Student Bill of Rights can seem virtually unimaginable, like something out of a dream. Their schools have never come
close to resembling anything quite like this. That, in brief, is why there is such
urgency to act, so that we can provide all students, parents, and communities
with the guarantee they deserve that their schools will be equipped with what
they need to create thriving families and neighborhoods.

Not only should we develop such a Student Bill of Rights, but we must also take
the steps necessary to ensure that it is put into action in ways that benefit all young
people. That will require developing a truly equitable school funding system that

aligns with students' developmental needs, prioritizing additional resources and supports for those young people who have been most affected and marginalized by systemic racism, and paying down our long-standing education debt that is owed to communities of color in particular. Anything less will never fully remedy the massive, multigenerational harm that has been done to these communities.

Of course, even top-notch schools can only do so much by themselves. We won't be able to maximize our schools' or our children's potentials unless we address the issues driving the inequitable developmental inputs that students are receiving outside of school, such as the shortage of living-wage jobs, affordable housing, adequate health care, prenatal care, affordable child care, and other vital social services.[171] We also need the policies and practices of all youth-serving institutions—including law enforcement and the child welfare and juvenile justice systems—to be aligned with the developmental focus of our education systems.

In short, we need to address these issues holistically. To pay for the necessary improvements in educational and developmental opportunities, we can start by reinvesting the approximately $50 billion in taxpayer dollars that are currently spent each year on school privatization. Beyond that, chapter 5 addresses how the implementation of a Student Bill of Rights and a comprehensive youth development agenda is eminently feasible if we finally make the education of all children a national priority.

This course of action may not be as sexy as launching a bunch of new charter schools and voucher programs. There is no billionaire-funded army of advocacy groups and think tanks that is pushing for it. It certainly doesn't benefit from a multimillion-dollar marketing campaign. But if we are serious about doing what is necessary to once and for all address our despicable system of separate and unequal education, then there are no shortcuts. Gimmicks won't undo the damage caused by generations of undereducating youth of color. And there is simply no magic that comes from restructuring the management of our schools.

There is only one viable path forward, and that requires making a commitment to every single child in the United States that we are going to dedicate the appropriate resources, and employ our most effective strategies, to ensure that they all get the education they deserve. We have been able to do that—or at least something very close to that—within predominantly white communities across the country, so we had better be able to do it within predominantly black and brown communities. If we do, we will finally be able close the book on our shameful legacy of education injustice. Then, at long last, we can usher in a new golden age of education equity in which demography will no longer equal destiny and our schools can be what we want them to be, not what a small group of billionaires wants them to be.

TOUGH-ON-CRIME FOR YOU, SERVE-AND-PROTECT FOR ME

One of the biggest hurdles in pursuing social justice is getting people to understand that social change is possible. Most people think that the dominant forces shaping our lives are largely unchangeable. However, if you pay close attention, you'll see that the public policies that most affect our lives are never static; they are always moving in one direction or the other. Typically, there are some forces pushing in the direction of making our public policies more humane, egalitarian, and focused on addressing the needs of individuals, families, and communities. However, there are also forces that attempt to push policies in the opposite direction, in ways that lead to more concentration of wealth and power, social inequality, and harm to large segments of the population. That has been a never-ending tug-of-war in US history. Unfortunately, in recent years, the latter group of forces has been prevailing far too often, so most of the changes we have been experiencing have dramatically expanded human suffering and widened societal inequities. There may be no better example of this trend, and just how much change can be created over time, than the US criminal justice system.

For example, at the beginning of the 1970s, after nearly two hundred years of existence as an independent nation, the United States had created a criminal justice system in which there were 325,618 people in prison or jail (or 1 out of every 624 US residents).[1] Nationwide, our criminal justice system employed 575,514 police personnel, 166,192 prosecutors and public judicial/legal employees, and 184,819 correctional employees in 1971.[2] Overall, in that year we spent what would be equivalent in today's dollars to $64 billion on the criminal justice system.[3]

While it took us nearly two centuries to steadily build what would be one of the largest criminal justice systems in the world if it still existed today, it took only a few decades to make that early 1970s criminal justice system seem almost incomprehensibly small in comparison. By 2015, we had increased our prison and jail population by almost 600 percent to 2,173,800 or 1 out of every 147 US residents (with another 4,650,900 individuals under the control of the correctional system through probation or parole). We employed 581,355 more police personnel than we did in 1971, 330,825 more prosecutors and public judicial/legal employees, and 565,216 more correctional employees. Overall, by 2015, we had increased our annual spending on the criminal justice system—after adjusting for inflation—by 361 percent.[4]

How did this happen? How did the "land of the free" wind up with both the largest incarcerated population and the highest incarceration rate in the world? And how did we, with just 5 percent of the world's population, become home to over 20 percent of its prisoners?[5]

Damar Garcia knows.

I met Damar in 2017, when she was a senior in high school in Sheridan, Colorado. By that time, she had already had a front row seat to observe the impact of our criminal justice system's exponential growth. She saw up close what it looks like when it expands to more and more areas of our lives. One of many such "growth industries" for the criminal justice system has been K–12 schools. "There are a lot of students in my school who have to deal with poverty and problems at home like domestic abuse and drug problems," Damar told me. "Those are a lot of the students who were constantly acting out or having behavioral problems. But it seems like nobody on the school staff had been trained to deal with students like that. They just send them to the police. Instead of police being the last resort, they're always the first option." As a result, Damar witnessed numerous classmates being brought into the justice system for a variety of minor offenses, such as talking back to a teacher. "These were all things that could have easily been resolved without involving the police," she said.

Damar has also seen what it looks like when we become overreliant on the criminal justice system to handle a wide variety of other social problems. For example, during her senior year, her family went through some tough times, and she wound up being homeless. She started spending her nights under some trees at the school's baseball field. For two months she kept it to herself. Finally, she confided in one of the school counselors whom she trusted, hoping that the counselor might be able to help her. "She didn't really provide anything," Damar said. "She just sent me to class. The next period I was called out of class to speak to an officer. The officer told me that she was going to press charges against my mother for negligence. They never asked me what I wanted. Nobody gave me any sort of support or provided any resources. They didn't provide me with any other way to deal with it. I wasn't being helped in any way. Instead, they turned to law enforcement, and they created all sorts of legal problems for me and my family." What was particularly demoralizing for Damar was how the response to her problems didn't seem to be focused on her interests. "In that moment I was turning to adults for help, but instead a problem was being created that was so much bigger than it should have been."

Damar's entanglements with the justice system didn't stop there. "After I had that incident with the police officer, I was scared to go back to school because I didn't want to create any more legal problems for my mom or myself. So I stopped going to school at all. And because I was classified as a runaway, I was constantly being watched by the authorities. They would always stop me on the street, but they weren't helping me—all they were doing was intimidating me. I felt like they were criminalizing me." To avoid being harassed by the police, Damar stopped sleeping at the baseball field—where she had felt relatively safe— and started spending her nights at bus stops and train stations, where she didn't feel safe at all.

As Damar reflected on her experiences, she was dismayed by the fact that the police and the justice system were viewed as the appropriate response to three entirely distinct problems in her life: disruptive behavior in her school, her family's struggles, and her homelessness. In all three cases, Damar was certain that the law enforcement approach was misguided and only made things worse. "It's pretty obvious that more time, energy, and money is being put toward strict law enforcement than is being put toward things like mental health resources in my school," she said. "And in my life, I've had more contact with police officers than I've had with people who can actually help me with my problems. It's really frustrating because you want to reach out for help, but you're scared to, because 'help' means the police."

The Other Side of the Tracks

There isn't a single person in the United States who hasn't been directly affected by the dramatic expansion of our current system of mass criminalization and incarceration, even if only financially. However, the range of that impact has been enormous, from relatively little nonfinancial impact within some predominantly white communities to utter devastation within many communities of color.

I grew up in communities closer to the low impact side of that scale. The local police force was relatively small, and the role of the criminal justice system in daily life was minimal. One could easily go weeks or even months without ever seeing a police officer doing anything other than operating a radar gun and looking for speeders. When my peers and I interacted with police officers, they were occasionally firm—though usually not unjustifiably so—but they were also typically quite understanding and helpful, and occasionally even kind. For the most part, they did seem to be there to "serve and protect" us. There was plenty of what could have been considered to be crime around, but the police and prosecutors never seemed inclined to use their power to criminalize us. If anything, they were often exceedingly lenient and went out of their way to *not* bring us into the juvenile or criminal justice systems when it would have been very easy to do so. Thus, through our personal interactions with them, the seemingly endless cop shows that were on TV, and the various other positive representations of the police, prosecutors, and judges we absorbed through popular culture, most of us developed a generally positive view of the justice system. In our eyes, like those of the residents of many predominantly white communities around the country, "police" became almost synonymous with "safety." We saw police officers, along with prosecutors and judges, as noble public servants looking out for our collective security.

It was only later in life that I learned that my experience with police and the justice system bore almost no resemblance to the experiences of many people of color. That only happened because my work allowed me to see the true mass criminalization and incarceration system up close and firsthand. Indeed, unless you have seen that system in action within communities of color, it can be hard to even believe that it exists.

The first thing you notice within many black and brown communities is just the sheer number of police officers who are deployed. I have been in neighborhoods that seemed to be teeming with officers. You could hardly walk a block down the street without having an officer pass by in a patrol car or on foot. On top of that, many of these communities have surveillance cameras on every block.[6] Thus, you *always* feel like you are being watched.

This is true in the schools within these communities as well. I have been in K–12 schools with up to eight police officers stationed on campus, with metal detectors at every entrance, surveillance cameras in every hallway, police cars parked menacingly right outside the entrance, and even police booking stations located inside the school.

If you have never experienced this type of policing, the picture you have in your head may be of a team of benevolent problem solvers patrolling the streets. You might even be imagining officers in the mold of Barney Fife from *The Andy Griffith Show*, Ponch from *CHiPs*, Jake Peralta from *Brooklyn Nine-Nine*, or Chief Wiggum from *The Simpsons*. In reality, the image projected by the criminal justice system in many of these communities is far closer to *Robocop* or even *Call of Duty* than it is to the Mayberry PD. The average patrol officer is often heavily armed, and many officers are outfitted as if they were in a war zone, with machine guns, assault rifles, body armor, helmets, masks, flashbang grenades, and various chemical agents. To further reinforce the war zone analogy, some of the police departments in these communities even have armored tanks, attack helicopters, and drones that they deploy regularly across the city.[7]

However, the biggest difference between how the criminal justice system operates in many communities of color compared to most predominantly white communities is how it engages with residents, and that starts with the police. It is jarring, as an outside observer, to see how much more aggressive officers are with residents. Verbally aggressive. Physically aggressive. Psychologically aggressive. In my entire life I have never had anyone speak to me with half as much contempt as some officers that I have seen confronting young men and women of color. I have also never had anyone feel nearly as entitled to put their hands on me as many officers do with respect to people of color. I have seen officers approach groups of young people who were just hanging out on the street and instantly turn them around to frisk them, sometimes without even uttering a word, as if it were an automatic reflex. What is particularly striking is the nonchalance with which they do it, the ease with which they assume they can perform such an invasive act. That can only come from those officers having a sense of dominion over the people they are searching, from having been made to feel empowered to treat the residents of black and brown communities the way most of us are only allowed to treat our personal property.

That aggression doesn't end with the police, however. The prosecutors in these communities have been granted enormous power over not only those individuals who are charged with crimes, but also their families and entire communities. Too often that power has been used with the force of a hammer against those communities when it should be used with the precision of a scalpel. Prosecutors have become far too quick to confine people to jail or prison cells, which are, of course, just human cages by another name. While the goal of any law enforcement agency should be to put itself out of business, in my experience it has frequently been the case that the apparent goal of prosecutors in communities of color was to bring people into the criminal justice system far more often, and keep them there far longer, than what is necessary, appropriate, or equitable when compared to other communities.

Overall, what is perhaps most striking about how criminal justice officials operate within many communities of color, compared to predominantly white communities, is the frequency with which they opt for hostile and degrading treatment of the people they are supposed to be serving and protecting. Over and over again, I have witnessed police officers and prosecutors treat community members not as valued citizens or partners in creating safe communities, but rather as adversaries or subordinates. There have been far too many occasions when I have seen law enforcement officials flaunt their power over community members, openly demanding the type of submissiveness and obedience that most of us would normally associate with an owner/pet relationship.

The harm these dynamics have wrought cannot be overstated. In many communities of color across the country, virtually everyone you meet has personal experience with demeaning and humiliating police behavior, if not even more egregious acts of police harassment and brutality. Virtually everyone can cite examples from their own lives, or those of their family members and friends, of being unnecessarily criminalized for precisely the same behaviors that happen regularly in predominantly white communities with very different consequences. Virtually everyone has been profoundly affected by the plague of mass incarceration that they see decimating their communities. Yet through it all, the criminal justice system has been almost shockingly unaccountable and nonresponsive to the needs and priorities of the residents of many of these communities.

Because of such dynamics, there are those who will, on occasion, refer to the United States as a "police state." That is understandable, considering that we now have an incarceration rate that is 85 percent higher than Russia's, 123 percent higher than Iran's, 268 percent higher than Venezuela's, and 441 percent higher than China's, all countries that US government officials regularly criticize as being repressive.[8] Nevertheless, I believe that the claim that we are a police state is demonstrably false and hyperbolic. It is quite easy to find numerous examples of communities where the role of the criminal justice system isn't overly repressive— namely, most if not all predominantly white communities. However, within many communities of color, there can be no doubt that we *have* created a police state. The highly concentrated police presence and hyperaggressive policing, surveillance, criminalization, and incarceration strategies within parts of New York, Los Angeles, Chicago, Miami, Oakland, Philadelphia, and numerous other communities of color are, in many respects, George Orwell's *1984* come to life. They are the end result of telling police officers, prosecutors, and judges for decades that they are at war, whether it be a "war on drugs," a "war on crime," or a "war on gangs." They are the effects of outfitting and arming police as if they were an occupying force in a war zone while encouraging them to adopt a "warrior's mentality."[9] They are the byproduct of convincing countless police officers, prosecutors, and judges that the people they are supposed to work for are instead the enemy.

In other words, in the United States, we pay public employees to wage war against our own people. (Let that sink in for a moment.) Over the years, that war has claimed millions of victims. However, perhaps the most significant outcome is that, like all wars, this one has resulted in a diminished view of the humanity of those on the opposite side of it. That, in short, is why the killings of Michael Brown, Freddie Gray, Eric Garner, Sandra Bland, Rekia Boyd, Tamir Rice, Walter Scott, Laquan McDonald, Philando Castile, Breonna Taylor, George Floyd, and so many others cannot be viewed as anomalies. *They are the predictable result of a series of criminal justice policies that haven't valued the lives of people of color enough to ensure that those lives aren't harmed, debased, or taken needlessly.*

If predominantly white communities were forced to endure the same law enforcement strategies as these communities of color, there would be an all-out political revolution in motion within a week. Yet when people of color such as those in the Black Lives Matter movement point out these realities, instead of coming together as a society around real solutions, the substance of what they are raising is largely ignored, and they are frequently attacked for being "anti-cop," "anti-American," or for ignoring "black on black" crime. (News flash: most crime against white people is "white on white." This is just the reality of racially segregated neighborhoods and the fact that most violent crime involves people who live with, or in close proximity to, one another.)[10]

Even more moderate individuals, including many readers of this book, will discount much of the above as unfortunate side effects of a sound law-enforcement strategy that is justified by higher crime rates in these communities and the need for public safety. (As discussed later, it isn't.) Or they will acknowledge the problems but point out that, thanks to the recent bipartisan consensus around the need for criminal justice reform, those excesses will be addressed through "community policing," body cameras for police, the various sentencing reforms that have been passed, and other comparable reforms. (They won't.)

Unfortunately, even after many decades of devastation caused by the mass criminalization and incarceration system, we still aren't having a real public conversation about how to address the problem. Instead, within the criminal justice debate, even some of the best-intentioned people have accepted certain premises as given. These premises include the following:

- Within our society, there are law-abiding citizens and there are criminals, and the former must be protected from the latter for our communities to be safe.
- The purpose of the criminal justice system is to achieve public safety, and public safety is achieved through a well-supported, well-resourced criminal justice system.
- There is a direct relationship between the size of our police force and the safety of our communities (i.e., more police = more safety; fewer police = more crime).

- Any concerns with regard to the performance of law enforcement personnel can be addressed through improving their relationships with the communities they serve.
- Criminals deserve punishment within the criminal justice system.
- While current incarceration levels may be too high, finding the appropriate level requires locating the tipping point at which further reductions would lead to increases in the crime rate.

As will be discussed later, not one of the bulleted statements stands up to scrutiny. Unfortunately, they are guiding much of the current debate around criminal justice policy. They are thus serving as obstacles to building a more just and effective criminal justice system because if you follow where these assumptions lead, you ultimately reach a lot of dead ends involving the same injustices our current system has created.

Instead of continuing to go around and around the same hamster wheel, we need to step back and ask ourselves a question that is very simple but nowhere to be found in the criminal justice debate: What are the best strategies available to us for both preventing and responding to crime and violence in a way that promotes safer, healthier, and more equitable communities across the country? At the end of this chapter, there are some strategies offered that can accomplish just that.

Additionally, to get to where we need to be, we must also confront the fact that our many misguided assumptions about public safety, along with all of the "tough on crime," "law and order," "zero tolerance," and "broken windows" policies that have been implemented over the past several decades, haven't come out of nowhere.[11] Relatedly, we must recognize that while these initiatives have been extraordinarily harmful and remarkably ineffective, they haven't been harmful and ineffective for everyone. On the contrary, our current system of mass criminalization and incarceration has been enormously advantageous and profitable for the ultra-wealthy. Many of these individuals have played substantial roles in creating and expanding that system, and they continue to actively impede efforts to fix it. So to have any chance of building a more equitable system that best meets the needs of all US communities, we must be aware of both the motives and the methods behind this form of strategic racism.

First, though, we must understand the primary mechanism that has been used to turn the often-violent suppression and caging of human beings into a wealth-building opportunity: the Criminalization Trap.

The Criminalization Trap

There are some basic choices that must be made in constructing a criminal justice system. First, how are we going to define "crime" and determine where it is happening? Second, who is going to respond to the crime that we find? And third, what is our response to that crime going to be? Each one of those questions presents us with a choice of numerous possibilities, and together those possibilities carry a wide range of potential outcomes that can dramatically alter the direction a society takes. So how have we in the United States answered them? With the following:

1. We have created policies that allow for the highly aggressive enforcement of extremely broad criminal laws, making it remarkably easy to identify "crimes" and ensuring that virtually every person can be considered a "criminal" at some point.
2. We have prioritized the use of law enforcement responses to these "crimes" over many other possible responses, despite the fact that there is a fundamental mismatch between what law enforcement is trained to do and the skills needed to best address the vast majority of these behaviors.
3. We have emphasized profoundly harmful and punitive consequences for criminal offenses rather than those that would be more effective at holding offenders accountable in meaningful ways, repairing the damage caused by crime, meeting the needs of survivors/victims, addressing the root causes of crime, and breaking the cycle of crime.

These are the decisions that have created what is arguably the largest criminal justice system in the history of the world. Moreover, our choices ensured that those who would be caught up in that system would be disproportionately people of color, because of the following:

1. The highly aggressive enforcement of extremely broad criminal laws has been especially focused on black and brown communities.
2. We have invested particularly heavily in the criminal justice system within black and brown communities while underinvesting in systems that could otherwise address the causes of crime and respond to incidents of crime.
3. Our desire to punish white "criminals" often doesn't rise to the same level as our desire to punish people of color.

I refer to these dynamics as the Criminalization Trap because we didn't have to criminalize people this way; we *chose* to. In other words, our current system of mass criminalization and incarceration isn't an accidental consequence or unfortunate side effect; the system is doing what it was designed to do. The policies and practices that have been instituted over the past several decades could not have produced anything other than a vastly oversized, overbroad, and destructive criminal justice system such as the one we have today.

Here is how the Criminalization Trap has been created, starting with how we have decided to define crime and where we have decided to look for it.

A Crime Is a Crime, Or Is It?

The Universality of Criminality

For many years, during presentations that I have given or training sessions I have facilitated, I have used one particular "icebreaker" exercise. I have everyone in the room—which typically includes mostly white teachers, school administrators, police officers, judges, and social services providers, among others—think back to when they were young and put themselves in one of three groups:

- Group One: those who never did anything wrong
- Group Two: those who were always getting into trouble
- Group Three: those who were generally "good" but got into occasional trouble

On the dozens of occasions that I have done this exercise, with thousands of adults, the distribution across groups has always been roughly the same: about 10 percent of participants go to Group One, another 10 percent go to Group Two, and the remaining 80 percent go to Group Three. I then ask those in Groups Two and Three to describe what they did that caused them to self-identify that way. Thus, I have had many very successful adults confess to automobile theft, drug dealing, criminal gang activity, numerous acts of violence, various property offenses, and an extensive history of unlawful alcohol and drug use. The only difference between Groups Two and Three—which together constitute 90 percent of participants—is the frequency with which they committed such offenses.

The next step is that I ask them whether they were ever arrested, suspended from school, or expelled from school for their actions. Every single time I do this, the entire (again, predominantly white) room stares back at me with the most befuddled looks on their faces, as if the thought that they could have been subjected to such consequences had never before crossed their minds. When I then ask what happened instead that allowed them to grow up to be successful adults, participants have sometimes cited parental interventions and the role of educators or coaches in helping to put them on a better path. But the most common response is that they were never caught, never faced any consequences, and simply grew out of it.

There are two basic facts to know about our criminal justice system and who is brought into it. First, behaviors that can be considered crimes under US criminal law happen constantly within every neighborhood in the country. Second, those behaviors only become crimes if law enforcement officers are there to see them, or are alerted to them, and decide to treat them as crimes.

The reality is that, at some point in their lives, almost all people steal, damage someone else's property, consume an illegal substance, engage in violence, or otherwise violate criminal law.[12] Most of us, particularly men, commit *many* such violations. (Just ask us. We usually *love* to talk about all the illicit stuff we did when we were young.) In fact, it is remarkably easy to witness rampant lawbreaking.

For example, virtually every K–12 school in the United States has regular incidents of students threatening each other, getting into scuffles, creating graffiti, and being unruly or defiant. The same is true for adults at most bars around the country. From the criminal law perspective, those incidents can be considered, in order, assault, battery, destruction of property, and disorderly conduct. You can go to any food court or restaurant with a self-service beverage machine and watch countless individuals perform "thefts" when they ask for a water cup and use it to get a soda instead. The same is true for the many small colonies of individuals who share the same Netflix passwords. You can drive around any neighborhood in the United States and find examples of people who meet the legal definition for loitering or unlawful assembly. You can go to any high-pressure work environment and find drug and alcohol violations. You can go to any college campus and find all of the above, plus any number of other violations of criminal law, at any time of day.

Some of these offenses are trivial; others are not. The point is that if you look closely enough, and long enough, you can see "crime" virtually anywhere, committed by almost everyone at some point. Thus, the idea that "criminals" are somehow different from the rest of us, the evil standing in opposition to our good, is pure fallacy. Note, however, that only a small fraction of what could be considered crime is policed. Behavior that may violate criminal law becomes "criminal" only when we decide to make it so, when policy makers decide to police that behavior or criminalize it once law enforcement is made aware of it.[13] In other words, crime is much less about behavior than it is about policy choices. Because we couldn't possibly bring everyone who violates the law into the criminal justice system, the question becomes: Which "crimes" do we, as a society, want to focus our resources on? How we answer that question can tell us a great deal about the behavior that we object to and the individuals whom we are comfortable turning into "criminals."

Notice, for example, that there is only a rough correlation between behavior that causes harm to others and the behavior we treat as criminal. We criminalize many types of behaviors that cause little to no harm to others—such as personal drug use—while not criminalizing, or only very rarely criminalizing, other behaviors that cause widespread death and destruction, such as manufacturing harmful or deadly products, polluting the environment with industrial waste, causing global financial meltdowns, and engaging in wars of aggression. Notice also that if you or I contaminate someone's food and they die of poisoning, then we will go to jail for murder. However, if the executives of a large corporation direct the manufacture of products that they know will result in thousands of unnecessary deaths, it can be difficult to impossible to sustain a civil lawsuit against them, much less any sort of criminal case.

As will be discussed more in the following, the decisions about where we choose to look for crime have typically been driven more by fear (usually the irrational sort), racism, and greed than by sound policy. Both policy makers and the media have spent the past several decades continually exploiting people's natural anxieties over their own safety and that of their loved ones. From President Nixon to President Trump, talking about crime, "crime waves," and the need for "tough on crime" and "law and order" strategies to address widespread criminality has been a consistent political winner. For the media, in movies like *Dirty Harry*, reality shows like *America's Most Wanted* and *Cops*, the dozens of police dramas that have been on TV, and the typically heavy concentration of crime coverage on the nightly news, sensationalizing crime and criminals has also been a major moneymaker.[14]

These descriptions and depictions of crime are typically only loosely connected with facts, at best. For example, while we are often encouraged to be fearful of violent criminals prowling our communities, the reality is that most violent crimes are committed by people known to the victims.[15] In the case of the "war on drugs," it took an extraordinary partnership between government officials and media to convince the public that drug use was a grave threat that necessitated aggressive police action.[16] Or if you watch many of the action-packed cop shows on TV, you would think that there is a perpetual crime wave. However, the reality is that most police work is very dull and sedentary. (Watching fictional officers fill out paperwork or sit in their patrol cars all day with radar guns waiting for speeders probably wouldn't get very good ratings.)

Nevertheless, these media and "public education" efforts shift and distort people's perception of crime in significant ways. Ultimately, they shape the behaviors and the people that we decide to criminalize. And while that process has taken many forms, perhaps the one constant has been that they tend to direct the public gaze toward black and brown communities.

For example, research has shown that the media overrepresents people of color as crime suspects and white people as crime victims. It is particularly popular to show incidents in which the offender was a person of color and the victim was white, even though such incidents in reality are far rarer than the media coverage would suggest. Crime coverage is also likelier to depict people of color in threatening ways, such as in mug shots or in handcuffs. The overall effect is that the public, especially the white public, associates crime with people of color, and people of color with crime.[17] When this association is paired with the egregious lack of context provided around the root causes of crime and the politics of crime, much of the white public starts to believe that people of color are more prone to criminality. Consequently, white people become more likely to call the police on people of color engaged in perfectly innocuous behavior, and they become convinced that communities of color should be targeted with particularly aggressive "tough on crime" strategies.

Occupied Territories

That is precisely what has happened. We have concentrated our criminal justice efforts within black and brown communities, ensuring that there are always law enforcement eyes nearby. As a result, behaviors there are criminalized far more easily than they are in predominantly white communities.

Consider that, across the entire United States, there are 0.18 police officers per square mile.[18] However, within communities of color, there are often several hundred times more than that. For example, in New York City there are 119.7 officers per square mile, or nearly 650 times as many as the national average.[19]

To further illustrate how much more significant the law enforcement presence is in communities of color compared to predominantly white communities, tables 12a to 12e list examples of five major cities—New York City, Chicago,

TABLE 12A

NY CITY OR TOWN	% OF PEOPLE OF COLOR	POLICE OFFICERS PER SQUARE MILE
New York City	68%	119.7
Bedford	23%	1.0
Eastchester	20%	9.5
New Castle / Chappaqua	16%	1.5
Scarsdale	23%	6.6

TABLE 12B

IL CITY OR TOWN	% OF PEOPLE OF COLOR	POLICE OFFICERS PER SQUARE MILE
Chicago	68%	52.5
Highland Park	15%	4.7
St. Charles	15%	3.6
Wheaton	18%	5.9
Winnetka	10%	7.3

TABLE 12C

FL CITY OR TOWN	% OF PEOPLE OF COLOR	POLICE OFFICERS PER SQUARE MILE
Miami	89%	33.5
Boca Raton	23%	6.2
North Palm Beach	14%	8.4
Palm Beach	6%	14.8
Palm Beach Gardens	21%	2.0

TABLE 12D

CO CITY OR TOWN	% OF PEOPLE OF COLOR	POLICE OFFICERS PER SQUARE MILE
Denver	47%	9.7
Castle Rock	16%	2.0
Cherry Hills Village	11%	3.7
Littleton	18%	5.4
Parker	17%	3.5

TABLE 12E

CA CITY OR TOWN	% OF PEOPLE OF COLOR	POLICE OFFICERS PER SQUARE MILE
Los Angeles	72%	21.0
Laguna Beach	16%	5.5
Newport Beach	20%	5.9
Redondo Beach	38%	14.8
Santa Barbara	46%	7.2

Miami, Denver, and Los Angeles—along with four nearby, predominantly white cities or towns, and the police densities within them.[20]

Note that Los Angeles has almost four times as many officers per square mile as Laguna Beach, Denver has almost five times as many as Castle Rock, Chicago has more than fourteen times as many as St. Charles, Miami has over sixteen times as many as Palm Beach Gardens, and New York has almost 120 times as many as Bedford.

In some ways, this actually understates the disparities. For example, while the citywide concentration in Chicago is 52.5 officers per square mile, in predominantly black neighborhoods within the city, it is often considerably higher. In Austin, a predominantly black neighborhood on the West Side, there are 91.7 officers per square mile, compared to other neighborhoods with smaller black populations where there are fewer than 10 officers per square mile.[21]

This may seem counterintuitive to some readers who have come to associate more police with greater safety. If that were so, one might reasonably expect these predominantly white communities, many of which are quite affluent, to have higher concentrations of police than the communities of color, many of which are low-income areas. After all, if high concentrations of police are so beneficial, then it would be reasonable to assume that the wealthier communities would want to devote their considerable resources to additional police. The reality, however, is that the "police = safety" idea only goes so far, and these communities don't want the same level of policing that communities of color often are forced to endure.

This is also true within schools. Over the past two decades, we have dramatically increased the number of police officers stationed in K–12 schools, especially within communities of color.[22] (This is painfully ironic considering that it was the tragedy at Columbine High School and other school shootings in predominantly white communities that were often the impetus for the buildup of school police forces in black and brown neighborhoods.) The typical justification offered for these changes has been that they are needed to protect students from outside threats. Within the predominantly white schools that have school resource officers (SROs), that has been largely how these officers have operated. However, in many other schools, particularly those within communities of color, the role of school police has often been quite different. In many schools, the primary function of these SROs hasn't been to protect students from threats coming from outside the school community but rather to aggressively police the students *within* the school community.[23]

Of course, the mere presence, or absence, of a police officer isn't the only factor contributing to the overpolicing of people of color. Police officers aren't robots capable of objectively identifying criminal acts. They, like all of us, bring their own sets of complications and biases into their work. Some of those biases may be explicit, most are likely to be implicit, but all of them can result in viewing the behavior of one person as criminal while the identical behavior of another person is viewed as noncriminal. Behavior that is deemed to necessitate a criminal justice response for one person can, for another person, be justified as an innocent mistake, a lapse in judgment, the result of just "having had too much to drink," a product of mental illness, an example of "boys being boys," or any number of other possibilities. Of course, those biases, in general, overwhelmingly disfavor people of color (not just with regard to police, but within the general population as well), such that even if white people and people of color faced identical police scrutiny and acted exactly the same, there would still be more people of color being brought into the criminal justice system.[24]

There are ways in which the effects of individual biases can be minimized. However, for police, we have often created environments in which the potential impact of bias is maximized. That is a result of giving them enormous discretion over which laws to enforce against which individuals. Consider our traffic laws.

Almost every single driver exceeds the speed limit on a regular basis. Police aren't going to stop every car, but they have a sound legal basis for stopping virtually any car they choose, meaning racial profiling becomes remarkably easy. Similarly, having broad criminal categories such as disturbing the peace, loitering, unlawful assembly, and disorderly conduct means that police officers are able to target large swaths of the population whenever they want. Having broad enforcement priorities around common behaviors, such as the use of illicit drugs, provides police with the opportunity to focus their efforts almost anywhere. Having officers stationed in schools means that when students fight, or scribble on the bathroom walls, or talk back to a teacher, the police often get to decide whether those typical adolescent behaviors constitute criminal violations or noncriminal school disciplinary matters. How all these decisions are made can be heavily influenced by officers' views concerning whom criminal law should be used against. Thus, discretion blends very easily into discrimination.[25]

The War at Home

Of course, police aren't just passive observers of criminal behavior or recipients of criminal reports. We have given them an expansive set of tools that allows for aggressive and often violent policing. We allow them to "stop and frisk" individuals based on a "reasonable suspicion" that a crime has been, or is about to be, committed and the person is "armed and dangerous." (In practice, they are often given even broader latitude.) We employ "broken windows" strategies that have police vigorously enforcing even the most low-level crimes. Of course, the more aggressive police are, the more likely their tactics will result in violence.[26] And as should be now obvious to anyone with even a passing interest in the news, we grant police considerable latitude in using force, including lethal force, against the public. That includes incidents in which it was the aggressive tactics of the police that created or escalated the situations that resulted in the use of force.

These techniques could be used to target crime anywhere in the United States. But they are not (at least not yet).[27] Such hyperaggressive and violent techniques are almost exclusively reserved for communities of color, where they are employed with shocking regularity. A few examples:

- New York City: Since 2002, New Yorkers have been subjected to more than five million incidents of stop and frisk that turned up no evidence of crime. Those stops have been overwhelmingly concentrated in communities of color, and almost 90 percent of those who have been stopped were people of color. In 2012, for instance, of the 532,911 reported stops, guns were discovered in just one out of every 714 stops.

While only 6 percent of those stops resulted in an arrest, force was used in 17 percent of them, meaning there were tens of thousands of New Yorkers who were put on the ground or against a wall, had a weapon drawn on them and/or pointed at them, or had manual force, a baton, handcuffs, or pepper spray used against them in circumstances that didn't even warrant an arrest. The individuals subjected to force during these stops have, again, been overwhelmingly people of color.[28]

- Chicago: During 2014 and 2015, there were 1.3 million reported "stops" of Chicagoans that resulted in no further action, and over 90 percent of them were of people of color (even though white people constitute 32 percent of the population in Chicago). Black individuals were far more likely than white individuals to be frisked after being stopped, even though white people were more likely to be found with weapons. Additionally, the Department of Justice found that Chicago police officers "engage in a pattern or practice of using force, including deadly force, that is unreasonable" and that results in "unnecessary and avoidable shootings and other uses of force." The Department of Justice also found that the "pattern or practice of unreasonable force and systemic deficiencies fall heaviest on the predominantly black and Latino neighborhoods on the South and West Sides of Chicago," with statistics showing that the police use force almost ten times more often against black residents than against white residents.[29]

- Miami Gardens, Florida: This town situated between Miami and Fort Lauderdale is home to around 110,000 residents, 97 percent of whom are people of color. Between 2008 and 2013, 250 individuals were stopped and frisked at least twenty times each. One man was stopped and frisked 258 times, including sixty-two times at the convenience store where he worked. Individuals as young as five years old and as old as ninety-nine were stopped because they were deemed to be suspicious.[30]

- Newark, New Jersey: During just a six-month period in 2013, there was nearly one stop by police for every ten Newark residents. In its 2014 investigation, the Department of Justice found that approximately 75 percent of reported police stops failed to articulate sufficient legal basis for the stop. They also found that police made thousands of stops of individuals who were described merely as "milling," "loitering," or "wandering," without any indication of reasonable suspicion of criminal activity. Black residents of Newark were at least two and a half times more likely to be subjected to a pedestrian stop or arrested than white residents.[31]

- Baltimore: Between January 2010 and May 2015, officers reported over three hundred thousand pedestrian stops that, according to the

Department of Justice, were "concentrated in predominantly African-American neighborhoods and often lack reasonable suspicion." Hundreds of individuals—nearly all of them black—were stopped on at least ten separate occasions during this period. Seven black men were stopped more than thirty times each. The DOJ also found that "officers regularly approach individuals standing or walking on city sidewalks to detain and question them and check for outstanding warrants, despite lacking reasonable suspicion to do so." They also found that officers "frequently pat-down or frisk individuals as a matter of course, without identifying necessary grounds to believe that the person is armed and dangerous." Only 3.7 percent of these stops resulted in officers issuing a citation or making an arrest. For example, in 2012, there were more than 123,000 reported stops that yielded a total of ten weapons and ten illegal drugs.[32]

This is, unfortunately, just a small sample of how these practices are used. There have been reports of similarly aggressive and violent practices being used in communities of color across the country, including in Boston, Milwaukee, New Orleans, Cleveland, Philadelphia, Seattle, Portland, Miami, and Ferguson, Missouri, among many others.[33]

As jarring as this data can be, it is critically important that we not get preoccupied with the numbers and lose sight of the *significant harm caused by every single one of these encounters*. They all have a cost associated with them, even those that don't result in arrests or uses of force. These are invasive and humiliating tactics. They represent an emphatic assertion of government power and dominance over a person. They send a message to the individuals being stopped that they are considered to be hostile and dangerous, that they are viewed as criminals, or at least criminals-in-waiting. They are an explicit reminder to the individuals being stopped that they are not trusted or valued as much as other members of the community. These harms are real, and when you begin to add up the cumulative effects of tens of thousands, hundreds of thousands, or even millions of such incidents within particular communities, the damage and trauma caused in the name of public safety are immense and devastating, while the corresponding benefits are minimal at best.

The US Criminal Justice System: Where All Are Welcome

This combination of a militant boots-on-the-ground strategy, considerable enforcement discretion, and hyperaggressive policing tactics has resulted in a deluge of people entering the criminal justice system each year. For example, in 2016, there were 10.7 million arrests in the United States. Given that policy makers typically attempt to justify heavy police presence and aggressive policing tactics by citing the need to crack down on violent crime, you might think that such offenses would constitute a large chunk of arrests. On the contrary, less than 5 percent of those arrests were for what the FBI classifies as violent offenses.[34] The vast majority of arrests were for offenses involving drugs or alcohol, property crimes, lower-level assault charges, disorderly conduct, and other relatively low-level behaviors. Not surprisingly, given the intensive focus on policing in communities of color, the black arrest rate was over twice as high as the white arrest rate.[35]

The same dynamics have played out in K–12 schools, especially those within black and brown communities. Behaviors that have long been considered school disciplinary issues, and still are in many predominantly white communities, are now criminalized, even for children as young as five or six years old.[36] As a result, in 2015–16, K–12 schools in the United States reported that 235,266 students were referred to law enforcement and 62,020 were arrested in school.[37] (Note that as striking as these numbers are, the actual numbers are likely far higher, as many school districts don't track and report this data.)

Again not surprisingly, most of these arrests came from schools with police officers on site. Schools that reported having sworn law enforcement officers on staff served 32 percent of students in the United States in 2015–16 but were responsible for 62 percent of the students arrested. Even if we exclude elementary schools (where there are few SROs or arrests), students in middle and high schools with police on site were 122 percent more likely to be arrested than those who attended schools without police.[38]

Because of how we have taken the "tough on crime" strategies used on adults and applied them to children, there are now school districts around the country in which hundreds or even thousands of students are referred to law enforcement and arrested each year. For example, table 13 shows the twenty-five districts with the most students referred to law enforcement during the 2015–16 school year, all but two of which have student populations that were at least 48 percent students of color.

The Tough-on-Crime Lie

It is time for us to admit that we have been lying to black and brown communities. For several decades, the dominant message from US policy makers to communities of color has been: We will keep you safe by being "tough on crime." By flooding your communities with law enforcement officers. By using stop and frisk.

TABLE 13 School districts with most students referred to law enforcement, 2015–16

NAME OF DISTRICT	CITY, STATE	% STUDENTS OF COLOR	NUMBER OF STUDENTS REFERRED TO LAW ENFORCEMENT
Los Angeles Unified	Los Angeles, CA	90%	8,416
Philadelphia City SD	Philadelphia, PA	86%	6,834
New York City Public Schools	New York, NY	84%	4,414
Chicago Public Schools	Chicago, IL	90%	3,041
Austin ISD	Austin, TX	73%	2,697
Polk County Public Schools	Bartow, FL	58%	2,481
Broward County Public Schools	Fort Lauderdale, FL	78%	2,407
Palm Beach County Public Schools	West Palm Beach, FL	67%	2,032
Wake County Schools	Cary, NC	53%	1,955
Hillsborough County Public Schools	Tampa, FL	65%	1,527
Etiwanda SD	Etiwanda, CA	76%	1,431
Prince George's County Public Schools	Upper Marlboro, MD	96%	1,379
Pittsburgh SD	Pittsburgh, PA	67%	1,299
Washoe County SD	Reno, NV	55%	1,235
Auburn City SD	Auburn, NY	19%	1,201
East Side Union High School District	San Jose, CA	94%	1,164
Prince William County Public Schools	Manassas, VA	68%	1,129
Chesterfield County Public Schools	Chesterfield, VA	48%	1,120
Clark County SD	Las Vegas, NV	74%	1,070
Jefferson County School District No. R-1	Golden, CO	33%	1,068
Richmond City Public Schools	Richmond, VA	91%	1,026
Raytown C-2	Raytown, MO	68%	987
Gwinnett County Public Schools	Suwanee, GA	74%	946
San Antonio ISD	San Antonio, TX	98%	939
Orange County Public Schools	Orlando, FL	72%	901

Source: US Department of Education, *Civil Rights Data Collection*.

By employing "broken windows policing" and cracking down on low-level offenses. By aggressively policing K–12 students in their schools. The consistent message to these communities has been that these were the most effective strategies for improving public safety.

However, if this were true, then wouldn't predominantly white communities have wanted the same things? Wouldn't they have been in the offices of their elected officials clamoring for the benefits of heavy-handed law enforcement strategies all these years?

Notice, though, that there is nothing comparable to the style of policing described here within predominantly white communities. There are no pre-dominantly white communities in the United States with police officers on every block, where people are routinely stopped and frisked, where police regularly initiate violent encounters with residents, and where the developmentally nor-mal behavior of children and youth in school is regularly criminalized. However, it must be noted that there could be. We could be enforcing the law far more aggressively against people in predominantly white K–12 schools, colleges, work-places, and neighborhoods. We could uncover more than enough criminal activ-ity to fill up our jails and prisons many times over with white teenagers, frat boys, Wall Street stockbrokers, corporate polluters, lawyers, Silicon Valley computer programmers, and others who have until now been "criming" with impunity.[39] If we really wanted to crack down on white crime, we could position undercover cops next to self-service beverage machines in predominantly white communi-ties all across the country and lock up tens of thousands of soda thieves in no time. You might think that is a ridiculous idea, but is it any more absurd than the fact that we bring tens of thousands of low-income people of color from New York and Los Angeles into the criminal justice system every year for not paying their fares on public transit?[40]

Even without adopting all these tactics in predominantly white communities, it would be easy to have an overwhelmingly white prison population that would be just as large or larger than our current one. For example, there were already well over four million white people arrested in 2016, and we weren't even making nearly as much of an effort to "get tough" on white crime as we were on crime committed by people of color.[41] If we were to simply shift our focus and reallocate some of the law enforcement resources currently dedicated to communities of color, the overall complexion of our prison population could take on a decidedly more pinkish hue rather quickly and dramatically.

These notions might strike you as unfathomable or even laughable, but they shouldn't. They represent totally reasonable approaches and outcomes—if we were to truly act on what we say we believe with regard to the criminal justice system and subtract our racial biases from the equation. All we have to do is rid ourselves of the automatic assumption that people of color will be overrepre-sented in our jails and prisons and, voilà, the possibility of an overwhelmingly white incarcerated population emerges as a completely plausible outcome.

Of course, the reality is that we don't truly believe what we say about our hyperaggressive law enforcement approach within communities of color. As will be discussed later, creating this type of police state doesn't represent anywhere close to our best option for improving public safety. In fact, it is probably our worst, and most harmful, option. Yet we continue to perpetuate the "tough on crime lie."

Even if the tough-on-crime approach did represent a high-quality strategy, there still wouldn't be a sound basis upon which to justify the differences between the law enforcement tactics used in communities of color and those used in predominantly white communities. It's not like these are subtle distinctions that can be justified by legitimate differences in crime rates between communities. The difference between how communities of color are policed and how predominantly white communities are policed is roughly the same as the difference between how the US military engages with civilians in Iraq and how it engages with the teenagers at your local high school career fair.

Nevertheless, it must be acknowledged that there are some communities of color that do have truly serious levels of crime and violence, and we need to be able to respond effectively in support of all who are affected. But first we need to be able to understand the root causes of the problem. We need to understand why it is that some communities of color struggle more with crime, and particularly violent crime, than other communities. This tends to be where people's biases about people of color being more prone to criminality come into play. However, unless you believe in the inherent inferiority of the residents of those communities, then you must acknowledge that there has to be something about their lived conditions that can explain the differences in crime rates.

Creating the Perfect Storm

There is a strong tendency in the United States to label people by their crimes. People who commit burglary are marked as "burglars." People who sell drugs become known as "drug dealers." People who commit murder become "murderers." We typically view crime through the lens of individual responsibility and are quite quick to demonize "criminals" for their moral failings. Yet, in reality, crime is just as much of a macro issue as it is a micro issue. No person, "criminal" or not, lives in a vacuum. We are all interconnected by the choices we make and the impact those choices have on others. And our public policies heavily influence the context in which we all make such choices. Thus, if you actually analyze any particular individual crime and seek to understand the causes of it, you will likely find the responsibility for it is far more diffuse than is typically acknowledged. In truth, for most of the individuals we describe as criminals, the collective "we" has failed them as much, or more, than they failed us.

No, that that doesn't mean that individual offenders aren't responsible for their actions. It does mean that we, the broader society, set the conditions that determine, in the aggregate, whether such actions become more or less likely. Unfortunately, the conditions we have created within many communities of color have made crime and violence far more likely and the creation of strong, thriving neighborhoods far less likely.

For example, when we fail to provide quality, equitable educational opportunities and wraparound supports for youth, crime becomes more likely. When we fail to provide enough living-wage jobs and a sufficient social safety net in a community, crime becomes more likely. When we allow significant physical, mental, and behavioral health needs to go unmet, crime becomes more likely. When people don't have access to quality, affordable housing, crime becomes more likely. When communities are decimated by decades of heavy-handed policing and incarceration strategies, crime becomes more likely. When many, or all, of these dynamics are allowed to linger across decades within particular communities, it often creates a downward spiral of trauma, toxic stress, family destabilization, and community deterioration that almost unavoidably produces profoundly destructive cycles of violence and crime.[42]

To put it another way, in most cases, what we call crime is best thought of as the product of unmet needs, whether they be health needs, the need to feel safe, the need for a sense of belonging, the need for financial stability, or some other fundamental need. And nowhere are there more unmet needs in the United States than in low-income communities of color. There have been far too few public investments that expand opportunity and well-being in these communities and far too many that have had the opposite effect.[43] And yet we act as if we are shocked and appalled when there are reports of crime and violence in those communities. What exactly did we think was going to happen? In what alternative universe are there communities that are similarly neglected, undermined, and destabilized for generations without the same outcomes?

The reality is that every person has a breaking point. There is only so much trauma, stress, and pain that people can be subjected to, and only so much fear and anger that can be triggered in them before they start engaging in behaviors that are harmful to themselves and others. What we have done is ratchet up those effects on entire communities of people through our public policies. Simply put, our neglect of people's basic needs has hurt people, and as the saying goes, hurt people hurt people. That is especially true when so many of the hurts are concentrated in particular communities.

This doesn't mean that all, or even many, of the people in a neighborhood will become more inclined to crime or violence. It only takes a small number of the most vulnerable individuals to be affected for entire communities to be transformed in negative ways. Think of it as if you are a Las Vegas oddsmaker. When the conditions that allow for the creation of safe, healthy communities are improved, the odds that any one person in that community commits a serious act of crime or violence go down. When those conditions are allowed to deteriorate, the odds go up. The longer they are allowed to deteriorate, the higher the odds go.

Again, that doesn't excuse people's individual choices, but at the macro level, it is practically a statistical certainty that these dynamics will occur, given the underlying conditions we have created within many communities of color. To be clear, none of the above should be read as pathologizing the residents of those communities. Overall, they don't respond any differently to the conditions they are presented with than anyone else would under the same circumstances. Indeed, if anyone deserves to be pathologized, it would be those who are responsible for creating the systemic inequities under which the residents of those communities must try to survive.

So, where there are communities struggling with the effects of crime and violence, the question becomes: What is the best way to respond? The obvious response would be to have our public safety strategies address the root causes of that crime and violence. However, the architects of the Criminalization Trap clearly had other ideas.

America ♥ Law Enforcement

It is important to recognize that none of the law enforcement dynamics described previously were necessary. It wasn't inevitable that we would overrun communities of color with police and grant those police broad discretion to enforce the law, often violently. We often act as if responding to concerns over crime and violence with a police-led suppression strategy is the only option, but it isn't. Nevertheless, just as there has been a concerted effort to convince the public of the need to "get tough" on crime, there has been a parallel effort to lead us to believe that vigorous law enforcement is the primary—or even the sole—solution to our public health and safety issues. Starting almost at birth, we are inundated with pro-law-enforcement messages from policy makers and popular media. For example:

- Anyone with small children can vouch for just how many children's books, TV shows, and movies include heavily favorable images of law enforcement.
- Local news programs tend to be dominated by criminal justice issues, and they are almost always presented from the perspective of law enforcement rather than from the perspective of those being policed, prosecuted, and imprisoned.
- There is very little that news producers and politicians value more than photo ops with police. (Somewhere, Rudy Giuliani's ears are burning.)
- At any time of day, you can find numerous TV stations airing shows or movies that glorify and romanticize the work of police and prosecutors.

(Believe it or not, but most police officers don't single-handedly annihilate international terrorist rings on a regular basis like John McClain does in the *Diehard* movies. Plus, I would be willing to bet that no matter where you live or what time it is where you are currently, if you checked your cable listings, there would be an episode of *Law and Order* on right now.)
- Many of those cop shows are just blatant propaganda. (I mean, have you ever seen an episode of *Blue Bloods*?)[44]

Almost invariably, these fictional pieces and news reports are supportive of heavy-handed law enforcement strategies, accept as given that the alternative to such an approach is rampant crime, and are strongly supportive of law enforcement even when police or prosecutors arguably abuse their authority or act recklessly.[45]

To be clear, there is nothing wrong with political statements or media coverage that recognizes the good work that law enforcement does or that sheds some light on the realities of those jobs. The problem is that the messaging is so heavily slanted and willfully unquestioning that it serves less of a public education purpose than a public miseducation purpose. Plus, when one professional field is featured so heavily within the public discourse and popular culture, it does raise one's eyebrows a bit. If you really stand back and examine it, you can begin to see that, taken as a whole, these efforts have a larger purpose than creating an informed public and generating mass entertainment. They represent a massive marketing campaign aimed at shaping the public's views on law enforcement and its role within our society. Ultimately, they have convinced us that our law enforcement system should be our one-stop shop for public health and safety issues.

Lots of Square Pegs and One Round Hole

Pop quiz: What do drug and alcohol use, street violence, school disruptions, mental illness, homelessness, street gangs, domestic violence, poor school attendance, organized crime, the drug trade, sex work, property offenses, immigration issues, financial crimes, and traffic infractions have in common? Answer: In many communities, and particularly communities of color, we have made police and the criminal justice system our primary response to all of them, among many other social ills.[46] Over the years we have added more and more to law enforcement's plate, often in a knee-jerk fashion. Whatever the social problem, our default answer to it is almost always to get law enforcement involved. It is now often viewed as the only acceptable response to any behavior that falls within our expansive definitions of crime. Thus, it should be no surprise that annual inflation-adjusted spending on policing at the local, state, and federal levels in the

United States rose from $37 billion in 1971 to $146 billion in 2016, an increase of 289 percent (see figure 1).[47]

If we structured our approach to individual health care the same way we structure our approach to addressing these public safety and public health issues, we would refer every type of health problem—whether it was chest pains, diabetes, cancer, a torn ACL, or an ingrown toenail—to an orthopedic surgeon. If home maintenance were treated similarly, we would be sending all our electrical, tiling, roofing, HVAC, masonry, and painting jobs to plumbers. Yet while those notions strike us as absurd, we seemingly have no problem funneling a staggering variety of public health and safety issues to law enforcement, often regardless of whether they are the individuals best equipped to address them. Thus, alongside the traditional law enforcement functions of addressing serious crime that threatens social stability, we have made the criminal justice system (1) our primary poverty management system; (2) our largest repository for individuals who use drugs or have mental health issues; and (3) our dominant method of warehousing those who have been failed by our education system and other youth-serving institutions.[48]

Imagine that you were designing a society from scratch. Any rational person would want to identify the needs of that society and match up the appropriately

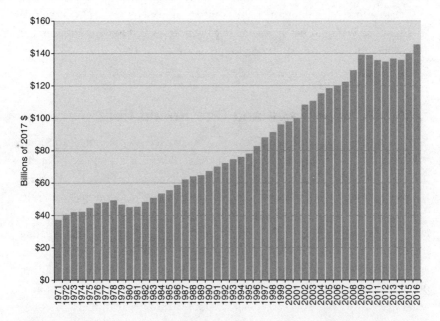

FIGURE 1.   US police spending, 1971–2016, in billions of 2017 dollars.
Source: Bureau of Justice Statistics, *Prisoners Series.*

skilled individuals to meet those needs. You would assess all of the problems that arise, or that could arise, and design solutions to each of them. When it came to public safety, you would recognize that the best way to address crime is to prevent it from ever happening. Thus, you would want to make the optimal use of your human capital to address the root causes of crime. When there were incidents of crime, you would want to be able to minimize both the harm they cause and the odds of their recurrence. So you would tailor your responses to the circumstances of the incident and ensure that your first responders had the right skill sets for the tasks at hand.

What you wouldn't do is make one group of people with a very specific and limited skill set your go-to resource for both preventing crime and being the first responders to all the many different crimes that arise. And you definitely wouldn't give that job to the group of people whose specific and limited skill set was centered on the use of force.

The primary tools in patrol officers' toolbox that distinguish them from other professionals are (a) their ability to incapacitate people through arrests and incarceration; and (b) their ability to employ violence, both lethal and nonlethal. In practice, of course, effective patrol officers regularly employ interpersonal, investigative, and analytical skills, among many others. However, their core competencies—what they are best equipped to do relative to everyone else—lie in the use of force. Thus, we shouldn't make the mistake of thinking that adding police to a community is the best—or even a good—strategy for preventing crime. It may produce temporary dips in certain types of crime, or displace some forms of crime from one location to another, but it is simply not effective at producing meaningful, long-term improvement. How could it be when the primary skill sets of police are nonresponsive to the root causes of crime? (The absurdity of this strategy should be intuitively obvious when you look at communities that have had a heavy police presence for a very long time and still have far higher crime rates than other communities with less of a law enforcement presence.)

Additionally, no one should be fooled into thinking that relying on law enforcement is an effective approach for addressing most of the public health and safety issues that do arise. While there are obviously circumstances in which the use or threat of force is necessary, those situations represent, at most, a small subset of the ones that law enforcement is tasked with addressing. For the vast majority of situations in which we have made them first responders, their core competencies simply aren't what is needed. They may be able to hide a problem for a period of time, or kick the can down the road so that someone else has to deal with it, but rarely do they actually provide real solutions to the issues at hand. That is because the standard law enforcement response to crime is simply to arrest and then sort it out later. However, almost every person who is arrested for a crime within a community sooner or later returns to that community. Without more strategic interventions, most of them are just as likely, if not more likely, to repeat the same behaviors or commit other offenses when they return.[49]

For example, if I am a heroin user and I steal to support that behavior, you can put me in jail for a while, but when I get out, I will probably still have the same underlying issue, only now I will probably be in an even worse financial situation. If I am selling drugs because it represents the most viable economic option available to me, then spending time in prison will only decrease my job prospects in the formal economy. If I commit a violent crime and you lock me up, my being put in a cage surrounded by other people who committed similar crimes certainly isn't likely to make me *less* inclined toward violence. Or if I am being extremely disruptive in school and I am arrested, when I get back to school I will probably be even more of a problem because nothing has been done to address the reasons for my behavior, and now I am feeling even more alienated because the adults responsible for my education have sent me a clear message that they don't value me or my educational opportunities.

We simply have to acknowledge that there is a fundamental mismatch between the law enforcement skill set and the problems police officers are often tasked to address. They are expected to be able to effectively respond to the myriad effects of intergenerational poverty, deep-seated trauma, domestic and international social inequality, and countless other issues, and it's just not realistic. Many officers try their best to address these issues, but they are often just not the right people for the jobs they are given. And there shouldn't be any shame in that; nobody else would be either. No one person or one profession has the type of skill set needed for effective problem solving in more than a small subset of the situations that police are tasked with addressing. Yet we charge them with cleaning up all these messes. We expect the police to be miracle workers when, quite often, the best they can realistically do is be janitors. Thus, not only does the fact that they are asked to be jacks-of-all-trades reflect mind-bogglingly bad social policy; it is also deeply unfair to the police. When there is no way you can succeed at the job you have been given, then you have been set up to fail.

Too often, and especially with regard to communities of color, we have seemingly forgotten that there are dozens of strategies that can be used to both prevent and respond to crime (discussed later in this chapter). We have neglected or underemphasized most of those in favor of the harshest and most potentially harmful option: we throw police at the problem and tell them to deal with it. But after all these years of employing that strategy, what do those communities have to show for it? Where are the heavily policed communities that are flourishing economically, politically, socially, and culturally? The answer is that there are none. It's a null set. There is simply no path to success with the heavy-handed law enforcement approach. It has proven to be effective at only two things: (1) causing the widespread criminalization of people of color; and (2) fueling the mass incarceration system.

Even the Dogs Get Criminalized

While he was chief of the Dallas Police Department, David Brown said, "We're asking cops to do too much in this country. We are. Every societal failure, we put it off on the cops to solve. Not enough mental health funding, let the cops handle it. . . . Here in Dallas we got a loose dog problem; let's have the cops chase loose dogs. Schools fail, let's give it to the cops. . . . That's too much to ask. Policing was never meant to solve all those problems."

Source: Brady Dennis, Mark Berman, and Elahe Izadi, "Dallas Police Chief Says 'We're Asking Cops to Do Too Much in This Country,'" *Washington Post*, July 11, 2016.

Normalizing the Use of Cages

In the United States, we have an unusual appetite, and in some cases lust, for punishment. We insist on extracting our pound of flesh to show "criminals" that we disapprove of their actions. "If you can't do the time," we say, "then don't do the crime." Interestingly, though, our desire for punishment doesn't typically extend to everyone. It usually applies only to those whom we don't know and care about.

For example, when our children misbehave, as parents we want to teach them accountability, to take responsibility for their actions. We seek to help them develop empathy and the ability to understand the impact of their actions. We try to teach them the importance of making amends and repairing the harm they have caused. We also take the long view and recognize that while we cannot undo the youthful mistakes that our kids make, we can help them learn from them and avoid repeating them in the future. What we don't do is respond to their misbehavior by kicking them out of the house, disenrolling them from school, or seeking out ways to inflict severe physical, psychological, or emotional pain on them. We don't do these things because we love them and don't want to harm them, particularly in ways that have long-term, negative impacts.

Similarly, when our adult loved ones engage in illicit or harmful activities, we often demonstrate a remarkable capacity for compassion and forgiveness. We generally have no problem understanding all the circumstances that led to their wrongdoing. We also recognize so easily that "to err is human," that all of us have a long history of mistakes behind us, and the best we can do is to learn from them and repair as much of the damage we have caused along the way as possible. Thus, we are often willing to show each other truly inspiring levels of mercy. We provide each other a virtually limitless number of "second chances." We all seem to understand intuitively that the right response in almost every situation is to not simply cast our loved ones out, or punish them harshly for their mistakes, but rather to find the best way forward to ensure that everyone is as healthy and safe as possible.

However, when it comes to people other than our loved ones (and ourselves), we take a very different approach to their wrongdoing. For them, there is seemingly no limit to how punitive we are willing to be. Thus, in the United States, we have implemented a variety of severe criminal justice practices—such as mandatory minimum sentencing, three-strikes laws, and truth-in-sentencing laws— that result in incarceration being used far more often, and for far longer periods, than in comparable countries.[50]

Perhaps most troubling is how such an extreme measure as incarceration has become so thoroughly normalized within US society. When we hear on the news that someone has been sent to jail or prison, most of us think almost nothing of it. If it registers at all, most of us simply assume that the person deserved it.

So how did we get to a point where we can be so understanding and compassionate with regard to our loved ones but so callous and punitive for everyone else? How do we reconcile that disconnect?

The answer is that we have been conditioned this way. These attitudes aren't something we are born with; they are learned behaviors. For the past several decades there has been a concerted campaign to shift how Americans respond to crime and violence. The overwhelming message that has been transmitted is that harsh consequences for criminals are necessary to show that we are "tough on crime" and committed to public safety. Republicans won election after election at the local, state, and federal levels by using such messages, and Democrats soon followed suit. Similarly, our news reporting and popular media reinforced the idea that crime must necessarily be followed by harsh punishment. As a result, this notion has become so deeply established within mainstream US culture that there is virtually no interest in questioning the efficacy of the punitive approach or exploring other methods. It is, in most cases, simply assumed that this is what we do. The result is that the US public has become both far more punitive than we once were and far more so than other people around the world.[51]

However, that sentiment isn't applied equally. Because we view punishment as being only appropriate for other people, the more you are seen as an "other," the more our society thinks you deserve to be punished. In particular, our desire for punishment is determined in significant part by our race and the race of the wrongdoer. When we see ourselves in the "criminal," we are more likely to reflect on the underlying circumstances of the crime and respond with empathy and compassion. However, when we perceive a racial gap between ourselves and those who commit crimes, we tend to be less merciful and more likely to react with anger and outrage. Thus, you will often see both white policy makers and the white public being quite understanding and lenient . . . when the wrongdoer is white. The strong desire to punish is generally (though certainly not exclusively) reserved for people of color, who are seen as being more culpable and more dangerous.[52]

Consider, for example, how drug use and drug dependence is typically treated as a crime in communities of color but a public health problem in white communities. Cocaine, crack, heroin, and marijuana use within communities of color led to a war on drugs and millions of people who use drugs being incarcerated. The response to the opioid epidemic—which has been more heavily concentrated within predominantly white communities—has been far more compassionate, focusing on prevention, treatment, and harm reduction.[53] In other words, the resources marshaled to address people getting high in communities of color were overwhelmingly police, prosecutors, and corrections officers, while in predominantly white communities, our investments have been focused on doctors, nurses, behavioral health specialists, and public health experts.

As a result of these dynamics, people of color tend to be punished far more often, and far more harshly, than white people for similar offenses.[54] According to the US Sentencing Commission, between 2007 and 2011, sentences for black males were 20 percent longer than those for white males who committed similar crimes. Furthermore, black men were 25 percent less likely to receive sentences below the sentencing guidelines associated with the crime for which they were convicted.[55]

To demonstrate just how deeply we have embraced the idea that punishment is for other people, note that while there are millions of people arrested every year from every race, ethnicity, and socioeconomic level, our incarcerated population is overwhelmingly composed of low-income people, and low-income people of color in particular.[56] While there are numerous mechanisms and dynamics that enable more affluent and white arrestees to avoid being incarcerated for their wrongdoing, they are all based on the widespread assumption that incarceration isn't really *for* them.

An American WMD

It is no small thing to deprive an individual of their liberty and confine them to a cage. The US Constitution even recognizes it as a form of slavery.[57] However, the consequences of incarcerating someone go far beyond the loss of their freedom. Incarceration is extraordinarily harmful not only to the individual involved, but to their family and their entire community. Here is a list of just some of the harms that frequently result from putting a person in jail or prison:[58]

Harms to the Individual

- Daily humiliations
- Living conditions that are deliberately poor and nonrehabilitative
- Severe trauma and toxic stress, producing high rates of depression, anxiety, and suicide
- High risk of psychological abuse, sexual harassment, physical abuse, and sexual assault
- Severe social and emotional withdrawal that can lead to extreme aggression and violence
- Lack of effective treatment for drug and alcohol dependence
- Adaptation to the cultural norms of prisons ("prisonization"), making the transition back to the community difficult
- Increased likelihood of contracting both infectious and chronic diseases
- Decreased life expectancy
- Missed births, deaths, anniversaries, birthdays, and other family milestones and events
- Damaged or severed relationships with family and friends
- Potential loss of parental rights
- Loss of employment and educational opportunities
- Loss of property
- Potential deportation for immigrants
- Financial debt due to fines and fees associated with the legal process and loss of income
- Extensive collateral consequences upon reentering the community, including barriers to getting a job, finding housing, receiving public benefits, accessing educational opportunities, serving in the military, and voting
- The stigma of being a formerly incarcerated person that makes every aspect of life more difficult and frequently results in numerous forms of discrimination
- Onerous probation requirements that can make it difficult to put one's life back together
- Increased likelihood of engaging in future crime (i.e., incarceration itself is criminogenic)

Harms to the Family

- Psychological and emotional strain on family members
- Weakened or disintegrated families
- Separation of parents from children, leading to lower levels of child well-being, academic difficulties, emotional and mental health issues, increased behavioral issues and delinquency (thus potentially deepening the cycles of crime), and decreased life expectancy
- Loss of income provided by the incarcerated person, leading to increased economic hardship and insecurity for the family
- Increased burdens on family members, such as those relating to child care responsibilities
- Loss of public benefits and public housing for family members
- Financial costs of keeping in touch with and supporting the incarcerated person, including for travel (many prisoners are incarcerated far from home) and often exorbitant charges for phone calls, video visitations, and other services within prisons

Harms to the Broader Community

- Undermining of social networks and support systems that stabilize communities
- Deepened cycles of crime that weaken neighborhoods and generate high levels of trauma and toxic stress
- Reintegration of formerly incarcerated persons who may have additional mental, physical, and behavioral health issues and may be more likely to commit crime than when they left
- Strain on community resources
- Deepening of intergenerational poverty
- Substantially reduced political power for communities with large numbers of formerly incarcerated persons
- Exposure to the infectious diseases contracted by formerly incarcerated individuals within prison
- Diversion of resources away from other efforts to improve community health and safety
- Substantial economic costs related to incarceration, the need for post-incarceration public support, and reduced ability of incarcerated and formerly incarcerated individuals to contribute in taxes

In other words, when we incarcerate an individual, it is not just about taking away their liberty for a period of time. The decision to incarcerate represents a public commitment to cause profound and often irreparable harm to that person, every member of that person's family and social circle, and every member of that person's community (particularly when the impacts of incarceration are concentrated geographically, as they often are).[59] Indeed, the impact of incarceration is often so severe that it can be *far more harmful* than the original crime for which the person was incarcerated.

Nevertheless, in justifying the frequent use of incarceration, policy makers and prosecutors will often say that it is a valuable "tool in the toolbox." Among many other problems with that defense, it is an insult to tools everywhere. Tools are used to fix or build things. Incarceration almost never fixes anything, and instead it usually makes things worse. It is also almost never effective at building anything positive. Thus, rather than a tool, incarceration is best thought of as a weapon of mass destruction. Far too often, that weapon has been used irresponsibly.

Of course, it is also true that, in some cases, incarceration has provided some benefits to individuals, families, and communities. But to say that something provided benefits isn't the same thing as saying it was the most beneficial strategy. Even in those instances in which incarceration did serve some positive purpose, the harms will usually outweigh the benefits, even if they might not be immediately apparent. Plus, there is almost always a better solution available. Because not only have our incarceration strategies been deeply harmful; they have also been shockingly ineffective.

Cutting Off Our Nose to Spite Our Face

The goal of any criminal justice strategy should be to create safe, healthy, and just communities in which harsh consequences like incarceration become less and less necessary. However, if you speak to the residents of the communities most affected by mass incarceration, "safe," "healthy," and "just" aren't words that are likely to come up in their descriptions of their neighborhoods. And the image in figure 2 is very nearly the precise opposite of what a high-functioning justice system looks like.

Additionally, in the most comprehensive study of the research on the topic, the National Research Council detailed the extensive evidence demonstrating the ineffectiveness of our sentencing policies. It found little connection, if any, between our incarceration strategies and crime rates and concluded that "lengthy prison sentences are ineffective as a crime control measure."[60]

Neither the widespread harm nor the ineffectiveness of the mass incarceration system is at all surprising to anyone who pays attention to criminal justice policy issues. This wasn't an "oopsie" that couldn't have been foreseen. In fact,

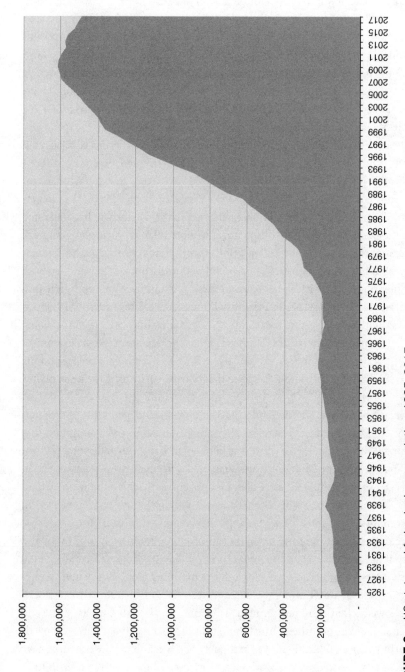

FIGURE 2. US state and federal prison population, 1925–2017.

Source: Bureau of Justice Statistics, *Prisoners Series.*

just prior to the rise of mass incarceration, the consensus among criminologists during the relatively low-incarceration days of the early 1970s was that the prison system would soon fade away.[61] In 1973, the National Advisory Commission on Criminal Justice Standards and Goals also recommended that no new prisons be built and that all juvenile detention centers be closed. It advised shifting away from our "pervasive overemphasis on custody" due to incarceration's "shocking record of failure" and the "overwhelming evidence that these institutions create crime rather than prevent it."[62] (Bear in mind that, at the time, there were 204,211 people in US prisons, compared to nearly 1.5 million today.)[63]

These ideas, which were grounded in hard facts and lived experience, lost out to lofty-sounding theories based on retributive justice and deterrence theory. Retributive justice states that crime is a moral wrong and that punishment for that crime is a moral good. Deterrence theory is based on the idea that by ratcheting up the consequences for criminal behavior, that behavior will become rarer. Both theories have the same bottom line: the more often crime is met with punishment of the criminal, the better.[64] Both theories are now thoroughly embedded within our criminal justice policies and public discourse. They are also both in contention with "trickle-down economics," "preemptive war," and perhaps a few others as the most destructive ideas within recent US history.

First, both ideas imagine incarceration as affecting only the individual going into jail or prison. However, as discussed earlier, incarceration is less reminiscent of a surgically precise missile strike than it is an indiscriminate nuclear bomb. Thus, retributive justice and deterrence theory wind up hurting the same people they purport to help.

Second, both ideas are based on a fundamental misunderstanding of the realities of crime and human behavior. They are grounded in the assumption that "criminals" are rational actors choosing between moral goods and moral wrongs. Perhaps in a far more equitable world than our own, where people's basic human needs were attended to far better than they are currently, this assumption would hold more water. The reality is that there is very little rationality involved in the commission of most of what we punish as crimes. Most of the people we incarcerate were, at the time of their crimes, acting impulsively, not rationally. Many, if not most, had their judgment compromised by drugs or alcohol, mental health issues, or physical, psychological, or emotional pain. Even when "crime" is the product of a well-thought-out choice, the reality is that those wrongdoers' choices were often extremely limited. They may know something is illegal and that they could be punished for it, but they decide that meeting their other needs is worth that risk. Thus, even our extremely harsh criminal consequences have little effect on people's choices, which is why, after all these years of retribution and deterrence, we still have individuals entering the criminal justice system over ten million times per year.

A third problem with these theories is that because they are not guided by any sound limiting principles, they are extremely susceptible to abuse. Indeed, as it has played out in practice, when it comes to deciding how much punishment is appropriate, the answer has usually been "more is better." It often looks something like this: We set the criminal penalties for a particular behavior at, let's say, one year of incarceration because we think that sends the message that the behavior is a moral wrong and that amount of time should be an effective deterrent for that behavior. But the behavior continues. So we set the criminal penalties at five years, which, we tell ourselves, will be an even more powerful message and an even more effective deterrent. But the behavior continues. So we set the penalties at ten years, and then fifteen years, and on and on until we wind up in a place where there is no sound rationale for any criminal penalty beyond how it might compare in a relative sense to similarly unprincipled decisions made around other crimes.

A fourth problem with the theories of retribution and deterrence is that they have led us to confuse punishment with accountability. As a result, our responses to crime are less effective, more harmful, and less likely to meet the needs of the victims and survivors of crime, while also frequently harming them as well.

When we hurt others, there should of course be consequences. However, when those consequences are centered on punishment, the result is often an endless cycle of harm and suffering. On the other hand, when those consequences are centered on what we might call "authentic accountability," the result is a much more meaningful form of justice.

By authentic accountability, I am referring to processes that prioritize offenders taking responsibility for their actions, the repairing of harm caused by wrongdoing, the promotion of healing, and the creation of healthier, safer communities through addressing root causes of crime and violence. These processes take a holistic view of human beings and human relationships and recognize how systemic factors intersect with individual behavior. They recognize that our top priorities should be doing everything we can to ensure that offenders don't reoffend and that all those involved with, or affected by, the offense have their needs addressed as fully as possible. They also recognize that many offenders are themselves crime survivors, and many survivors will be future offenders if their needs aren't met appropriately. While achieving authentic accountability is often a very difficult process for offenders (often far more difficult than simply accepting a punishment), it is grounded in positive values and comes from our best features as human beings, such as our capacity for empathy and compassion and our ability to problem solve. (Examples of authentic accountability in action include the many high-quality restorative justice and transformative justice initiatives under way across the country.)

Punishment, on the other hand, is typically grounded in some of our worst and basest instincts as human beings. It is often the product of anger, the desire for vengeance, our capacity for cruelty, a myopic view of humanity, and our frequent inability or unwillingness to understand or care about a wrongdoer. It is also frequently antithetical to accountability. It doesn't require that offenders take real responsibility for their actions and truly face the human impact of what they have done.[65] It doesn't, in most cases, require them to repair the harm they have caused or build the skills necessary to avoid repeating the same behavior. Instead, it casts people out, typically provides little relief for the survivors/victims, and often increases the likelihood that the wrongdoer will reoffend. If you think about it, you will note how rare it is that punishment truly fixes a problem. More often it just hides the problem while often creating many others. Thus, the impulse toward punishment never fully addresses anyone's needs; not the survivor's or victim's, not the broader community's, and certainly not the offender's or the offender's family's.

A fifth way in which retributive justice and deterrence theory have tarnished US society is particularly insidious. They have led us to lose sight of the obvious: *our government shouldn't be harming us, the people it serves, unless that harm is absolutely necessary.* We have allowed our justice system to engage in wanton and needless destruction of people's lives because we have been made to believe that incarceration is necessary to give "criminals" what they deserve and to deter future crime. In the process, we have enabled those who are responsible for protecting us and serving us to, instead, abuse us.

To be clear, none of the above should be interpreted as suggesting that we should immediately abolish all jails and prisons. It would be naïve to ignore the devastating impact that various systemic injustices have had on many people and communities and how that has resulted in there being some individuals who have both caused serious harm to others and, if they were to simply be released from prison without any other interventions, would put others at risk of additional harm. While those individuals represent just a small segment of the incarcerated population, we must acknowledge that we currently don't have many well-developed alternatives to our system of jails and prisons for addressing their particular needs and the needs of the broader communities that are affected by them. But we could have such alternatives, and we should.

Everyone should be able to agree that the abolition of prisons and jails should be our collective goal. We should all want to live in a society in which it doesn't become necessary to lock each other in cages. Unfortunately, the story of the past forty-plus years is that an overwhelming majority of our decisions have moved us in the wrong direction, further from that goal. Instead of phasing out incarceration, we have allowed it to grow exponentially. Instead of building alternatives to the use of cages, we largely pretend that such options don't even exist. Instead of building safe, healthy, and equitable communities that require little to no assistance from the correctional system, we have built a system of mass incarceration that is incompatible with the creation of safe, healthy, and equitable communities.

To be fair, there has been progress in addressing overincarceration in numerous states within recent years.[66] A number of sentencing reforms have been passed and have been vital to shifting the momentum around this issue. Thus, instead of continuing the virtually unimpeded upward trajectory of our incarcerated population, we have actually made some small reductions in recent years. However, as encouraging as some of these shifts have been, we must also face the fact that, for the most part, they have only addressed the low-hanging fruit such as the most egregious sentencing practices and the lowest-level, nonviolent crimes.[67] Of course every journey has to begin somewhere, so these initial steps have been both necessary and commendable. However, we must also all be very clear that they represent only a very small fraction of the total distance that we must travel to get this right. In fact, at our current pace, it would take seventy-five more years to even cut our incarcerated population in half.[68]

We can do so much better than that, and indeed we must. Incarceration is so frequently ineffective, and so profoundly destructive, that most people would never subject someone they loved or cared about to it unless they had absolutely no other option. Thus, what it ultimately comes down to is that we, as a society, simply don't care enough about most of the people we have put inside our jails and prisons. We don't value them enough to find another way to deal with their offenses. We don't love them enough to spare them the devastation associated with being caged. And most of those people whom we don't care for, value, and love enough are people of color.

The Racism of the Criminalization Trap

Through our public policy decisions, we shape the contours of what our criminal justice system will look like. We create the conditions under which there will be more, or fewer, of the behaviors that we call "crimes." We create the conditions under which there will be more, or fewer, people who are treated as "criminals" after engaging in those behaviors. We also create the conditions under which there will be more, or fewer, of those "criminals" who wind up being incarcerated. The Criminalization Trap is a result of innumerable policy decisions being made over the past several decades that opted for "more." More "crime," more "criminals," and more incarceration.

Of course, we also get to decide who is going to be ensnared by that trap. We could have placed it anywhere, but we weren't so indiscriminate. We could have placed it everywhere, but we weren't that inclusive. No, we were both precise and discerning in our approach. We set the Criminalization Trap where we knew without a doubt that it would catch people of color far more than others.

Some of the innumerable policy decisions that produced this result were undoubtedly racially motivated; others may not have been. What is more important than that historical analysis is an understanding that, taken as a whole, the mass criminalization and incarceration system has been deeply racist in that it has quite obviously valued the lives and freedom of the residents of black and brown communities far less than those of other US residents. What is perhaps even worse is that the evidence of that racism has been apparent for decades, yet there has been very little public support offered to those who have continuously pointed that out or tried to fix it. To put it another way, we know—for certain—that the policies that are still in use across the country will continue to decimate communities of color in particular, and yet we haven't been willing to do what is necessary to stop it from happening. Instead, we have, for the most part, willfully ignored these gross inequities, simply accepted them, or have even gone to great lengths to justify them. That unwillingness to fully address the conditions that have been so obviously and disproportionately devastating to communities of color may be the most racist aspect of the whole system.

The Criminal Justice Money Pit

We have also made increasingly enormous investments over the past several decades to build this racist system. For example, figure 3 illustrates the annual expenditures (local, state, and federal) on the criminal justice system in the United States since 1971, adjusted for inflation.[69]

While we spent $64 billion in 1971, by 2016 that annual spending had increased to $302 billion. To give a sense of just how costly this shift has been, we can calculate how much we have spent cumulatively over time beyond what we would have spent if the justice system had stayed the same size. In other words, if we had continued to spend $64 billion per year from 1972 to 2016, our total spending on the criminal justice system over that period would have been $2.9 trillion. However, what we actually spent from 1971 to 2016 was $8.2 trillion. Thus, the cost to US taxpayers of expanding our criminal justice system so dramatically has been *$5.3 trillion* (see figure 4).

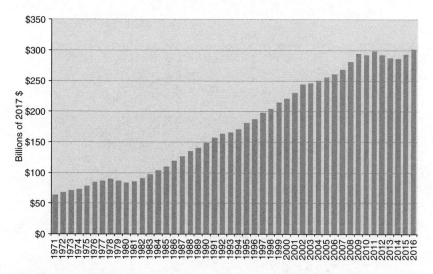

FIGURE 3. US criminal justice spending, in billions of 2017 dollars.
Source: Bureau of Justice Statistics.

The impact of this can be seen most clearly at the local level. Figure 5 provides some examples of how the criminal justice system has expanded dramatically for the same five cities profiled earlier: New York City, Chicago, Miami, Denver, and Los Angeles.[70]

Not only were these investments into the criminal justice system profoundly harmful; there has also been an enormous opportunity cost. Just imagine what else we could have done with $5.3 trillion. So many of the major social problems we face today could have been addressed long ago if we had allocated our resources differently.[71] We could have substantially improved the lives of every single US resident, created a far more equitable society, and advanced public safety in far more sensible ways. To make matters worse, what we did instead was pay for our criminal justice expansion by using funds that otherwise could have gone toward addressing vital community needs. In particular, in the communities where the criminal justice system has been exploding in size, essential strategies for addressing the root causes of crime and violence (educational opportunities, wraparound supports for youth, living-wage jobs, health care, affordable housing, etc.) are often severely underfunded.[72] Thus, rather than investing properly on the front end in strategies to prevent crime and violence, we have been making enormous investments on the back end to criminalize the behaviors that would predictably occur as a result.

In short, for virtually everyone, the Criminalization Trap has been an unconscionable waste of national wealth. However, not for the ultra-wealthy. For them, it has been an opportunity to accumulate even more personal wealth.

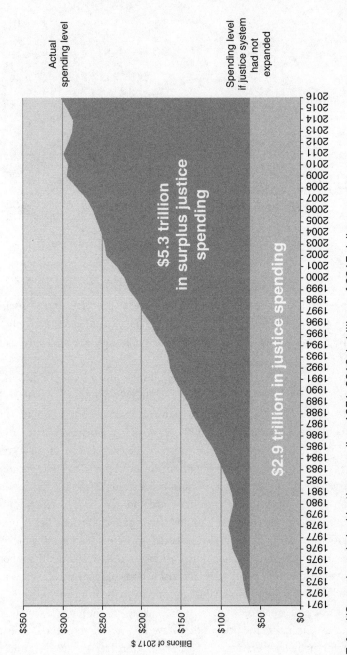

FIGURE 4. US surplus criminal justice spending, 1971–2016, in billions of 2017 dollars.

Source: Bureau of Justice Statistics.

New York City

Criminal justice spending:
$3.2 billion in 1980 $8.2 billion in 2016

# of NYPD employees:
28,549 in 1980   53,943 in 2016

# of correctional employees,1980–2016: ↑6,505

Chicago/Cook County

County correctional spending,1980–2016: ↑200%

Chicago Police Department spending
(including annuity and benefit fund):
$1.2 billion in 1982 $2.0 billion in 2017

# of correctional employees,1980–2016: ↑205%

Miami/Dade County

County correctional spending,1980–2016: ↑666%

City of Miami Police Department spending:
$70 million in 1980 $204 million in 2016

# of county correctional employees,1980–2016: ↑334%

Denver

Criminal justice spending:
$177 million in 1980 $410 million in 2016

DA annual spending, 2004–17: ↑$6.7 million

# of police/correctional employees,1980–2016: ↑889

Los Angeles

County criminal justice spending,1980–2016: ↑203%

LAPD spending:
$766 million in 1980 $2.3 billion in 2016

# of county police/correctional employees,1980–2016: ↑6,000

FIGURE 5.   Criminal justice system growth—local level (all dollar figures adjusted for inflation to 2017 dollars).

The Wizards behind the Curtain

When the harms of mass criminalization and incarceration policies had become apparent to anyone who cared enough to look, why weren't these approaches immediately discontinued? Why, instead, were they allowed to proliferate all across the country and become even more harmful over time?

The short answer is because there has been no shortage of people who have benefited from the creation of a police state within communities of color and the mass caging of our people. Most are what we might call short-term beneficiaries, such as those people who might feel safer with the knowledge that a massive police force is patrolling particular neighborhoods, or who feel a sense of relief that a certain individual or group of people is locked up, or who gain some competitive advantage over the individuals living in neighborhoods treated as occupied territories by law enforcement. In truth, the Criminalization Trap can produce minimal improvements in the quality of life for this group of beneficiaries—who are of course mostly white. However, what those of us in this group usually fail to recognize is that, over the long term, these policies are deeply harmful to ourselves as well. In fact, the harms to our own long-term interests related to public safety, public health, government spending, civil rights, and civil liberties, among other priorities, typically far outweigh whatever short-term benefits we receive. Nevertheless, we are often complicit in creating and perpetuating mass criminalization and incarceration, and in the process, we unwittingly assist the *long-term beneficiaries*.

The individuals who are the real winners from the Criminalization Trap are the ultra-wealthy. They receive the overwhelming share of the benefits from our current criminal justice system. In fact, these Corporate America and Wall Street executives have discovered that an oppressive criminal justice system is one of the keys to accumulating wealth and power.

This isn't the typical story that most of us have been told about the origins of mass incarceration. That story focuses on politicians, particularly Republican politicians and later Democratic ones, and how they have used "tough on crime" rhetoric and policy over the past several decades to drive this change. Most of the time that story attributes those policy decisions to legitimate concerns over crime and thus affirms that they were reasonable attempts to address a serious issue. What that story typically omits is how those policies got onto the desks of those politicians in the first place so that they could be voted on, and why they were put there.

As with many policies that have been especially harmful to low-income, working-class, and middle-class families, a critical component of this underlying story has been ALEC. ALEC and its hundreds of corporate members have been at the forefront of the mass criminalization and incarceration effort. If you have ever wondered how virtually every state adopted the same sort of harsh criminal sentencing reforms, ALEC is your answer. It is the common thread running through many of the laws that drove the growth of our criminal justice system. ALEC created model three-strikes laws, mandatory minimum sentencing laws, and truth-in-sentencing laws that they were able to spread like wildfire all across the country.[73] To give a sense of how effective ALEC was in getting its agenda implemented, in just one year (1995), its Truth in Sentencing Act was signed into law in twenty-five states.[74]

ALEC has also been instrumental in pushing legislation that treats "juvenile offenders" as adults, increases criminal penalties for retail theft, discourages alternatives to incarceration, and promotes the use of for-profit bail bond companies, among many other efforts that expand the criminal justice system.[75] In short, ALEC's corporate members have created, and continue to create, much of the legal infrastructure that has allowed mass criminalization and incarceration to flourish.

ALEC's agenda has been heavily supported by so-called "free market," pro-corporate think tanks that have aggressively sold this agenda to both policy makers and the public. One particularly prominent contributor was the Manhattan Institute for Policy Research. The Manhattan Institute even claims to have pioneered the hyperaggressive broken-windows style of policing discussed earlier. It also takes credit for inventing CompStat, the data collection and performance management tool used by police departments all across the country that has been instrumental in justifying the overpolicing of communities of color.[76] The Manhattan Institute continues to defend those initiatives, as well as other policies responsible for the Criminalization Trap (such as mandatory minimum sentencing), with vigor.[77] It not only worked closely with the NYPD in implementing these policies in New York City; it was instrumental in disseminating them across the country, and even around the world.[78] While its work on these issues has evolved over time, many of its efforts continue to be almost shockingly out of touch with real-world conditions. For example, one of the Manhattan Institute's senior fellows, Heather Mac Donald, is one of the leading champions of mass criminalization and incarceration policies. In her book *War on Cops*, she vehemently defends practices such as stop and frisk, argues for even more aggressive criminal justice practices, calls the Black Lives Matter movement a "fraud," and claims there is a "false narrative" of racial discrimination in policing.

Other right-wing think tanks that have been highly influential on these topics include the Heritage Foundation and the Reason Foundation. The Heritage Foundation's advocacy in support of for-profit, private prisons beginning during the Reagan administration helped pave the way for the expansion of the prison system and the severe cost-cutting that led to a marked deterioration of inmates' living conditions.[79] The Reason Foundation has also taken on that mantle and continues to aggressively defend prison privatization today.[80]

Additionally, the Heritage Foundation has been among the most vocal defenders of hyperaggressive policing.[81] It published a report in 2017 strongly defending stop and frisk, asserting that "allegations of 'systemic racism' are false and hurtful," and lamenting the lack of "political support" for police. It offered no substantive reforms for addressing the many high-profile police shootings and clear evidence of systemic failures. Instead, it proposed that police follow the example of the military and invest in "marketing, branding, and media relations" in order to take control of the narrative and "enhance [their] reputation among the public."[82]

While these "free market" think tanks provide the intellectual rationale for harmful criminal justice policies that organizations like ALEC support, someone still needs to do the legwork to get them passed. Among the leaders of that effort are the two largest private prison companies, CoreCivic (formerly the Corrections Corporation of America) and the GEO Group. At the federal level, since 1998, CoreCivic and the GEO Group have spent more than $31 million in lobbying to advance their corporate interests, which are of course centered on keeping their prisons filled and increasing the number of prison beds even further.[83] At the state level, from 2003 to 2012, CoreCivic hired 272 lobbyists across thirty-seven states, while the GEO Group hired 142 lobbyists in twenty-five states.[84] Together, they have also combined for at least $16 million in federal and state political campaign contributions.[85] They were also both members of the task force within ALEC that was responsible for pushing the mandatory minimum, three-strikes, and truth-in-sentencing laws that created additional demand for their "product" and led to the dramatic expansion of their corporations.[86]

The "ground game" of these corporate-led efforts to expand mass criminalization and incarceration has also been heavily supplemented by the National Rifle Association (NRA). While the NRA enjoys touting its list of individual dues-paying members, its operations over the years have been heavily subsidized by large corporations and the ultra-wealthy. These outside benefactors recognized that the NRA had something they didn't: the ability to mobilize voters.[87] Dating to the early 1990s and continuing today, the NRA has been among the most aggressive supporters of "tough on crime" policies such as mandatory minimums, three-strikes laws, harsher parole standards, aggressive policing methods, treating "juveniles" as adults, and prison expansion.[88] The NRA is also a longtime member and longtime funder of ALEC.[89]

While ALEC, the Manhattan Institute, the Heritage Foundation, the Reason Foundation, CoreCivic, the GEO Group, and the NRA have all played a key role in creating and sustaining mass criminalization and incarceration, to truly understand the origins of our current criminal justice system, one must examine who funds those organizations. When you start to peel back the onion a bit, you soon find that the true drivers of our current criminal justice system all come from Corporate America and Wall Street.

Following the Money

ALEC's funds come primarily from four sources: (1) membership dues from legislators (which represented less than 1 percent of its revenues in 2016); (2) corporate dues and contributions; (3) donations from corporate trade groups; and (4) donations from philanthropic foundations.[90] Its corporate dues and contributions come from a broad range of companies, including consumer products manufacturers, tech companies, big banks, media companies, oil and gas companies, drug companies, insurance companies, defense contractors, and health care providers.[91] ExxonMobil, for example, has given over $1.4 million to ALEC in dues and other contributions.[92]

The undisclosed donations that ALEC has received from corporate trade groups also run the gamut, covering well over one hundred industries, such as the American Petroleum Institute, the US Chamber of Commerce, the American Bankers Association, the Pharmaceutical Research and Manufacturers of America (PhRMA), and the American Bail Coalition, which represents the for-profit bail bond industry.[93]

The philanthropic foundations that have donated to ALEC include many of the most prominent right-wing, pro-corporate funders in the United States. Many of those foundations have also donated heavily to the Manhattan Institute, the Heritage Foundation, and the Reason Foundation. Here are just some of the foundations that have donated to at least two of those organizations (along with information on the source of the foundation's wealth):[94]

- Adolph Coors Foundation / Castle Rock Foundation (formed from wealth generated by the Coors Brewing Company)
- Bill & Melinda Gates Foundation (Microsoft)
- Walton Family Foundation (Walmart)
- Lynde and Harry Bradley Foundation (Allen-Bradley, a manufacturer of factory automation equipment)
- Scaife Foundations (the Mellon oil, aluminum, and banking fortune)
- Roe Foundation (Builder Marts of America, a building materials supply company)

- Rodney Fund (Detroit Forming, a plastics company)
- JM Foundation (Borden Milk Company)
- Ruth & Lovett Peters Foundation (oil and gas industry)
- William H. Donner Foundation (real estate investments, the National Tin Plate Company, and Union Steel)
- John Templeton Foundation (banking and managing mutual funds)
- Jaquelin Hume Foundation (Basic American Foods, a producer of dried food products)
- William E. Simon Foundation (banking)
- John M. Olin Foundation (chemical and munitions inventions and manufacturing)

Meanwhile, as public companies, CoreCivic and the GEO Group have a wide variety of shareholders. However, a sizable percentage of their shares are owned by just a small number of entities. For example, here is the value of CoreCivic and GEO Group stock owned by the following investment firms and big banks as of the end of 2017:[95]

- Vanguard Group—$885 million
- BlackRock—$533 million
- Cohen & Steers—$274 million
- State Street Corporation—$154 million
- Barrow, Hanley, Mewhinney & Strauss—$153 million
- FMR LLC—$132 million
- Prudential Financial—$127 million
- Bank of New York Mellon Corporation—$101 million
- Northern Trust—$100 million

As for the NRA, it has raised tens of millions of dollars from gun manufacturers and undisclosed, "dark money" political donors over the years.[96]

Together, this collection of donors represents every major industry and wealth center in the United States. However, perhaps the individuals most responsible for supporting the organizations driving these extreme criminal justice policies haven't been mentioned yet in this chapter: the Koch family and their network. Here are just some of the ways that Charles Koch and his organized collection of billionaires and multimillionaires have supported these efforts:[97]

- ALEC: The Koch network has donated at least $4.4 million to ALEC, while Koch Industries has also made undisclosed donations. Koch Industries formerly chaired ALEC's corporate board, was a member of the board for many years, and currently plays a major role within many organizational task forces. The Kochs have even funded interns and fellows at ALEC and once bailed out the organization with a loan of nearly half a million dollars in the 1990s.[98]

- Manhattan Institute: The Koch network has donated at least $5 million directly and has also donated at least $30 million to the State Policy Network, of which the Manhattan Institute is an associate member.[99] Plus, a member of the Koch network, Paul Singer, is the chairman of the board of the Manhattan Institute.[100]
- Heritage Foundation: The Koch network has donated at least $8.1 million directly, and Heritage is also an associate member of the State Policy Network.[101]
- Reason Foundation: The Koch network has donated at least $6.0 million directly, and Reason is also an associate member of the State Policy Network.[102] Additionally, David Koch was formerly one of Reason's trustees.[103]
- NRA: The Koch network donated at least $8.4 million directly to the NRA in 2012 and 2014.

On top of that are the Kochs' extensive political donations to the policy makers responsible for our web of criminal justice policies. For example, just at the federal level, between 1998 and 2020, Koch Industries spent almost $62 million on political contributions, primarily for Republicans, plus almost $146 million on lobbying.[104] It is impossible to know exactly what influence that money bought, but it is certainly safe to say that the politicians passing and preserving our various "tough on crime" laws have been doing so with their pockets lined with Koch money.

Simply put, the Kochs and their ultra-wealthy allies have been at the forefront of the effort to fund the creation of the mass criminalization and incarceration system. Their efforts have been supported by a large and diverse set of major US corporations, big banks, Wall Street firms, investment companies, and foundations created from amassing extreme wealth across numerous industries. These individuals and organizations are collectively responsible for funding and leading many of the organizations that have created, and continue to advance, mass criminalization and incarceration. Our deeply racist criminal justice system can be attributed in significant part to them. Perhaps the most twisted aspect of this dynamic is that the executives and shareholders of these organizations have become extravagantly wealthy off the consumption and labor of the American people, and in return they have used that wealth to then oppress the very people who made it possible.

How the Ultra-Wealthy Benefit and Profit from Mass Criminalization and Incarceration

One might reasonably wonder why this has been the agenda of the ultra-wealthy. It may not be immediately intuitive how Corporate America and Wall Street benefit from mass criminalization and incarceration and why they would devote so many resources to organizations that support such policies. The reality, though, is that the wealthiest and most powerful individuals in the United States have learned that they can become even more wealthy and powerful through hyperaggressive policing and a large prison system.

Here are just some examples of the many ways in which they benefit from the mass criminalization and incarceration system:

1. Provides Preferential Treatment and Protection

As discussed previously, behaviors that are treated as criminal aren't always harmful to others, and the behaviors that cause the most harm are quite often not treated as criminal. Where these lines are drawn usually correlates with the wealth and political power of those engaging in the particular behavior. Both our lawmaking process and the criminal justice system it creates are structured to better insulate the ultra-wealthy from having their wrongdoing be considered crimes and to ensure that they face less law enforcement scrutiny for the criminal acts that they do commit.

This is oftentimes a privilege that they pay for, such as through donations to the police or the political campaigns of prosecutors. For example, in New York, the investment bank JPMorgan Chase donated $12 million to the NYPD in 2011–12, and large New York law firms (whose clients are typically quite affluent) donated millions of dollars to the campaign of Manhattan district attorney Cyrus Vance Jr.[105] Such practices are commonplace across the country. Thus, when these police and prosecutors make their policy decisions about which of the many criminal laws to enforce against which people, does anyone not think that millions of dollars in donations from wealthy donors make it less likely that the gaze of law enforcement will settle in their direction?

The preferential protection received by the ultra-wealthy can even go much further than that. Law enforcement has a long history of prioritizing the protection of the property rights of corporations and the affluent over other interests. In a particularly glaring example, many cities have "paid detail units" in which corporations pay for armed, uniformed, on-duty police officers to serve their interests. Among the largest consumers of these services have been Wall Street banks.[106]

2. Generates Profits from Privatization and Expansion of the Criminal Justice System

As discussed in chapter 2, Corporate America and Wall Street are always look-ing for new markets and expandable markets from which they can profit. The dramatic growth of the criminal justice system has been, for them, a gold mine of economic opportunities.

At the most basic level, locking up so many more people means that we needed new jails and prisons to be built. That provided a number of economic opportunities for real estate investors and construction companies, among many others. As a result, prison construction today represents a $3.3 billion industry. As large at that is, it is still smaller than it was in the 1990s when many of our current jails and prisons were built. For example, in 1991, spending on prison construction, renovations, and major repairs totaled $4.6 billion. By 1996, there were 122 federal and state prisons under construction across the country. Many of the largest Wall Street banks seized on this growth as an opportunity to finance prison construction through bond issues, allocating $2 billion to $3 billion per year to this endeavor during the 1990s.[107]

New prison construction represents just the tip of the iceberg. The creation of our bloated incarcerated population opened up numerous opportunities, dur-ing the 1980s and '90s in particular, to profit off the privatization of criminal justice functions (much like the privatization of schools has been creating similar opportunities more recently within the education field). To put this "industry" in perspective, our prison and jail population of 2.2 million is larger than the entire population of fifteen US states.[108] What Corporate America has realized is that incarcerating that many people requires an enormous collection of goods and services, each one of which can generate profits for private companies.

Among the countless examples of the prison industrial complex in action are the following:

- Private prisons: Private prisons have grown to the point that they now house over 120,000 people at a time.[109] US taxpayers now spend $3.9 billion annually on private prisons, and in 2016, CoreCivic and the GEO Group made a combined $361 million in profits.[110] Large banks such as Bank of America, JPMorgan Chase, Wells Fargo, BNP Paribas, SunTrust, US Bancorp, and Barclays have invested heavily over the years in financing the expansion of this industry through underwriting bonds, making loans, and providing hundreds of millions of dollars in revolving credit.[111]
- Prison telecommunications: Companies charge incarcerated individuals outrageous rates—including up to thirty dollars for a fifteen-minute

phone call or half-hour video visitation—creating a $1.6 billion industry.[112]

- Prison health care: Providing the health care for 2.2 million individuals represents a $12.3 billion industry. For example, Corizon Health currently works in more than 110 correctional facilities, generating $1.6 billion in annual revenue.[113]
- Prison food: Feeding the incarcerated generates $2.1 billion in revenue annually.[114]
- Prison commissary: Vendors that sell goods to incarcerated people—usually with heavy markups for them and their families (resulting in prices up to five times higher than non-incarcerated people would pay)—bring in $1.6 billion annually.[115]
- For-profit bail bonds: These companies bring in $1.4 billion annually in nonrefundable fees from defendants and their families.[116]
- Supervision and surveillance: The development of surveillance and tracking equipment using biometric and radio frequency identification (RFID) technology has generated millions of dollars in sales to prisons for numerous technology companies such as 3M and Hewlett-Packard.[117]
- Prisoner transportation: The job of busing incarcerated people to and from facilities, court appointments, and medical visits has created multimillion-dollar transportation businesses.[118]

There are many, many more examples of private companies making money off mass incarceration. Simply providing uniforms for the nearly three million people who are incarcerated or work in prisons or jails is a major industry. There are also now companies dedicated to creating prison-safe writing utensils, eating utensils, electronic tablets, and drinks, as well as "law-enforcement-designed" e-cigarettes. There are even companies, such as JailBedSpace.com, that work with jail and prison administrators as "correctional concierges," finding available beds when their facilities are over capacity.[119]

This merely represents the profit-making opportunities within prisons and jails. There are a wealth of other such economic opportunities that companies are happy to exploit across the rest of the criminal justice system. Perhaps the fastest-growing market is "community corrections." With nearly five million people under the control of the justice system through probation or parole, many companies, and especially private prison operators like the GEO Group and CoreCivic, have been dramatically expanding their products in this increasingly lucrative area. This new "treatment industrial complex" includes drug and alcohol treatment facilities, electronic monitoring services, mental health treatment facilities, day reporting centers, job training programs, reentry programs and services, home confinement services, and private probation services, among many others.[120]

Additionally, the police now purchase more goods from private businesses than ever before. For example, a number of companies, including IBM, have developed the "predictive policing" technology that is being sold to police departments around the country.[121] The police are also increasingly using biometric technology products and other expensive "crime-fighting" technology from private companies, including those from within the defense industry.[122]

Additionally, the more police there are on the street, the more gear they can be sold. There are currently over one million people employed in police and sheriff's departments across the country, creating the need for a massive supply of firearms and other weapons, and thus a huge market for gun manufacturers.

In short, mass criminalization and incarceration are big business, and there is no shortage of private companies that are willing to profit from it.

3. Ensures a Large Supply of Cheap Labor

There is very little that is more valuable to Corporate America and Wall Street than (a) the ability to depress wage levels, and (b) having an abundant supply of workers for low-wage jobs. The ultra-wealthy have used overwhelming resources over the years to fight to both keep wages for many workers at poverty levels and—as discussed in chapter 2—maintain education inequities, thus ensuring that there will be millions of poorly educated, low-skill individuals who are essentially forced to accept those wages to survive. Through the money they save from paying poverty wages at the lower tiers of the labor market and the downward pressure that can put on wages within the rest of the labor market, this has been a critical wealth-accumulation strategy for Corporate America and Wall Street.[123]

Mass incarceration is a critical component of that strategy. It has produced tens of millions of people entering, or reentering, the workforce with criminal records, interrupted labor histories, a wide variety of legal entanglements and collateral consequences they must navigate, a whole host of social, emotional, and health issues that have been created or exacerbated by incarceration, and the stigma of incarceration around their necks. In other words, they are extremely vulnerable and thus ripe for exploitation. Much of the time these individuals are not in a position to refuse even the lowest-paying and most degrading jobs. Many struggle to find any job at all.[124] While virtually all of Corporate America benefits from the enormous burdens that we put on formerly incarcerated individuals, those that benefit the most are the companies that employ large number of workers at very low wages—such as ALEC members like Walmart and Home

Depot—as well as those who are heavily invested in such companies (e.g., Wall Street).

Nevertheless, in recent years, companies such as Koch Industries, Walmart, and Home Depot have received glowing media attention around their efforts to hire formerly incarcerated persons.[125] While at the superficial level these have been nice and even heartwarming stories, at a slightly deeper level they represent a classic example of how extreme wealth and power can turn virtually any situation into a heads-I-win, tails-you-lose situation. For each formerly incarcerated person that these companies hire, they receive federal tax credits, plus they are indemnified for loss due to any crime the person commits.[126] Thus, not only were these companies responsible for many of the laws that led to so many people with criminal records needing jobs, but they can now expand their profits further by paying even less for labor.

4. Generates Profits from Ultra-Cheap Prison Labor

The benefits to Corporate America and Wall Street from cheap labor provided by those who have been criminalized aren't limited to individuals who have left prison. There is a long history of companies benefiting from extremely low-wage labor performed by those who are in prison. An early example was the practice of "convict leasing" following the Civil War in which plantation owners essentially replaced black slave labor with black prison labor. The penal institutions of the day would lease out black "convicts" to plantations and other businesses. This widespread practice was highly profitable for both the states providing the labor and the companies benefiting from it, and much of the southern economy was rebuilt on the backs of forced black labor.

Those practices aren't much different from the use of prison labor today, which is at least a $2 billion industry. The prison laborers of today work in poultry plants, sew garments, manufacture guided missile parts and solar panels, work in mines, fight wildfires, and perform dozens of other jobs across multiple industries. During his presidential campaign in 2019, Michael Bloomberg used inmates to make campaign calls. Some prison laborers in the South even pick cotton.[127] (If the symbolic significance of that is lost on you, please go back one paragraph.) The contractors of prison labor are also seemingly not without a sense of irony, as many of our American flags are manufactured by, yes, people who are incarcerated.[128]

Some may view this as a potentially beneficial practice for incarcerated individuals who want to take some initiative to gain job skills and make a little money. However, in many facilities, this isn't voluntary; prisoners are forced to work. They can lose visitation or phone privileges, or even be placed in solitary confinement, if they refuse. Plus, the amount they are paid is often comparable to the levels we associate with the most exploited child laborers in desperately poor countries. Wages in some states can be as low as twelve cents an hour. In others, prison laborers aren't paid at all.[129]

The practice of private companies using prison labor was actually barred for many years. That changed, however, in large part through the efforts of ALEC, which made the expansion of such opportunities a priority in the 1990s. As a result, a whole host of corporations have benefited from these practices, including Starbucks, Whole Foods, Microsoft, Walmart, Victoria's Secret, Boeing, Nike, and Verizon, among numerous others.[130]

5. Provides a Cheaper Alternative to Meeting People's Basic Human Needs

It is quite common to see graphics that compare what it costs to incarcerate a person for a year versus what it costs to instead pay for a year of college tuition at an elite school. The argument being made by such comparisons is that incarceration isn't cost-effective, represents an irrational policy choice, and that we should therefore be prioritizing education over corrections spending. We should, of course, be placing a far higher value on high-quality, equitable education than we do on incarceration, but that doesn't mean that our criminal justice spending is irrational. While the mass criminalization and incarceration system is certainly expensive, it would be a mistake to think that it is not economically sound from a certain morally warped perspective.

Imagine you are an extremely wealthy person with outsize influence over public policy, and you have two choices about how to use that influence. Choice A would be to ensure that every single child receives a world-class education, every adult is guaranteed a living-wage job, and every person has access to high-quality health care, housing, parks, and community centers. Choice B would be to create a more inequitable society in which large numbers of people had substantially fewer resources devoted to their education, little to no access to living-wage jobs, and limited access to those other community benefits. Instead of allocating resources in those areas, Choice B would have a far larger criminal justice system to manage the effects of underinvesting in segments of the population. As pricey as those additional police, prosecutors, courts, jails, and prisons would be, they are still likely to cost far less than what Choice B would save from reduced spending on education, jobs, and other community investments.* Thus,

---

*While incarcerating someone for a year may be cheaper than tuition at a private university, it is not cheaper than providing someone with a living-wage job in a well-resourced community. For

if you are not particularly invested in the quality of life enjoyed by the people who are affected by your decisions, and your top priority is reducing your own tax bill and labor costs, Choice B represents the better choice.

This type of logic also explains why we have dramatically reduced the services available to people who are incarcerated and have so many laws limiting their opportunities and the public support they receive when they leave prison. As it turns out, rehabilitation and putting people on a path to a better life are more expensive than not doing those things.

In short, the ultra-wealthy have learned that mass criminalization and incarceration can save them money by serving as a substitute for efforts that actually meet people's basic human needs.

6. Limits Democratic Action through Social Control

If you have ever had to train a dog, you know that there are a variety of methods that people use. Certain "old school" methods rely on asserting your dominance over your dog. The goal is to achieve obedience through intimidation, physical coercion, and putting the dog "in its place." Your dog is expected to comply with your authority or else face punishment or correction, sometimes involving harsh and painful consequences.

Our criminal justice system often treats US residents, and particularly those within communities of color, the same way—like dogs that need to be taught obedience. This is evident in a couple of ways.

First, whenever democratic efforts have threatened the power of the ultra-wealthy, it has been the criminal justice system that has been deployed to "keep the rabble in line." They are the ones who were sent in to arrest Martin Luther King Jr. in Birmingham, Rosa Parks in Montgomery, the lunch counter sit-in leaders in Greensboro, and countless others who were pushing for social change (including, more recently, Black Lives Matter protestors). The police have a long history of ensuring that protests don't go beyond the point at which they pose a real challenge to the dominant social order.[131] We are allowed to gather peacefully, and maybe even blow off a little steam, but beyond that, if any acts of protest

---

example, imagine that under Choice A, a young person would have an average of $10,000 more public dollars dedicated annually to their care and education until they reach the age of twenty-two; they are able to work at a job that provides them $60,000 in salary and benefits each year for fifty years; and they receive another $5,000 in annual benefits from the other community investments (for high-quality health care, housing options, parks, and community centers) for the duration of their eighty-year lives. Under Choice B, that same person doesn't receive the enhanced educational opportunities, wages, or other investments, but is instead incarcerated for fifty years at a cost of $30,000 per year. Choice A would cost $3.6 million. Choice B would cost $1.5 million.

become confrontational, people will start getting arrested, the riot gear is probably coming out, and the odds of violence go up dramatically. Not only does this limit the effectiveness of any one collective action; it discourages future actions because participants become disenchanted with political activity when they see that their efforts don't bear much fruit. Thus, the criminal justice system serves as the enforcer of the existing power structure, which obviously benefits those at the top of that structure, namely the ultra-wealthy.

More broadly, though, the use of aggressive and harsh law enforcement tactics by a highly visible police force has a deeper psychological impact on the public. It is a form of low-intensity warfare that produces a more fearful and compliant population. When we are told that crime is out of control, we become more willing to defer to the criminal justice system to protect us. When the power of the criminal justice system seems so overwhelming, we become less likely to question authority. When law enforcement has made it evident that failure to comply with their demands can lead to one's death, we become less likely to resist oppression. The larger and more heavy-handed the criminal justice system becomes, the more collectively docile and submissive we become, thus limiting efforts to pursue social change that could challenge the dominance of wealthy Corporate America and Wall Street executives.

7. Impedes Racial and Class Solidarity

Wedge issues are a powerful political tactic, and they have been used expertly by the ultra-wealthy to create divisions between people and thus prevent the type of broader unity that could begin to address some of the major systemic issues that we face. The most valuable wedge issues are those that produce race- and class-based tension because the creation of broader interracial and interclass unity represents the most significant threat to the power of the ultra-wealthy.[132] Thus, the issues surrounding crime and punishment have been a godsend to these individuals.

Because the operation of our criminal justice system is so heavily influenced by both race and class, and because our "tough on crime" approach has made us so willing to shun those who are deemed to be criminals, it has become very easy for our communities to be pitted against each other. There is almost always some other community with a higher real or imagined crime rate that we fear, look down upon, resent, or hate. Sometimes that occurs along racial lines, such as when predominantly white communities set themselves apart from communities of color, or when Latinx communities distance themselves from black communities. Sometimes we are set against each other along socioeconomic lines, such as when middle-class and affluent communities of all races distance themselves from low-income and working-class communities. In either case, the dynamics that have been spurred on by mass criminalization and incarceration have pushed apart communities that should be natural allies in addressing the true root causes of the systemic injustices we all face.

8. Preserves the System of Racial Hierarchy

It is important to recognize that the criminal justice system has essentially placed many communities of color across the country in a chokehold. It is simply impossible for these communities to substantially improve their social, economic, and political conditions when they have to deal with the profound set of harms that add up day after day as a result of our current criminal justice policies. These policies complicate even the most mundane daily aspects of life within a community, severely limit the wealth that can be accumulated, and prevent communities from engaging in the democratic process on an equal footing because so many people have been stripped of their voting rights following incarceration and are otherwise marginalized politically.[133] On top of that, there are deep psychological effects associated with being regularly humiliated and demeaned by our criminal justice system. One can even start to believe that such treatment is normal, and even deserved.

Black and brown communities had, of course, already been severely oppressed prior to the rise of mass criminalization and incarceration. What that system has done is ensure that they remain so by reinforcing their subordination and limiting their possibilities for upward mobility. It is not a coincidence that this shift in criminal justice strategy occurred immediately following the 1960s, the period of the greatest social and political advancement made by people of color during the twentieth century. The mass criminalization and incarceration system is, in many ways, a direct response to the civil rights movement and other democratizing movements of that era. (Nor is it a coincidence that, following the rise of the Black Lives Matter movement, the 2016 Trump campaign adopted extreme pro–law enforcement positions and then-candidate Trump regularly advocated for violence against protesters.)

Sometimes the actions taken by the criminal justice system to limit the progress of people of color have been even more direct. There is a long, well-documented history of law enforcement agencies infiltrating and undermining organizations fighting for racial justice. The best-known example is the FBI's enormous investment of resources over many years to discredit and destabilize Martin Luther King Jr. and the Southern Christian Leadership Conference, Malcolm X and the Nation of Islam, and the Black Panther Party, among others.[134] In some of the most shameful episodes of US history, law enforcement officers have gone even further and either killed, or assisted in killing, movement leaders.[135]

All throughout US history, whenever organized groups of people of color have dared to suggest that they are entitled to equality, they have been met with extreme force. Sometimes that force has come in the form of immediate, overwhelming violence. Other times that force has come in the form of protracted oppression. But in almost all cases, the criminal justice system has been charged with being the tip of the spear in efforts to ensure that our racial hierarchy is preserved and that the privileged status of the ultra-wealthy isn't disturbed.

The War on Drugs and Social Movements

John Ehrlichman, a top aide to President Nixon, had this to say about the launch of the war on drugs: "You want to know what this was really all about? The Nixon campaign in 1968, and the Nixon White House after that, had two enemies: the antiwar left and black people. You understand what I'm saying. We knew we couldn't make it illegal to be either against the war or black, but by getting the public to associate the hippies with marijuana and blacks with heroin, and then criminalizing both heavily, we could disrupt those communities. We could arrest their leaders, raid their homes, break up their meetings, and vilify them night after night on the evening news. Did we know we were lying about the drugs? Of course we did."

Source: Tom LoBianco, "Aide Says Nixon's War on Drugs Targeted Blacks, Hippies," CNN, March 24, 2016.

---

9. Helps Their Preferred Political Candidates Win Elections

It was no coincidence that the Republican Party began focusing on crime and "law and order" in their policies and rhetoric during the early 1970s, the same time that they were becoming far more aligned with the priorities of Corporate America and Wall Street.[136] "Tough on crime" policies both served the interests of the ultra-wealthy directly and, by exploiting the fears and anxieties of the public around issues of crime and public safety, enabled the politicians who supported their other economic priorities to win elections. These policies enabled the Republican Party to attract a voter base that wasn't as motivated by corporate profits and wealth accumulation as their corporate benefactors were.[137] This was a trend that started with Richard Nixon and continued on through the Reagan years, George H. W. Bush and the infamous Willie Horton ad, Newt Gingrich and the Contract with America, and up to the 2016 elections and Donald Trump's recycling of Nixonian "law and order" rhetoric. The Democratic Party was slower to adopt these tactics but eventually signed on as well, which was perhaps best exemplified by Bill Clinton's support of the devastating 1994 Violent Crime Control and Enforcement Act.

This has long been, and continues to be, a winning formula for the ultra-wealthy and the politicians they support: Scare the public, get elected, and implement policies favored by Corporate America and Wall Street. Lather, rinse, repeat.

Keeping Our Eye on the Ball

In short, the primary agenda driving the massive expansion of the US criminal justice system wasn't about creating sound policy that best served the American people; it was about expanding the wealth and power of Corporate America and Wall Street executives. It some cases, these individuals profited directly from the Criminalization Trap. In other cases, the profiteering was more indirect, such as when ultra-wealthy individuals who may not have contributed directly to mass incarceration nevertheless realized substantial financial gains from investing in companies that did.

This doesn't mean that each of the individuals, corporations, and organizations mentioned earlier has diabolically concocted this agenda with this goal in mind. It is impossible to know what each person involved thought about these issues at any moment in time. What is clear is that they have either directly produced the policies that created our existing criminal justice system or supported the organizations that were directly responsible, and they have benefitted tremendously from the results.

In recent years, many of these prominent ultra-wealthy individuals—such as Charles Koch—have joined right-wing politicians in attempting to "rebrand" themselves as criminal justice reformers. There have been countless glowing media reports of their partnerships with more progressive organizations such as the ACLU.[138] However, no one should be fooled into thinking that these are altruistic efforts on their part. Their primary motivations have quite obviously been to advance their own economic and political interests, not the interests of the people and communities that have been harmed by mass criminalization and incarceration. You will notice, for example, that they don't prioritize issues such as overpolicing, addressing the root causes of crime and violence, repairing the harm that has been caused, or even necessarily reducing the size and scope of the criminal justice system. Instead, their work has been primarily directed at initiatives they can profit from, such as reducing incarceration costs and using cheaper—and often privatized—methods to manage the flow of people coming into the criminal justice system.[139] Plus, they are still actively investing in the organizations that continue to defend the mass criminalization and incarceration system. Thus, any optimism that collaborations with these individuals will address these issues in anything but a relatively superficial way is, unfortunately, misplaced.

Nevertheless, these are the types of efforts that have dominated the criminal justice policy reform conversation in recent years. As a country, we are simply not talking about real solutions to mass criminalization and incarceration. The ultra-wealthy have successfully embedded their agenda so deeply that almost all of the Republican Party, a sizable percentage of the Democratic Party, and much of the public reflexively supports the primary drivers of the Criminalization Trap. Corporate America and Wall Street no longer even have to play as much of an active role in promoting these policies, which are now effectively on autopilot. Thus, the ultra-wealthy can claim ignorance over their actions from decades past, or merely assert that they were good-faith efforts to address urgent public safety issues.[140]

Let's be clear: whether corporate executives and Wall Street bankers actively contributed to the creation of the mass criminalization and incarceration system or have just taken advantage of the benefits it provides them, they are still profiting from the unnecessary and deeply harmful oppression and captivity of people, and particularly people of color. While millions of individuals are being routinely dehumanized and forced to live in cages, the bank accounts of the ultra-wealthy are getting fatter as a result of this "racism industrial complex." This form of strategic racism may not be the precise moral equivalent of slavery, but it is uncomfortably close to it. Indeed, it is arguably more repugnant than any of the criminal acts committed by our 2.2 million incarcerated persons.

And it must be changed.

Bringing Justice into the Justice System

If ever there was a clear sign that dramatic action was needed to address the abuses and excesses of the criminal justice system, it had to have been on June 12, 2013. That was the date on which *Sesame Street* introduced the character of Alex, whose father was in prison. When the children of incarcerated parents become such a large demographic that they need to be represented in toddler-friendly puppet shows, you know it is time to collectively take a long, hard look in the mirror. (And at one out of every twenty-eight children, they are a significant demographic.)[141]

If that wasn't enough of a telltale sign for you, then perhaps it would be the fact that many women's prisons around the country now have nurseries within them so that incarcerated mothers can raise their babies behind bars.[142]

As disgusted as we might be by such dynamics, and the Criminalization Trap more generally, the challenge for most of us is envisioning something different. We have become so accustomed to our current set of policies and practices that it can be difficult to imagine something better than our mass criminalization and incarceration system.

Allow me to suggest that this really shouldn't be that difficult. Considering how our criminal justice system operates within communities of color, we shouldn't have to work too hard to imagine something better. There are superior options virtually everywhere we look.

For example, it wasn't that long ago that here, in the United States, our criminal justice system was radically different from its current form. As stated at the beginning of the chapter, in the early 1970s our incarcerated population was a small fraction of what it is currently, and we had less than 40 percent of the number of police officers, prosecutors, correctional officers, and other justice system employees that we do now.

We don't even have to time travel to identify examples from which we can learn. There are already numerous places in the United States where we have somehow been able to advance public safety without creating a police state— namely, virtually every predominantly white community in the country. The fact is that if the criminal justice system merely engaged with the residents of communities of color the same way it has engaged with me and almost all the other white people I have known throughout my life, that would go a long way toward fixing the mess we have made. (For example, think about the difference it would make if we simply policed the residents of communities of color the way we treat the students at many predominantly white colleges and universities: as if there were a giant protective bubble around them.)

In fact, if we are looking for other models of places that don't rely on incarceration as much as we do, we can just pull out a map and throw a dart. Any other country in the world that we hit is going to have a lower incarceration rate than we do.

The fact is that almost every other place in the world, at almost every point in history, has used criminalization and incarceration less than the United States does within communities of color. So it shouldn't be that hard to envision something better.

Actually implementing that change will of course be more complicated. There are many, many policies and practices that will have to be changed. But they can all be essentially boiled down to the following four solutions, all of which come out of the work being led by black and brown communities from across the country that are most impacted by mass criminalization and incarceration.[143]

Solution 1: Do No Harm

We have become so myopically focused on our misguided approach to achieving public safety that we have lost sight of the fact that while safety is necessary, it is far from sufficient. Communities can be "safe" but wholly undesirable places to live, particularly when safety is defined as requiring an oppressive law enforcement presence. We have to collectively acknowledge that there are other values in play beyond this narrow notion of safety. For example, we want our communities to be both safe *and* healthy. In fact, true safety cannot be achieved without ensuring basic community wellness. Additionally, we all want communities in which all people can feel like they are cared for and can find happiness. We want just and equitable communities, where all people can thrive. Without that, there can be no truly safe spaces. One thing that all those values have in common is that they are incompatible with mass criminalization and incarceration policies. You simply cannot find true health, happiness, and justice in a police state.

Of course, the US criminal justice system often claims to produce these outcomes. Within certain communities—particularly predominantly white communities—sometimes it does. However, its primary product within communities of color isn't health, happiness, or justice; it's harm. While there are instances in which criminal justice professionals may be necessary or helpful, the benefits they sometimes provide have become severely outweighed by the damage being done on a daily basis by mass criminalization and incarceration. This isn't a problem that can be pinned on individual police officers or prosecutors. It is the system overall that routinely produces poorly designed responses that are delivered by individuals with the wrong skill sets for the tasks they are asked to perform. Thus, for every good result they help to create, there are many more instances in which the involvement of police, prosecutors, courts, jails, and prisons is actually detrimental.

There are circumstances in which causing some degree of harm is unavoidable, but those circumstances are rare. Far more often, our criminal justice system is inflicting *avoidable harm*. Indeed, its functions have become so grossly misaligned with its stated purpose that it is difficult to come up with another comparable institution.

If, for example, the medical profession functioned this way, doctors would be assigning us toxic medications that we don't need, lopping off random body parts without cause, performing routine cancer screenings by opening us up and poking around for tumors, and quarantining the sick for excessive and even indefinite lengths of time. They don't do these things because, among other reasons, doctors adhere to a set of ethical principles. Among the most widely recognized and respected principles is to "do no harm." It is the idea that, whatever else they do for their patients, they shouldn't take any action that will affirmatively harm them. If we ask professionals armed with stethoscopes and thermometers to take such an oath, shouldn't we also ask our professionals armed with guns and the ability to put us in cages to do the same? To put it another way, before we allow the public employees and institutions that we pay for with our tax dollars to harm us, shouldn't they have to exhaust all other options first? Shouldn't harming us be the absolute last resort?

To prevent any more of us from suffering avoidable harm at the hands of the criminal justice system, we desperately need that system, and all the individuals employed within it, to adopt their own form of a "do no harm" principle. Here are some examples of what such an ethical criminal justice system would look like:

- The role of police officers would be limited to only those functions that could not be fulfilled by other community-based resources (described more in solution 3), such as responding to truly dangerous situations in which other interventions would be inadequate to protect people from harm. No community would be treated as an occupied territory with a heavy, militarized police presence, and hyperaggressive tactics such as stop and frisk that target people indiscriminately would be abolished. Arrests and other uses of force could be employed only when individuals posed an imminent threat of serious harm to someone else, and when there were no other available alternatives for addressing the threat. In all cases, officers would be required to use the least amount of force necessary to resolve dangerous situations.[144]
- Students wouldn't be policed inside their schools.[145] Instead, the day-to-day duties currently fulfilled by school-based officers would be assumed by administrators, teachers, social workers, psychologists, restorative justice practitioners, unarmed security guards, and other support staff.
- All youth prisons would be closed in favor of community-based alternatives.[146]
- To send an adult to jail or prison, or keep them there, prosecutors and courts would have to prove that there were no other acceptable alternatives to protect others from an imminent threat of serious harm. The purpose of any period of incarceration would be to provide that individual with the treatment, rehabilitation opportunities, and skills training needed to resolve that threat as quickly as possible. The length of jail and prison sentences would be limited to the amount of time needed for that process to occur, and extensive reentry supports would be provided to those

returning to their communities after being incarcerated. All profit motive would be removed by ending the privatization of correctional functions and the outsourcing of prison labor. Plus, the death penalty and all punitive collateral consequences that are associated with incarceration would be eliminated.

- Criminal offenders wouldn't be kept under the control of the justice system through probation or parole unless there were no other alternatives outside the justice system for appropriately addressing their wrongdoing and particular needs.
- Poverty would no longer be criminalized through onerous fines, fees, and money bail requirements.
- Given the history of systemic racism within the criminal justice system, all policy decisions would be developed, implemented, and monitored using a comprehensive racial justice analysis to ensure that the mechanisms responsible for racial inequities are systematically dismantled and a truly just system can be created in its place.[147]

Community Policing Is Not the Answer

For decades there are those who have been pushing "community policing" as the answer to concerns over aggressive and violent policing practices within communities of color. In other words, instead of eliminating the police state that exists within many of these communities, the solution offered is to create a somewhat kinder, slightly gentler police state where officers use more "soft skills." Yet they are still armed, their core competencies still revolve around the use of force, and thus they cannot help but represent a threat to many of the people they encounter. Additionally, while police can be trained to perform the various tasks they are assigned more effectively, that doesn't mean that they should have even been assigned those tasks in the first place.

Plus, why is it that communities of color get only two choices for how they are policed: (a) a heavy law enforcement presence focused on suppression, and (b) a heavy law enforcement presence focused on "community policing?" Why can't there be an option (c), as there is for predominantly white communities?

Certainly, a criminal justice system that commits to "do no harm" would produce dramatically different realities for all, or nearly all, of the nearly seven million people currently under control of the correctional system. It would also lead to very different day-to-day experiences for the millions of individuals who are routinely demeaned, traumatized, and criminalized through their interactions with law enforcement. It is also worth pointing out that if we had adopted this approach just a few years ago, then Michael Brown, Eric Garner, Freddie Gray, Sandra Bland, Rekia Boyd, Tamir Rice, Walter Scott, Laquan McDonald, Philando Castile, Breonna Taylor, George Floyd, and so many others would still be alive. That in itself should be more than enough justification to make this change with the utmost urgency.

Solution 2: Defund All Elements of the Criminal Justice System

Obviously, the adoption of a "do no harm" principle would result in a criminal justice system with a far more limited role than the one we have currently. That role would be centered on its core competencies—the functions that it is better positioned to handle than other systems. Beyond those tasks, however, we need to start looking elsewhere for solutions to the challenges we face. And because a more narrowly tailored criminal justice system would only require a fraction of its current budget to perform its duties, all elements of the existing system should be right-sized and defunded according. We should be able to roll back our spending to at least the levels that existed prior to the rise of mass criminalization and incarceration in the early 1970s, if not more. That would create at least $238 billion per year that could be used to pursue community-led "justice reinvestment" (or "divest/invest") efforts: the reallocation of funds from police, prosecutors, courts, prisons, and jails to repair the harm caused by mass criminalization and incarceration and implement more effective prevention and intervention strategies.[148]

Solution 3: Reinvest into Multidisciplinary Prevention, Intervention, and Systems of Care

As anyone who has been personally affected by crime or violence can attest, the experience can be deeply traumatic, with profound and long-lasting effects. It can be almost like getting infected with a highly resilient and extremely contagious virus. Not only are you harmed personally, but it can be very easy to then pass that harm along to others. Once others around you become affected, they often pass it along to more people, who pass it along to more people, and then quite often the effects of that initial harm circle back around to affect you negatively again, creating a vicious cycle of crime and violence that can be difficult to interrupt.

But it can be interrupted. Doing so, however, requires that we ask the right questions. Currently, our typical approach after a crime is committed is to merely ask, "What should the punishment for that crime be?" The question we should be asking is: "How could we have prevented the crime from happening in the first place, and what is the best way to respond to it that meets the needs of everyone involved and makes it less likely to happen again?"

In other words, we should be looking at crime the same way epidemiologists look at diseases. Their focus is on examining the causes of a disease, how it spreads, and how it can be prevented and minimized. They focus on the big picture and try to insulate their decisions from irrational fears, anxieties, and biases. For them, diseases that pop up are clues to be followed. They recognize that such outbreaks are actually symptoms of larger, underlying problems, and the key to creating a healthier society is to attack the root causes while managing the symptoms with the most effective treatments available.

Similarly, the types of crimes being committed can be clues that tell us quite a lot about where the most pressing unmet needs are in our society. We should be following those clues and directing our attention to addressing the issues they uncover. While we cannot eliminate all the wrongdoing that we inflict on each other, we can make it far less frequent and far less damaging. That comes from how we choose to allocate our resources and how we choose to respond to crimes when they happen. In other words, to create truly safe communities, we need to move from a reactive public safety approach to a proactive, preventive, and holistic public safety approach.

To do so, we need to start with an honest assessment of community needs. We must analyze what is driving crime and violence and proceed from there. Within many communities of color, in particular, what we will find is that while we have been overinvesting in the justice system, we have also been underinvesting in, or divesting from, strategies that are critical for stopping crime before it starts, including the following:

- Improving educational opportunities
- Creating more living-wage jobs and financial supports for low-income families
- Providing higher-quality, trauma-informed physical, mental, and behavioral health care
- Expanding early childhood education, afterschool programs, job opportunities for youth, and other wraparound supports for young people
- Increasing affordable housing options
- Providing extensive wraparound supports for crime survivors/victims

Not only are such investments necessary to address underlying causes of crime, but studies also show that they are far more effective than police or prisons at preventing crime.[149] (By the way, many law enforcement leaders agree. For example, Fight Crime Invest in Kids is a national organization of police chiefs, sheriffs, and prosecutors who advocate for greater investments in pre-K, child care, and K–12 education because of the clear link to public safety. Similarly, the Law Enforcement Action Partnership recommends investments in housing, drug treatment, and education to lower crime.)

Alongside these investments, we must also rethink how we respond to crime. Instead of making police the first responders to almost all public safety and public health issues, we need to start using all the tools in our toolbox. Our responses should be tailored to fit the problems that arise, and in all cases, the goals in responding to crime should be minimizing the harm, promoting healing, providing for authentic accountability, and preventing such incidents from recurring. Thus, instead of criminalizing people who use drugs, we should be connecting them with treatment and support. Instead of criminalizing those suffering from mental illness, we should be connecting them with mental health professionals who can help treat their underlying conditions. Instead of criminalizing those experiencing homelessness, we should be connecting them with social workers, nurses, and opportunities to improve their quality of life. Instead of criminalizing violent acts, we should be using restorative and transformative justice practitioners and other violence intervention experts whenever possible to break the cycle of violence and ensure that both offenders and survivors/victims get the support they need. Instead of criminalizing K–12 students, we should be providing them with the developmental supports they need. And yes, when the need arises for someone trained in the use of force, and there are no other options for handling the situation appropriately, then we can bring in the police, but only in the most carefully considered and narrowly focused way.

The operative question should always be: Who is best equipped to solve the problem at hand? Most of the time, that is not going to be the police and prosecutors. Even though there will be circumstances within the near future in which they will continue to be the right call, we should be actively working as a society to build communities' capacity to address public safety issues without having to rely on the incapacitation of people or the threat of violence.

The notion that we should be using alternatives to the criminal justice system for addressing our social problems isn't a radical one. Public polling has demonstrated that the vast majority of US residents agree with these ideas. Even crime survivors/victims agree. That may seem counterintuitive, but the reality is that survivors/victims often have the most at stake in these decisions, and thus they tend to focus less on ideology and more on their own pragmatic self-interest. In short, perhaps more than anyone else, they want to do what works.[150]

The ones lagging behind in recognizing the need for a more comprehensive and nuanced problem-solving approach to public safety are policy makers. They seem to intuitively understand the need to be multidisciplinary in other areas, but not in this one. For example, nobody has any problem understanding that in schools, you have teachers who specialize in different subjects, support personnel like social workers, psychologists, and nurses to address nonacademic needs, special education teachers to assist students with disabilities, specially trained teachers to meet the language needs of English learners, and so on. As described previously, the same is true for home maintenance and health care services, where we have dozens of particular specialties designed around the variety of needs that exist in the population. However, with regard to public safety, our policy makers continue to be one-trick ponies. Not only do they rely too much on police departments; they also fail to see that even the idea of a police department as the filter through which public safety and health issues must pass is outdated, unnecessary, and ineffective.

Rather than a local police department, shouldn't each community have a public health and safety department? Police wouldn't lead such a department; they would be at most just one spoke within a comprehensive, community-problem-solving wheel that creates a system of care for residents. For example, such a department would have the full spectrum of professionals who have been identified to best address the needs of the community, such as social workers, psychologists, substance use counselors, conflict mediators, mental and behavioral health specialists, nurses, restorative and transformative justice practitioners, violence intervention experts, public health specialists, harm reduction practitioners, gang intervention workers, and trauma-informed healing practitioners. Rather than just having police on patrol throughout the community, you would have a variety of trained professionals with a diverse set of skills available to respond to and, more importantly, prevent crime and violence. When you called 911, switchboard operators would have a menu of options available to craft the appropriate response, depending on the circumstances.[151] Crime survivors/victims would have access to a far more robust set of resources to better meet their needs. Rather than simply meting out punishment as a reflexive response to crime, we would develop capacity to address and resolve such threats within communities while holding offenders responsible for their actions in more meaningful ways. In schools, educators would have access to the same collection of support services to meet the full array of student needs instead of simply resorting to out-of-school suspensions, expulsions, arrests, and referrals to the juvenile justice system. Ultimately, not only would we wind up criminalizing far less behavior; we would become far more effective at solving community problems and improving community health and safety. Thus, we could expect that what we currently think of as the criminal justice system would progressively shrink over time, in contrast to the steady growth of the past several decades.

Many of the component parts of this idea are already in existence. There are highly effective restorative justice and transformative justice programs in existence across the country.[152] There are numerous jurisdictions with initiatives that refer what had long been law enforcement matters to community-based services.[153] There are some cities that are expanding the notion of who can be a first responder to public health and safety issues.[154] There are others that have been effectively deploying violence intervention and gang intervention workers to address persistent issues of street violence.[155] A number of cities are also taking a far more holistic and prevention-focused approach around issues of crime, violence, and trauma.[156] Many cities and states are also pursuing justice reinvestment or divest/invest efforts.[157] In particular, following the killing of George Floyd in 2020 and the uprising that ensued, a number of jurisdictions made significant progress in these areas.[158]

The problem remains, though, that no cities, counties, or states are doing all these things in a robust, comprehensive way. So many of our resources have gone into mass criminalization and incarceration that we haven't invested appropriately in community-based responses to crime and violence. Even where we have developed effective alternatives to criminal justice system involvement, we have often unnecessarily positioned police and prosecutors as the gatekeepers to those services. Moreover, in the jurisdictions that have made a commitment to justice reinvestment, in almost all cases it hasn't been truly led by the most impacted communities but rather by policy makers who have been either unwilling or unable to fully confront the mass criminalization and incarceration system. Thus, the actual amount of money being reinvested within these initiatives is almost embarrassingly small, and much of it has been directed back into other areas of the criminal justice system.[159]

Nevertheless, reinvestment from the criminal justice system into meaningful prevention efforts and multidisciplinary public health and safety departments is something that can be done in every locality and state in the United States. And just to give a sense of what is possible, with $238 billion in annual savings from right-sizing the criminal justice system, we could do all the following:

- Increase education funding for the twenty-five million US students who qualify for free or reduced-price lunches by 25 percent
- Create a universal pre-K system for all three- and four-year-olds

- Provide over fifteen million children with quality afterschool programs
- Extend health care coverage to three million uninsured individuals
- Create half a million new jobs for the variety of professionals needed to staff public health and safety departments[160]

Because of how heavily concentrated the effects of the mass criminalization and incarceration system have been in certain communities, and particularly communities of color, it is only appropriate that whatever reinvestment is decided upon would be heavily focused on those communities as well. That would allow us to begin to repair the harm caused by decades of profoundly harmful criminal justice policies and address some of the blatant racial inequities that we have allowed to persist.

Moreover, as will be discussed in chapter 5, the reinvestment described in the preceding pages is just scratching the surface of what could be achieved with a more sensible allocation of our resources. The important thing to understand is that once we decide to align our resources with community well-being and equity, there are virtually limitless possibilities for creating truly transformative change that could dramatically improve the health, safety, and quality of life for all US residents.

The true test is this: Ask yourself how such an approach could improve your life. How would it have changed your own experience with crime and violence? Think about the public safety, public health, racial equity, civil rights, civil liberties, and fiscal ramifications of a more strategic, prevention-focused, problem-solving approach versus the mass criminalization and incarceration approach, and whether that would benefit you, your family, and your community. I think you will find that the answer is quite clear.

Solution 4: Ensure True Democratic Control over the Criminal Justice System

When it comes to how criminal justice policy decisions are made, in many communities around the country, and particularly communities of color, the tail usually wags the dog. Instead of the public deciding how police and prosecutors should be enforcing the law to best meet community needs and advance community priorities, it is often law enforcement officials who decide how they will be enforcing the law against the public. Plus, police and prosecutors are granted enormous power to actually make the law.

This might strike many readers as odd. You might think that the role of law enforcement is to do just that: enforce the laws that the rest of us come up with. You might also think that while legislators would understandably rely to a certain extent on law enforcement to provide advice on criminal justice policy issues, the police and prosecutors wouldn't be engaging in advocacy around those issues. However, you would unfortunately be wrong on both counts. The reality is that law enforcement groups have become a major political force that is both extremely active in making policy and extremely protective of the Criminalization Trap and the outsize power and budgets that come with it.[161] In fact, when it comes to criminal justice policy issues, law enforcement groups are often far and away the most impactful voices—exponentially more influential than any ordinary citizens who will be the ones subjected to those policies and who pay the salaries of police and prosecutors. Law enforcement officials are so powerful, in fact, that many lawmakers won't support any bill that they oppose. Thus, as I can attest to from extensive personal experience, even relatively modest reforms directed at addressing overpolicing or racial inequities in the criminal justice system are routinely and swiftly shut down through police or prosecutor intervention in the legislative process.

This gross distortion of the political process needs to stop. First, the power granted to law enforcement institutions to influence policy making around criminal laws and how they should be enforced should be immediately revoked. Their perspective may be useful at times in an advisory capacity, and there may be issues on which they have as much right to engage in legislative advocacy as anyone else (such as around their labor rights), but the notion that those charged with enforcing the laws should also have so much influence over the process of making those laws is patently absurd. Instead, there should be robust and inclusive community-led processes in every state and locality to revise criminal justice laws to ensure that they serve community interests, not those of the ultra-wealthy.

Second, communities that have historically not been well served by their law enforcement agencies should be granted immediate control over those agencies.[162] Every community should have a right to self-determination on these matters. In many predominantly white communities, this is so obviously self-evident that it doesn't even have to be mentioned. Yet for many black and brown communities, these types of law enforcement decisions are typically made by policy makers who are more beholden to predominantly white neighborhoods within their jurisdiction and virtually nonresponsive to the concerns of people of color. Black and brown communities are almost never provided meaningful opportunities to influence the criminal justice policies that have an enormous impact on their lives. Moreover, there is almost no recognition that law enforcement should be accountable to those communities.

Thus, within such communities, there should be civilian-controlled, representative bodies that are empowered to determine agency funding, set law enforcement policies, establish agency priorities, make hiring and firing decisions, conduct internal investigations, and determine disciplinary actions in the event of misconduct. In some cases, that may require revising the jurisdictional lines of law enforcement agencies or breaking up agencies into smaller units to ensure that they are truly accountable to the communities of color they serve. Regardless of what it takes, after decades of being devastated by the Criminalization Trap, there can no longer be any legitimate justification for denying these communities democratic control over the institutions that are supposed to be serving them.

The fact is that safety doesn't come from police, prosecutors, jails, and prisons. True safety comes from healthy, well-resourced, and equitable communities employing the best available strategies for both preventing and responding to crime and violence. The four solutions presented in this chapter—"do no harm," defunding, reinvestment, and community control—would create that kind of safety. They would dramatically improve the quality of life for every person in the United States. They would replace the tough-on-crime approach with one that truly serves and protects the interests of black and brown communities. They would ensure that our public safety strategies are meeting community needs, not generating profits for Corporate America and Wall Street. And they would allow the United States to finally eliminate the devastating systemic racism within the criminal justice system that has needlessly harmed and taken so many lives, so that at long last we could make a credible claim on the title "land of the free."

FROM JIM CROW TO JUAN CROW

In the United States, we have, over the course of generations, developed our own system of values. These are the ideas that dominate our culture and shape how each of us views the world beginning at a very young age. There are a number of such values that we can identify as being commonly held across generations and across regions of the country. However, there may be none that are more central to the American identity than (1) liberty; (2) equality; and (3) family. Those three, in particular, are at the very core of what we profess to stand for as Americans. These values are so near and dear to our hearts that when we perceive something that infringes upon them, our sense of injustice and outrage can be triggered very quickly.

Expert filmmakers have learned this lesson well. They know that they can almost instantaneously shift our loyalties and manipulate our emotions by even just briefly tapping into these values. Thus, in the *Star Wars* movies, all it takes are short depictions of the Empire's authoritarian tactics to immediately identify them as the villains and the Rebels as the freedom fighters. In *Braveheart*, a few brief scenes that depicted Scots as second-class citizens of the British Empire were enough to turn much of the audience into rabid defenders of Scottish independence. The horrors of being forcibly separated from one's family members are so evocative for us that Liam Neeson was somehow able to make three *Taken* movies, and the four *The Hunger Games* movies grossed nearly $3 billion.[1]

These values also have more practical applications, of course. For example, as a country we have a rich tradition of humanitarianism toward individuals suffering from oppressive conditions elsewhere around the world. We have an asylum process for individuals who demonstrate that they were "persecuted or fear persecution due to race, religion, nationality, political opinion, or membership in a particular social group."[2] In other words, when lack of liberty or unequal treatment threatens the well-being of people around the world, we have often been willing to provide safe haven for them. Plus, for over fifty years, our immigration policies have prioritized "family unification," meaning that we have given preference to the family members of US residents. Through these and a variety of other means, we have put our core values into practice, allowing countless individuals to enjoy higher-quality lives in the process.

This is the cultural tradition in which I was raised. It was a source of pride that, when it came to immigration issues, my country was willing to stand up for individual liberties, the fundamental equality of all people, and the importance of familial bonds. I was, of course, educated enough to know that our track record on these matters was nowhere close to perfect, but I still believed that the US's approach to immigration was truly guided by the famous quote on our Statue of Liberty: "Give me your tired, your poor, your huddled masses yearning to breathe free." I believed that, even with all our flaws, we still generally treated people here and around the world better than other countries, and that there was something to this idea of "American exceptionalism."

Then I began spending time within immigrant communities around the United States. In particular, I began working very closely with predominantly Latinx but also Caribbean and South Asian immigrant communities in New York, California, Colorado, Virginia, Illinois, Florida, and numerous other parts of the country. I witnessed how, across the George W. Bush, Obama, and Trump administrations, we have implemented public policies that have caused millions of people to live in constant, abject fear that they or their loved ones will be detained or deported. I observed how we have expanded the Criminalization Trap described in chapter 3 to terrorize immigrant communities with the threat of not only criminal justice consequences but immigration consequences as well. I watched as we created bands of law enforcement officials charged with hunting down brown-skinned people who don't have legal immigration status. I have seen how, as a nation, we have been deliberately cruel to some of the most dispossessed people in the world as a matter of policy.

Those descriptions may seem overblown to you. That is what I would have thought if I had read those words years ago. Before I saw these dynamics for myself, I was resistant to accepting the truth about how we treat migrants in this country. I didn't want to believe that this was such a significant part of who we are as a country right now. Thus, even as I began working with immigrant communities, I rationalized the injustice I was seeing as the actions of a few misguided public officials. However, as I became more acquainted with how routinely and comprehensively we mistreat undocumented immigrants, I realized that what I was seeing weren't aberrations; they were the norm. I learned that those core American values of liberty, equality, and family are far from absolute. Though they may be deeply rooted within us, we Americans can, under the wrong influences, abandon them entirely. We can be made to support, or at least accept, severe limitations on people's liberties, thoroughly unequal treatment of particular groups of people, and the wanton destruction of families. In other words, we have shown ourselves to be more than capable of permitting our public policies to systematically devalue the lives of millions of people of color who migrate to the United States from around the world.

The reality is that most Americans have virtually no knowledge of the policies and dynamics that I am describing. Most of us have never witnessed the devastation caused by our immigration policies on a daily basis. Most of us have no direct experience with the impact that this type of agonizing fear and anxiety can have on a person. We have never been on the sharp end of discrimination that is widely deemed to be acceptable simply because of where we were born. If you don't live or spend a great deal of time within immigrant communities, it is quite easy to live your life unburdened by the realities of what is being done by our policy makers. To be sure, one can easily find extensive coverage of a variety of immigration issues within mainstream media. However, what is almost never highlighted within that coverage is what is most important: that for many years the United States has been implementing a set of public policies that target the undocumented members of our society with a barrage of unequal and unjust treatment that virtually ensures that their lives will be filled with fear, trauma, and suffering. In other words, despite our stated commitment to aiding individuals who face persecution abroad, we are *actively persecuting millions of people in our own country solely because of their race, ethnicity, country of origin, and immigration status.*

Of course, there is plenty of room for disagreement on the particulars of immigration policy. The decisions about who gets to come here and stay here are often both difficult and complex. But at the core of this thorny set of issues there is actually a very simple question that we are called to answer: How are we going to treat the people who are already here but who don't have legal status? There are approximately eleven million such undocumented immigrants (or about one out of every thirty people in the United States).[3] They have migrated here over the past several decades for a wide variety of reasons. Many faced horrendous conditions in their home countries—some of which were created or exacerbated by US policies—that essentially "pushed" them here. Most were also "pulled" here by job opportunities and the possibility of a higher quality of life. What they all share in common is that they would have all preferred to enter the country legally and be "documented." Given the choice, no one would opt to be undocumented, not with all the consequences and risk that has come to entail (including, for many, having to cross one of the most brutal deserts in the world, a trek that has claimed thousands of lives).[4] However, for the vast majority of undocumented immigrants, there was no real choice. Hardly any of those eleven million people had any viable path to come here legally. Those opportunities have simply not been provided by US law.[5]

So that leaves the rest of us with a choice to make. One would hope that in making that choice, we would live up to our core values and opt for the humane treatment of those who have migrated here and now make their homes here. Sometimes—such as with the Deferred Action for Childhood Arrivals (DACA) program—we have. However, far too often we have instead opted for brutal and heartless treatment of migrants. As a country, we often act as if their lack of US citizenship grants us a license to abuse them for our own benefit. Thus, rather than putting our core values into practice, we have extended the worst of our American traditions: that of setting ourselves apart from, and above, those we define as being different from "us." In other words, our modern-day treatment of undocumented immigrants follows in the same line of some of the most shameful chapters from US history, including the internment of Japanese Americans during World War II, the forced displacement of Native Americans, and Jim Crow segregation, among others.

How have so many of us been led to view migrants as the "other," to actually value their lives less than those of other people? And who benefits from that? By this point in the book, I am sure you can guess that our collective ignorance and failure to address such a long-standing example of systemic racism aren't accidental. Our treatment of immigrants may be a flagrant betrayal of core American values, but it is also a prime example of the strategic racism employed by the ultra-wealthy. As will be discussed later in this chapter, a small group of Corporate America and Wall Street executives have been instrumental in creating and preserving the immigration policies that have forced millions of people to live "in the shadows" as far less than equal members of our society. While the stated rationales for our many harsh, anti-immigrant policies have been that such policies are necessary to protect public safety, uphold the rule of law, and avoid the overextension of limited public resources, these are, for the most part, merely smokescreens. The primary purpose behind our cruelty toward migrants is to advance the wealth accumulation of billionaires and multimillionaires.

Thus, while there are many immigration issues that contribute to racial injustice, in this chapter the focus will be quite narrow. It centers on whether we, as a country, are going to continue allowing undocumented residents of the United States to be ruthlessly exploited and treated as a virtually permanent underclass, or not. To put it another way, we have to decide how we are going to treat millions of people who made the same decisions that we likely would have made had we been in their shoes (that is, if we hadn't had the luxury of never having to consider transnational migration as a means of survival).

To address that issue, and demonstrate how the ultra-wealthy profit off immigrants' pain, it may help to start by understanding how our immigration policies work in practice. And there may be no better place to exemplify how hostile and degrading such policies can be toward immigrants than Arizona.

The Eye of the Storm

The population of Arizona has experienced two dramatic demographic shifts in recent decades. First, it has become home to the largest number of aging baby boomers anywhere in the United States outside of Florida.[6] Drawn by the warm weather, dry air, relatively low cost of living, and "senior friendly" communities, Arizona has become a prime destination for retirees and "snowbirds."

Second, the undocumented population in Arizona increased dramatically as the state became by far the most heavily traveled passageway through which undocumented immigrants pass over the border from Mexico. That shift was attributable, in significant part, to federal immigration policy. Because of stricter enforcement policies along the border in California, New Mexico, and Texas beginning in the 1990s, migrant crossings were essentially funneled into Arizona.[7] The thought was that the harsh desert along the Arizona-Mexico border would serve as a natural deterrent to border crossings. In reality, and because of how desperate many migrants are, it just made the journey to the United States far more dangerous while concentrating many of the effects of migration within one particular region.[8] Obviously, many of the migrants entering the United States through Arizona continue on to other states around the country. However, many others choose to stay in the state. As a result, it is estimated that the number of undocumented immigrants in Arizona increased from ninety thousand in 1990 to half a million in 2007.[9]

Thus, the state was simultaneously inundated with both older, predominantly white Americans, and mostly young Mexicans and Central Americans.[10] In one sense, you can see how these two groups were on a collision course. The seniors who relocated to Arizona were sold a vision of perpetual tans, immaculate golf courses, low taxes, and simple living. What wasn't included in the shiny brochures were the realities associated with large numbers of migrant individuals and families who are struggling to survive and gain their own toehold on a better life. Thus, many of Arizona's light-skinned transplants saw the state's darker-skinned transplants as intruders within their retirement paradise.

While such conflict was perhaps unsurprising, there has also been a codependence that has developed between these two populations. Meeting the needs of an expanding community of retirees requires workers who can build new senior living facilities, provide home-based health care services, and handle all the lawn mowing, housecleaning, and other domestic chores that many seniors can no longer do themselves. Those jobs have often been filled by immigrants. Thus, Arizona's senior community is often just as reliant on the undocumented workers helping to meet their geriatric needs as those workers are on them for their jobs.

Nevertheless, beginning in the 1990s, the response to the influx of undocumented immigrants in Arizona (and elsewhere) was to institute what essentially amounted to a "tough-on-immigrants" strategy. Just as our so-called tough-on-crime approach in the criminal justice system used hyperaggressive enforcement tactics and severe criminal consequences for offenders, our immigration policies began to single out undocumented immigrants for severe mistreatment while also ratcheting up the penalties for unauthorized border crossings. Many of these tough-on-immigrants policies came from the federal government, such as the militarization of the US-Mexico border and the creation of a massive "deportation machine" directed at undocumented individuals already within the country.[11] While these federal initiatives were devastating to countless migrant families, many states and localities still took it upon themselves to layer on additional anti-immigrant policies. Arizona, in particular, took up this mantle with extreme vigor. Here is just a sample of Arizona's crackdown on the undocumented:

- 1996: Until the 1990s, undocumented immigrants were able to get driver's licenses anywhere in the United States. California was the first state to revoke that access in 1993, and then Arizona followed suit in 1996. (Forty-five other states joined them in subsequent years.)[12]
- 2000: Proposition 203, which banned bilingual education in Arizona public schools in favor of so-called "immersion" strategies, was passed with 63 percent of the vote.[13]
- 2004: Proposition 200, which passed with 56 percent of the vote, prohibited undocumented immigrants from receiving any public benefits.[14]
- 2006: Proposition 103, which passed with 74 percent of the vote, made English the official language of the state and prohibited most government business from being done in other languages. Proposition 300, passed with 72 percent of the vote, made undocumented persons ineligible for

child care assistance, adult education, in-state college tuition, and financial aid. Proposition 100, passed with 78 percent of the vote, singled out undocumented immigrants as being ineligible for bail for certain criminal offenses. Proposition 102, passed with 74 percent of the vote, singled out undocumented immigrants as being ineligible to receive punitive damages in the event they win a civil lawsuit.[15]

- 2010: The state legislature passed SB 1070, arguably the most comprehensive anti-immigrant law ever passed in the United States up to that point. Its stated purpose was to pursue "attrition through enforcement," meaning that the legislators wanted to make living conditions so bad for undocumented immigrants that they would leave the state voluntarily.[16] It included a number of provisions designed to achieve that effect, including making it a state crime to reside or work in the United States without legal permission, requiring law enforcement officers to verify the legal status of all individuals who were arrested or detained, and making it a crime to transport or "harbor" an undocumented immigrant. (Thus, driving one's grandmother to the doctor or having her live with you would be a crime if she were undocumented.) The law also required law enforcement officers to determine a person's immigration status during stops, detentions, and arrests if there was a "reasonable suspicion" that the person was undocumented (thus legalizing blatant racial profiling).[17] Less than six weeks after SB 1070 was signed into law, the state also banned the teaching of ethnic studies classes.[18]

On top of these state-level anti-immigrant measures, many localities instituted additional policies targeting undocumented immigrants. In Maricopa County, which includes Phoenix and over 60 percent of the total state population, Sheriff Joe Arpaio carved out a national reputation for himself owing to the extreme anti-immigrant policies he instituted during his twenty-four-year tenure.[19] For example, the self-styled "America's toughest sheriff" detained individuals charged with immigration offenses in an outdoor jail called Tent City where the temperatures reached as high as 145 degrees during the day. Arpaio referred to this jail as his own "concentration camp." He seemed to delight in demeaning those he incarcerated, such as by forcing men to wear pink underwear and denying women menstrual hygiene products and forcing them to sleep on their own blood-stained sheets. He also reinstated chain gangs and ran a twenty-four-hour webcast from within his jails that showed people being arrested, strip searched, and held in cells. He even had webcams mounted in bathrooms and streamed live footage of women using the toilet.[20]

Arpaio's efforts to target the Latinx community with immigration enforce-ment actions escalated in 2007 when his department became the first in the country to partner with ICE to implement on a large scale what is known as a 287(g) agreement. This agreement allows state and local law enforcement officials to become deputized as, and perform the duties of, federal immigra-tion officers. Arpaio used this newfound authority to conduct perhaps the most tyrannical sweeps and raids in modern US history. For many years, the Sheriff's Department would target Latinx communities, establish a perimeter, and send in over one hundred officers, who over the course of several days would stop everyone who was suspected of being undocumented (which in reality often meant everyone who was brown-skinned). Arpaio recruited nearly one thou-sand civilians to become part of an armed "posse" that would assist with these immigrant roundups.[21]

Each one of these state- and local-level policies had a profoundly harmful impact on people around the state. The English-only law and the ethnic stud-ies ban created shame around people's language and cultural identity. The ban on public benefits meant that many people could no longer access professional health care services, and as a result a number of individuals were subsequently deported directly from hospitals because they had a health care emergency and they weren't able to cover the charges out of pocket. The ban on educational services sent an unmistakable signal that an entire community of people wasn't going to be allowed to improve upon its social and economic status. The ban on bail meant that a certain class of people was truly treated as guilty until proven innocent. The bans on punitive damages and driver's licenses reinforced the notion that undocumented immigrants weren't to be afforded the same protec-tions and privileges as Americans. The raids and sweeps made people so fearful that they would lock themselves in their houses for three or four days at a time, not even leaving to take their children to school. SB 1070 made every minute of every day a minefield of potential encounters with police that could lead to being permanently separated from one's family.

When viewed in isolation, each one of these policies has been rather vicious. Taken as a whole, they represent an all-out assault on every aspect of life for Arizona's undocumented population. Each one of them creates or expands the divide between "them" and "us." Each one of them ramps up the degree of difficulty of living in Arizona as an undocumented person. Each one of them increases the likelihood that undocumented individuals, and families with one or more undocumented members, will become trapped in a vicious cycle of inter-generational poverty and criminalization. Overall, the end result for most of the people targeted by these policies is either (a) their lives are made to be so miser-able that they leave the state voluntarily; or (b) they stay in Arizona, continue to work largely menial jobs, but are forced so far into the shadows that the rest of society barely has to account for them.

In other words, Arizona essentially decided to abuse people so thoroughly and repeatedly that they would either reach a point where they couldn't take it anymore or they would have to accept being continually demeaned and exploited. Go ahead and try to reconcile that approach with your understanding of American values. The deliberate creation of an aggressively inhospitable environment is what you do to address an infestation by mice or roaches in your house, or what a petulant teenager does to register unhappiness over having a new step-parent. It is far beneath any country that purports to exercise moral leadership across the globe—or at least it should be.

To understand how dehumanizing this collection of laws has been on Arizona's undocumented residents, it is of course best to listen directly to those who have been affected by them. Thus, I visited Arizona in February 2018 to meet with undocumented residents and hear their stories about how the policies described here have intersected with their lives. For example, I met Josefina, a mother of four with a broad smile and a magnetic personal warmth that makes even strangers feel like they have known her for their whole lives.[22] She and her family had, by that point, lived in Phoenix for sixteen years. She told me that for her, and many families like hers, the reality of being targeted by Arizona's anti-immigrant policies could be felt every minute of every day.

"We leave the house as infrequently as possible," she said. "You never know what's going to happen, so we really only are out to go from home to work, and then from work to home. When we have to go to the grocery store, no one ever goes alone. The entire family goes together. That is the level we have come to— that one person cannot go to the store alone because of the fear of being stopped. We all go together; we all leave together. It's because of the fear that one of us could go and not come back."

Josefina's husband was deported in 2017, and as with most deportations, the impact went far beyond the person being moved to the other side of the border. Josefina's oldest daughter, Elena, who had acquired legal status under the DACA program, had to leave college to get a job in order to help support the rest of the family following her father's deportation. Josefina was heartbroken over the impact this had on Elena. She explained, "It's very sad because my daughter said to me, 'Mommy, this would have been the year I would have graduated if not for what happened to Daddy. Because of that, my dreams have been broken.' It's very sad to hear that from one of your kids." As a result of this episode, Josefina said that Elena was so devastated and so perpetually fearful that she would no longer speak to anyone she didn't know.

The impact was perhaps even more severe for Josefina's ten-year-old son, Manuel. She told me that she worried about him incessantly, and said that his spirit was broken by losing his father. "He's often very afraid," she said. "He tells me, 'Mommy, don't go to work.' He says the same thing to his sister. And he doesn't want to go to school either because he's afraid of what might happen." After her husband was deported, Josefina said that Manuel would implore her, "'No one can go anywhere, Mommy—we all have to stay here inside in the house. I don't want to ever be separated from the family.'"

Anyone who has ever been a parent of a young child and had the experience of being out in a public place and suddenly realizing that you had lost track of your child, even for only a few seconds, knows how terrifying that can be. Maybe you are out shopping or at a park watching them play and you turn your head, just for a moment. Then, when you turn back, you don't see them anymore, and you panic. Your heart starts racing, adrenaline starts coursing through your veins, and whatever capacity you once had for rational thought has now vanished. Those can be the worst moments of a person's life. Yet people like Josefina are forced to confront similar fears every single day. She explained, "I have to live with this uncertainty that one day I'm going to go to work and be detained and then won't be able to return home to see my kids. I am so afraid, my body trembles to even think about them arriving to take me away and not being able to see my kids again. It's the worst thing that could possibly happen to me. I wouldn't be able to endure that, to be without them. So every day when I leave the house I pray, 'God, please take care of us, protect us, help ensure that nothing happens at my job and that I can arrive home safely, and that nothing happens to anyone.' I shudder just thinking about these things; so many things go running through my mind."

Because of how aggressively we police, detain, and deport immigrants, particularly in places like Arizona, the possibilities that Josefina's worst nightmare will occur are far from remote. Thus, she constantly has to walk on eggshells. "Every time I'm in the car and see a police officer," she said, "I pray to God that they don't stop me. You never know how they're going to react. Maybe they'll just give you a ticket, or maybe . . ." She wasn't able to finish the sentence as she wept at the thought of what could occur.

Families all over Arizona have stories like this. I met a man named Miguel who moved to the United States fourteen years earlier with his wife and their two kids. Miguel is the type of strong, dignified man who looks you squarely in the eyes the entire time he is speaking with you and, when you meet him, makes you realize that too many years of working behind a computer have left you with a weak handshake. Three years earlier, just as he got home from work one evening, several police cars emerged, and officers swarmed around him on his front lawn as his family watched in horror. He was detained for an immigration violation and taken to Mexico that night. It was nearly two years before Miguel was able to rejoin his family while the court system considered his petition for legal status.

That separation took a huge toll on the whole family. "Our family life has been completely devastated," he said. "The fear, the uncertainty, having to find a way to subsist that we weren't accustomed to; you can't take that away. That is going to be permanent. It's always going to be part of the story of our lives. They're going to be sad stories, but that's what they are. You lose part of yourselves. For me, I was separated from my family for two years. I can't get those back. I missed a lot of important things in my kids' lives. Their growth, their education, a lot of planning, and all of that ends, right? So we're starting over again now, but always with that 'yesterday' that was missed in mind."

I asked Miguel what it was like being apart from his family for that length of time. He said, "It's like your life ends. You're still alive, and you're still walking down the street, but you're only walking because you need to walk. You're only breathing because your body does it for you. You don't really exist anymore; you're no longer in your own body. You're somewhere else, thinking only of your family. It's a very sad daily life. Every moment you're thinking of them. Of your wife, and how will she be able to provide for the family? And what will happen to your kids if they wind up detaining your wife? And what are the two of you going to do if you're both deported?"

As difficult as it was for Miguel, he too was most concerned about the effects it had on his children. "You could say that I was the victim of what happened," he said, "but in reality it was my kids who were the victims. They were harmed more than I was. That's what hurts me the most." He explained to me that the entire family suffered from depression. He said that his son Joel wouldn't leave his room for a long time. "He would only go into the kitchen," he said, "and he ate a lot, and put on a lot of weight. Same for my daughter. She shut herself in her room and wouldn't leave. She used to be very involved in school. She was the student council president and a cheerleader. She stopped all of that. And that has left a mark on me."

As Miguel describes the impact of his removal from the United States on his children, tears streamed down his face. He was deeply concerned about them being put at greater risk because of his absence. "Here I was, in Mexico and then in a detention center," he said, "and meanwhile my kids are abandoned here, away from their father, and as a result they can make mistakes that can result in *them* entering a prison or a detention center." He was also troubled by the impact of these immigration policies on other children and youth in his community. "A lot of kids are being separated from their families," he said. "They're alone, and so they have to leave school to get a job. And now they're on the path to detention, to being hurt, even to being killed."

Even though Miguel's family was back together when I met them, they were still living in a constant state of apprehension that the immigration system would again upend their lives. According to Joel, they would use the "Find My iPhone" app to monitor each other's location throughout the day and make sure that no one had been picked up by ICE. He told me that they also called to check on each other regularly throughout the day. When I asked how often, he answered "a lot!" though with far less annoyance than a typical twenty-one-year-old who constantly has to explain his whereabouts to his parents.

For Joel, what was most difficult was seeing the impact that the anti-immigrant climate in Arizona had on his parents. "My parents are always afraid to leave the house," he said. "If my parents see a car they don't recognize, they freak out. They turn off the lights and start looking through the window. When they're out and they arrive back at the house, they still stop for a minute just to look around. They get really nervous, even though my dad has legal status. They still freak out when they see a police officer."

When you talk to undocumented Arizona residents, one after another has stories like those of Josefina and Miguel, stories that should horrify every American. Most of the people I met were reluctant to leave their houses unless absolutely necessary, and most would take precautions such as only going out in groups. Many have known parents who were picked up by ICE while simply taking their kids to school, so they are hesitant to even do that anymore.[23] According to Carlos Garcia, a Phoenix City Council member and former executive director of Puente Human Rights Movement, a grassroots migrant justice organization, "most families have an 'on your way home you're calling us' rule and a 'when you get home you're calling us' rule. It's a constant check-in. A constant fear that you're going to get home that night and not everyone is going to be at the dinner table. That's literally everyday life for the majority of our people."

I met people who are filled with regret because our immigration policies led to their missing important milestones in their children's lives or prevented them from being with loved ones as they were dying in their native countries. I met families in which someone got sick with a disease that would normally be easily treatable or curable, but because the family didn't have access to health insurance and had to rely on home remedies, their loved ones suffered severe, permanent harm, or even died. Person after person had stories of almost unimaginable cruelty by immigration officials and law enforcement officers, such as the woman who went into labor as she was picked up by Sheriff Arpaio's deputies for an immigration violation and then was forced to give birth while still in handcuffs. Virtually every family I met lived in such a precarious state that they had a written plan in place that identified, in the event one or more parents were detained by ICE, who would pick their kids up from school and care for them.

Perhaps the most damaging aspect of Arizona's immigration policies is how they have shattered people's hopes and dreams for their lives and their children's lives. Many parents I spoke with told me how disillusioned their children had become as they got older and realized how many education and employment opportunities had either been taken away or were never available to them in the first place. They expressed how agonizing it was to watch their children lose hope that a better life was possible. According to Garcia, "Most of the folks will tell you that they came here for a better future for their kids. But all of those roads have been blocked because of the conditions that have been created for them. So you're seeing this loss of spirit. Because they're not with their people, they're not happy, they're not practicing their traditions, and their culture is being taken from them because they had to move here. But now their hopes and dreams of their kids becoming something else and then maybe going back or being able to recuperate some sort of happiness or find a better way of life are also not happening. Because the youth are living in the barrios and being pushed into the criminal justice system. So now a lot of their kids are on probation, in jail, in prison, getting killed, all the same things that black and brown folks with papers go through. So now they're getting the worst of both worlds. The whole reason they risked their lives to go through the desert and put up with all this injustice isn't turning out the way they intended. They put themselves through this horrible trajectory, and now the outcomes are even worse than they would have been if they hadn't left."

For those who have never experienced anything similar to these dynamics, it can be difficult to put into context the cumulative impact that Arizona's immigration laws have had. It is just not that common for a single group of people to be targeted by so many destructive policies at one time. One analogy for these anti-immigrant laws would be to the effects of chronic pain. If you have ever suffered from chronic pain, you know how all-consuming it can be. You know how it dominates your thoughts almost every second of every day, how it disrupts every aspect of your life, from your eating and sleeping to your overall mood, stress, and energy levels. You also know about how it frequently leads to other physical, mental, and behavioral health issues, producing a downward spiral that can be extremely difficult to break. Now imagine those dynamics affecting hundreds of thousands of people living in close proximity to each other, and you would have a rough approximation of the effects of Arizona's anti-immigrant policies. These laws have produced entire communities of severely traumatized individuals, many of whom suffer from excruciating and debilitating levels of toxic stress, depression, and anxiety.[24]

The only other analogies to Arizona's anti-immigrant policies that come to mind are from the historical no-fly zones, those chapters in world history that aren't supposed to be discussed because their mere mention is deemed to be inflammatory and beyond the pale. Nevertheless, as person after person told me how they were forced to hide in their houses for fear of being discovered by ICE and forcibly removed from their family, it was impossible not to be reminded of *The Diary of Anne Frank*. Indeed, there is very little that a government can do to its residents that is worse than terrorizing them to such an extent that they become afraid to leave their own houses. Throughout history, there have only been a relatively small group of members of that ignominious club. It just so happens that the Third Reich was one of them, and modern-day Arizona is another. If that happens to fall outside the lines of civil discourse, then so be it, because it represents a truth that we must confront as a country.

The American Gestapo

In the event you think I might be overstating the aggressiveness and intentionality of our anti-immigrant policies, consider this chilling warning issued by Thomas Homan, then-acting director of ICE, in 2017: "If you're in this country illegally and you committed a crime by entering this country, you should be uncomfortable. You should look over your shoulder. And you need to be worried."

Source: Maria Sacchetti and Nick Miroff, "How Trump Is Building a Border Wall That No One Can See," *Washington Post*, November 21, 2017.

A Thousand Points of Darkness

While Arizona may be the worst example of American xenophobia, it is by no means an outlier. All across the country, immigrant families have been encountering similar, or even worse, mistreatment from state, local, and federal government officials for many years.[25] For example, after Arizona's SB 1070 was passed in 2010, two dozen copycat bills were introduced in state legislatures across the country, and five of them passed, in Alabama, Georgia, Indiana, South Carolina, and Utah.[26] Overall, a total of 164 anti-immigrant laws were passed by state legislatures in just 2010 and 2011. The election of President Trump in 2016 spurred yet another wave of state immigration laws.[27]

At the local level, Hazleton, Pennsylvania, passed an ordinance in 2006 that was similar to SB 1070 and sought to limit the ability of undocumented immigrants to work and find housing in the city. Over one hundred other localities around the country subsequently passed some version of the same law.[28] (Note that many of these laws, or portions of these laws, have, like sections of SB 1070, been struck down by federal courts in recent years. Nevertheless, their impact prior to being struck down was still devastating, and those effects linger on in those communities and beyond.)

At the federal level, our nationwide deportation force, ICE, regularly conducts raids across the country, sometimes detaining people by the hundreds.[29] ICE also pursues more individualized enforcement actions, tracking down undocumented immigrants in their homes or at work. In 2017, ICE expanded its target areas to include schools, hospitals, churches, and courthouses, so that there is nowhere for people to feel safe.[30] Nationwide, we have been deporting between 165,000 and 435,000 people per year since the beginning of the George W. Bush administration.[31]

Additionally, ICE now partners with 133 law enforcement agencies across twenty-four states through the same types of 287(g) agreements that Sheriff Arpaio used to terrorize the Latinx community in Maricopa County.[32] Moreover, through a program called "Secure Communities," whenever individuals are taken into custody anywhere in the United States, the FBI cross-checks their fingerprints with immigration databases to determine if they are eligible to be turned over to ICE.[33] In other words, we have essentially deputized all law enforcement officers across the country to assist in advancing ICE's agenda.

Thus, the same type of fear and anxiety experienced by the undocumented residents of Arizona has been exported to the rest of the country. Contrary to popular understanding, those effects haven't been limited to brown-skinned Mexican and Central American immigrants, either. Black immigrants from Africa, the Caribbean, and Latin America have disproportionately been targeted for ICE enforcement, and Asians, Muslims of all races and ethnicities, and other immigrants of color have all been deeply affected by our tough-on-immigrants policies.[34]

The Criminalization Trap: Immigrant Edition

As discussed in chapter 3, the United States has, in recent years, favored the highly aggressive enforcement of extremely broad criminal laws, making it remarkably easy to identify "crimes" and ensuring that virtually every person can be considered a criminal at some point. Additionally, we have greatly prioritized the use of law enforcement responses to these "crimes" over many other possible responses, while also attaching profoundly harmful, punitive consequences to them. The focus of the preceding chapter was on the impact that this Criminalization Trap has had on US citizens. However, these dynamics haven't been limited to those born within the United States, nor have the consequences meted out been restricted to those administered by the US correctional system.

Our national addiction to criminalization has carried over to the immigration system and our treatment of immigrant communities as well. In recent years, the criminal justice system and the immigration system have become so thoroughly intertwined that it is often impossible to say where one ends and the other begins. However, it wasn't always this way. In fact, for most of US history, immigration issues were largely treated as matters of economic and labor policy, or as humanitarian concerns. It has only been over the past few decades, and particularly over the past fifteen years, that immigration has been handled through the same destructive and ineffective "law and order" approach that characterizes our criminal justice system. The result has been that we have stopped viewing and treating undocumented immigrants for what they are: fellow human beings who are doing their best to play the often lousy hand they have been dealt. Instead, we have lumped them in that ever-growing box marked "criminals" that contains all the other members of our society we have become so quick to discard.

For example, in 1994, the average number of people we incarcerated at any one time in immigrant detention centers was around 5,000. By 2019, that had skyrocketed to an average of 50,165 people behind bars for immigration matters every day. Overall, ICE incarcerated 510,854 immigrants in their detention centers that year.[35] In other words, we are now putting over half a million immigrants behind bars every year on top of those we put in jails and prisons as part of the largest incarcerated population in the world.

This process has been fueled by a massive investment in immigration enforcement that virtually mirrors our ballooning expenditures on the criminal justice system. To illustrate, our projected 2021 budget for federal immigration enforcement was $28.6 billion.[36] If we adjust for inflation, that is ten times more than what we spent in 1994 and thirty-two times more than what we spent in 1975 (see figure 6).[37]

This explosion of resources devoted to immigration enforcement has been used to criminalize immigrants in much the same way that we have criminalized US citizens, and particularly people of color. That criminalization has been achieved through a variety of mechanisms, including increased use of all the following tactics: (1) treating the act of crossing the border without documentation as a criminal act; (2) imposing incarceration as a consequence for immigration violations; (3) targeting immigrant communities with heavy police presence and hyperaggressive law enforcement tactics; and (4) using even the flimsiest suspicions of criminality to trigger severe immigration consequences.[38]

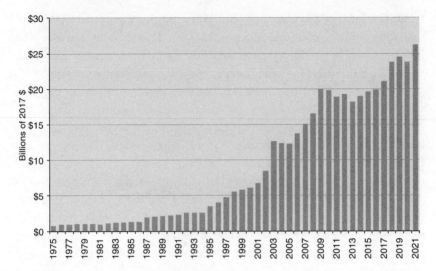

FIGURE 6. US Immigration Enforcement spending, in billions of 2017 dollars. *Sources:* Department of Homeland Security, Department of Justice.

Moreover, because of federal programs like 287(g) and "Secure Communities," the law enforcement officers who are charged with criminalizing US citizens are also often at the front lines of the criminalization of immigrants.[39] In short, the criminal justice and immigration systems have become seamlessly integrated in ways that put all noncitizens at high risk of devastating consequences such as incarceration and deportation.

Just as the mass criminalization and incarceration system brings severe and needless harm to the lives of countless individuals, families, and communities, so too does this approach to immigration enforcement. For example, while the public rhetoric around immigration enforcement often centers on "violent" or "dangerous" immigrants, the reality is that most of the individuals being deported have no criminal convictions.[40] Even where there is an underlying criminal violation, it is often the result of the same overly punitive law enforcement approach that afflicts US citizens. In other words, the "criminal" acts don't necessarily indicate that the person is a genuine threat to public safety.

Consider the impact of the war on drugs on immigrant families. For undocumented immigrants as well as legal permanent residents, we have created policies in which any drug law violation can trigger automatic detention and deportation, often without the possibility of return. Thus, more than 250,000 people have been deported from the United States for drug law violations every year since 2007. Many of those offenses were for some of our lowest-level drug charges. For example, in 2013, the fourth most common cause of deportation for any criminal offense was simple marijuana possession. That charge led to the deportation of more than thirteen thousand people in 2012 and 2013.[41]

The criminalization of immigrants also hasn't been limited to adults. In the previous two chapters, we have discussed the school-to-prison pipeline, which refers to the widespread use of education and law enforcement policies that push young people out of school and into the juvenile and criminal justice system. Tying immigration consequences to criminal justice matters escalates this crisis even further, creating a school-to-deportation pipeline that threatens undocumented youth and mixed-status families across the country. Now a routine disciplinary infraction can, for some students, result in not only an out-of-school suspension, expulsion, or arrest—it can also lead to them being ripped from their family and their community for detention and deportation. Thus, the school-to-deportation pipeline is, in some ways, the ugly culmination of all the deep, systemic injustices discussed thus far within this book. It combines the worst elements of our education, criminal justice, and immigration systems and centers them on children and youth of color to absolutely devastating effect.

Peeling Back the Onion

There are many who feel compassion for the plight of immigrants but who aren't inclined to object very strongly to their criminalization. "They broke the law by crossing the border illegally," they often say, "and the law is the law!" However persuasive you may find such arguments—and putting aside for the moment that just because something is illegal doesn't mean that any set of consequences attached to that illegality is just—it is still worth considering why those particular laws are broken so frequently.

If history has taught us anything, it is that wherever there are people suffering from a relatively low standard of living or unsafe conditions, and there is a perception that opportunities are substantially better elsewhere, migration is inevitable. That, in a nutshell, is why the ancestors of most US citizens wound up moving here from other countries; it is why many of those ancestors moved westward across the United States during the 1800s; and it is why children who grow up in suburban or rural areas still tend to congregate in major cities after their education is completed. Some of the factors that influence such migration are out of our control. However, quite often the United States exerts considerable influence over many of the factors that drive migration into our country, including a long history of economic and political destabilization of Latin America.

One significant component of that history is the aggressive pursuit of economic policies that primarily advance the interests of US corporations abroad, often at the expense of low-income and working-class families in other countries (as well as those in the United States).[42] For example, after the North American Free Trade Agreement (NAFTA) went into effect in 1994, American corn exports to Mexico increased by over 400 percent, flooding the market and severely harming Mexico's two million corn farmers. Overall, 1.5 million agricultural jobs in Mexico were lost. Additionally, US pork exports to Mexico rose twenty-five-fold, eliminating 120,000 Mexican jobs. During this period, the number of Mexicans living in extreme poverty surged by more than fourteen million. Not surprisingly, the number of undocumented Mexicans entering the United States increased by 185 percent between 1992 and 2011.[43]

The United States also has an extensive track record of supporting right-wing Latin American political leaders who align themselves with the interests of our large, multinational corporations, while opposing left-wing politicians who prioritize addressing social and economic inequality in their countries.[44] Additionally, it is well documented that the United States has supported brutal regimes in Guatemala, Nicaragua, Honduras, and El Salvador—including in some cases backing atrocities perpetrated by those governments against their own people.[45] It is not coincidental that a large percentage of the migrants now crossing, or attempting to cross, our borders originate from those countries.[46]

In other words, when it comes to international relations and immigration, the United States often tries to have its cake and eat it too. We use our clout to advance US-specific interests, often to the detriment of extremely vulnerable communities in nearby countries, and then act surprised when residents from those countries show up on our doorstep.

It is also true that, until very recently, US policy makers haven't demonstrated much genuine interest in discouraging undocumented migration into the United States. As will be discussed later in the chapter, this is intimately related to the fact that most US corporations are more than happy to benefit from an expanded and more easily exploitable labor market. Thus, not only do these corporations often welcome undocumented workers; they recruit them. US businesses frequently advertise for workers in Mexico and have even set up bus lines to transport them to the United States.[47] Examples of particularly aggressive efforts to bring undocumented workers to the United States include the effort to prepare Atlanta for the 1996 Summer Olympics and to help rebuild New Orleans following Hurricane Katrina. In both cases, undocumented workers were integral to advancing US interests, though after the jobs were done those workers often found themselves encountering extremely hostile treatment from their new country of residence.[48]

In short, one cannot credibly lament the so-called "flood" of undocumented immigrants trying to enter our borders without also recognizing that our own policies helped to turn on the tap. Indeed, the mass migration across the US-Mexico border is the predictable result of taking too many actions that destabilize and take advantage of our regional neighbors, and too few to promote vibrant democracies and social justice in the region. That doesn't necessarily mean that we have to allow entry to every oppressed person who seeks entry to the United States. It does mean, however, that our efforts to criminalize and otherwise demean such individuals are extraordinarily callous.

How Human Beings Become "Illegals"

While it became fashionable during the Trump administration to blame the president for the widespread anti-immigrant sentiment within the United States, that view underestimated the depths of the problem. These efforts have long had bipartisan support and have been substantially advanced over the past twenty-five years by both Democrats (including Presidents Clinton and Obama) and Republicans (including Presidents George W. Bush and Trump). Anti-immigrant efforts have also garnered substantial support from the public. So how was it that so many of us became accustomed to drawing such a sharp distinction between "Americans" and "illegals"?

Much of that answer can be attributed to how our policy makers discuss these issues and how the media covers them. A variety of tactics has been used over the years:

- Demonizing immigrants, and particularly undocumented immigrants, for a wide variety of social ills, regardless of whether the facts support the assertions being made[49]
- Engaging in "dog whistle politics" by using race-neutral language in strategic ways to trigger racist views against immigrants[50]
- Highlighting individual acts of wrongdoing by undocumented immigrants and suggesting that they are representative of all such migrants[51]
- Defining an entire group of people by a particular violation of the law— that is, "illegals" or "illegal immigrants"
- Turning national origin into a defining distinction between people (in the United States we seem to care far more than much of the rest of the world about where someone happens to have been born)
- Providing a large media platform for those who create or support anti-immigrant policies, while largely neglecting the perspective of those who are most affected by those policies[52]
- Failing to provide critical analysis of anti-immigrant policies and positions[53]

As a result, some segments of the population are driven to irrational fear or hatred of undocumented immigrants, and virtually everyone's perspective on the issue becomes confused, overly narrow, and infected with at least a little moral ugliness. Even compassionate and thoughtful consumers of the news become inclined to support deeply harmful anti-immigrant policies when they absorb enough images and sound bites of trusted public officials and news programs discussing the harms allegedly being committed by migrants. Many of our policy makers have become quite proficient at keeping the public's attention focused on the supposed scourge of "illegal immigration" while ignoring the fact that our policies are having a far more harmful impact on millions of undocumented immigrants than those individuals are having on the rest of us. The end result is that enough doubt is sown about whether or not our policies are unwarranted or unjust that relatively few US citizens become motivated to forcefully object to them.

Here is a dirty little secret of both the legal profession and the public relations field: Every policy, no matter how despicable, can be successfully sold to the public if it is made to appear as if there is room for debate on the topic. Not only that, but for skilled practitioners, there are always multiple strategies available to create that uncertainty. There are numerous, sophisticated-sounding justifications that can be crafted for even the most appallingly racist policies.[54] These strategies are especially potent if one's critique of the alternatives can successfully stoke the public's fear. We have a mountain of evidence demonstrating that there is no shortage of audiences who are receptive to those arguments. Indeed, it is remarkably easy to divert attention from the most important issues—such as the thorough dehumanization of large groups of people—toward far less important matters, or even issues that are entirely unrelated. All you have to do is make it seem as if there are at least two sides to the story.

However, there are some things that are so clearly wrong and so obviously morally reprehensible that there can be no justification for them. Consider the actions of former sheriff Arpaio. His crusade against Maricopa County's Latinx population was so horrific that it actually met some legal definitions of domestic terrorism.[55] It should have been easy for us, as a society, to denounce and bring a swift end to such disgusting abuses of authority. There is simply no "other side of the story" that can come close to validating the routine degradation of hundreds of thousands of people. Yet Arpaio was repeatedly provided with a largely uncritical national platform to defend his policies and spread misinformation.[56] For example, over the course of the one-year period following the launch of his immigration sweeps—which wouldn't have looked out of place within the most notorious fascist regimes of the twentieth century—he appeared on CNN seventeen times to share his perspective.[57] Over the years he has appeared on Fox News and Fox Business at least sixty-five times.[58] Thus, while it would be difficult to find more than a handful of people in the United States who have caused more harm to more people than Arpaio, he won six elections in a row, garnered substantial public support, and was even pardoned by President Trump for a 2017 criminal conviction resulting from his refusal to comply with a judge's order to end racially motivated traffic stops. He continues to have enough supporters that in 2018 he ran for Arizona's US Senate seat and in 2020 ran for his old job as the sheriff of Maricopa County.

How effectively has the wool been pulled over the public's eyes on immigration issues? A large percentage of the US population continues to blame undocumented immigrants for "taking American jobs" or "using resources that should be going toward Americans." But who is really to blame: the undocumented men and women who are typically making poverty wages doing jobs that are often excessively dangerous and demanding, or the executives in charge who were more than happy to increase their profits by hiring often desperate and vulnerable migrants for those jobs? And who is more responsible for the increasingly inadequate educational and health care opportunities that are provided for low-income, working-class, and middle-class families, the undocumented immigrants who are forced to fight for the same crumbs as other marginalized populations in the United States, or those who consistently try to minimize such services for others and decrease their own tax bills in the process?

And here is a related question: Who do you think benefits the most from the fact that so many of us do direct our anger over these realities toward immigrants?

The Spoils of Xenophobia

Back in 2009, a Republican state senator in Arizona named Russell Pearce had a problem. For five years in a row he had attempted to pass legislation that would have escalated the criminalization of undocumented immigrants, but each time he had been unable to garner enough votes. He realized that he needed something to push his bill over the hump, so he took it to ALEC. There, among the high-powered corporate titans who had been so influential in the rise of "tough on crime" criminal justice policies and school privatization, Pearce found the support he needed. In fact, Pearce got more than just support. ALEC proceeded to adopt his "No Sanctuary Cities for Illegal Immigrants Act" as one of its model bills in December 2009. One of Pearce's key champions within ALEC was the for-profit prison company Corrections Corporation of America (CCA) (now known as CoreCivic). CCA had identified immigrant detention as a profit center important for its future growth, speculating that "a significant portion" of its future revenues would come from detaining immigrants. This new model bill represented such a potential financial boon for CCA and others in the industry that after Pearce returned home to Arizona and introduced it in the Arizona legislature under a new name, thirty of the thirty-six legislators he had recruited to be cosponsors of the bill promptly received campaign contributions from for-profit prison companies.[59]

Shortly thereafter, in April 2010, Pearce finally got his victory. Owing in significant part to the endorsement of ALEC and the active and tacit support of its members, Arizona passed one of the most aggressively racist laws in modern US history, SB 1070 (which was described earlier).

To understand what motivated such efforts, it can be helpful to put yourself in the shoes of those represented by organizations like ALEC. Think of it this way: If you were an extraordinarily wealthy business executive or investor and you wanted to continue to maximize your own wealth, what would be the best possible set of immigration policies to serve your interests? You would want enough low-wage workers to handle all the various menial jobs that needed to be done, but not so many that there would be a surplus of people requiring various life-sustaining services that would have to be paid for with public dollars. You would also want all of those workers' lives to be unstable enough that they would be motivated to work hard and wouldn't be inclined to push back against any injustice they faced, engage in any activism, or otherwise rock the boat in any way. In other words, you would want to create the most favorable conditions possible for exploiting immigrants. Thus, you would be agreeable to, and even supportive of, federal, state, and local policies—such as SB 1070—that criminalize migrants and target them for mistreatment, so long as those policies didn't go so far as to drive away too many of the low-wage workers you desire. At the same time, you would want the federal government—which is charged with creating the overall structure of our immigration system—to keep undocumented families in limbo. You wouldn't want there to be a broadly accessible path to citizenship, which would eliminate much of your leverage over undocumented workers, but you also wouldn't want the type of mass deportation that hardcore nativists would prefer. Finally, you would want as many opportunities as possible to profit off the oppression and criminalization of immigrants that would ensue.

This is precisely the system that has been created over the past quarter century. Over that time, our immigration system has become remarkably aligned with the interests of the ultra-wealthy. Thus, while there has been widespread consensus for many years that a path to citizenship is urgently needed for undocumented immigrants, Congress has consistently failed to deliver. And that failure has the fingerprints of Corporate America and Wall Street all over it.

For example, outside of SB 1070 and the dozens of copycat laws that were introduced across the country (and were also based on ALEC's model bill), ALEC has adopted a number of other immigration-related model bills intended to shape both public policy and the public dialogue around the issue. Two examples:

- "Resolution against Amnesty": This bill explicitly urges Congress "to strongly oppose any legislation supporting amnesty or the granting of lawful status to any person that has entered or remained in the United States illegally."
- "Resolution to Enforce Our Immigration Laws and Secure Our Border": This ALEC bill would require states to eliminate "sanctuary policies" in order to combat the "illegal alien invasion" that, the bill alleges, has produced an increase in "violent crime, gangs, threat to public health, billions in cost to the taxpayer, [and] jobs taken from Americans."[60]

Additionally, some of the most ardent and influential opponents of immigration reform have been heavily funded by Corporate America and Wall Street donors. Among them is the Heritage Foundation, which, as profiled in previous chapters, has received millions of dollars from ultra-wealthy donors such as the Koch network and the Bradley Foundation. The Heritage Foundation has also received tens of millions of dollars from the Scaife family, which is the primary bankroller of numerous anti-immigrant organizations (using wealth that, as mentioned in chapter 3, comes primarily from the Mellon oil, aluminum, and banking fortune).[61] The Heritage Foundation has been actively opposing legislative efforts to provide a path to citizenship for undocumented individuals and has even put out a toolkit to assist like-minded members of the public.[62] Additionally, in 2013, while Congress was considering a comprehensive immigration reform proposal that included a path to citizenship, Heritage released a widely publicized report (written by someone who had previously argued in his doctoral dissertation that Latinx immigrants have lower IQs than the "white native population") strongly condemning such a step as a fiscally irresponsible approach.[63]

Of course, outside of the obvious influence of organizations like ALEC and the Heritage Foundation, a direct line cannot always be drawn between the ultra-wealthy and the profoundly harmful and racist immigration policies that have been enacted over the years. Political causes and effects are rarely so transparent. Nevertheless, some trends evident within the political process can be illustrative.

For example, ever since the early 1970s, when Corporate America and Wall Street executives began promoting their interests far more aggressively within the political process, primarily through enormous political contributions, their priorities have been increasingly reflected in political platforms, and particularly those of the Republican Party.[64] Up until that era, Republican presidential platforms had typically been supportive of liberal immigration policies and silent on issues related to the treatment of undocumented immigrants. Consider Dwight Eisenhower's 1956 presidential platform: "The Republican Party supports an immigration policy which is in keeping with the traditions of America in providing a haven for oppressed peoples, and which is based on equality of treatment, freedom from implications of discrimination between racial, nationality and religious groups, and flexible enough to conform to changing needs and conditions."[65] Considering the tenor of modern-day Republican rhetoric on immigration, reading this today is nothing short of jaw-dropping.

However, by 1972, Republicans had changed course, as illustrated by Richard Nixon's presidential platform that vowed to "increase our efforts to halt the illegal entry of aliens into the United States." Note, however, that in a nod to the interests of Corporate America, the platform still advocated for "selective admission of the specially talented."[66] Positions combining strict enforcement practices with business-friendly exceptions have been a consistent hallmark of Republican priorities ever since (though, notably, "illegal entry" has never come close to being halted).

Notice also that whenever any federal legislative efforts that would disrupt this status quo do progress, such as several recent efforts to provide a path to citizenship for undocumented immigrants, they have been consistently thwarted by those members of Congress who are remarkably well-funded by Corporate America and Wall Street executives. These individuals serve as the backstop against any efforts that would threaten the interests of the ultra-wealthy. For example, in recent years one of the most outspoken critics of so-called "amnesty" for undocumented residents has been Senator Ted Cruz (R-Texas). While his reasons for adopting this position are ultimately inscrutable, it takes very little investigation to notice that Senator Cruz's views on immigration matters seem to have evolved in direct relation to the tens of millions of dollars in contributions that he has collected from billionaire donors.[67]

Yet perhaps the most important piece of evidence against the ultra-wealthy is their collective silence on addressing this issue. They have never joined together as a group—as they have around dozens of other issues—to support a legalization process for undocumented immigrants. As a result, despite immigration being consistently highlighted as a key legislative priority by multiple presidents, much of Congress, and the general public, there has been no significant legislative action around immigration issues for decades.

Think about it: As a group, the ultra-wealthy have collectively invested unfathomable amounts of resources in the political process in order to influence policy making around a huge range of issues, and they have been remarkably successful at it. On every single area of public policy that has a direct impact on their economic interests, they exert enormous and often overwhelming influence.[68] Quite simply, if they had wanted the immigration system to be fixed, it would have been fixed. (Who would have stood in their way? Which organized political constituency would have had enough clout to stand up to Corporate America and all the other supporters of a path to citizenship? The small band of angry xenophobes? Not a chance.)

There is absolutely no reason to think that immigration is the one area of US policy in which these Corporate America and Wall Street executives haven't gotten their way. But instead of using their immense political muscle to create a more humane set of immigration policies, they have chosen instead to largely sit back and enjoy the enormous benefits our racist immigration system has provided them for many years.

So what are the benefits to this form of strategic racism? They are virtually identical to those that the ultra-wealthy enjoy as a result of the criminal justice policies described in chapter 3. Almost everything covered in that section (how mass criminalization has expanded opportunities for privatization, limited democratic action by promoting social control, reinforced the system of racial hierarchy, and so on) is also applicable to our anti-immigrant policies. Indeed, the wealth-generating effects of the criminal justice system are substantially broadened by our treatment of undocumented residents. By expanding the scope of our mass criminalization system to include the undocumented, we have also expanded the benefits that can be accrued from that system by the ultra-wealthy. In other words, the more people who are subject to criminalization and oppression, the more Corporate America and Wall Street executives profit.

While the full descriptions of how these types of policies benefit the ultra-wealthy won't be repeated here, there are some additional elements and subtle differences within the immigration context that are important to understand. Thus, here are some examples of additional ways in which the ultra-wealthy benefit from the persecution of migrants:

1. Generates Profits from the Privatization and Expansion of Immigration Enforcement

Just as in the criminal justice system, the mass criminalization and incarceration of immigrants creates a highly lucrative racism industrial complex. For-profit prison companies such as CoreCivic and the GEO Group are certainly a large part of that equation. These two corporations operate over 60 percent of all immigrant detention facilities, making them even more prominent in the immigration sector than they are in the criminal justice sector.[69] As CoreCivic predicted in relation to SB 1070, the expansion of immigrant detention has been highly profitable for private prison companies in recent years, and the extreme anti-immigrant policies of the Trump administration were great for business.[70]

For-profit companies have also invested heavily in alternatives to detention for immigrants, such as GPS monitoring through electronic ankle bracelets and "intensive supervision programs." Many of these programs are operated by Behavioral Interventions Incorporated and other subsidiaries of the GEO Group.[71]

Just as Wall Street has benefited extensively from the use of for-profit prisons and privatized "community corrections" within the criminal justice system, firms such as Wells Fargo, JPMorgan Chase, Bank of America, and BlackRock, among others, have profited greatly from these dynamics in the immigration enforcement context as well.[72] Additionally, when former President Trump promised to build a US–Mexico border wall, many of these companies positioned themselves to enjoy an additional windfall as it was constructed.[73]

Numerous Silicon Valley tech companies have also been enthusiastic partners with the federal government on these issues. For example, Microsoft, Palantir, Hewlett Packard Enterprise, Thomson Reuters, and Motorola all had active contracts with ICE as of 2018. Microsoft had a $19.4 million contract to help ICE develop its surveillance operations with data-processing and artificial-intelligence technology. Palantir, whose chairman is billionaire Peter Thiel (the cofounder of PayPal and the first outside investor in Facebook), had a $39 million contract to use its proprietary intelligence database to track immigrants' records and relationships. Hewlett Packard Enterprise had a $75 million contract with US Customs and Border Protection to manage their network operations center.[74]

In short, anti-immigrant policies have been a fertile cash cow for Corporate America and Wall Street.

2. Ensures a Large Supply of Cheap Labor

As has been discussed previously, Corporate America is on a never-ending search for strategies to reduce costs. For most companies, labor costs represent by far the largest component of their total expenses. Thus, large corporations are constantly on the lookout for ways to pay people less money to do the work that they need. Sometimes that results in relocating operations or outsourcing to other parts of the United States, or other parts of the world, where they can pay lower wages. Sometimes that results in using technology to eliminate jobs or hold employees accountable for completing their work at ever-increasing speeds. That almost always results in support of so-called "right to work" laws and opposition to labor unions. And for well over one hundred years, that has meant relying on workers who migrate across the US-Mexico border.[75]

US businesses have always sought out cheap bodies to fill the least desirable jobs and pad their bottom lines. Thus, from their perspective, a healthy supply of undocumented immigrants is invaluable. In fact, during many points in our history, there has been too little migration to serve their purposes, and they have supplemented the undocumented workforce with massive "guest worker" programs such as the Bracero Program, which resulted in two million Mexicans being recruited to work in the United States.[76] So if you ever go looking for a reason why the United States has, for decades, had such a deeply anti-Mexican public dialogue but has never actually closed down the US-Mexico border, you need look no further than the immense benefits that US corporations enjoy from having a consistent supply of easily exploitable foreign workers.

3. Generates Profits from Ultra-Cheap Labor in Immigrant Detention Centers

One of the arguments frequently made by the advocates for private prisons is that they are often cheaper to operate than their public counterparts. What rarely goes mentioned is that one of the reasons they are cheaper, and their profit margins are so great, is that—just like within the US prison system—they often force the immigrants detained inside to do the work required to operate the facility. In other words, rather than paying employees to prepare the food, clean the facility, do the laundry, and so on, many immigrant detention centers demand that the detainees themselves do those jobs, often for as little as one dollar a day, and sometimes for no pay at all.[77] At some facilities, detainees who refuse to work are threatened with solitary confinement and the withholding of basic necessities like food and soap.[78]

In other words, we are now incarcerating hundreds of thousands of people every year for the "crime" of wanting to improve their quality of life—a crime that US businesses frequently aid and abet—and then, while they are in captivity, we force them to work for little to no money so that for-profit prisons and their investors can increase their profit margins. (Of all the ways in which our mass criminalization and incarceration systems have created modern-day parallels to slave plantations, none may be more disconcertingly close to the mark than this.)

4. Provides a Cheaper Alternative to Meeting People's Basic Human Needs

To humanize people who are unfamiliar to you, to fully recognize their humanity and how they are fundamentally equal to yourself and all other people, isn't easy. It requires that we not only value their lives appropriately but that we also recognize what they need to lead good, full lives. That means we have to be able to look at ourselves in the mirror and acknowledge that just as we need high-quality education, health care, housing, and the other basic building blocks of a happy, healthy life, so too do all other people. That also means that we must recognize that the failure to ensure that all people have their basic needs met is unjust. Then, just as you would expect others to object to injustice committed against you, in order to demonstrate full respect for the humanity of others you must be willing to stand up against injustice committed against them. Thus, true humanization requires that we take some responsibility for each other's well-being.

The dehumanization of someone, however, is far simpler. When the public can be convinced that a person, or group of people, is less worthy of having the same opportunities to thrive that the rest of us enjoy, then it becomes quite easy to abdicate any responsibility for that person's, or that group's, well-being. That is why so many of the right-wing think tanks and advocacy organizations funded by the Koch network and other ultra-wealthy individuals—such as the Heritage Foundation and the Cato Foundation—invest so much time and energy in disparaging low-income and working-class people and place such an enormous emphasis on "personal responsibility." If other people's struggles are seen as their own fault, then the collective capacity to recognize the roots of injustice and then address them diminishes considerably. Such ideas have been critically important to establishing an intellectual foundation for systemic racism, including the long-standing undereducation and overcriminalization of black and brown communities discussed earlier.

So it is with regard to our treatment of undocumented immigrants as well. They have been so thoroughly dehumanized in much of the public's eyes that it has become difficult to discern if there are even any limits to the injustices we are willing to heap upon them. Plus, the multitude of anti-immigrant laws passed in Arizona and elsewhere throughout the country made it crystal clear that there is no widespread sense of responsibility for the well-being of undocumented individuals. On the contrary, these laws send the unmistakable message that "we" don't want to invest in, or be accountable for, "them." They draw a line in the sand signaling that "our" resources are for "us" and us alone, and not the millions of undocumented immigrants who will suffer as a result of these laws.

Not only is it disturbingly easy to dehumanize millions of people, from the perspective of many of the most influential shapers of public policy it is also cheaper than the alternative. If the public doesn't care that an undocumented immigrant is receiving a poor-quality education or being paid a substandard wage, then imposing such inequities becomes, from a certain (morally vacuous) perspective, a valuable cost-cutting approach. (This also explains why the conditions in immigrant detention centers are so abysmal—perhaps even worse than they are in our jails and prisons.)[79]

Thus, the main beneficiaries of this approach are once again the ultra-wealthy, as they have the most to gain from reducing public spending and the most to lose if we did recognize our common humanity with undocumented residents and assumed collective responsibility for ensuring their basic human needs are met.

5. Limits Democratic Action through Social Control

While the US criminal justice system has effectively quashed many positive social change efforts and created a more docile and compliant population, that pales in comparison to how our array of federal, state, and local immigration policies has affected our immigrant population. It has long been the case in the United States that undocumented immigrants were expected to simply do the jobs they are given and otherwise neither be seen nor heard. What ICE's hyperaggressive enforcement actions and laws like SB 1070 have done is dramatically increase the threat to any migrants who aren't so submissive. The end result is that our immigration policies have ensured that millions of people will be too fearful and traumatized to ever stick their necks out to demand the type of justice that would challenge the existing power structure.

6. Impedes Racial and Class Solidarity

Just as issues of crime have effectively pitted communities against each other, so too has immigration been used to breed resentment against undocumented immigrants among US-born low-income and working-class people, in particular. This becomes quite easy to do when there is severe underinvestment in low-income communities and a lack of commitment to meeting the needs of all people, as there is across the United States. A critical element of that systemic neglect is that employment opportunities and public services are often treated as zero-sum competitions, meaning that any progress made by immigrants can seem to, and in many cases actually does, result in losses for other residents. Even when there are no such direct causal effects, if people are struggling to survive, the perception that "their gain is our loss" can easily take hold. Within such an environment, where people are put into direct competition around the means of survival, anti-immigrant rhetoric and action will almost invariably find a welcoming audience.

This tactic of pitting the newcomers against the "native population" has perhaps the longest history of any wedge issue in the United States, dating back to the early colonial period.[80] It has been especially popular during any economic downturn. The idea is simple: if low-income, working-class, and middle-class people are fighting each other, then they are less likely to come together and direct their anger at those who are most responsible for their common plight.

7. Preserves the System of Racial Hierarchy

Just as the US criminal justice system has substantially reinforced the subordination of African Americans and other US-born people of color, our various anti-immigrant policies have virtually ensured that immigrant communities will be unable to advance socially, economically, and politically. It is simply impossible for the residents of a community to avoid becoming an underclass when the oppression they face is so overwhelming that they become afraid to even leave their homes. And, obviously, the more difficult it is for those who occupy the lower strata of our racial hierarchy to advance, the more benefits there are for those who occupy the upper strata.

8. Helps Their Preferred Political Candidates Win Elections

The tough-on-immigrants approach has been perhaps even more valuable to the ultra-wealthy than tough-on-crime criminal justice policies were in attracting a voter base that could win elections for corporate-friendly candidates. The most obvious example is the presidential campaign of Donald Trump. One of the key pillars of his campaign involved stoking anti-immigrant sentiment and promising to build a wall on the US-Mexico border. Yet by far the most noteworthy legislative initiative of his first year in office had nothing to do with immigration but rather involved passing massive tax cuts that overwhelmingly benefit the ultra-wealthy.[81]

The politics around immigration have now become so extreme that, on the Republican side, policy makers are seemingly competing with each other to see who can be the most strenuously anti-immigrant, and there is almost no support for any humane immigration policies.[82] On the Democratic side, the dynamics have been remarkably similar to what happened with criminal justice policy. Starting with the Clinton administration and then continuing on during the Obama administration, the Democratic Party has largely followed in the anti-immigrant footsteps of its political rivals out of fear that being labeled "soft on immigration" will have the same effect as being labeled "soft on crime."[83] Thus, the two primary political parties have effectively been working in concert over the past twenty-five years to create the thoroughly vicious environment that undocumented immigrants experience today.

Bidding Farewell to All Members of the Crow Family

It wasn't that long ago that it was lawful in the United States to treat people differently on the basis of their race. Jim Crow segregation was permissible, it was said, because African Americans were fundamentally different from white Americans. Thankfully, we don't do that anymore. We have decided that creating legal distinctions solely on the basis of someone's race is barbaric and beneath us. We like to think that we have evolved beyond such glaring bigotry as a society. However, the reality is that we have simply moved from discriminating on the basis of race and ethnicity to discriminating on the basis of national origin and immigration status *combined* with race and ethnicity. Plus, while we no longer try to justify Jim Crow by making the case that white people and black people are intrinsically different, there is no shortage of those who will defend "Juan Crow" discrimination by claiming that "illegals" are fundamentally different from Americans. One of them happens to have been the forty-fifth president of the United States.[84]

The fact is that there is very little difference between our current federal, state, and local Juan Crow policies and the Jim Crow system of the early twentieth century, beyond the fact that one legalizes discrimination on the basis of where one was born and the other legalized discrimination based on where one's ancestors were born. Yet whereas Jim Crow represents, for most of us, an embarrassing chapter of our history, the Juan Crow story is still being written, and there appears to be very little embarrassment about what it contains. On the contrary, Donald Trump was elected in significant part on a promise to pick up a pen and write a chapter himself.

Quite simply, we have to be better than this. We, like all people, want to believe that we live in a great country. However, there can be no greatness alongside such disgracefulness. They are incompatible. We cannot claim to be superior to any other country when we treat the people of those countries as if they were inferior to us.

Fortunately, our wrongs can easily be corrected. We can put ourselves on a different path, one that is more compatible with the values for which we claim to stand. Liberty. Equality. Family. These need not be merely the foundation for meaningless political rhetoric or Hollywood movies. We can rediscover these values in ways that have real meaning and that can elevate us all to higher ground. But that requires that we listen closely to those communities that have been most affected by our anti-immigrant policies, as they are in the best position to educate us on how we have gone astray from our core values and how we can reconnect to them.[85] Here are four recommendations that have emerged from those communities:

Solution 1: Eliminating Juan Crow Discrimination

This should be easy. The fact that there is even a debate about the righteousness of our systemic discrimination against undocumented residents speaks to how morally bankrupt our politics have become. There are really only a few options with regard to how we treat the millions of undocumented people who have decided to make the United States their home: (a) we maintain the status quo and continue to force them to live in the shadows as inferior members of our society; (b) we forcibly deport them, creating unimaginable human suffering; or (c) we legalize their status and start treating them like full-fledged members of the United States who can openly contribute to their communities, enjoy all our country has to offer, and live their lives in peace. That should be just about the easiest multiple choice question any of us has ever had to answer, and yet it has proved to be too difficult for our policy makers thus far. Far too many of them, both Republican and Democrat, have treated the lives of undocumented people as little more than political bargaining chips to be used to extract concessions from the other side of the aisle or score cheap political points.

This reckless disregard for people's basic humanity has to stop. The Juan Crow system, and all the various federal, state, and local laws that uphold it and allow discrimination against undocumented persons, needs to be systematically dismantled. Second, US immigration policy must also open up more paths of legal immigration for people of color around the world, particularly for family members of US residents who have encountered disproportionate barriers to being with their loved ones.[86] Third, those who have been separated from their families in recent years through needless deportations should be allowed to return. Fourth, as we construct the path to legalization for undocumented residents, unlike many of the comprehensive immigration reform proposals that have been discussed, but not passed, in Congress over the years, there shouldn't be exclusions for those who have been needlessly caught up in our Criminalization Trap. Fifth, unlike many previous efforts, the path to legalization also shouldn't be made contingent on the implementation of heightened border security measures or any other issue that is immaterial to the urgent needs of current US residents.

Finally, contrary to what has been included in previous reform proposals, there shouldn't be any onerous fines, fees, or administrative procedures involved in the legalization process, as they would only serve to limit access to legal status and thus perpetuate the problem. While there are those who demand that we impose these sorts of penalties as the pound of flesh for the "wrongs" committed by undocumented residents, at this point, the wrongs committed by the US government in this area vastly exceed those committed by those who seek to legalize their status. Thus, instead of focusing on the penance to be paid for these supposed wrongs, we should, at long last, simply do what's right.

Solution 2: Do No Harm

Just as the US criminal justice system should adopt a "do no harm" approach (as discussed in chapter 3), so too should the immigration enforcement system. The same principles should apply regardless of someone's country of origin. Simply put, the US government shouldn't be in the business of inflicting avoidable harm on people and making millions of people feel unsafe through cruel policies. Yet we have routinely acted in ways that have been devastating to individuals, families, and entire communities without any reasonable justification.

Here are some examples of what a "do no harm" approach to immigration enforcement would entail:[87]

- ICE would be abolished. US tax dollars shouldn't be going toward immigration shock troops whose primary purpose is to target, imprison, and exile people.
- Migration wouldn't be treated as a criminal act. There are innumerable ways to address the challenges of migration without criminalizing migrants for crossing the border and thus adding immigration enforcement to the long list of issues that have been inappropriately tasked to the criminal justice system.
- Criminal justice violations would not be used to justify the deportation of those who have made their home in the United States. Consistent with the more narrowly tailored role of law enforcement agencies outlined in the last chapter, the functions of the criminal justice system shouldn't become confused with those of the immigration system. Thus, even if there is a serious criminal act committed by an undocumented resident of the United States, it can be addressed just as any similar infraction committed by a US citizen would be addressed. There is no need to potentially cause exponentially greater harm—such as by breaking up a family—through the imposition of immigration consequences like deportation.
- We would eliminate all immigrant detention centers. Just as US citizens shouldn't be kept in cages unless there are no other acceptable alternatives to protect others from an imminent threat of serious harm, the same holds true for migrants. Even in the rare circumstances in which that condition was met, once again there is no reason why we would need a separate incarceration infrastructure beyond the prisons and jails within the criminal justice system.

- We would not under any circumstances be incarcerating children and youth who migrate here.
- The US-Mexico border would be demilitarized. The vast majority of individuals attempting to cross into the United States are doing so because they are suffering in their home country and are desperate for a better quality of life. They are also often severely physically compromised from the journey across the desert. It doesn't speak well of our country that they are then greeted by a heavily fortified border patrolled by a massive force of armed and often hyperaggressive officers who have been trained to treat the border area as a war zone. Thus, rather than welcoming migrants with fences, guns, and surveillance cameras, our response should be to provide them with the humanitarian aid they need to be safe before ever delving into the various issues of residency and legal status.
- US employers wouldn't be allowed to exploit undocumented workers and other immigrants. While we have been hypervigilant and punitive with regard to the alleged transgressions of immigrants, far too often we have ignored employers who have taken advantage of vulnerable undocumented workers and guest workers to pay them substandard wages, subject them to deplorable and abusive working conditions, and often fail to even pay them what they are owed.

An immigration enforcement system that committed to do no harm would lead to far less criminalization and incarceration, far less violence, far fewer deaths, and far more humane treatment toward millions of thoroughly marginalized undocumented immigrants. It would also free up considerable resources that are currently being misused to implement tough-on-immigrants policies but could instead be repurposed for more admirable and effective initiatives.

Solution 3: Reinvestment

Rather than investing taxpayer dollars in the criminalization and deportation of migrants, we could be allocating those funds to addressing many of our most urgent education, economic, health, and housing needs. For example, if we were to roll back our immigration enforcement spending to what it was in the mid-1970s, that would save nearly $28 billion per year that could be used to address far more urgent priorities. Just imagine how much good could be done with those resources that are currently causing so much pain and suffering. As just one possibility, we could be using those resources to invest $1 billion annually in comprehensive community development strategies within twenty-eight of the immigrant communities across the United States that have been most harmed by anti-immigrant policies over the years. Alongside the life-altering direct effects of such an initiative, the positive ripple effects would be staggering, producing benefits for all US residents. Some of the resources could also be leveraged to not only address the needs of those who have migrated, but the causes of their migration as well.

Solution 4: Responsible Global Citizenship

There are many US residents who favor closing the borders. They want to make America an impenetrable fortress. Others, including many economists, argue for relatively open borders so that people can move as freely across nations as capital is allowed to move. They point out that this is already how much of the world operates.[88] Wherever one might fall on that spectrum, hopefully we can all agree on two things: (1) people should always be able to move when their health, safety, or even their very survival depends on it; and (2) we can no longer tolerate, and even exacerbate, severe global inequality and then be surprised when migrants show up at our borders.

Far too often we act like a schoolyard bully trying to take as much for ourselves as we can while disregarding the well-being of everyone around us. But if our foreign policy continues to support repressive governments across Latin America and the Caribbean while also destabilizing governments that propose to tackle long-standing social, economic, and political inequities, then we can expect mass migration to continue. If our trade agreements and other economic policies continue to allow US corporations to exploit people around the world, then mass migration will continue. If the United States doesn't make a far more concerted effort to raise the standard of living within neighboring countries, then mass migration will continue.

The United States has been on a long crusade to achieve global economic, political, and military dominance, and however one might feel about that approach, it must be recognized that the long lines of immigrants at our borders are, in many ways, a consequence of it.

Simply put, we have to start playing nicer in the sandbox. While we cannot, by ourselves, eliminate global inequality, we can make substantial inroads in reducing such inequities by becoming more invested in the well-being of our Latin American and Caribbean neighbors.[89] The more we can help those nations thrive, the less reason their residents will have to uproot their lives and take the uncertain and often dangerous journey to the United States. Thus, in the future, however and whenever we decide to allow people from around the world into the United States, we can make it far more likely that migrants come here because they want to, and less likely that they do it because they have to.

One of the most common questions asked of all people who were alive during a major human rights violation perpetrated by their government is some version of "How could you have let it happen?" It was asked of Germans alive in the 1940s, it was asked of white Americans alive during the era of legalized slavery, and one day it will be asked of us because of our treatment of undocumented immigrants. There is no avoiding that at this point. All that is left to determine is what comes next. Will we allow this institutionalized cruelty and discrimination to continue? Will we replace one form of oppression with another, the way slavery was replaced with Jim Crow? Or will the history books report that we finally reached the point where we stopped making deeply harmful distinctions based on characteristics like immigration status and instead we began to discover just how much shared prosperity could be achieved once we recognized that all of our lives have equal value?

DEFEATING GOLIATH

As we have explored in the previous three chapters, the ultra-wealthy have been instrumental in developing and advancing the education, criminal justice, and immigration policies that continue to oppress people of color on a massive scale. However, their strategic racism is certainly not limited to those three systems. We could conduct the same type of analysis around low-wage labor, environmental degradation, health care inequities, voter suppression, and numerous other issues. What we would find in each case is a similar story: a small group of racism profiteers has been aggressively implementing an agenda that, while enormously beneficial for them, has been devastating to communities of color.[1]

The tyranny of the ultra-wealthy hasn't been limited to just domestic issues either. Consider how we have chosen to use, and dramatically expand, our military and national security apparatus. No matter how old you are, the United States has been at war for at least a substantial portion, or even a majority, of your lifetime.[2] Indeed, there are currently college students who have never known a world in which the United States wasn't engaged in a war. The United States now has around eight hundred military bases around the globe, and we spend more on our military than any other country in the world. In fact, our military budget is roughly the same size as the combined military budgets of the next seven countries on the list.[3] While we like to think of ourselves as a force for peace and democracy around the globe, because of our propensity toward perpetual war and aggressive military involvement, the rest of the world tends not to share that perspective. Instead, multiple opinion polls of people around the world, taken over many years, have found that the United States is perceived as the greatest threat to world peace of any country.[4] (In other words, for anyone who has ever seen *Star Wars* and rooted for the Rebel Alliance against the evil and tyrannical Empire, it is worth reflecting on the fact that from the perspective of much of the world, *we* are the Empire.)

None of this is new, of course. In his famous "Vietnam Speech" in 1967, Martin Luther King Jr. made the case for linking the civil rights movement to the antiwar movement by stating, "I knew that I could never again raise my voice against the violence of the oppressed in the ghettos without having first spoken clearly to the greatest purveyor of violence in the world today: my own government." What Dr. King recognized is that our militarism abroad is thoroughly intertwined with our systemic racism here at home, and even worse, we have obviously prioritized investments in the former over addressing the latter. ("I knew that America would never invest the necessary funds or energies in rehabilitation of its poor so long as adventures like Vietnam continued to draw men and skills and money like some demonic destructive suction tube.")[5] Those dynamics have only deepened over time, such that our annual defense spending is now over $316 billion more than it was during the mid-1970s (after adjusting for inflation).[6] And in 2016, $630 billion of our federal discretionary spending went toward the military, but only $183 billion went toward education, housing, jobs, health care, and other antipoverty programs.[7]

Additionally, we all have to recognize that the ideology used to defend the harming of US residents through mass criminalization is the same as that which is used to defend our militarism and the harming of people abroad. The so-called war on terror that we have been fighting for twenty years is essentially our "tough on crime" criminal justice approach applied to the people of other countries. It is, in many ways, the Criminalization Trap: International Version. It should also be noted that, just as in our domestic version, most of the people who are harmed by our military policies—including both our soldiers and the citizens of other countries around the world—are people of color.

Plus, as with the issues discussed in previous chapters, perhaps the biggest winners from the use of military aggression to expand US power overseas have been the ultra-wealthy.[8] They are the primary beneficiaries of all the new markets, expanded markets, and international access and influence that our military interventions have provided. The ultra-wealthy have also engaged in rampant profiteering off the privatization of national security functions, mirroring the dynamics around the privatization of education, criminal justice, and immigration enforcement.[9] In short, our hyperaggressive use of the military has been, much like the other issues covered earlier, a key wealth accumulation strategy for Corporate America and Wall Street.[10] (It should come as little surprise that large defense contractors like Northrop Grumman and Boeing were early members of ALEC.)[11]

This again demonstrates that while the primary target of the unjust policies being advanced by the ultra-wealthy has been people of color, they certainly haven't been the only target. Just as white Americans suffer the effects of underinvestment in education and overinvestment in criminalization, so too do they suffer when the ultra-wealthy are able to implement such an extreme anti-worker, anti-environment, anti-health-care-reform, anti-democracy, and pro-military agenda. While these are all racial justice issues, they are also responsible for many of the most significant challenges faced by white Americans. In other words, racial justice issues are "white issues" too. The overall effects on white folks aren't identical to, or as severe as, the effects on people of color, but they are real and they are significant. And whether we choose to admit it or not, they demonstrate clearly that the interests of low-income, working-class, and middle-class white people and people of color are aligned and that we all have much to gain by working together to defeat the ultra-wealthy agenda.

The Nightmare Scenario

It is difficult to imagine any greater threats that our population could face than the challenges outlined previously. It is indeed a scary time. The only thing scarier is that the ultra-wealthy are seemingly not content with dominating US policy making within Congress, the White House, and at the state and local levels in order to advance their own interests. What should be truly frightening is that they are attempting to reshape the "supreme law of the land" to ensure that their agenda is forever enshrined as our national system of values and priorities.

There are currently two efforts being led and financed by ALEC, the Koch network, and other billionaires and multimillionaires that propose to make substantial changes to, and perhaps completely rewrite, the US Constitution. They are attempting to convene an Article V constitutional convention, which is one of two methods outlined within the Constitution for making changes to its contents. It has never been done before (unlike the second method—the amendment process—which has been done successfully seventeen times). To convene a constitutional convention, thirty-four states must pass resolutions through their state legislatures calling for such a convention. Regardless of what the stated purpose of these resolutions is and how narrowly they are framed, constitutional scholars have long warned that if a convention is called, there will be virtually nothing to prevent a "runaway convention," or an expansion of the scope of the convention to completely rewrite the Constitution.[12] In short, once the contents of the Constitution are opened up, everything could be up for grabs.

There have been right-wing efforts to call such a constitutional convention for decades. However, owing to the investment and support these efforts have received from the ultra-wealthy, they have escalated dramatically in recent years. Indeed, there is a significant likelihood that one of them will be successful in convening a constitutional convention within the near future.

The most advanced is the effort to call a constitutional convention around a "balanced budget amendment" (BBA). As of April 2020, backers had already secured twenty-eight states, leaving them just six short of the thirty-four needed, with at least another eight states that are actively considering proposals to join the effort.[13] ALEC has been a key driving force behind this effort. It has produced three model resolutions for states to pass, done extensive behind-the-scenes work to push states to pass these resolutions, actively recruited state legislators to join its effort, and even begun drafting proposed rules for when and if such a convention does occur.[14]

Another effort, which is more recent but expanding quickly, is from an organization called Convention of States (COS). Thus far, fifteen states have passed the COS resolution since 2014, another seven states have passed it within one legislative chamber, and an additional fourteen state legislatures were actively considering it in 2020.[15] COS is very well funded, having received millions of dollars in recent years from the Koch network and affiliated organizations, as well as other prominent Republican donors such as the Mercer family. There are also extensive ties to the Koch network and ALEC within COS leadership, including former Heritage Foundation president and US senator Jim DeMint. The COS effort has generated so much momentum and excitement within certain circles that supporters even held a mock convention in 2016 to come up with proposed amendments to the Constitution.[16]

The stated justifications for these two efforts are to limit federal spending and federal power, both of which tend to be effective talking points with the great many people who—justifiably—don't feel like Congress and the White House have traditionally served their needs very well. However, let's be clear: the primary purpose of these efforts to convene an Article V convention is to create a US Constitution that better serves the interests of the ultra-wealthy at the expense of the overwhelming majority of US residents. First, to believe otherwise would require that we ignore the well-established track record of the primary supporters and organizers of these efforts.[17] Second, the types of limits on federal spending and power that are included in these Article V resolutions would, if implemented, clear the path for Corporate America and Wall Street to implement even more of their agenda (including the Doctrine of Corporate Greed discussed earlier) and would thus be disastrous for low-income, working-class, and middle-class people. Third, if the Constitution were opened up entirely, the possibilities would become even more terrifying. All the policies that are favored by the ultra-wealthy and that they have been so successful in getting passed through state legislatures and Congress could be formalized and protected within the Constitution. This would be devastating for virtually all US residents. And, again, this is a very real possibility *as early as this year*.

Time to Circle the Wagons

We all desperately need to understand the gravity of the threat posed by the ultra-wealthy to the rest of us. The constitutional convention effort, alongside their other policy reform efforts described earlier, demonstrate that they are going for the political jugular, nothing less than a radical reshaping of our laws and policies to fully align with their agenda. Though the adherents to this vision may be few in number, they are strategic, they are methodical, and they are of course extraordinarily well funded. In 2016, the Koch network alone employed sixteen hundred paid staffers across thirty-five states, all dedicated to advancing their agenda.[18]

This isn't to say, however, that their victory is inevitable. The ultra-wealthy *can* be stopped. We *can* reverse the damage their agenda has already wrought and begin to craft policies that truly meet the needs of all our people. But the question is: How does David beat Goliath?

There is much that is going to be required to get out of this mess, but if we had to boil down what we need most into just one word, it would be democracy.

In order to move away from a government that is overwhelmingly controlled by Corporate America and Wall Street executives, there is, unfortunately, no simple policy solution. There is no magic bullet that will address the plutocracy we have created. Those individuals will certainly not give up their power willingly, nor will our policy makers be willing or able to solve the problem unless they are made to by their constituents. Thus, the only solution is for more people to get involved and demand something different. In other words, we need more democracy, and lots of it. This isn't the kind of democracy that involves showing up for elections and then tuning out until the next election and hoping that our elected representatives do a good job. Hopefully it is obvious by now that we cannot depend on the benevolent paternalism of the ultra-wealthy or the politicians they fund so heavily to meet the needs of low-income, working-class, and middle-class people. No, the type of democracy that is needed involves ongoing, active participation by far more people in far more ways than perhaps we have ever had before. It entails diverse groups of people from all sorts of backgrounds and walks of life coming together to make their communities stronger. It demands a collective recognition that to solve community problems most effectively, and to make sure that public resources are being used in alignment with community needs and priorities, we need many more voices at the table than we have currently. And it requires that communities are actively holding policy makers accountable for their actions (and inactions).

There may be nothing more threatening to the ultra-wealthy than this type of participatory government. From the very beginning of US history, the ruling class has sought to limit democracy, not expand it. The affluent and politically powerful members of our society have always been afraid of what would happen if the rest of us ever activated our enormous—yet largely latent—political power around our common interests. For example, in the debates that produced the US Constitution, James Madison—aka the "Father of the Constitution"—argued that the major concern of any society has to be to protect "the minority of the opulent against the majority." That is why the original US Constitution rested so much power in the members of the Senate, who were, at that time, unelected appointees of state legislatures (and were largely wealthy white men).[19] It is also why we have an Electoral College that can select a president who lost the popular vote. These antidemocratic tendencies have continued to this day, with campaign finance rules that allow the ultra-wealthy to dominate political giving, numerous restrictions on voting, and political processes that are generally inaccessible for most people, among many other strategies for limiting the political participation of low-income, working-class, and middle-class people.

The primary justification for the various antidemocratic measures that have been implemented has always been that the general public couldn't be trusted to act in the best interests of the country, that the wealthy would be more responsible protectors of our national interests. However, I suspect that this rationale is inconsistent with most readers' experiences. It certainly has been with mine. Most of my career has involved assisting groups of community members of various races, ethnicities, socioeconomic levels, and backgrounds to come together and address community problems. I have found that when they are provided the factual information they need and the opportunity to work collaboratively, communities have a remarkable ability to solve even the most difficult of problems. Plus, the collective wisdom of low-income, working-class, and middle-class people produces far more humane results than the policies advocated by the ultra-wealthy. In fact, most of the community-based groupings I have worked with were formed only because of the need to address the devastation that had been caused by the ultra-wealthy and their favored policies.

So how do we create a government that is truly "of the people, by the people, and for the people"? First, it will require an army. Not a violent, military-style army, but an army of people committed to participatory democracy, justice, and equality. An army of people who recognize the immense power of collective action. An army of people who refuse to be pitted against each other on the basis of race, ethnicity, national origin, or any other demographic characteristic.

The reason I say that an army is needed is that, whether we like it or not, we are in a fight. The ultra-wealthy have been taking that fight to us for decades, so the only question is whether or not we decide to fight back and demand that they end their assault on the greater good so that we can all find a better way forward together.

To be clear, the type of army I am referring to isn't one that is centered on any particular political party. While there are those who say that the path forward is through the Democratic Party, note that in all three examples of systemic racism discussed in previous chapters—within our education, criminal justice, and immigration systems—what started out as far-right and Republican priorities were subsequently embraced by Democrats as well. Thus, relying on that or any other political party as the primary means of advancing racial justice would be unwarranted, to say the least.

Similarly, there are a great many people who resist the notion that we face an adversarial situation with regard to the ultra-wealthy. They insist that the path forward is to collaborate and find common ground with the Corporate America and Wall Street executives who are responsible for the conditions we face. Included within this group are the many politicians who determine their own positions on issues by seeing which way the wind is blowing at any given moment. They stick their fingers in the air, and whichever direction they feel the breeze heading, that is the direction they go. What they don't know is that, most often, the ultra-wealthy are out of eyesight with a giant fan.

What we all must recognize is that there is no relief to be found from compromising with those who promote, or are indifferent to, your destruction. Or, as Malcolm X put it, "If you stick a knife in my back nine inches and pull it out six inches, there's no progress. If you pull it all the way out that's not progress. Progress is healing the wound that the blow made. And they haven't even pulled the knife out much less heal the wound."[20] Thus, merely following the direction of wind that has been created in large part by the ultra-wealthy will never produce the results we need. Instead of following the wind, we need to get to work in shifting the wind by creating our own gusts. We need low-income, working-class, and middle-class people of all races and ethnicities to come together around real, transformative change. This doesn't mean that everyone has to all of a sudden become politically active, but we do need enough of a critical mass of change makers that, in the future, whenever policy makers decide to stick a finger in the air and check the wind, they will notice that it is blowing in a far more just direction.

In short, we need to build stronger, multiracial mass movements.

The Movement Moment

There are many misconceptions about how social change actually happens. One particularly popular one is that change happens as a result of charismatic leaders or random acts of individual courage. Thus, within our sound-bite versions of history, we typically mythologize or romanticize individuals such as Martin Luther King Jr., Cesar Chavez, and Rosa Parks. While these individuals' place within the pantheon of our greatest social justice leaders is unquestionable, focusing such a disproportionate amount of attention on them as individuals does a great disservice to the massive social movements that were built around them. It was only because tens of thousands, hundreds of thousands, or even millions of others devoted some portion of themselves to these collective efforts that they were able to succeed and the leaders of those efforts became household names.

While there are many ways to create social change, by far the most effective way to create transformative and sustainable change is through grassroots-led social movements. This is true now, and it has always been true. To illustrate, think about every issue area in which we have seen significant, progressive social change over the years. What they all had in common is that each had been the subject of strong nationwide grassroots organizing, activism, and communications efforts for many years prior to policy makers taking action. Meaningful change didn't just come out of nowhere. Our political leaders didn't just decide one day to magnanimously implement dramatic policy changes. In all cases, there was a long-term, collective effort to apply the kind of political pressure needed, and to change public opinion enough, that the government ultimately felt compelled to respond.

Thus, when we think about how we can turn the tide on the political agenda being advanced by the ultra-wealthy, our strategy should reflect that history. Here is one formulation of such a "theory of change": *Transformative and sustainable social change occurs when those who are most directly impacted by oppression take collective action, lead their own social movements, and build power with other impacted individuals to change the conditions that produce their oppression.*[21]

What does it mean to "build power"? In this context, it refers to the ability to shape the world in ways that match your priorities. Currently, despite being few in number, the ultra-wealthy have far more ability to shape the agenda around education, criminal justice, and immigration issues, as well as all the other issues discussed previously. While this is profoundly unfortunate and unjust, it shouldn't be discouraging. Just as David prevailed against Goliath, so can we if we are strategic and intentional about building solidarity with each other.

For example, if the low-income, working-class, and middle-class people of all races who are currently active politically were all pulling in the same direction and were able to aggregate their power, the public policies of the United States would be dramatically different, and far more just, than the ones we have currently. On top of that, there are massive, largely untapped sources of grassroots power all across the country, especially within communities that are currently marginalized politically or that haven't traditionally been active on racial justice issues. Effectively engaging those communities represents the key to dramatically expanding our collective power and allowing us to create a system in which resources and decision-making power are allocated equitably across the population.[22] (After all, the goal isn't for roles to be reversed and the oppressed to all of a sudden become the oppressors. The goal is justice, not an inverted form of injustice.)

Of course, this is also why divide-and-conquer strategies have such appeal for the ultra-wealthy. If they can pit white people against people of color, middle-class people against low-income and working-class people, African Americans against Latinx people, and so on, then our collective power becomes diffuse. We become so consumed with interracial and interclass conflict that we are unable to consolidate our existing power or build new power. Ultimately, we become far less than the sum of our parts. Thus, we squander our capacity to mount an effective opposition to the ultra-wealthy and never reach our full potential as a unified group.

Plus, the reality is that if you analyze where power lies with regard to these large, systemic problems, no matter how you do the math, there is no scenario under which a US populace that is so thoroughly divided by race and class will be able to build enough power to win those fights. We simply won't be able to get there. The power imbalances are simply too great, and the ultra-wealthy have demonstrated many times over that they will devote extraordinary resources to defend these systems that have been so profoundly beneficial for them. Thus, the primary purpose of forming a unified, multiracial force isn't so that we can all join together and bask in our collective "wokeness." It's a necessity to overcome the extraordinarily well-financed effort to uphold the thoroughly unjust system that affects all of us. It's how we win.

While there are always a multitude of voices out there suggesting that this type of movement building is impossible, or that it is a waste of time to even try, the reality is that these kinds of unified, grassroots efforts are being formed constantly in ways that both prevent the worst abuses of the ultra-wealthy and move our country forward. There are innumerable examples of this throughout history, including the creation of Social Security, Medicare, and the rest of the social safety net; winning forty-hour workweeks and other labor protections; ending Jim Crow segregation and various other racial justice victories; and passing the Nineteenth Amendment and numerous other advances in women's rights, among many, many others. We need not look to the distant past for examples of these dynamics in action, either. In the past ten years, there have been strategic mass movements that have passed living-wage policies, expanded the rights of undocumented youth, advanced marriage equality, raised awareness of workplace sexual harassment and sexual assault against women, and begun to dismantle the school-to-prison pipeline, among many other important victories. Plus, every day, in communities across the country, there are people coming together to solve a wide variety of problems in powerful and authentically democratic ways. These stories aren't told very often, and even when some attention is given to them, the real story about how those changes came about is almost never discussed. But they are out there, and they can show us the way forward.

And here's the exciting part: While there is no denying that the challenges we face in defeating the ultra-wealthy agenda are substantial, there are no limits to what can be accomplished once we start to embrace multiracial, grassroots movement-building strategies. There are no problems too large or intractable once we begin to play with all the pieces on the chessboard. There are no unwinnable advocacy campaigns. For every system of oppression in existence, there is far more than enough latent grassroots power to dismantle it. All that is required is that we join together and be strategic about building the power needed, and the possibilities for building a more just and equitable society become endless.

Calling All White People

Fortunately, there is a great foundation upon which to build such movements. All across the country, there is more organizing, activism, and coalition building under way than we have seen in decades. That is not to say that there aren't some complexities involved, however. The most significant of them involves the role of white people. To win this fight, large numbers of us are going to have to come to terms with the reality that modern-day systemic racism is, in significant part, our fault.

Obviously, the ultra-wealthy are disproportionately responsible for the racial injustice described in previous chapters. However, they couldn't have succeeded in their efforts without their predominantly white group of minions. Whether we want to admit it or not, white Americans carry a great deal of responsibility for millions of people of color suffering from education inequities, mass criminalization and incarceration, dehumanizing immigration policies, and numerous other injustices. It is our votes that are overwhelmingly responsible for translating the priorities of the ultra-wealthy into policies that oppress communities of color in particular. It is mostly our views that shape the public dialogue in ways that support racial injustice. And it is our advocacy and activism that has been the largest barrier to fixing these problems.

The fact that we are complicit—often unwittingly, but complicit nonetheless—in the perpetuation of systemic racism doesn't mean that we have to walk around with our heads hanging in shame, riddled with "white guilt." It does mean that we have a responsibility to acknowledge it and then get to work in fixing it. All white Americans should be taking a rigorous self-inventory of how their actions, or inactions, have contributed to systemic racism. Then we should all be modifying our voting patterns, charitable giving, career decisions, political activity, and overall behavior accordingly.

Beyond that, we must also recognize that if white folks continue to sit out the fight for racial justice, the potential path to victory against the broader ultra-wealthy agenda disappears. It ceases to exist. The numbers simply no longer add up. So we simply have to start pulling our weight.

Of course, while the marriage equality and #MeToo campaigns demonstrated that white people are capable of propelling major social change efforts when they come out in force, it must also be acknowledged that we have a long history of undermining and destabilizing social movements and potential social movements, often despite having good intentions. Dr. King warned us all of the destructive tendencies of well-meaning white liberals in his "Letter from Birmingham Jail" in 1963, and the ensuing fifty-plus years have provided an abundance of evidence to reinforce the point he was making. Thus, it is worth repeating the theory of change mentioned above: transformative and sustainable social change occurs when those who are most directly impacted by oppression take collective action, lead their own social movements, and build power with other impacted individuals to change the conditions that produce their oppression.

In other words, white people shouldn't expect to achieve significant social change when their advocacy efforts are disconnected from grassroots-led social movements (which happens often). They shouldn't expect people of color to become the on-the-ground foot soldiers in support of their social change goals (also quite common). And they shouldn't expect to be successful when their advocacy fails to speak to the issues of greatest importance to communities of color (which almost *always* happens).

There can be dynamic and compelling advocacy campaigns around education inequities, mass incarceration, the criminalization of immigrants, and other systems of oppression, but if the individuals and communities who are bearing the brunt of those injustices aren't at the forefront of the efforts to address them, then those campaigns will rarely achieve anything more than superficial, symbolic, or short-lived victories. The leadership and authentic engagement of those most directly impacted are absolutely essential to building the level of public support, and thus the level of power, needed to dismantle oppressive systems.

Additionally, the centering of grassroots leadership from the most affected communities is absolutely essential to truly solving these problems at their roots. Communities of color are typically the "miner's canary" of unjust policies; they are the ones who are affected first and most severely, thus alerting the rest of us to the dangers we all face.[23] If we fix those issues, then everyone benefits. However, the inverse isn't true. If we fail to employ a racial justice analysis and merely address the issues that are most salient for white communities, the challenges faced by communities of color typically go unaddressed. This, in short, is why so many of even the most well-meaning progressive reform efforts have actually widened racial inequities.[24]

None of this should be read as suggesting that predominantly white communities don't have their own vested interests in tearing down oppressive systems. It is also not meant to suggest that there isn't a place for white leadership within these fights. On the contrary, we need "leader-ful" movements in which both people of color and white folks are exercising many different forms of leadership to address these injustices. There must also necessarily be processes by which predominantly white communities and communities of color explore the unjust conditions they face and jointly address the root causes that lie at the intersection of them. But to create the type of change that is both necessary and possible, white people are going to have to join the fight for racial justice, not take it over. In other words, while we desperately need more white people to prioritize the dismantling of systemic racism, we also need them to avoid doing so in ways that essentially gentrify racial justice movements.

Building a Counterweight to the Power of Extreme Wealth

There are two primary ways to move public policy: with money, and with people. The ultra-wealthy obviously have massive advantages with regard to the former, but the rest of us overwhelm them with regard to the latter. So why has their strategic advantage been so much more effective than ours?

Say what you will about these Corporate America and Wall Street executives, but you have to admit that they are supremely organized. They are using their wealth in highly strategic ways to advance their priorities. In particular, they have recognized that the key to moving their agenda is building organizational power. They have invested heavily in the creation and growth of organizations to represent their interests within local, state, and federal policy making. These organizations include ALEC, Americans for Prosperity, the Club for Growth, Americans for Tax Reform, the LIBRE Initiative, the NRA, and FreedomWorks, among numerous others.

The ultra-wealthy have also recognized that these organizations need a supportive infrastructure. Thus, they have invested heavily in organizations that can provide their advocacy organizations with the research, policy, communications, and legal support they need to be effective in shaping policy and shifting the public dialogue. Among the many organizations within that infrastructure are the Cato Institute, the Heritage Foundation, the American Enterprise Institute, the State Policy Network and its affiliates, and the Federalist Society. Overall, this group of Corporate America and Wall Street executives has effectively leveraged its wealth to create a massive network of organizations that largely operates from the same playbook.[25]

There is only one effective counterweight to the power of such organized wealth, and that is the power of organized people. To resist the Corporate America and Wall Street agenda and ultimately advance an agenda that is more favorable to low-income, working-class, and middle-class families, we must take a page out of their playbook and invest far more deeply in organizations. However, unlike their organizations, which are fueled primarily by money, we need to build people-powered organizations.

Building strong mass organizations represents the difference between winning and losing; between having a powerful, organized force pushing for change and merely having a large number of isolated voices in the wilderness. There may be a million protesters out in the streets yelling about various injustices, but if those million protesters are a million atomized individuals, then whatever impact is created by their actions will quickly dissipate. If, however, those million protesters are members of organizations that can build off the momentum created by that protest and channel it into positive social change, then we start to collectively shift the needle.

Building the types of organizations that can form the organizing, policy, communications, and legal infrastructure of successful social movements is complex, long-term work. However, for the average person, the two most important action items are actually quite simple.

Action Item 1: Show Up for Racial Justice Base-Building Organizations

It is critically important that low-income, working-class, and middle-class people who support racial justice have a consistent, organized presence to advance that agenda. Fortunately, there are already numerous grassroots racial justice organizations all across the United States, within every single state. Unfortunately, these organizations are typically severely underresourced relative to their opposition. Thus, to truly build the type of unified grassroots force that can defeat the ultra-wealthy agenda, we are going to have to make a collective investment in these types of organizations. Certainly that includes financial investments, as all of these organizations would greatly benefit from donations, even small ones.

Beyond that, these organizations need people who can invest their time, their skills, and their perspective to advancing racial justice efforts. They need people who can conduct research, analyze data, assist with public relations and communications, and provide policy and legal assistance. They need visual artists, musicians, and dancers. They need cooks, fund-raisers, and people who are good at just getting things done. They need people who can share their lived experiences with the systems of oppression that they are confronting on a daily basis. Whatever skills or knowledge you have accumulated in your life, it is virtually guaranteed that at least some of it would be of great value to an existing or potential mass movement. And even if you don't want to contribute in any of those ways, grassroots organizations also just need people who will consistently show up for public events.

Thus, if you are inclined to want to advance racial justice, start by finding an organization near you and seeing what you can do to help move its agenda forward. If you need a place to start, table 14 provides a list of some of the best and most strategic racial justice organizations in the country. There may be nothing more valuable that individuals could do to advance racial justice than contribute whatever time, energy, and money they have available to support the work of these or other like-minded organizations.

In other words, what we need is for more people to show up. And to keep showing up. Even if the work gets hard. Even if you get uncomfortable, frustrated, or offended. Take it from someone who has been to hundreds of community meetings, rallies, protests, and strategy sessions all across the country. At most of those gatherings, I felt like I was being welcomed into a family. At others, I felt like an outsider. Many of the convenings were inspiring, invigorating, and highly productive. Some of them were not. On occasion, at some of these meetings, my feelings got hurt. At others, it was my ignorance that offended others. But I kept coming back, kept trying to build relationships, kept trying to learn, kept trying to do better, and at the end of the day, the rewards for just the simple act of showing up—on both a movement-building level and on a personal level—have been extraordinary.

TABLE 14

SELECT RACIAL JUSTICE BASE-BUILDING ORGANIZATIONS

Puente Human Rights Movement (AZ)	Urban Youth Collaborative (NY)
Labor/Community Strategy Center (CA)	Desis Rising Up & Moving (NY)
Black Organizing Project (CA)	Youth United for Change (PA)
Dignity and Power Now (CA)	Philadelphia Student Union (PA)
Justice Teams Network (CA)	Tenants & Workers United (VA)
Coleman Advocates for Children and Youth (CA)	Make the Road (NY, NJ, CT, PA, NV)
Ella Baker Center for Human Rights (CA)	New Virginia Majority (VA)
Community Coalition (CA)	Southerners on New Ground (SONG) (Southern US states)
Youth Justice Coalition (CA)	Black Lives Matter (national and local)
Californians for Justice (CA)	Movement for Black Lives (national)
Causa Justa: Just Cause (CA)	Journey for Justice Alliance (national and local)
Padres & Jóvenes Unidos (CO)	Poor People's Campaign (national and local)
Dream Defenders (FL)	Mijente (national)
Power U Center for Social Change (FL)	Right to the City (national and local)
New Florida Majority (FL)	NAACP (national, statewide, and local)
Communities United (IL)	United We Dream (national, statewide, and local)
Voices of Youth in Chicago Education (VOYCE) (IL)	Black Youth Project 100 (national and local)
Southern Echo (MS)	Color of Change (national)
Baltimore Algebra Project (MD)	Black Alliance for Just Immigration (national and local)
CASA (MD)	Million Hoodies Movement for Justice (national and local)
Beloved Community Center (NC)	Sunrise Movement (national)
SpiritHouse (NC)	Formerly Incarcerated Convicted People and Families Movement (national and local)

Action Item 2: Create Community Equity Assemblies

Beyond plugging into the racial justice infrastructure that has already been built, we also need to create new structures for more people to become involved, particularly for the members of communities that have been systematically excluded from the political process for generations. In every community in the United States that struggles with equity issues (which is to say, every community in the United States), we need to create "community equity assemblies" where regular people can come together to learn about systemic racism and other forms of oppression and then get to work in dismantling them. These need not be formal bodies, particularly initially; just places where community members can gather together and find ways to collaborate. They also don't have to be large. As is demonstrated every day all across the country, even small groups of dedicated advocates can have a remarkable impact within a community. However, over time, if we can grow these assemblies by bringing in more like-minded people from

our neighborhoods, workplaces, community groups, churches, mosques, syna-
gogues, student groups, labor unions, volunteer organizations, and other forma-
tions, then the possibilities for what we can accomplish together begin to grow
dramatically. All of a sudden, the many people of all races and ethnicities who
care about these issues can become transformed from a collection of individuals
into a powerful political force. From there, they can start influencing policy decisions, they can demand a seat at the table for budgetary decisions, they can hold
policy makers accountable in far more meaningful ways, and in relatively short
order they can create truly transformative change in their communities.

There are innumerable benefits to building and expanding these types of people-
powered organizations—both existing base-building organizations and community equity assemblies. They create stronger, tighter-knit communities, they give
people a stronger sense of purpose, and participating in them also tends to be
a lot of fun. Most people find that those reasons alone are more than enough
justification to commit one's time and energy. Beyond that, though, these types
of organizations represent the only way that we will be able to create the type
of power needed to defeat the ultra-wealthy and achieve racial justice. They are
simply essential for bringing more people into these fights, shifting the public
narrative around these issues, advancing more just public policies, building a
more participatory democracy, and creating public institutions that are accountable to the needs of all people.

If there are any doubts in your mind about how effective and necessary this type
of community organizing is, consider this: The Koch family and their network
have themselves begun investing heavily in their own grassroots organizing efforts
in recent years, even creating a "Grassroots Leadership Academy" modeled after
progressive community organizing efforts.[26] Plus, they and other ultra-wealthy
corporate executives have created a large network of "astroturf" organizations
that are designed to convince the public and policy makers that they represent
authentic grassroots efforts.[27] In other words, the ultra-wealthy have recognized
that there is so much power in the strategies available to the rest of us that they
are actively co-opting them.

Looking for Answers

As we strengthen the network of organizations pushing for racial justice, the next
question becomes: What are the policies that we should be advancing to create
more just and equitable communities? Obviously, one place to start would be
with the solutions identified in the previous chapters. However, it is important

to understand that those ideas were all the product of many years of collaborative work within communities of color around the country. I offered them as a way to advance the conversation, but they are not "my" ideas, per se. They come from the many black and brown communities that I have been fortunate to work with and that have been severely impacted by the worst our education, criminal justice, and immigration systems have to offer. It was large groups of community leaders who identified the solutions to the challenges they face; my contribution has involved little more than passing them along.

In other words, there won't be the typically long list of specific policy proposals that you find at the end of most policy-focused books. The goal here isn't to get people to listen to my ideas about how to address various social problems. It's to get more people to listen far more closely to those who are most affected by systemic racism and then find ways to support efforts to address those injustices. Thus, rather than trying to provide all the answers to our numerous racial justice issues, this book is intended to spur more multiracial community collaborations so that people can discover the answers for themselves. My hope is that through authentic participatory processes, groups of community members can improve and expand upon the solutions I have offered, while also tackling the numerous other racial justice issues that weren't covered at length here.

What I will suggest is that, regardless of the particular policy proposals that are eventually identified, the focus of our collaborative work moving forward should be centered squarely on redefining what it means for all of us to find true freedom.

Liberatory Communities

There may be no word in the English language whose meaning has been more thoroughly distorted in recent years than "freedom." The network of far-right organizations that has been propped up by the ultra-wealthy has long attempted to redefine freedom as being about the individual's relationship to government regulation. Thus, imposing a minimum wage that is enough for people to live on is portrayed as an attack on "American freedom." Expanding health care protections is an assault on liberty. Preserving or expanding the social safety net is un-American socialism that will make us all less free. You will notice that the litany of mass criminalization policies—those that literally deprive millions of people of their most basic freedoms—aren't typically included within the laundry list of policies that are considered by these organizations to be anti-freedom. The most oppressive education, health care, employment, voting, reproductive rights, and anti-LGBTQIA+ policies also tend not to even make it onto that list.

What usually separates the policies that make the cut from those that don't is (a) they benefit low-income, working-class, and middle-class families; and (b) they lead to diminished profits and power for Corporate America and Wall Street executives. In other words, the concept of "freedom" has been reduced to the freedom of the ultra-wealthy to accumulate extreme wealth on the backs of the rest of us. And those who talk the most about freedom tend to be the ones who are also most responsible for passing policies that oppress low-income, working-class, and middle-class people.

We need to rediscover a more authentic notion of freedom, one that is centered on all people having the ability to lead full, rewarding lives. Despite what ALEC and the Koch network would have us believe, government regulation isn't necessarily the enemy of that type of freedom.[28] There are both policies that foster that type of freedom and those that stifle it. However, the latter category is quite different from the far right's conception of anti-freedom policies. For example, when our policies limit the healthy education and development of youth, hinder families' health and economic security, promote criminalization, fail to address injustice or discrimination, undermine our democracy, or compromise the environment, then our collective ability to lead fulfilling lives is diminished, and we all become less free. Our task is to eliminate such policies and replace them with those that will allow all people to live within Liberatory Communities.

Liberatory Communities are those in which all public policy decisions are centered on what is needed to help all people thrive and enjoy health, safety, and happiness. They embrace participatory democracy and providing all people with meaningful and equitable opportunities to shape the public policy decisions that affect their lives. They recognize that there is nothing more valuable than people's lives, and that all people's lives have equal value.[29] They seek to maximize community wellness and minimize community harm. In short, they are communities designed around the needs of the people who live there, by the people who live there.

To ensure that all people are able to live within Liberatory Communities, we need to reassess how we allocate our public resources. We all have to recognize that every community is, in significant part, the product of the investments that have been made into it. There are positive investments—such as those for education, health care, living-wage jobs, and wraparound supports for youth—that address the essential needs of individuals, families, and communities and advance people's liberation. There are also harmful investments—such as those connected to mass criminalization—that make communities less liberatory. In many communities, we have supplied residents with a heavy dose of positive investments while making relatively small harmful investments.[30] In other communities, however, this relationship is reversed. The positive investments are far too small to meet the needs of residents, while a disproportionate share of resources is devoted to harmful investments. It is of the utmost importance that we remedy these discrepancies and ensure that our public dollars are aligned with community needs instead of exacerbating those needs, as is often the case currently.

This may seem pie-in-the-sky to some. One might understandably question whether it is feasible to align public resources with these goals, and whether we could even afford to pay for the types of policies being alluded to earlier. However, even if we accept the perhaps dubious notion that government spending must come from a fixed set of resources, it is not that difficult to imagine a policy landscape that would support the creation of Liberatory Communities across the country.[31]

As one example, we could reduce the harmful investments we have made in school privatization, the criminal justice system, and the immigration enforcement system, as discussed in chapters 2, 3, and 4. Then, if we roll back military spending to post–Vietnam War levels and implement Senator Elizabeth Warren's proposed "wealth tax" and the modest tax reforms on Wall Street, Corporate America, and other extremely wealthy individuals that have been proposed by Senator Bernie Sanders, we would create $1.3 trillion in additional annual revenue that could be reinvested in other priorities (see table 15).[32]

With those resources, we could be dramatically expanding our positive investments into families and communities across the country. Merely as an illustration of what could be done with these funds in a given year, consider the reinvestment possibilities presented in table 16.[33]

Under this scenario, millions of additional living-wage jobs would be created, and the most urgent needs of tens of millions of families would be addressed.[34] Countless children, families, and communities would experience dramatic improvements in their quality of life. Hundreds of struggling communities would be revived. Many of the most significant root causes of crime, violence, poverty, and war would be addressed. The health of our planet would finally be given the attention it deserves. We would be making investments that would

TABLE 15

POTENTIAL ANNUAL SAVINGS FROM DIVESTMENT IN HARMFUL POLICIES AND SENSIBLE TAX REFORMS

Roll back criminal justice spending	$238 billion
Roll back immigration enforcement spending	$28 billion
Roll back defense spending	$316 billion
Eliminate public funding of school privatization	$50 billion
Impose wealth tax and modest tax reforms on Wall Street, Corporate America, and other extremely wealthy individuals	$704 billion
Total annual savings and additional revenue	**$1.3 trillion**

TABLE 16

POTENTIAL ANNUAL INVESTMENTS IN LIBERATORY COMMUNITIES

Increase public school spending by 50% to implement Student Bill of Rights and address education debt owed to communities of color	$327 billion
Make investments in clean and renewable energy sources that, if continued over time, would allow us to completely eliminate our reliance on fossil fuels	$391 billion
Eliminate tuition costs at every public college and university	$82 billion
Replace mass criminalization and incarceration system with multidisciplinary public health and safety departments by hiring one million new social workers, psychologists, substance use counselors, conflict mediators, mental and behavioral health specialists, nurses, restorative and transformative justice practitioners, violence intervention experts, public health specialists, harm reduction practitioners, gang intervention workers, and trauma-informed healing practitioners	$68 billion
Create a universal pre-K system for all three- and four-year-olds that would be free for low-income families	$20 billion
Provide over 15 million children living in poverty with quality afterschool programs	$69 billion
Invest $1 billion in comprehensive community development strategies within 200 historically marginalized communities around the US	$200 billion
Invest in comprehensive poverty-reduction strategies around the world to address causes of global inequality and mass migration	$150 billion
Total annual spending	**$1.3 trillion**

actually produce taxpayer savings instead of the typical downward financial spiral of our harmful investments.[35] Plus, if these types of investments were continued over time, intergenerational poverty—which is now generally accepted as a permanent feature of American life—could be eliminated. And if we were intentional about addressing racial inequities instead of just hoping that "universal" reforms would benefit everyone, the systematic underinvestment in communities of color could finally be remedied.

Process all of that for a moment. Then consider how the types of alternative investments listed earlier could benefit you, your family, and your community. Ask yourself: Would you be better off under our current system of government spending, or under this one? Which one would best support the overall health and well-being of you, your family, and your community? Which would make you safer on a day-to-day basis? Which would allow you to live a happier and more fulfilling life?

The simple truth is that there is no good reason why, in the United States, we can't guarantee every person a high-quality education, a living-wage job, an adequate social safety net, a public safety system that doesn't criminalize people, and a clean and healthy environment. Yet over time most of us have been convinced that these things are unattainable. We have been operating from a scarcity model in which we act as if there aren't enough of these things to go around and thus only some of us are able to enjoy them. Yet in reality we have all the resources we need to ensure that all US residents are able to thrive and be free from numerous unnecessary challenges, struggles, and abuses that they currently face. The only real question is whether enough of us are willing to demand that our country be made to serve our interests, and not the interests of those who have been exploiting it, and us, for far too long.

When the "Supreme Law of the Land" Isn't Supremely Aligned with People's Needs

Whether we are able to achieve our collective liberation is ultimately dependent on whether we can build the level of power necessary to prevail over those who benefit from oppression. While that is eminently feasible, one must also acknowledge that the ultra-wealthy have a number of built-in advantages over low-income, working-class, and middle-class people. Among them are our campaign finance laws that overwhelmingly favor wealthy interests, our heavily gerrymandered legislative districts, our court system stacked with far-right judges, the significant legal hurdles that have been put in place to limit social justice advocacy and organizing, and the fact that the ultra-wealthy own much of the media that we all consume on a daily basis. All these elements, among many others, serve as obstacles that protect the overwhelming power of wealthy Corporate America and Wall Street executives even in the face of popular resistance. While these challenges certainly aren't insurmountable, the fact that the ultra-wealthy have been strategically stacking the deck in their own favor for decades makes it far more difficult than it should be to provide all people with an equal say in our democracy. (It is also why purely electoral strategies—that is, just focusing on electing better people into office—are insufficient to address the challenges we face.)

That brings us back to the US Constitution and the efforts to convene an Article V constitutional convention discussed previously. Because of the enormous structural advantages currently enjoyed by the ultra-wealthy, there is justifiable concern that if an Article V convention were to be called in the near future, the results would likely be extremely damaging and perhaps catastrophic for low-income, working-class, and middle-class people. Thus, many social-justice-focused organizations have understandably taken the position that the calls for a constitutional convention should be defeated.[36] This is likely a wise strategy in the short to medium term. However, we must still prepare ourselves to participate in the rewriting of some or all of the US Constitution in the event that either the BBA or COS initiatives are successful. If that were to happen, it would be vitally important not only that those who receive the overwhelming share of the benefits from our current legal system aren't allowed to advance their interests any further, but that the rest of us are able to mount an affirmative strategy around our interests as well. In other words, we should be getting ready to play offense as well as defense.

Beyond that, it is worth noting that the ultra-wealthy clearly don't believe that the Constitution is set in stone, so perhaps the rest of us shouldn't either. While the BBA and COS initiatives could hardly be more wrong in their analysis of what ails our country and how it should be fixed, the one thing that the organizers and funders of those initiatives have gotten right is their assertion that our Constitution isn't doing enough to serve the interests of the American people. Indeed, the very reasons why the prospect of an Article V constitutional convention is so terrifying—namely, the hugely disproportionate influence of the ultra-wealthy over the political system, legal system, and mass media—may be the best of all possible justifications for reshaping our governing documents. Thus, rather than just waiting around until the BBA and COS initiatives get the votes they need, it may be worth considering the possibility of our own grassroots-led call for a constitutional convention centered on addressing these inequities and advancing the interests of low-income, working-class, and middle-class people. While this would almost certainly be a long-term strategy, there may be no more effective approach to addressing our deep, long-standing systemic injustices. In fact, while there are of course substantial gains to be made irrespective of the Constitution, it may not be possible to fully address these issues without modifying the "supreme law of the land."

Believe me when I say that I don't offer this up lightly. Not long ago I would have scoffed at the idea that we should consider revising the Constitution. I, like most everyone else in the United States, was raised to revere that document. I went to law school in large part because of my desire to learn the Constitution and constitutional law inside and out. For years, I even carried a copy of the Constitution around with me in my computer bag. I will also continue to assert that, for whatever flaws it may have, it represented a major achievement for its time. It has been a model for countless other constitutions and legal documents around the world. The mere fact that it has held up this long, when virtually every other country in the world has updated its governing documents, is remarkable. Nevertheless, when I read the document now with fresh eyes, and particularly in comparison to the constitutions of other countries around the globe, I must admit that some of the shine has come off the apple. I now realize that perhaps the Constitution shouldn't be considered quite so sacrosanct.

Consider this: How effective is the US Constitution at protecting individual rights and promoting justice when millions of people have been suffering from the effects of under-education, mass criminalization, and other dehumanizing policies for generations? How successful is it in promoting basic human equality when deep racial inequities persist throughout the country more than two centuries after it was written? Indeed, if we are being honest about it, it must be acknowledged that our Constitution has served as a barrier to the change that is needed across a wide range of issues, including education, criminal justice, democratic rights, environmental protection, women's rights, and workers' rights, among others. Sometimes that is because of what the document says, but far more often it is because of what it doesn't say. There just isn't much language in the Constitution that speaks to the issues of greatest importance to low-income, working-class, and middle-class people. In other words, our Constitution often serves not as an instrument of justice, but as an impediment to achieving it.

As a result of these deficiencies, there is a certain absurdity to how we use the Constitution in modern times. Judges deciding issues of constitutional law are often basing their decisions on a document that doesn't even speak directly to those issues. In fact, if you convened a group of non-lawyers and asked them to read the text of the Constitution, they would probably question—rightfully—its relevance to the major challenges facing our country. If you then told them that they had to use the text of the Constitution to decide cases, they would likely become extremely confused. How do you decide cases involving the use of automatic weapons capable of firing hundreds of rounds per minute by relying on two-hundred-plus-year-old language that was concerned with militias armed with muskets and bayonets? How do you decide cases involving the right of privacy from government surveillance using a document that couldn't possibly have imagined police officers collecting digital data from people's cell phones to determine their location?[37] How do you decide cases around issues of public education, abortion rights, climate change, and labor rights when the Constitution doesn't even speak directly to any of those issues (along with many other important issues)? It's like asking someone to learn how to fix a computer by reading *War and Peace*. It's just not the right tool for the job. So those non-lawyers would have to go through a series of analytical and logical gymnastics to find some tenuous relationship between whatever decisions they make and the text of the Constitution, just as judges often have to do. While the legal profession has developed a series of customs and interpretive methods that provide some semblance of order and reason to this process, that shouldn't blind us to the reality that constitutional decisions are often only loosely connected, at best, to the document on which they are supposedly based.

One's response to this might be to suggest that this isn't a problem with the Constitution, but rather it is a problem with the judges we appoint and elect. You might think that if only we had better judges, then we would have better law, and thus the solution is a political one. However, as long as we provide judges with such extraordinary latitude to interpret the Constitution, we as a country run a terrible risk that it will be used in ways that are contrary to our national interests. That is why we devote so much collective energy to the fights over Supreme Court nominations, because we recognize that the unelected, lifetime-appointed justices have enormous power over the rest of us, with very little language in the Constitution to prevent them from using that power in deeply harmful ways (or to guide them in using it in beneficial ways).

But what if they didn't have quite as much room for interpretation? What if, like most other countries around the world, we provided them with a document that actually had guidance that was germane to the cases they had to decide? What if we didn't have to be quite so concerned about how the ideological or political leanings of judges would factor into their decisions?

For example, out of the 202 constitutions in use around the world that have been cataloged by the Comparative Constitutions Project, consider how many of them have explicit language in them that the US Constitution does not:

- 149 recognize a right to education.
- 145 recognize a right to health care.
- 101 recognize the right to equal pay for equal work.
- 167 recognize a right to environmental protection or conservation.
- 91 recognize the right to a reasonable standard of living.
- 158 recognize a right to join a union.
- 86 recognize a right to rest and leisure.
- 166 prohibit the use of torture.[38]

The truth is that, for as groundbreaking as the US Constitution was in its time, most countries around the world now have constitutions that advance the rights of their citizens and promote justice and equality far more than our own. Here are some examples:

- Sweden: "Public power shall be exercised with respect for the equal worth of all and the liberty and dignity of the individual. The personal, economic and cultural welfare of the individual shall be fundamental aims of public activity. In particular, the public institutions shall secure the right to employment, housing and education, and shall promote social care and social security, as well as favorable conditions for good health. The public institutions shall promote sustainable development leading to a good environment for present and future generations. The public institutions shall promote the ideals of democracy as guidelines in all sectors of society and protect the private and family lives of the individual. The public institutions shall promote the opportunity for all to attain participation and equality in society and for the rights of the child to be safeguarded. The public institutions shall combat discrimination of persons on grounds of gender, color, national or ethnic origin, linguistic or religious affiliation, functional disability, sexual orientation, age or other circumstance affecting the individual."

- Pakistan: "The State shall: (a) secure the well-being of the people, irrespective of sex, caste, creed or race, by raising their standard of living, by preventing the concentration of wealth and means of production and distribution in the hands of a few to the detriment of general interest and by ensuring equitable adjustment of rights between employers and employees, and landlords and tenants; (b) provide for all citizens, within the available resources of the country, facilities for work and adequate livelihood with reasonable rest and leisure; (c) provide for all persons employed in the service of Pakistan or otherwise, social security by compulsory social insurance or other means; (d) provide basic necessities of life, such as food, clothing, housing, education and medical relief, for all such citizens, irrespective of sex, caste, creed or race, as are permanently or temporarily unable to earn their livelihood on account of infirmity, sickness or unemployment; (e) reduce disparity in the income and earnings of individuals, including persons in the various classes of the service of Pakistan."
- Belgium: "Everyone has the right to lead a life in keeping with human dignity. . . . These rights include among others: . . . the right to social security, to health care, and to social, medical and legal aid; the right to decent accommodation; the right to the protection of a healthy environment; the right to cultural and social fulfillment."
- Brazil: "The following are rights of urban and rural workers, in addition to any others designed to improve their social condition: . . . a national uniform minimum wage, fixed by law, capable of meeting a worker's basic living needs and those of his family, for housing, nourishment, education, health, leisure, clothing, hygiene, transportation and social security, with periodic adjustments to maintain its purchasing power . . .; normal working hours not to exceed eight hours per day and forty-four hours per week . . .; paid weekly rest, preferably on Sundays . . .; an annual paid vacation, at a rate at least one-third higher than normal pay; maternity leave without loss of job or wages for a period of one hundred-twenty days; paternity leave, as provided by law . . .; free assistance for children and dependents from birth to five years of age in day-care centers and preschools . . .; prohibition of any difference in pay in performance

of duties and in hiring criteria by reason of sex, age, color or marital status . . .; prohibition of any distinction among manual, technical and intellectual work or among the respective professionals."

- Democratic Republic of the Congo: "All Congolese have the right to enjoy the national wealth. The State has the duty to redistribute it equitably."
- Bolivia: "Every person has the right to health. The State guarantees the inclusion and access to health for all persons, without any exclusion or discrimination. There shall be a single health system, which shall be universal, free, equitable, intra-cultural, intercultural, and participatory, with quality, kindness and social control. The system is based on the principles of solidarity, efficiency and co-responsibility, and it is developed by public policies at all levels of the government."
- Switzerland: "Men and women have equal rights. The law shall ensure their equality, both in law and in practice, most particularly in the family, in education, and in the workplace. Men and women have the right to equal pay for work of equal value."
- Ecuador: "Education will focus on the human being and shall guarantee holistic human development, in the framework of respect for human rights, a sustainable environment, and democracy; education shall be participatory, compulsory, intercultural, democratic, inclusive and diverse, of high quality and humane; it shall promote gender equity, justice, solidarity and peace; it shall encourage critical faculties, art and sports, individual and community initiatives, and the development of competencies and capabilities to create and work. . . . Education shall be for general welfare of the public and shall not be at the service of individual and corporate interests. Universal access, permanence, mobility and graduation without any discrimination shall be guaranteed. . . . Public education shall be universal and secular at all levels and shall be free of charge up to and including the third level of higher education [postsecondary undergraduate schooling]."
- Egypt: "Every individual has the right to live in a healthy, sound and balanced environment. Its protection is a national duty. The state is committed to taking the necessary measures to preserve it, avoid harming it, rationally use its natural resources to ensure that sustainable development is achieved, and guarantee the rights of future generations thereto."
- Angola: "The Republic of Angola shall . . . establish friendly and cooperative relations with all states and peoples on the basis of the following principles: (a) Respect for sovereignty and national

independence; (b) Equality amongst states; (c) The rights of peoples to self-determination and independence; (d) Peaceful solutions to conflicts; (e) Respect for human rights; (f) Non-interference in the affairs of other states; (g) Reciprocal advantages; (h) Repudiating and combating terrorism, drug trafficking, racism, corruption and people and human organ trafficking; (i) Cooperation with all peoples for peace, justice and progress. The Republic of Angola shall defend the abolition of all forms of colonialism, aggression, oppression, domination and exploitation in relations between peoples."[39]

Obviously, these countries don't always live up to the standards set in their constitutions. However, at least they set their sights high. The US Constitution has nothing comparable to the protections and value statements just listed. Instead, what most distinguishes our Constitution from others around the world are the sections that are more shameful than admirable, such as the three-fifths clause (referring to the value of a slave in determining a state's population), and the fact that it was written entirely by white men, many of whom were slave owners. Even the sections that most people would cite as the most important parts of our Constitution—such as the First Amendment right to free speech—no longer stand up that well to scrutiny. (After *Citizens United* declared that political spending equals protected free speech, it is difficult to argue that the First Amendment is serving our collective interests as well as it could, or should.)

While it might strike some as blasphemous, when the US Constitution is viewed in context and in comparison to other constitutions in use throughout the world, it is difficult not to be at least a little embarrassed by how outdated it looks in comparison. It is also hard not to be a little jealous of the many ways in which other countries' constitutions do far more to promote social justice and protect the interests of low-income, working-class, and middle-class people.

The contents of the "supreme law of the land" should be aligned with our values, priorities, and needs as a country, and yet nobody could legitimately argue that the US Constitution is so aligned. At some point, the question must be asked: How long are we going to continue to rely on the same document? How long is long enough? Another hundred years? Another two hundred years? Forever?

Of course, there are many provisions of the Constitution that have served us well and should be preserved. However, our Constitution clearly doesn't do nearly enough to protect individual rights, address racial inequality, advance participatory democracy, promote the freedom and well-being of all people, and establish a direction for the country that best serves our collective interests. Thus, it is worth considering whether an authentic, grassroots-led alternative to the BBA and COS initiatives—that brings together the racial justice, economic justice, gender justice, LGBTQIA+ justice, climate justice, and other social justice movements—could allow us to reshape our governing documents with more meaningful language around issues of key national importance, such as democratic rights; educational and developmental opportunities for children and youth; health care; protection of the environment; corporate accountability; workers' rights; criminal justice; social safety net; women's rights; LGBTQIA+ rights; immigrants' rights; rights of people with disabilities; Native American tribal rights; equality and nondiscrimination; gun control; the right to privacy; and international relations.

These are all vitally important issues, and yet our Constitution is either silent on them or constitutional law has, for much of US history and increasingly in modern times, tended to reflect only the views of a small subset of the most privileged among us. That has been holding us back as a country for far too long. Thus, an inclusive, unified, and democratic process to revise the United States Constitution may be precisely what is needed to help create a far more inclusive, unified, and democratic United States.

Making Politics "Our Thing"

As I mentioned in chapter 1 of this book, my key epiphany came once I finally realized that the continued existence of systemic racism wasn't due to older generations of Americans or the small minority of hateful bigots. Instead, I realized that it hinged entirely on normal, everyday white people. We are by far the single largest force propping up systemic racism. Of course, the flip side of that is that we are uniquely well positioned to help tear it down. The question is whether enough of us are going to choose to join the multitudes of people of color who have been in the fight since the beginning. If we do, then the dreams of every person in the United States about what we want for our lives can get a whole lot bigger. If we don't, then the ultra-wealthy will continue testing the limits of how much injustice and social, economic, and political inequality we can all tolerate before we reach our breaking point.

Nevertheless, many people tend to say things like "I'm not that into politics," or "Politics isn't really my thing." Indeed, it would be nice not to have to devote so much energy to such things. But the reality is that while we might not be that involved in politics, the people who own the companies we work for, the banks we use, the insurance companies we send our premiums to every month, and the makers of the products we rely on are *very* involved in politics. While we are focused on other things, they are putting their resources—the money we make for them or give to them—to use in advancing policies that harm us in a multitude of ways. And they are really hoping that we all continue to say things like "I'm not that into politics," or "Politics isn't really my thing."

Ultimately, there are only two things that can happen from this point forward. Either we are going to collectively make things better, or they are going to continue to get worse. So when it comes to deciding whether or not to get involved, do we really even have an option?

A DECLARATION OF INTERDEPENDENCE

In 1776, a group of revolutionaries drafted a document that would forever alter the course of history. They wrote,

> We hold these truths to be self-evident, that all men are created equal, that they are endowed by their creator with certain unalienable rights, that among these are life, liberty and the pursuit of happiness. That to secure these rights, governments are instituted among men, deriving their just powers from the consent of the governed, that whenever any form of government becomes destructive of these ends, it is the right of the people to alter or to abolish it, and to institute new government, laying its foundation on such principles and organizing its powers in such form, as to them shall seem most likely to effect their safety and happiness.

These words still ring true today. Can there be any doubt that our current government has been "destructive of these ends," greatly limiting the rights of millions of people to life, liberty, and the pursuit of happiness, and obscuring our fundamental equality? Based on the principles established by Jefferson, Adams, Franklin, and their colleagues, it is thus the "right of the people" to "alter" that form of government. To do so, we will need to be just as audacious as the "Founding Fathers" were when they drafted their statement of rebellion. However, instead of making a Declaration of Independence as they did in the late eighteenth century, what is needed to address the severe challenges that we face today is a Declaration of *Inter*dependence.

In the United States, we often like to think of ourselves as rugged individual-ists. In reality, though, we are far more interdependent than we are independent. Our lives are all deeply interconnected within a web of both obvious and not-so-obvious threads. For example, if you asked me about my children and what makes them the unique individuals that they are—and I look deeply enough—I see that they are really a combination of countless influences from innumerable individuals. They are a product of genetic material passed down from genera-tions, what my wife and I have instilled in them, what they learn from our friends and family members, the influence of their friends and teachers, interactions with people they encounter out in the world, and all of the books, movies, TV shows, and other media that they ingest, which are produced by thousands of people around the world. (And of course all those people have their own sets of influencers, who have their own sets of influencers, and out it spirals from there.) What often determines the outcome of all those factors are the public policies that shape my children's lives and those of all the people they encounter or are influenced by on a daily basis. There are countless education, health care, labor, environmental, economic, child care, housing, voting, media, and criminal justice policies that intersect with their lives, either directly (such as through the impact of budgetary decisions on their schools) or indirectly (such as if one of their classmates' parents is incarcerated or deported and how that trauma sub-sequently affects them, the rest of the class, their teacher, and so on). If I look closely, I can see how all these factors play a role in their actions from day to day. I can also appreciate how delicate this cocktail of influences can be, and how even the smallest of shifts in inputs can produce enormous differences in outputs.

The same is true when viewing the impact of policies at the broader, systemic level. We all need to get to the point where we can clearly see that education inequities, mass criminalization, anti-immigrant policies, and other racial justice issues don't just harm those who attend the underresourced schools, suffer the effects of overpolicing, and face the prospect of being deported. If we examine our own lives closely, we will all find evidence of harm caused by the reverbera-tions from these unjust systems. On the flip side, we also all need to recognize that addressing those issues doesn't just help those people of color who have the burden of systemic racism lifted off them. We all stand to benefit when our neighbors are able to live higher-quality lives and the rot of injustice is purged from our public systems.

There is immense power that comes from acknowledging this interdepen-dence. Because when we start to see that my health, safety, and happiness are intimately connected to your health, safety, and happiness, the possibilities for what we can accomplish together begin to increase exponentially. If we can go beyond that and reach the point where we care enough about each other that we are able to recognize that whatever we want for ourselves, we should want for all people, then true freedom within the United States, and true greatness for the United States, start to become real possibilities.

Those are ultimately the prizes at stake here: American freedom and American greatness. While there is little evidence to suggest that we are, as we often claim, the greatest or freest country in the world, we *could* be. We could build the most advanced, inclusive, and equitable democracy the world has ever seen. We could build a country that is truly deserving of the love, devotion, and patriotism of all its residents and that people around the world would respect and even revere. America could be that "shining city on a hill," but it is ultimately on us to make it worthy of that distinction. Each of us is going to have to decide what we want our country to be and how we want to live. Do we want our public policies centered on creating opportunities for a small number of people to amass extraordinary wealth at the expense of everyone else, or do we want to use our resources to address the essential needs of individuals, families, and communities? Do we want to continue to allow our lives to be devalued and our voices to go unheard on the decisions that most affect our lives, or do we want to create a new, more humane world in which all people have a right to self-determination? Do we want to live our lives in a never-ending competition where we are always trying to get a leg up on other people, or do we want to find another way that involves working together for our mutual benefit? Do we want our children, grandchildren, and great-grandchildren to have to address the same issues of systemic racism that we face now, or do we finally want to address our inequities so that all people can be on equal footing and race will never again determine a person's chances of living a good life?

These are our choices. True American freedom and greatness are achievable, but to attain them, many more of us will have to recognize our fundamental interdependence and embrace our shared humanity. That is how we will ensure that racism is never again a source of profit. And that is how David will beat Goliath. Or more accurately, how the hundreds of thousands of Davids there are for every Goliath will be able to realize and actualize their true strength so that they can prevail and build a better, stronger, and more just America in the process.

Acknowledgments

I have been profoundly fortunate to spend my career working to support and help build social movements. Over that time, I have learned that groups of people can accomplish truly amazing things when they are all pulling in the same direction. I have also had more fun than I thought was possible as part of one's job. Yet the most valuable part of this experience has been getting to meet, work with, and learn from hundreds of extraordinary and inspiring people who dedicate themselves each and every day to serving the people in their communities. Every valuable insight in this book is most likely the product of the wisdom that they have graciously shared with me over the years. Every less-than-valuable portion of this book is most likely the result of my not having done a good enough job of learning from them.

I want to thank all my brilliant colleagues, teachers, mentors, and friends who have inspired, shaped, and sharpened my thinking on these issues over the years, including Roger Bertling, Allison Brown, Matt Cregor, Leigh Dingerson, Chris Edley, Dan Farbman, Alana Greer, Lani Guinier, Damon Hewitt, John Kim, Chinh Le, Dan Losen, Maxine Phillips, Lewis Pitts, Bill Quigley, Brooke Richie, Alexa Shabecoff, Purvi Shah, Anita Sinha, Marbre Stahly-Butts, and Elizabeth Westfall. In particular, I want to offer my deep gratitude to Judith Browne Dianis, Penda Hair, Eddie Hailes, and Monique Dixon, who gave so much of themselves in helping me grow into this work. They, more than anyone, helped me to discover that it was possible to work in the exact space in which my head meets my heart, and there is very little that is more valuable than that.

Nobody has shaped the ideas in this book more than the many community organizers and community leaders who have been my tour guides into the ugly depths of systemic racism, including Mónica Acosta, Jenny Arwade, Raul Botello, Jitu Brown, Oona Chatterjee, Manuel Criollo, Patrisse Cullors, Maria Degillo, Ruth Dinzey, Nijmie Dzurinko, Marsha Ellison, Juan Evangelista, Kesi Foster, Fred Ginyard, Joyce Johnson, Nelson Johnson, Daniel Kim, Sarah Landes, Dale Landry, Jon Liss, Tammy Bang Luu, Pam Martinez, Ricardo Martinez, Charles McDonald, Lalo Montoya, Marco Nuñez, Adora Obi Nweze, Andi Perez, Francisca Porchas, Hiram Rivera, Leidy Robledo, Elsa Oliva Rocha, Bill Schiebler, Jonathan Stith, Mustafa Sullivan, Marlyn Tillman, Evelin Urrutia, and Geoffrey Winder. These individuals, and so many others whom I have been fortunate to collaborate with, are constantly working to bring people together and help them understand how much power they truly possess to change the world. They are my heroes.

I also want to offer my sincere thanks to Fran Benson, who gave me perhaps the three greatest gifts an editor can give: (1) an immediate and precise understanding of what I wanted to say and why I wanted to say it; (2) genuine enthusiasm for helping me to actually say it; and (3) the remarkable ability to know exactly how to nudge me to say it better.

I want to extend my deepest appreciation to my family, my network of friends, and all the other members of the communities I have been a part of that I probably took for granted for far too long. I now appreciate with far more clarity that no one is able to achieve anything worthwhile without a great many others helping, encouraging, and investing in them. We all need that support system. We all need ladders of opportunity. We all need a safety net when we fall off track or make mistakes. I have spent most of my adult life working with people who have never been able to enjoy the type of supportive infrastructure that was built for me and others around me, and it is not lost on me that without it, my life's journey could have gone very differently.

Finally, I want to thank Lexi, Cheyson, and Charley, who have brought far more joy into my life than I ever thought was possible. Of all the many privileges I have enjoyed in my life, the one I am most thankful for is being able to live with my three absolute favorite people on the planet.

Notes

INTRODUCTION

1. Throughout this book, I use "black and brown communities" to describe those parts of the United States in which the residents are primarily people of color of African, Latin American, Caribbean, Native American, and South Asian descent.

2. "'Segregation Forever': A Fiery Pledge Forgiven, but Not Forgotten," NPR, January 10, 2013.

3. Smithsonian Institution, "Spotlight: Dr. Martin Luther King, Jr.," accessed March 20, 2018, https://www.si.edu/spotlight/mlk?page=4&iframe=true.

4. Eugene Scott, "Six Times President Trump Said He Is the Least Racist Person," *Washington Post*, January 17, 2018.

5. I am using "white" as shorthand to describe people who are typically of European descent, aren't of Latin American descent, and identify as, and are perceived as, "white" within US culture.

1. THE RACISM PROFITEERS

1. "Chicago Board Votes to Close 50 Schools," CNN, May 22, 2013.

2. The interview I conducted with Anna Jones has been supplemented by information she provided in the article "Anna Jones: Hunger Striker," *Chicago Reader*, December 9, 2015.

3. Inequality.org, "Facts: Wealth Equality in the United States," accessed March 5, 2018, https://inequality.org/facts/wealth-inequality/.

4. Center for Media and Democracy, "What Is ALEC?," ALEC Exposed, accessed March 5, 2018, https://www.alecexposed.org/wiki/What_is_ALEC%3F.

5. Center for Media and Democracy, "What Is ALEC?"

6. Center for Media and Democracy, "ALEC Corporations," SourceWatch, accessed March 5, 2018, https://www.sourcewatch.org/index.php/ALEC_Corporations.

7. Center for Media and Democracy, "Corporations That Have Cut Ties with ALEC," SourceWatch, accessed March 5, 2018, https://sourcewatch.org/index.php?title=Corporations_that_Have_Cut_Ties_to_ALEC.

8. eHistory.org, "The Invasion of America," YouTube video, June 2, 2014, https://www.youtube.com/watch?v=pJxrTzfG2bo/.

9. Laura Meckler, "Report Finds $23 Billion Racial Funding Gap for Schools," *Washington Post*, February 26, 2019.

10. Actual disparities can be much greater than this. US Department of Education Office of Civil Rights, "2015–16 Civil Rights Data Collection."

11. David Cooper, "Workers of Color Are Far More Likely to Be Paid Poverty-Level Wages Than White Workers," Economic Policy Institute, *Working Economics Blog*, June 21, 2018, https://www.epi.org/blog/workers-of-color-are-far-more-likely-to-be-paid-poverty-level-wages-than-white-workers/.

12. Don Gonyea, "Majority of White Americans Say They Believe Whites Experience Discrimination," NPR, October 24, 2017.

13. American Values Institute, *Transforming Perception: Black Men and Boys*; Perception Institute, https://perception.org/; Kirwan Institute for the Study of Race and Ethnicity, http://kirwaninstitute.osu.edu/.

14. David Armiak and Alex Kotch, "ALEC Leading Right-Wing Campaign to Reopen the Economy Despite COVID-19," Center for Media and Democracy, April 30, 2020, https://www.exposedbycmd.org/2020/04/30/alec-leading-right-wing-campaign-to-reopen-the-economy-despite-covid-19/.

15. Morgan Jerkins, "Too Many Kids: School Districts Are Packing More and More Kids into Classrooms—and That's Pushing Teachers Out," *Atlantic*, July 1, 2015; Tim Walker, "The Testing Obsession and the Disappearing Curriculum," *NEA Today*, September 2, 2014.

16. Michael Mitchell, Michael Leachman, and Kathleen Masterson, *A Lost Decade in Higher Education Funding*, Center on Budget and Policy Priorities, August 23, 2017.

17. Dave Gilson, "Overworked America: 12 Charts That Will Make Your Blood Boil," *Mother Jones*, July/August 2011; G. E. Miller, "The U.S. Is the Most Overworked Developed Nation in the World," 20 Something Finance, January 2, 2018.

18. Morgan Haefner, "Medical Bills Account for 1 in 3 GoFundMe Campaigns," *Becker's Hospital Review*, July 3, 2018.

19. Adam Gopnik, "The Caging of America," *New Yorker*, January 30, 2012; Communities United et al., *The $3.4 Trillion Mistake: The Cost of Mass Incarceration and Criminalization, and How Justice Reinvestment Can Build a Better Future for All*, 2016; Electronic Frontier Foundation, "NSA Spying," accessed March 5, 2018, https://www.eff.org/nsa-spying.

20. National Priorities Project, "Federal Budget Tipsheet: Pentagon Spending," accessed March 5, 2018, https://www.nationalpriorities.org/guides/tipsheet-pentagon-spending/.

21. Danny Hakim and Michael Wines, "'They Don't Really Want Us to Vote': How Republicans Made It Harder," *New York Times*, November 3, 2018; Elizabeth Tandy Shermer, "The Right to Work Really Means the Right to Work for Less," *Washington Post*, April 24, 2018; Michelle Chen, "America's Right to Protest Is under Attack," *Nation*, June 6, 2017; see also In the Public Interest, https://www.inthepublicinterest.org/.

22. "'The Future of the Negro': Clip from 'I Am Not Your Negro,'" PBS, https://www.pbs.org/video/i-am-not-your-negro-future-negro-clip-uppanz/.

23. Howard Zinn, *A People's History of the United States* (New York: Harper & Row, 1980).

24. Relatively recent examples include directing the ire of white people against black "welfare queens" squandering taxpayer dollars, "illegal immigrants" stealing "our" jobs, "thugs" and "gangbangers" tearing up inner cities, "America-hating Muslims," and "superpredator" kids terrorizing our schools. These are all direct descendants of much older tactics, such as pushing the narrative around the need to protect white women from "black brutes."

25. "James Baldwin: How Much Time Do You Want for Your 'Progress?'" uploaded by UnaffiliatedCritic, YouTube video, https://www.youtube.com/watch?v=OCUlE5ldPvM.

26. The potential examples are endless, but the "triangulation" strategies of centrist politicians in the mold of Bill Clinton, Joe Biden, and Rahm Emanuel are a good place to start.

27. For example, almost fifty-two million white people performed volunteer work in 2015; the median amount of time spent volunteering was fifty-two hours. In other words, white people literally spent billions of hours volunteering in their communities or surrounding communities. Bureau of Labor Statistics, Economic News Release, "Volunteering in the U.S., 2015," February 25, 2016.

28. There are nearly 200 million white Americans, meaning that the mobilization of half a million white racial justice advocates would require getting only about one out of every four hundred white people.

2. THE SQUANDERED BRILLIANCE OF OUR DISPOSABLE YOUTH

1. As the great community organizer Ricardo Martinez has said many times.

2. The names of all children and youth in this book have been changed to protect their identities.

3. Naomi Klein, *The Shock Doctrine: The Rise of Disaster Capitalism* (New York: Picador, 2007), 5.

4. Alliance to Reclaim Our Schools, *Confronting the Education Debt: We Owe Billions to Black, Brown and Low-Income Students and Their Schools*, September 2018.

5. Journey for Justice Alliance, *Death by a Thousand Cuts: Racism, School Closures, and Public School Sabotage*, May 2014; Communities United for Quality Education, *Fact Sheet on Chicago Public Schools' Proposed Charter School Expansion*, January 15, 2014; Susan Saulny, "Board's Decision to Close 28 Kansas City Schools Follows Years of Inaction," *New York Times*, March 11, 2010; Dominic Adams, "Half of Closed Flint Schools Over Last 10 Years in Predominantly Black Neighborhoods in Northwest Quadrant," *MLive*, May 12, 2013; Theresa Harrington and Aly Tadayon, "Oakland School Board's Vote to Close Schools Draws Ire from Parents, Teachers," *Mercury News*, September 12, 2019.

6. Kevin Hesla, Jamison White, and Adam Gerstenfeld, *A Growing Movement: America's Largest Public Charter School Communities*, 13th annual ed., National Alliance for Public Charter Schools, March 2019; National Alliance for Public Charter Schools, *A Growing Movement: America's Largest Charter School Communities*, 5th annual ed., November 2010, 1.

7. Arianna Prothero, "Alabama Governor Signs Measure to Allow Charter Schools," *Education Week*, March 19, 2015.

8. National Alliance for Public Charter Schools, National Association of Charter School Authorizers, and 50Can, *A Call to Action to Improve the Quality of Full-Time Virtual Charter Public Schools*, June 2016.

9. Diane Ravitch, "North Carolina Relaxes Oversight for Charters, Launches ASD to Turn More Public Schools Over to Charters," *Diane Ravitch's Blog*, July 3, 2016, https://dianeravitch.net/2016/07/03/north-carolina-relaxes-oversight-for-charters-launches-asd-to-turn-more-public-schools-over-to-charters/; Vivian Lee and Jesse McKinley, "Legislature Reaches Deal to Extend Mayoral Control of New York's Schools for a Year," *New York Times*, June 17, 2016; Jonathan Pelto, "Cha-Ching! Wealthy Charter School Backers Give Big to Malloy—Malloy Gives Big to Charter Schools," *Wait What?* (blog), February 7, 2016, http://jonathanpelto.com/2016/02/07/cha-ching-wealthy-charter-school-backers-give-big-to-malloy-malloy-gives-big-to-charter-schools/; Valerie Strauss, "What Gov. Scott Walker Is About to Do to Wisconsin's Public Schools," *Washington Post*, July 8, 2015; Darcie Cimarusti, "Christie Breaks the Law (Again) to Overfund State's Charter Schools," NJ Spotlight, June 25, 2015; Mike Klonsky, "Rauner's Dream: A State with No Unions and More Charters," *Mike Klonsky's Blog*, February 5, 2015, https://michaelklonsky.blogspot.com/2015/02/rauners-dream-state-with-no-unions-and.html; Erin Richards, "Walker Budget Proposal Would Virtually Upend Education Status Quo," *Milwaukee Journal Sentinel*, February 3, 2015.

10. Center for Popular Democracy, *State Takeovers of Low-Performing Schools: A Record of Academic Failure, Financial Mismanagement & Student Harm*, February 2016.

11. Center for Popular Democracy, *State Takeovers of Low-Performing Schools*; Alliance to Reclaim Our Schools, *Out of Control: The Systematic Disenfranchisement of African American and Latino Communities through School Takeovers*, August 2015; Alliance to Reclaim Our Schools, *The Facts about State Takeovers of Public Schools*, 2015.

12. Education Commission of the States, *50-State Comparison: Vouchers*, March 6, 2017; see also Alliance to Reclaim Our Schools, "Resources," accessed March 5, 2018, http://www.reclaimourschools.org/resources.

13. Network for Public Education and Schott Foundation for Public Education, *Grading the States: A Report Card on Our Nation's Commitment to Public Schools*, June 2018.

14. Tim Walker, "Beware of School Voucher Doublespeak," *NEA Today*, May 26, 2017; Evie Blad, "Trump Pushes Tax Break to Promote School Choice in State of the Union Address," *Education Week*, February 4, 2015.

15. Andrew Marra, "Schools Chief Wants Freedom from State Rules to Rival Charters," *Palm Beach Post*, July 30, 2015.

16. Howard Blume, "Backers Want Half of LAUSD Students in Charter Schools in Eight Years, Report Says," *Los Angeles Times*, September 21, 2015.

17. Gary Miron, William J. Mathis, and Kevin G. Welner, review of *Separating Fact & Fiction: What You Need to Know about Charter Schools*, National Education Policy Center, February 2015; Diane Ravitch, *Reign of Error: The Hoax of the Privatization Movement and the Danger to America's Public Schools* (New York: Knopf, 2013), 156, 206.

18. Arianna Prothero and Alex Harwin, "In Many Charter High Schools, Graduation Odds Are Slim," *Education Week*, February 26, 2019.

19. Unless otherwise noted, the following information on the effects of charter school and voucher expansion comes from the following sources: Journey for Justice Alliance, *Death by a Thousand Cuts*; *Envisioning the Future of Newark Public Schools: Excellent Neighborhood Public Schools for All*, May 17, 2014; Great Public Schools–Pittsburgh, *Creating a District of Last Resort: The Community Perspective on Pittsburgh Public Schools' Proposed "Corporate-Style" Reforms*, October 2013; Philadelphia Coalition Advocating for Public Schools, *The Philadelphia Community Education Plan: Excellent Schools for All Children*, 2012; Network for Public Education, *Charters and Consequences: An Investigative Series*, November 2017; Network for Public Education, *NPE Toolkit: School Privatization Explained*; Ravitch, *Reign of Error*; Diane Ravitch, *The Death and Life of the Great American School System: How Testing and Choice Are Undermining Education* (New York: Basic Books, 2011); Molly F. Gordon et al., *School Closings in Chicago: Staff and Student Experiences and Academic Outcomes*, University of Chicago Consortium on School Research, May 2018; Brett Robertson, "NPR Series Exposes the Numerous Problems with Trump and DeVos' Push for Private School Vouchers," Media Matters for America, May 25, 2017; Alliance to Reclaim Our Schools, "Vouchers: What the Research Says," April 7, 2017; Alliance to Reclaim Our Schools, "Myths and Facts about Vouchers," April 7, 2017; Network for Public Education, *NPE Toolkit*; and interviews with members of the Journey for Justice Alliance.

20. Network for Public Education, *NPE Toolkit*; David Lapp, Joshua Linn, Erik Dolson, and Della Moran, *The Fiscal Impact of Charter School Expansion: Calculations in Six Pennsylvania School Districts*, Research for Action, September 2017; Bruce D. Baker, *Exploring the Consequences of Charter School Expansion in U.S. Cities*, Economic Policy Institute, November 30, 2016; In the Public Interest, *Breaking Point: The Cost of Charter Schools for Public School Districts*, May 2018.

21. Kevin G. Welner, "The Dirty Dozen: How Charter Schools Influence Student Enrollment," *Teachers College Record*, April 2013, http://www.tcrecord.org.

22. Great Public Schools–Pittsburgh, *Creating a District of Last Resort: The Community Perspective on Pittsburgh Public Schools' Proposed "Corporate-Style" Reforms*, October 2013, 5; Journey for Justice Alliance, *Death by a Thousand Cuts*, 17.

23. For example, when Chicago closed fifty schools in 2013, over fifteen thousand students were displaced, and 40 percent of them weren't attending their designated welcoming schools the following year and were unaccounted for. Linda Lutton, "Only 60 Percent of Students from Chicago's Closed Schools Turn Up at 'Welcoming Schools,'" WBEZ, October 14, 2013.

24. Network for Public Education, *Charters and Consequences*; Network for Public Education, *#AnotherDayAnotherCharterSchoolScandal*; Jeff Bryant, "The Truth about

Charter Schools: Padded Cells, Corruption, Lousy Instruction, and Worse Results," *Salon*, January 10, 2014.

25. Network for Public Education, "California Charters Gone Wild: Part 2—Storefront Schools," October 17, 2016.

26. Jess Clark, "Department of Education Awards $13 Million to Train New Orleans Teachers," New Orleans Public Radio, November 13, 2017; Eric Westervelt, "Where Have All the Teachers Gone?," NPR, March 3, 2015.

27. Daniel J. Losen et al., *Charter Schools, Civil Rights and School Discipline: A Comprehensive Review*, Center for Civil Rights Remedies at the Civil Rights Project, March 2016; NAACP Task Force on Quality Education, *Quality Education for All . . . One School at a Time*, July 2017; Frank Adamson, Channa Cook-Harvey, and Linda Darling Hammond, *Whose Choice? Student Experiences and Outcomes in the New Orleans School Marketplace*, SCOPE, September 2015; Joe Davidson, "Feds Cite D.C. Charters for High Suspension Rates, Particularly for Black Students," *Washington Post*, February 14, 2017.

28. "Bruce Baker: The Relationship between States' Charter Schools and Fiscal Effort," Diane Ravitch's Blog, May 23, 2017, https://dianeravitch.net/2017/05/23/bruce-baker-the-relationship-between-states-charter-schools-and-fiscal-effort/; Michael Leachman, Kathleen Masterson, and Eric Figueroa, *A Punishing Decade for School Funding*, Center on Budget and Policy Priorities, November 29, 2017; National Education Association, *Wraparound Services*, accessed July 31, 2020, http://www.gpsnetwork.org/assets/docs/Wraparound-Services-05142013.pdf.

29. Center for Popular Democracy, *Charter School Vulnerabilities to Waste, Fraud, and Abuse*, May 2017; Valerie Strauss, "What Taxpayers Should Know about the Cost of School Choice," *Washington Post*, January 26, 2017; Jonathan Pelto, "Loosely Regulated, Charter Schools Pose Fiscal Risk," The Hill, November 1, 2016; Network for Public Education, *Charters and Consequences*; Network for Public Education, *Still Asleep at the Wheel: How the Federal Charter Schools Program Results in a Pileup of Fraud and Waste*, December 6, 2019.

30. Journey for Justice Alliance, *Death by a Thousand Cuts*, 21.

31. Journey for Justice Alliance, *Death by a Thousand Cuts*, 4.

32. National Alliance for Public Charter Schools, "About Charter Schools," accessed July 29, 2020, https://www.publiccharters.org/about-charter-schools (indicating that there are 3.3 million students in charter schools); Patrick J. Wolf et al., *Charter School Funding: Inequity in the City*, School Choice Demonstration Project (Fayetteville, AR: University of Arkansas Department of Education Reform, 2017), 11 (calculating weighted average per-pupil expenditure at charter schools across fourteen cities to be $14,200); Drew Catt, "The States Ranked by Spending on School Choice Programs, 2020 Edition," EdChoice, January 28, 2020, https://www.edchoice.org/engage/the-states-ranked-by-spending-on-school-choice-programs-2020-edition/ (calculating total spending on voucher and voucher-like programs to be $2.7 billion).

33. Eve L. Ewing, "Phantoms Playing Double-Dutch: Why the Fight for Dyett Is Bigger Than One Chicago School Closing," Seven Scribes, August 26, 2015; Nadia Prupis, "'Reclaim Our Schools': Cities Rally Nationwide to Save Public Education," Common Dreams, February 17, 2016; Naomi Nix, "Newark Student Protestors to End Four-Day Sit-In against Superintendent," NJ.Com, February 20, 2015; News Advisory, "CTU to Lead Picket before Chicago Board of Education Meeting Calling for Halt to Charter School Expansion," May 26, 2015.

34. John Mooney, "Newark Civil-Rights Probe Mirrors Investigations in Other U.S. Cities," NJ Spotlight, July 24, 2014.

35. Diane Ravitch, *Slaying Goliath: The Passionate Resistance to Privatization and the Fight to Save America's Public Schools* (New York: Knopf, 2020).

36. Ravitch, *Slaying Goliath*; United Teachers Los Angeles, "Our Contract Agreement: What We Won & How It Builds Our Future."

37. All of the Forbes rankings and net worth figures come from one of the following two sources: Luisa Kroll and Kerry A. Dolan, "The Forbes 400: The Definitive Ranking of the Wealthiest Americans," *Forbes*, https://www.forbes.com/forbes-400/#15dbd 2177e2f; Kerry A. Dolan, "Billion-Dollar Clans: America's Richest Families 2016," *Forbes*, June 29, 2016, https://www.forbes.com/sites/kerryadolan/2016/06/29/billion-dollar-clans-americas-25-richest-families-2016/#72e3881e32f5.

38. Meaning they (a) donated to charter schools or prominent school privatization organizations; (b) have made their money primarily from a company that is, or was until recently, a member of ALEC (per "ALEC Exposed," a project of the Center for Media and Democracy), which has been instrumental in advancing the school privatization agenda at the state level; or (c) were part of the Koch network of donors that have also adopted school privatization as a major priority (per Gavin Aronsen, "The Koch Brothers' Million-Dollar Donor Club," *Mother Jones*, September 6, 2011). Luisa Kroll, "Forbes 400 2017: Meet the Richest People in America," *Forbes*, https://www.forbes.com/forbes-400/#4d419 2887e2f.

39. Walton Family Foundation, "K–12 Education," accessed March 5, 2018, https://www.waltonfamilyfoundation.org/our-impact/k12-education.

40. Bill & Melinda Gates Foundation, "Who We Are: Annual Reports," accessed March 5, 2018, https://www.gatesfoundation.org/Who-We-Are/Resources-and-Media/Annual-Reports.

41. Aronsen, "Koch Brothers' Million-Dollar Donor Club."

42. All the figures provided in tables 2 through 5 and 7 through 10 are based on the 990 tax filings available from Guidestar since 1998 for the following foundations: Broad Foundation, Michael & Susan Dell Foundation, Laura and John Arnold Foundation, Robertson Foundation, Tiger Foundation (also operated by Julian Robertson), Lynde and Harry Bradley Foundation, and Doris & Donald Fisher Fund / Doris & Donald Fisher Foundation. For the Bill & Melinda Gates Foundation and the Walton Family Foundation, donation amounts were compiled from their organizational websites. For the Silicon Valley Community Foundation, the available tax filings don't allow for each person's individual investments to be disaggregated, so the foundation's donations are presented in total. For the Fisher family, the available tax filings were supplemented with information on Don Fisher's donations to KIPP and Teach for America in "Philanthropy Roundtable Hall of Fame: Don Fisher," accessed March 25, 2020, https://www.philanthropyroundtable.org/almanac/people/hall-of-fame/detail/don-fisher. "Koch Network" includes the following organizations: Charles G. Koch Charitable Foundation, David H. Koch Foundation, Claude R. Lambe Charitable Foundation, Freedom Partners, Donors Trust, Donors Capital Fund, and TC4 Trust. PRWatch Editors, "Meet the Network Hiding the Koch Money: 'Donors Trust' and 'Donors Capital Fund,'" Center for Media and Democracy's PRWatch, October 29, 2012; Mike Allen and Jim Vandehei, "The Koch Brothers' Secret Bank," Politico, September 11, 2013; SourceWatch Editors, "Koch Family Foundations," Center for Media and Democracy's SourceWatch, accessed March 5, 2018, https://www.sourcewatch.org/index.php/Koch_Family_Foundations#Contributions_of_the_Claude_R._Lambe_Foundation. Because these organizations are not required to precisely disclose the source of their funding, it is impossible to know precisely what the role of Charles and David Koch has been in each of them. However, all these organizations have clear, deep ties to the Kochs, including sizable amounts of Koch money passing through them. Donation amounts were compiled from both 990 tax filings available from Guidestar and from the Center for Media and Democracy's SourceWatch.

43. Donations from NewSchools Venture Fund and Charter School Growth Fund were compiled from 990 tax filings available from Guidestar. The US Department of

Education grants were compiled from information on the department's website. "Charter School Program Grants for Replication and Expansion of High-Quality Charter Schools," accessed March 26, 2020, https://oese.ed.gov/offices/office-of-discretionary-grants-support-services/charter-school-programs/charter-schools-program-grants-for-replications-and-expansion-of-high-quality-charter-schools/awards/; "Charter Schools Program Non-State Educational Agencies Dissemination Grants," accessed March 26, 2020, https://www2.ed.gov/programs/charternonsea-dissemination/awards.html; "Charter Schools Program Non-State Educational Agencies Planning, Program Design, and Initial Implementation Grant," accessed March 26, 2020, https://www2.ed.gov/programs/charternonsea/awards.html.

44. Kayla Lattimore, "DeVos Says More Money Won't Help Schools; Research Says Otherwise," NPR, June 9, 2017.

45. Walton Family Foundation, "Investing in Cities," accessed March 5, 2018, https://www.waltonfamilyfoundation.org/our-impact/k12-education/investing-in-cities.

46. "About Education Matters Funding," *Los Angeles Times*, accessed March 5, 2018, http://www.latimes.com/local/education/la-me-edu-about-education-matters-funding-20151120-story.html.

47. Valerie Strauss, "Mark Zuckerberg Is Giving $120 Million to Bay Area Schools (after His Last Education Reform Effort Didn't Go So Well)," *Washington Post*, May 30, 2014.

48. Network for Public Education, *Hijacked by Billionaires: How the Super-Rich Buy Elections to Undermine Public Schools*; "The $1M School Board Race," *Economist*, November 9, 2017; Valerie Strauss, "Dark Money Just Keeps on Coming in School Board Races," *Washington Post*, October 29, 2017; "The 96 Billionaires Who Decided to Buy Local School Board Elections," *Diane Ravitch's Blog*, June 13, 2017, https://dianeravitch.net/2017/06/13/the-96-billionaires-who-decided-to-buy-local-school-board-elections/.

49. Howard Blume and Ben Poston, "How L.A.'s School Board Election Became the Most Expensive in U.S. History," *Los Angeles Times*, May 21, 2017; Peter Dreier, "Big Money Wins Big in L.A. School Board Race," L.A. Progressive, May 17, 2017.

50. Joanne Barkan, "Charitable Plutocracy: Bill Gates, Washington State, and the Nuisance of Democracy," *Nonprofit Quarterly*, April 11, 2016.

51. Matt Rosoff, "Steve Ballmer Spends $425,000 Fighting Bill Gates over Income Tax in Washington," Business Insider, November 1, 2010.

52. Russell Berman, "'You Better Learn Our Lesson,'" *Atlantic*, October 11, 2017; Mitch Smith and Julie Bosman, "Kansas Supreme Court Says State Education Spending Is Too Low," *New York Times*, March 2, 2017.

53. Danica Coto, "Puerto Rico's Gov Seeks Charter Schools, Raises for Teachers," *Washington Post*, February 5, 2018; Merrit Kennedy and Lauren Migaki, "School Closures Loom in Puerto Rico as Enrollment Shrinks after Maria," NPR, January 4, 2018.

54. Sarah Lahm, "Billionaires Are the Biggest Threat to Public Schools," Common Dreams, May 15, 2020, https://www.commondreams.org/views/2020/05/15/billionaires-are-biggest-threat-public-schools; Katie Ferrari, "Disaster Capitalism is Coming for Public Education," *Jacobin*, May 14, 2020.

55. *Envisioning the Future of Newark Public Schools*; Great Public Schools–Pittsburgh, *Creating a District of Last Resort*; Philadelphia Coalition Advocating for Public Schools, *The Philadelphia Community Education Plan*.

56. Matt Levin, "Bill Gates, Angelina Jolie Top List of Most Admired People in the World," *Houston Chronicle*, May 12, 2016.

57. Jane Mayer, *Dark Money: The Hidden History of the Billionaires behind the Rise of the Radical Right* (New York: Anchor Books, 2016), 33–41.

58. Marc Sternberg, "Our $1 Billion Plan to Create Opportunities for U.S. Students," Walton Family Foundation, January 7, 2016, https://blog.waltonfamilyfoundation.org/2016/january/our-$1-billion-plan-to-create-opportunities-for-us-students.

59. James Hohmann, "The Daily 202: Koch Network Laying Groundwork to Fundamentally Transform America's Education System," *Washington Post*, January 30, 2018; Andrew Ujifusa, "Koch Network Announces New Education Lobbying Group, Walton Funding Pact," *Education Week*, June 29, 2019.

60. Center for Media and Democracy, "ALEC Exposed," accessed March 5, 2018, https://www.alecexposed.org/wiki/ALEC_Exposed. In the past few years, Microsoft, Facebook, and Dell all claim to have ended their ALEC membership. Center for Media and Democracy, "Corporations That Have Cut Ties with ALEC," SourceWatch, accessed March 5, 2018, https://sourcewatch.org/index.php?title=Corporations_that_Have_Cut_Ties_to_ALEC.

61. Brendan Fischer and Zachary Peters, "Cashing in on Kids: 172 ALEC Education Bills Push Privatization in 2015," Truthout, March 9, 2016.

62. National Alliance for Public Charter Schools, "Charter School FAQ," accessed March 5, 2018, http://www.publiccharters.org/about-charter-schools/charter-school-faq.

63. Center for Education Reform, "Just the FAQs—Charter Schools," accessed March 5, 2018, https://www.edreform.com/2012/03/just-the-faqs-charter-schools/.

64. Foundation for Excellence in Education, "Charter Schools," accessed March 5, 2018, http://www.excelined.org/opportunity/charter-schools/.

65. Colorado Department of Education, "Charter School Waivers 2017–18," https://www.cde.state.co.us/cdechart/report-waiversbycharterschool-0.

66. Democrats for Education Reform, "Statement of Principles," accessed March 5, 2018, https://dfer.org/about-us/statement-of-principles/ (referencing public schools' "top-down monopolies").

67. National Alliance for Public Charter Schools, "Data Dashboard," accessed March 15, 2019, http://data.publiccharters.org (listing six charter management organizations with more than fifty thousand students); Monica Disare, "Eva Moskowitz Looks Back at Her Turn Away from District Schools, as She Plans for 100 Schools of Her Own," Chalkbeat, October 16, 2017.

68. Journey for Justice Alliance, *Death by a Thousand Cuts*, 7.

69. Democrats for Education Reform, "Statement of Principles" (referencing how school systems have "become captive to powerful, entrenched interests that too often put the demands of adults before the educational needs of children").

70. Journey for Justice Alliance, *Death by a Thousand Cuts*, 7.

71. Tal Axelrod, "DeVos: Teachers Union Has a 'Stranglehold' on Many Federal, State Politicians," The Hill, November 27, 2018.

72. Center for Popular Democracy, *Charter School Vulnerabilities*; Strauss, "What Taxpayers Should Know about the Cost of School Choice"; Pelto, "Loosely Regulated, Charter Schools Pose Fiscal Risk"; Network for Public Education, *Charters and Consequences*; Network for Public Education, *Still Asleep at the Wheel*.

73. Monte Whaley, "'Historic' Colorado Charter School Funding Measure Headed for Governor's Signature," *Denver Post*, May 10, 2017.

74. Miron, Mathis, and Welner, review of *Separating Fact & Fiction*; Welner, "Dirty Dozen."

75. Noble's 990 forms were accessed via Guidestar.

76. Journey for Justice Alliance, *Death by a Thousand Cuts*, 16.

77. Lynne Marek, "How the Noble Charter Network Connected with Chicago's Business Elite," *Crain's*, February 22, 2014.

78. Marek, "How the Noble Charter Network Connected."

79. Melissa Sanchez and Kalyn Belsha, "Inside Noble," *Chicago Reporter*, February 8, 2016.

80. US Department of Education Office of Civil Rights, "2015–16 Civil Rights Data Collection," https://ocrdata.ed.gov. It should be noted that Noble doesn't operate elementary schools, while the national averages do include those schools.

81. Chicago Public Schools, "School Data," accessed March 5, 2018, https://cps.edu/SchoolData/Pages/SchoolData.aspx.

82. Dusty Rhodes, "Culture Shock: Teachers Call Noble Charters 'Dehumanizing,'" NPR Illinois, April 3, 2018.

83. James Warren, "Some Students Really Pay for Breaking the Rules," *New York Times*, February 17, 2012.

84. Carol Caref et al., *The Black and White of Education in Chicago's Public Schools: Class, Charters & Chaos; A Hard Look at Privatization Schemes Masquerading as Education Policy*, Chicago Teachers Union, November 30, 2012, 4, 35–37.

85. KIPP, accessed March 26, 2020, http://www.kipp.org.

86. KIPP-New Orleans, "Schools Overview," accessed March 26, 2020, https://www.kippneworleans.org/apps/pages/schoolsoverview.

87. US Department of Education Office of Civil Rights, "2015–16 Civil Rights Data Collection" (based on the KIPP schools that reported data).

88. Tim Tooten, "Number of Suspended, Expelled Students Raises Concern," WBAL TV, November 15, 2016.

89. George Joseph, "Where Charter-School Suspensions Are Concentrated," *Atlantic*, September 16, 2016.

90. Alejandra Matos, "New Scrutiny on Suspension Rates in Some D.C. Charter Schools," *Washington Post*, February 17, 2017; 2015–16 DC Charter Schools with Suspension Rates of 10% or Higher, https://www.nonpartisaneducation.org/Review/Resources/DC_Charters_GAO_Susp_Rpt_17_0209.xls.

91. Losen et al., *Charter Schools, Civil Rights and School Discipline*, 10.

92. Sarah Carr, "How Strict Is Too Strict? The Backlash against No-Excuses Discipline in High School," *Atlantic*, December 2014.

93. Welner, "Dirty Dozen" (describing methods used by charter schools to exclude students).

94. Journey for Justice Alliance, *Death by a Thousand Cuts*, 4.

95. Editorial Board, "The NAACP Opposes Charter Schools. Maybe It Should Do Its Homework," *Washington Post*, October 11, 2016.

96. Shane Goldmacher, "Daniel Loeb, a Cuomo Donor, Makes Racial Remark about Black Leader," *New York Times*, August 10, 2017.

97. Dave Powell, "No, Education Isn't the Civil Rights Issue of Our Time," *Education Week*, May 15, 2017; Susan Berry, "Jeb Bush Calls Education a 'Civil Rights Issue,' Quiet on Support of Common Core," Breitbart, January 18, 2016.

98. Journey for Justice Alliance, *Death by a Thousand Cuts*, 19.

99. Dustin Beilke, "New Grants Announced: ED Continues to Pour Millions into Charter School Black Hole," PR Watch, September 29, 2016.

100. Julian Vasquez Heilig, "Truth: Why Vouchers and School Choice Were Created," *Cloaking Inequity* (blog), January 13, 2017, https://dianeravitch.net/2017/02/12/julian-vasquez-heilig-the-sordid-truth-about-vouchers/.

101. Sean Cavanagh, "George W. Bush Defends Legacy of No Child Left Behind at Education Business Conference," *Education Week*, April 17, 2018.

102. Based on a December 14, 2017, Westlaw search for the following terms: "failing schools," "failing school system," "failing public schools," "failing public school system," "public schools are failing," "crisis in education," "crisis in public education," and "education crisis."

103. Sarah Darville, "Echoing Bush and Obama, Trump Calls Education 'The Civil Rights Issue of Our Time'—and Asks for a School Choice Bill," Chalkbeat, February 28, 2017.

104. Frank Luntz, *Words That Work: It's Not What You Say, It's What People Hear* (New York: Hyperion, 2007), 287.

105. Jonas Persson, "ALEC Admits School Vouchers Are for Kids in Suburbia," Center for Media and Democracy, July 22, 2015.

106. Based on a search of these organizational websites on March 5, 2018.

107. Ballotpedia, "Massachusetts Authorization of Additional Charter Schools and Charter School Expansion, Question 2 (2016)," https://ballotpedia.org/Massachusetts_Authorization_of_Additional_Charter_Schools_and_Charter_School_Expansion,_Question_2_(2016).

108. Michael Levenson, "Pro–Charter School Group Pays State's Largest Campaign Finance Penalty," *Boston Globe*, September 11, 2017.

109. Levenson, "Pro–Charter School Group"; Ravitch, *Slaying Goliath*, 203.

110. Gates Foundation, "Awarded Grants," accessed March 5, 2018, https://www.gatesfoundation.org/How-We-Work/Quick-Links/Grants-Database.

111. Journey for Justice Alliance, *Death by a Thousand Cuts*, 13.

112. "After Success Academy's Annual Lottery, 14,000 Children Are Left on Waitlist," press release, Success Academy, April 6, 2017.

113. "After Success Academy's Annual Lottery"; Great Schools Massachusetts, "Governor Charlie Baker—YES on 2 HD," accessed March 5, 2018, https://ballotpedia.org/Massachusetts_Authorization_of_Additional_Charter_Schools_and_Charter_School_Expansion,_Question_2_(2016).

114. Charter School Capital, *Digital Marketing 101 for Charter Schools*, March 17, 2015, https://www.slideshare.net/CharterSchoolCapital/digital-marketing-101-for-charter-schools; Colorado League of Charter Schools, *Stand Out: A Guide to School Marketing*, 3, accessed March 5, 2018, https://charterschoolcenter.ed.gov/sites/default/files/files/field_publication_attachment/StandOut-Marketing-Tookit-2015.pdf; Six Degrees Digital Media, "Marketing Your Charter School Online: What to Keep in Mind," March 11, 2015, https://sixdegreesdigitalmedia.com/marketing-your-charter-school-online-what-to-keep-in-mind/; Dustin Dwyer, "Some Charter Schools Focus on Quality. Others Focus on Marketing. Guess Which Ones Are Winning," State of Opportunity, April 24, 2013; Hayleigh Colombo, "Charter School Offered $100 Reward to Anyone Who Referred Students Who Enrolled," Chalkbeat, January 29, 2015.

115. "Online Charter Schools Spent Millions of Taxpayer Dollars on Advertising to Recruit New Students," Huffington Post, November 29, 2012.

116. Colorado League of Charter Schools, *Stand Out*, 3.

117. Great Schools Massachusetts, "Yes on 2—Absurd," YouTube video, September 27, 2016, https://www.youtube.com/watch?time_continue=30&v=QqXUr3N7lcw.

118. Democrats for Education Reform, accessed March 5, 2018, https://dfer.org/.

119. Stand for Children, accessed March 5, 2018, http://stand.org.

120. Peter Marcus, "U.S. Education Secretary Betsy DeVos Calls School Choice Protestors 'Defenders of the Status Quo,'" Colorado Politics, July 21, 2017.

121. Based on a search in Westlaw.

122. Based on a search in Westlaw.

123. Based on a search in Westlaw.

124. Based on Westlaw searches for media hits within major US newspapers that included both the person's name and organization.

125. Persson, "ALEC Admits School Vouchers Are for Kids in Suburbia"; Diane Ravitch, "The Great Retreat Now Begins: Choice Is No Longer about 'Saving Poor Children from Failing Schools,'" *Diane Ravitch's Blog*, May 6, 2017, https://dianeravitch.net/2017/05/06/the-great-retreat-now-begins-choice-is-no-longer-about-saving-poor-children-from-failing-schools/; Arianna Prothero, "Extending Vouchers into Middle Class Is Florida's Next Move," *Education Week*, April 16, 2019.

126. Valerie Strauss, "The 'Walmartization' of Public Education," *Washington Post*, March 17, 2016.

127. Stephanie Condon, "Jeb Bush Pitches 'Total Voucherization' at Education Summit," CBS News, August 19, 2015; Laurie Roberts, "Koch-Funded Group Spends Six Figures to 'Educate' on Vouchers," AZ Central, November 16, 2017; Kye Martin, "Chicago Teachers Union Opposes School Funding Plan's 'Extremist Voucher Tax Credit,'" NBC Chicago, August 28, 2017.

128. Naomi Klein, *The Shock Doctrine: The Rise of Disaster Capitalism* (New York: Picador, 2007); See also Jan Resseger, "'One Newark' Exemplifies the Shock Doctrine," *The Progressive*, April 28, 2015.

129. The American Presidency Project, "Political Party Platforms," "Parties Receiving Electoral Votes, 1840–2016," accessed March 5, 2018, http://www.presidency.ucsb.edu/platforms.php.

130. For much more on this agenda see Mayer, *Dark Money*; Nancy MacLean, *Democracy in Chains: The Deep History of the Radical Right's Stealth Plan for America* (New York: Viking, 2017); Gordon Lafer, *The One Percent Solution: How Corporations Are Remaking America One State at a Time* (Ithaca, NY: Cornell University Press, 2017); Klein, *Shock Doctrine*.

131. Mayer, *Dark Money*; MacLean, *Democracy in Chains*; Lafer, *One Percent Solution*; see also Center for Media and Democracy, "ALEC Exposed," accessed March 5, 2018, https://www.alecexposed.org/wiki/ALEC_Exposed.

132. Network for Public Education, *Charters and Consequences*, 1; see also Diane Ravitch, "Worldwide, Public Education Is Up for Sale," *U.S. News & World Report*, August 9, 2016; Ravitch, *Reign of Error*, 180–97.

133. Reuters, "Privatizing Public Schools: Big Firms Eyeing Profits from U.S. K–12 Market," Huffington Post, August 2, 2012.

134. Reuters, "Privatizing Public Schools."

135. Journey for Justice Alliance, *Death by a Thousand Cuts*, 24.

136. Abby Jackson, "The Walmart Family Is Teaching Hedge Funds How to Profit from Publicly Funded Schools," Business Insider, March 17, 2015.

137. Valerie Strauss, "The Big Business of Charter Schools," *Washington Post*, August 17, 2012; Peter Grant, "Charter-School Movement Grows—for Real-Estate Investors," *Wall Street Journal*, October 13, 2015.

138. Bruce D. Baker and Gary Miron, *The Business of Charter Schooling: Understanding the Policies That Charter Operators Use for Financial Benefit*, National Education Policy Center, December 10, 2015.

139. Ravitch, *Reign of Error*, 161.

140. Ravitch, 161.

141. Mercedes Schneider, "Tax Credit Scholarships: 'Neovoucher' Profiteering Disguised as Philanthropy," *Deutsch29* (blog), April 8, 2017, https://deutsch29.wordpress.com/2017/04/08/tax-credit-scholarships-neovoucher-profiteering-disguised-as-philanthropy/.

142. Journey for Justice Alliance, *Death by a Thousand Cuts*, 24.

143. Matt Barnum, "An Integration Dilemma: School Choice Is Pushing Wealthy Families to Gentrify Neighborhoods but Avoid Local Schools," Chalkbeat, March 16, 2018; Arun Gupta, "How Education Reform Drives Gentrification," Al Jazeera America, March 17, 2014; Pauline Lipman, *The New Political Economy of Urban Education: Neoliberalism, Race, and the Right to the City* (London: Routledge, 2011); Pauline Lipman and Nathan Haines, "From Education Accountability to Privatization and African American Exclusion—Chicago's 'Renaissance 2010,'" *Educational Policy* 21, no. 3 (2007); see also

Data and Democracy Project, accessed March 5, 2018, http://ceje.uic.edu/publications/ (mapping school closings onto areas of gentrification).

144. Lafer, *One Percent Solution*, 129.

145. For one recent example in a very long line see Alyson Klein, "Betsy DeVos: There's a 'Disconnect' between K–12 Schools and the Economy," *Education Week*, January 25, 2018. The Trump administration's plans to merge the Department of Education and the Department of Labor to better align education policies with employer needs is another. Danielle Douglas-Gabriel, "Merging the Labor and Education Departments Won't Accomplish Much, Say Experts," *Washington Post*, June 21, 2018.

146. Valerie Strauss, "How to Fix the Charter School Movement: Ravitch," *Washington Post*, July 16, 2012.

147. See ALEC's model bills at Center for Media and Democracy, "Bills Affecting Americans' Rights to a Public Education," accessed March 5, 2018, https://www.alec exposed.org/wiki/Bills_Affecting_Americans%27_Rights_to_a_Public_Education; see also Matthew Ladner, *Report Card on American Education: State Education Rankings*, ALEC, November 10, 2015.

148. Center for Media and Democracy, "K12, Inc.,"; K12, Inc., *2017 Annual Report*.

149. Andrew Ujifusa, "Trump Seeks to Cut Education Budget by 5 Percent, Expand School Choice Push," *Education Week*, February 12, 2018; Curtis L. Decker, "DeVos to Remove Key Discipline Protection for Children," Huffington Post, January 4, 2018; Scott Sargrad, "Rolling Back Rights for Students," *U.S. News & World Report*, March 7, 2018; see also Andrew Ujifusa, "Trump Seeks to Slash Education Budget, Combine 29 Programs into Block Grant," *Education Week*, February 10, 2020; Valerie Strauss, "In State of the Union, Trump Makes Clear His Aversion to Public Schools," *Washington Post*, February 4, 2020.

150. Diane Ravitch, "The Demolition of American Education," *New York Review of Books*, June 5, 2017.

151. Miron, Mathis, and Welner, review of *Separating Fact & Fiction*, 5.

152. Journey for Justice Alliance, *Death by a Thousand Cuts*, 22.

153. Mayer, *Dark Money*; MacLean, *Democracy in Chains*; Lafer, *One Percent Solution*; Center for Media and Democracy, "ALEC Exposed."

154. MacLean, *Democracy in Chains*, 154–68.

155. Condon, "Jeb Bush Pitches 'Total Voucherization'"; Roberts, "Koch-Funded Group Spends Six Figures to 'Educate' on Vouchers."

156. Bernie Sanders, "What Do the Koch Brothers Want?," accessed March 5, 2018, https://www.sanders.senate.gov/koch-brothers.

157. Mayer, *Dark Money*; MacLean, *Democracy in Chains*.

158. Adamson, Cook-Harvey, and Hammond, *Whose Choice?*; "Faking the Grade," editorial, *New Orleans Tribune*, https://theneworleanstribune.com/faking-the-grade/; Equity in All Places, *Considering the Impact of Education Reform on High-Risk Neighborhoods*, 2016; "Bill Quigley: Outraged Parents and Students in New Orleans Blast Charter School System," *Diane Ravitch's Blog*, April 28, 2017, https://dianeravitch.net/2017/04/28/bill-quigley-outraged-students-and-parents-in-new-orleans-blast-charter-school-system/; Ravitch, *Slaying Goliath*, 219.

159. Frank Adamson, *Privatization or Public Investment in Education?*, SCOPE, November 2016, 3–4.

160. Adamson, *Privatization or Public Investment in Education?*; Jennifer Pribble and Jennifer L. Erkulwater, "Betsy DeVos Wants 'School Choice.' Chile Tried That Already," *Washington Post*, January 17, 2017; Amaya Garcia, "Chile's School Voucher System: Enabling Choice or Perpetuating Social Inequality?," New America, February 9, 2017; Martin Camoy, "Lessons of Chile's Voucher Reform Movement," Rethinking Schools, http://rethinkingschools.aidcvt.com/special_reports/voucher_report/v_sosintl.shtml.

161. Adamson, *Privatization or Public Investment in Education?*; MacLean, *Democracy in Chains*, 167.

162. Adamson, *Privatization or Public Investment in Education?*

163. Adamson, *Privatization or Public Investment in Education?*; MacLean, *Democracy in Chains*, 167.

164. Mary Ann Ahern, "Emanuel Disavows 25% of School Kids, Says CTU," NBC Chicago, February 27, 2012.

165. For an example of what this looks like in practice see the Boston Consulting Group plan for Philadelphia Public Schools. Philadelphia Coalition Advocating for Public Schools, *The Philadelphia Community Education Plan*.

166. Sanders, "What Do the Koch Brothers Want?"; Hohmann, "Koch Network Laying Groundwork to Fundamentally Transform America's Education System."

167. Deborah Meier and Emily Gasoi, *These Schools Belong to You and Me: Why We Can't Afford to Abandon Our Public Schools* (Boston: Beacon, 2017).

168. Of the 202 constitutions made available by Constitute (https://www.consti tuteproject.org, accessed April 7, 2018), 149 include an explicit right to an education.

169. For examples of what this looks like in practice, the work of Dr. James Comer from Yale University over the past fifty-plus years is the best place to start. See also Linda Darling-Hammond and Channa M. Cook-Harvey, *Educating the Whole Child: Improving School Climate to Support Student Success*, Learning Policy Institute, September 2018.

170. Jeannie Oakes, Anna Maier, and Julia Daniel, *Community Schools: An Evidence-Based Strategy for Equitable School Improvement*, National Education Policy Center and Learning Policy Institute, June 5, 2017; Journey for Justice Alliance, *Death by a Thousand Cuts*, 25–32; Journey for Justice Alliance, *The Journey for Justice Alliance Education Platform*, accessed March 5, 2018, http://beta.j4jalliance.com/wp-content/uploads/sites/2/2017/02/J4J_Final_Education_Platform.pdf; Center for Popular Democracy, *Community Schools: Transforming Struggling Schools into Thriving Schools*, February 10, 2016.

171. See Broader, Bolder Approach to Education, https://www.boldapproach.org, for more information.

3. TOUGH-ON-CRIME FOR YOU, SERVE-AND-PROTECT FOR ME

1. Sentencing Project, "Criminal Justice Facts," accessed March 20, 2018, https://www.sentencingproject.org/criminal-justice-facts/; Margaret Werner Cahalan, *Historical Corrections Statistics in the United States, 1850–1984*, Bureau of Justice Statistics, December 1986, 76; US Census Bureau, *A Look at the 1940 Census*, accessed June 26, 2020, https://www.census.gov/newsroom/cspan/1940census/CSPAN_1940slides.pdf.

2. Bureau of Justice Statistics, *Justice Expenditure and Employment in the U.S., 1971–79*, August 1984, 37.

3. Bureau of Justice Statistics, *Justice Expenditure and Employment in the U.S., 1971–79*, 36; Robert Sahr, "Individual Year Conversion Factor Tables," Oregon State University, accessed March 27, 2020, http://liberalarts.oregonstate.edu/spp/polisci/faculty-staff/robert-sahr/inflation-conversion-factors-years-1774-estimated-2024-dollars-recent-years/individual-year-conversion-factor-table-0.

4. Danielle Kaeble and Lauren Glaze, *Correctional Populations in the United States, 2015*, Bureau of Justice Statistics, December 2016; Bureau of Justice Statistics, *Justice Expenditure and Employment in the U.S., 2015—Preliminary*; Bureau of Justice Statistics, *Justice Expenditure and Employment in the U.S., 2015—Final*; Sahr, "Individual Year Conversion Factor Tables"; Robert Schlesinger, "The 2015 U.S. and World Populations," *U.S. News and World Report*, December 31, 2014.

5. World Prison Brief, accessed June 27, 2020, http://www.prisonstudies.org/highest-to-lowest/prison_population_rate?field_region_taxonomy_tid=All; NAACP, *Criminal Justice Fact Sheet*, accessed March 20, 2018, http://www.naacp.org/criminal-justice-fact-sheet/.

6. Gaynor Hall and Pam Grimes, "Are Surveillance Cameras Making Chicago Safer?," WGN, February 22, 2016; Edward Ericson Jr., "Watching the CitiWatcher: The Night Shift Monitoring Baltimore's Security Cameras," *City Paper*, January 27, 2016.

7. Radley Balko, *Rise of the Warrior Cop: The Militarization of America's Police Forces* (New York: Public Affairs, 2014); American Civil Liberties Union, *War Comes Home: The Excessive Militarization of American Policing*, January 2014.

8. World Prison Brief, accessed March 20, 2018, http://www.prisonstudies.org/highest-to-lowest/prison_population_rate?field_region_taxonomy_tid=All.

9. Seth Stoughton, "Law Enforcement's 'Warrior' Problem," *Harvard Law Review* 128, April 10, 2015.

10. Rachel E. Morgan, *Race and Hispanic Origin of Victims and Offenders, 2012–15*, US Department of Justice, October 2017.

11. "Broken windows policing" refers to the theory that police should be aggressively enforcing even the lowest-level criminal offenses to prevent community deterioration and more serious crime.

12. Substance Abuse and Mental Health Services Administration, *Results from the 2016 National Survey on Drug Use and Health*, table 1.1B (finding that almost half of all Americans over the age of twelve admit to using an illicit drug sometime in their life); Tanya Basu, "1 in 6 Young Americans Have Stolen Something in the Last Year, Study Finds," *Time*, October 12, 2015; Child Trends, *Physical Fighting by Youth*, accessed March 20, 2018, https://www.childtrends.org/indicators/physical-fighting-by-youth/.

13. Only half of all crimes are even brought to the attention of police. National Research Council of the National Academies, *The Growth of Incarceration in the United States: Exploring Causes and Consequences* (Washington, DC: National Academies Press, 2014), 133.

14. Angela Y. Davis, *Are Prisons Obsolete?* (New York: Seven Stories, 2003), 91; Loïc Wacquant, *Prisons of Poverty* (Minneapolis: University of Minnesota Press), 154.

15. Jennifer L. Truman and Lynn Langton, *Criminal Victimization*, 2014, Bureau of Justice Statistics, September 29, 2015, table 1.

16. Alyssa Rosenberg, "The Drug War's Most Enthusiastic Recruit: Hollywood," *Washington Post*, October 27, 2016; Michelle Alexander, *The New Jim Crow: Mass Incarceration in the Age of Colorblindness* (New York: New Press, 2012), 52, 105.

17. ColorOfChange.Org, *Not to Be Trusted: Dangerous Levels of Inaccuracy in TV Crime Reporting in NYC*, March 2015; Sentencing Project, *Race and Punishment: Racial Perceptions of Crime and Support for Punitive Policies*, 2014.

18. Federal Bureau of Investigation, "2016 Crime in the United States," table 25, accessed March 20, 2018, https://ucr.fbi.gov/crime-in-the-u.s/2016/crime-in-the-u.s.-2016/topic-pages/tables/table-25/; US Census Bureau, "State Area Measurements and Internal Point Coordinates," accessed March 30, 2020, https://www.census.gov/geographies/reference-files/2010/geo/state-area.html (land area only).

19. Federal Bureau of Investigation, "2016 Crime in the United States," table 26, accessed March 20, 2018, https://ucr.fbi.gov/crime-in-the-u.s/2016/crime-in-the-u.s.-2016/tables/table-26/table-26-state-cuts/table-26-new-york.xls; US Census Bureau, "QuickFacts: New York City, New York," accessed March 20, 2018, https://www.census.gov/quickfacts/fact/table/newyorkcitynewyork/PST045216.

20. Federal Bureau of Investigation, "2016 Crime in the United States," table 26, accessed March 20, 2018, https://ucr.fbi.gov/crime-in-the-u.s/2016/crime-in-the-u.s.-2016/tables/

table-26/table-26.xls/view; US Census Bureau, "QuickFacts." The police data was unavailable in the FBI files for Winnetka and Highland Park; the number of police officers was gathered from the following: City of Highland Park, *Police Department Annual Report 2016*, accessed March 20, 2018, https://www.cityhpil.com/government/city_departments/police/docs/2016%20Annual%20Report%20PD.pdf; Village of Winnetka, "Police: Divisions," accessed March 20, 2018, http://www.villageofwinnetka.org/departments/police/divisions/.

21. Heather Cherone, "Here's How Many Officers Are Patrolling Your Neighborhood," DNA Info, April 17, 2017.

22. US Department of Education Office for Civil Rights, *2015–16 Civil Rights Data Collection*; Kristen Harper and Deborah Temkin, "Compared to Majority White Schools, Majority Black Schools Are More Likely to Have Security Staff," Child Trends, April 26, 2018.

23. Advancement Project and Alliance for Educational Justice, *We Came to Learn: A Call to Action for Police-Free Schools*.

24. German Lopez, "How Systemic Racism Entangles All Police Officers—Even Black Cops," Vox, August 15, 2016.

25. For this line of reasoning I owe an enormous debt of gratitude to my former criminal law professor, Bill Stuntz.

26. Prison Policy Initiative, "The Hidden Cost of Stop and Frisk," accessed March 20, 2018, https://www.prisonpolicy.org/graphs/stop_and_frisk.html.

27. Louis Nelson, "Trump Calls for Nationwide 'Stop-and-Frisk' Policy," Politico, September 21, 2016.

28. Delores Jones-Brown, Jaspreet Gill, and Jennifer Trone, *Stop, Question, and Frisk Policing Practices in New York City: A Primer*, John Jay College of Criminal Justice, Center on Race, Crime and Justice, July 2013; New York Civil Liberties Union, "Stop-and-Frisk Data," accessed March 20, 2018, https://www.nyclu.org/en/stop-and-Frisk-data; Prison Policy Initiative, "NYC Police Use of Force without Arrest 2010," accessed March 20, 2018, https://www.prisonpolicy.org/graphs/nyc_police_use_of_force_without_arrest_2010_rates.html.

29. ACLU of Illinois, *March 2017 Stop & Frisk Report*; US Department of Justice Civil Rights Division and US Attorney's Office Northern District of Illinois, *Investigation of Chicago Police Department*, January 13, 2017.

30. Alice Brennan and Dan Lieberman, "Florida City's 'Stop and Frisk' Nabs Thousands of Kids, Finds 5-Year-Olds 'Suspicious,'" Fusion; Adam Weinstein, "Meet Miami Gardens: The Stop-and-Frisk Capital of America," Gawker, May 29, 2014; Conor Friedersdorf, "The City Where Blacks Suffer under 'Stop and Frisk on Steroids,'" *Atlantic*, May 30, 2014.

31. Udi Ofer and Ari Rosmarin, *Stop-and-Frisk: A First Look*, ACLU of New Jersey, February 2014; US Department of Justice Civil Rights Division and US Attorney's Office District of New Jersey, *Investigation of Newark Police Department*, July 22, 2014.

32. US Department of Justice Civil Rights Division, *Investigation of the Baltimore City Police Department*, August 10, 2016; NAACP, *Born Suspect: Stop-and-Frisk Abuses & the Continued Fight to End Racial Justice in America*, September 2014, 24.

33. ACLU of Massachusetts, "Ending Racist Stop and Frisk," accessed March 20, 2018, https://aclum.org/our-work/aclum-issues/racial-justice/ending-racist-stop-and-frisk/; American Civil Liberties Union, "ACLU Challenges Milwaukee Police Department's Unconstitutional Stop-and-Frisk Program Conducted without Reasonable Suspicion and Based on Racial Profiling," February 22, 2017; US Department of Justice, "Special Litigation Section Cases and Matters: Law Enforcement Agencies," accessed March 20, 2018, https://www.justice.gov/crt/special-litigation-section-cases-and-matters0#police.

34. Federal Bureau of Investigation, "2016 Crime in the United States," table 18.

35. Federal Bureau of Investigation, "2016 Crime in the United States," table 21A; US Census Bureau, "ACS Demographic and Housing Estimates," 2012–16 American Community Survey 5-Year Estimates, DP05, accessed March 20, 2018, https://data.census.gov/cedsci/table?g=1600000US4033300&tid=ACSDP5Y2016.DP05&q=DP05.

36. Alex Horton, "Body-Cam Video Shows 6-Year-Old Crying for Help as Officers Zip-Tie Her," *Washington Post*, February 25, 2020; Advancement Project and Alliance for Educational Justice, *We Came to Learn*.

37. US Department of Education Office for Civil Rights, *2015–16 Civil Rights Data Collection—Flat File*.

38. US Department of Education Office for Civil Rights, *2015–16 Civil Rights Data Collection—Flat File* (analyzing schools that reported having either seventh grade students or tenth grade students).

39. "Wall Street Millenials Living Fast and Hard," *Barron's*, March 9, 2017; Emily Chang, "'Oh My God, This is so F—ed Up': Inside Silicon Valley's Secretive, Orgiastic Dark Side," *Vanity Fair*, February 2018.

40. Safety beyond Policing, accessed March 20, 2018, http://www.safetybeyondpolicing.com (stating that one hundred thousand New Yorkers are arrested annually for not paying transit fares); Labor/Community Strategy Center, "The Strategy Center Submits DOJ & DOT Civil Rights Complaint against the LACMTA," November 14, 2016.

41. Federal Bureau of Investigation, "2016 Crime in the United States," table 21A.

42. California Endowment, *Community Safety: A Building Block for Healthy Communities*, January 2015; Jamecca Marshall, *Comprehensive Violence Reduction Strategy (CVRS), A Framework for Implementing the CVRS in Your Neighborhood*, Advancement Project, April 2011; Danielle Sered, *Accounting for Violence: How to Increase Safety and Break Our Failed Reliance on Mass Incarceration*, Common Justice, 2017.

43. Center for Popular Democracy et al., *Freedom to Thrive: Reimagining Safety & Security in Our Communities*; see also Schott Foundation for Public Education, *Loving Cities Index: Creating Loving Systems across Communities to Provide All Students an Opportunity to Learn*, February 2018; Advancement Project California, "Healthy City," http://www.healthycity.org; Haas Institute for a Fair and Inclusive Society, https://haasinstitute.berkeley.edu.

44. Color of Change and USC Annenberg Norman Lear Center, *Normalizing Injustice: The Dangerous Misrepresentations That Define Television's Scripted Crime Genre*, January 2020.

45. Alyssa Rosenberg, "In Pop Culture, There Are No Bad Police Shootings," *Washington Post*, October 26, 2016; Adam Johnson, "6 Elements of Police Spin: An Object Lesson in Copspeak," FAIR, January 30, 2018.

46. Karen Dolan and Jodi L. Carr, *The Poor Get Prison: The Alarming Spread of the Criminalization of Poverty*, Institute for Policy Studies, 2017; United Nations Human Rights Office of the High Commissioner, "Statement on Visit to the USA, by Professor Phillip Alston, Special Rapporteur on Extreme Poverty and Human Rights," December 15, 2017; Peter Edelman, "More Than a Nuisance: How Housing Ordinances Are Making Poverty a Crime," *New Republic*, April 10, 2018; "Governor Scott Announces Major Action Plan to Keep Florida Students Safe following Tragic Parkland Shooting," press release, Office of the Governor of Florida, February 23, 2018 (calling for "a mandatory law enforcement officer in every public school"); Dana Goldstein, "Inexcusable Absences," *New Republic*, March 6, 2015.

47. Bureau of Justice Statistics, *Justice Expenditures and Employment Extracts Series*; Sahr, "Individual Year Conversion Factor Tables."

48. For example, nearly 60 percent of middle-aged African American men without a high school degree have served time in prison. Sentencing Project, *Race and Punishment*, 5.

49. Sered, *Accounting for Violence*, 23.

50. Justice Policy Institute, *Finding Direction: Expanding Criminal Justice Options by Considering Policies of Other Nations*, April 2011; Connie de la Vega, Amanda Solter, Soo-Ryun Kwon, and Dana Marie Isaac, *Cruel and Unusual: U.S. Sentencing Practices in a Global Context*, University of San Francisco School of Law, Center for Law and Global Justice, May 2012. "Mandatory minimum sentencing" refers to policies that require a pre-determined term of incarceration for a particular crime, regardless of any surrounding circumstances. "Truth in sentencing laws" refers to those that attempt to eliminate, or at least limit, the possibility of parole, thus lengthening criminal sentences and reducing the ability to tailor sanctions to fit particular circumstances. "Three strikes laws" refers to the imposition of very severe criminal penalties on crimes committed when the offender had at least two prior convictions. Under many of these laws, a "third strike" involving a broad array of crimes would automatically result in a life sentence without the possibility of parole.

51. Sentencing Project, *Race and Punishment*, 7; Marc Mauer, *Incarceration Rates in an International Perspective*, Sentencing Project, June 28, 2017.

52. Sentencing Project, *Race and Punishment*, 8–9; "Black Boys Viewed as Older, Less Innocent Than Whites, Research Finds," press release, American Psychological Association, March 6, 2014; "People See Black Men as Larger, More Threatening Than Same-Sized White Men," press release, American Psychological Association, March 13, 2017.

53. Chris Hayes, *A Colony in a Nation* (New York: W. W. Norton, 2018), 209; Josh Katz, "How a Police Chief, a Governor and a Sociologist Would Spend $100 Billion to Solve the Opioid Crisis," *New York Times*, February 14, 2018; "Race and the Gentler War on Drugs," Color of Pain, http://www.colorofpain.org.

54. C. Eugene Emery Jr., "Hillary Clinton Says Blacks More Likely to Be Arrested, Get Longer Sentences," PolitiFact, February 26, 2016.

55. Jamal Hagler, "8 Facts You Should Know about the Criminal Justice System and People of Color," Center for American Progress, May 28, 2015.

56. Adam Looney and Nicholas Turner, "Work and Opportunity before and after Incarceration," Economic Studies at Brookings, March 14, 2018.

57. William J. Stuntz, *The Collapse of American Criminal Justice* (Cambridge, MA: Harvard University Press, 2011), 44.

58. National Research Council of the National Academies, *The Growth of Incarceration in the United States*, 157–319; Movement for Black Lives, "End the War on Black People," accessed March 20, 2018, https://policy.m4bl.org/end-war-on-black-people/; John F. Pfaff, *Locked In: The True Causes of Mass Incarceration and How to Achieve Real Reform* (New York: Basic Books, 2017), 119–23; Human Rights Watch and American Civil Liberties Union, *Every 25 Seconds: The Human Toll of Criminalizing Drug Use in the United States*, 132–79; Kim Gilhuly et al., "Rehabilitating Corrections in California: The Health Impacts of Proposition 47, Research Summary," Human Impact Partners, September 2014, 8–9; Ella Baker Center for Human Rights, Forward Together, and Research Action Design, *Who Pays? The True Cost of Incarceration on Families*, September 2015; Alec Karakatsanis, "Policing, Mass Imprisonment, and the Failure of American Lawyers," *Harvard Law Review Forum*, April 10, 2015; Ernest Drucker, *A Plague of Prisons: The Epidemiology of Mass Incarceration in America* (New York: New Press, 2013).

59. Justice Mapping Center, https://www.justicemapping.org; Million Dollar Hoods, https://milliondollarhoods.pre.ss.ucla.edu/.

60. National Research Council of the National Academies, *The Growth of Incarceration in the United States*, 130–56. Quote on 156.

61. Alexander, *New Jim Crow*, 8.

62. Wacquant, *Prisons of Poverty*, 133.

63. US Department of Justice, Bureau of Justice Statistics, *Prisoners: 1925–81*, December 1982.

64. Stuntz, *Collapse of American Criminal Justice*, 51.

65. Sered, *Accounting for Violence*, 17–19.

66. Pew Charitable Trusts, *Justice Reinvestment Initiative Brings Sentencing Reforms in 23 States*, January 22, 2016.

67. Pew Charitable Trusts, *Justice Reinvestment Initiative*.

68. Nazgol Ghandnoosh, "Can We Wait 75 Years to Cut the Prison Population in Half?," Sentencing Project, March 8, 2018.

69. Bureau of Justice Statistics, *Justice Expenditures and Employment Extracts Series*; Sahr, "Individual Year Conversion Factor Tables." Note that judicial/legal expenditures weren't available for 1980 and 1981 so they were estimated by assuming that they increased by the same amounts as police and corrections spending in those years.

70. Bureau of Justice Statistics, *Justice Expenditures and Employment Extracts Series*; City of Chicago, *2017 Budget Overview*, 113, accessed March 20, 2018, https://www.cityofchicago.org/content/dam/city/depts/obm/supp_info/2017%20Budget/2017.Budget.Overview.pdf; City of Chicago, *1982 Annual Appropriations*, 108, accessed March 20, 2018, http://docs.chicityclerk.com/budget/Annual%20Appropriation%201982optimize.pdf; City and County of Denver, *2017 Mayor's Budget*, 53, accessed March 20, 2018, https://www.denvergov.org/content/dam/denvergov/Portals/344/documents/Budget/Mayors_2017_Budget.pdf.

71. Communities United et al., *The $3.4 Trillion Mistake: The Cost of Mass Incarceration and Criminalization, and How Justice Reinvestment Can Build a Better Future for All*, 2016.

72. Center for Popular Democracy et al., *Freedom to Thrive*; Justice L.A., Center for Popular Democracy, and Law 4 Black Lives, *Reclaim, Reimagine and Reinvest: An Analysis of Los Angeles County's Criminalization Budget*, 1; ACLU, *Cops and No Counselors: How the Lack of School Mental Health Staff Is Harming Students*.

73. Mike Elk and Bob Sloan, "The Hidden History of ALEC and Prison Labor," *Nation*, August 1, 2011; Center for Media and Democracy, "Minimum-Mandatory Sentencing Act Exposed," accessed March 20, 2018, https://www.alecexposed.org/w/images/e/eb/7D6-Minimum-Mandatory_Sentencing_Act_Exposed.pdf; Brigette Sarabi, "ALEC in the House: Corporate Bias in Criminal Justice Legislation," *Prison Legal News*, January 15, 2002.

74. Elk and Sloan, "Hidden History of ALEC and Prison Labor."

75. Center for Media and Democracy, "ALEC Exposed: Guns, Prisons, Crime, and Immigration," accessed March 20, 2018, https://www.alecexposed.org/wiki/Guns,_Prisons,_Crime,_and_Immigration.

76. Manhattan Institute, "Urban Policy: Crime," accessed March 20, 2018, https://www.manhattan-institute.org/urban-policy/crime; Joseph L. Giacalone and Alex S. Vitale, "When Policing Stats Do More Harm Than Good," *USA Today*, February 9, 2017.

77. Heather Mac Donald, "Mandatory Minimums Don't Deserve Your Ire," *Wall Street Journal*, May 25, 2017.

78. Wacquant, *Prisons of Poverty*, 10.

79. Dana Joel, *A Guide to Prison Privatization*, Heritage Foundation, May 24, 1988; David Dayen, "The True Cost: Why the Private Prison Industry Is About So Much More Than Prisons," TPM, http://talkingpointsmemo.com/features/privatization/two/.

80. Reason Foundation, "Criminal Justice Reform," accessed March 20, 2018, https://reason.org/topics/criminal-justice-reform/; SourceWatch Editors, "Reason Foundation," Center for Media and Democracy's SourceWatch, accessed March 31, 2020, https://www.sourcewatch.org/index.php/Reason_Foundation.

81. Paul Larkin, "Reviewing the Rationale for Stop-and-Frisk," Heritage Foundation, March 24, 2014.

82. Edwin Meese III and John Malcolm, *Policing in America: Lessons from the Past, Opportunities for the Future*, Heritage Foundation, September 18, 2017.

83. Center for Responsive Politics, accessed June 27, 2020, https://www.opensecrets.org.

84. SourceWatch Editors, "GEO Group," Center for Media and Democracy's Source-Watch, accessed March 20, 2018, https://www.sourcewatch.org/index.php/GEO_Group; SourceWatch Editors, "Corrections Corporation of America," Center for Media and Democracy's SourceWatch, accessed March 20, 2018, https://www.sourcewatch.org/index.php/Corrections_Corporation_of_America.

85. Center for Responsive Politics, accessed June 27, 2020, https://www.opensecrets.org; SourceWatch Editors, "GEO Group"; SourceWatch Editors, "Corrections Corporation of America."

86. SourceWatch Editors, "GEO Group"; Sourcewatch Editors, "Corrections Corporation of America."

87. Peter Stone, "Inside the NRA's Koch-Funded Dark-Money Campaign," *Mother Jones*, April 2, 2013.

88. Tim Murphy, "The Big House That Wayne LaPierre Built," *Mother Jones*, February 8, 2013; Alex Yablon, "The NRA Is Talking Tough on Crime Again, Bipartisan Prison Sentencing Reform Be Damned," Trace, June 6, 2016; Jewelle Taylor Gibbs and Teiahsha Bankhead, *Preserving Privilege: California Politics, Propositions, and People of Color* (Westport, CT: Praeger, 2001), 53–58.

89. SourceWatch Editors, "National Rifle Association," Center for Media and Democracy's SourceWatch, accessed March 20, 2018, https://www.sourcewatch.org/index.php/National_Rifle_Association.

90. SourceWatch Editors, "American Legislative Exchange Council," Center for Media and Democracy's SourceWatch, accessed March 20, 2018, https://www.sourcewatch.org/index.php/American_Legislative_Exchange_Council.

91. SourceWatch Editors, "ALEC Corporations," Center for Media and Democracy's SourceWatch, accessed March 20, 2018, https://www.sourcewatch.org/index.php?title=ALEC_Corporations.

92. SourceWatch Editors, "American Legislative Exchange Council."

93. SourceWatch Editors, "ALEC Trade Groups," Center for Media and Democracy's SourceWatch, accessed March 20, 2018, https://www.sourcewatch.org/index.php/ALEC_Trade_Groups.

94. Center for Media and Democracy's SourceWatch, https://www.sourcewatch.org/index.php/SourceWatch.

95. Nasdaq, "GEO Group Inc (The) REIT," accessed December 29, 2017, https://www.nasdaq.com/symbol/geo/institutional-holdings; Nasdaq, Core Civic, Inc. Institutional Ownership, accessed December 29, 2017, https://www.nasdaq.com/symbol/cxw/institutional-holdings.

96. Walter Hickey, "How the Gun Industry Funnels Tens of Millions of Dollars to the NRA," Business Insider, January 16, 2013; Peter Stone, "'Your Fight Has Become Our Fight,'" *Mother Jones*, April 2, 2013; Stone, "Inside the NRA's Koch-Funded Dark-Money Campaign."

97. All the donations listed are based off the 990 tax filings available from Guidestar and information compiled by the Center for Media and Democracy's SourceWatch for the following organizations: Charles G. Koch Charitable Foundation, David H. Koch Foundation, Claude R. Lambe Charitable Foundation, Freedom Partners, Donors Trust, Donors Capital Fund, and TC4 Trust.

98. Lisa Graves, "A CMD Special Report on ALEC's Funding and Spending," Center for Media and Democracy's PRWatch, July 13, 2011; SourceWatch Editors, "ALEC Corporations"; SourceWatch Editors, "American Legislative Exchange Council."

99. State Policy Network, "Directory," accessed March 20, 2018, https://spn.org/directory/.

100. Manhattan Institute, "About: Board of Trustees," accessed March 20, 2018, https://www.manhattan-institute.org/board-of-trustees.

101. State Policy Network, "Directory."

102. State Policy Network, "Directory."

103. Reason Foundation, "Reason Trustees and Officers," accessed March 20, 2018, https://reason.org/trustees-and-officers/.

104. Center for Responsive Politics, accessed June 27, 2020, https://www.opensecrets.org.

105. Joe Catron, "Gentrifiers and Prison Profiteers Are 'Re-Engineering' the NYPD," MintPress News, May 19, 2015; Jacob Sloan, "JP Morgan Chase Donates $4.6 Million to NYPD on Eve of Protests," Disinfo, October 3, 2011; James C. McKinley Jr., "A Growing Call to Limit Lawyers' Donations to Prosecutors," New York Times, November 15, 2017.

106. Justice Police Institute, Rethinking the Blues: How We Police in the U.S. and at What Cost, May 2012, 10; Naomi Wolf, "NYPD for Hire: How Uniformed New York Cops Moonlight for Banks," Guardian, December 17, 2012.

107. Peter Wagner and Bernadette Rabuy, "Following the Money of Mass Incarceration," Prison Policy Initiative, January 25, 2017; Lauren-Brooke Eisen, Inside Private Prisons: An American Dilemma in the Age of Mass Incarceration (New York: Columbia University Press, 2018), 71; Wacquant, Prisons of Poverty, 143.

108. Wagner and Rabuy, "Following the Money of Mass Incarceration."

109. Sentencing Project, "Private Prisons in the United States," August 28, 2017, https://www.sentencingproject.org/publications/private-prisons-united-states/.

110. Wagner and Rabuy, "Following the Money of Mass Incarceration"; In the Public Interest, "How Private Prisons Take Tax Dollars Away from Fixing Our Criminal Justice System," February 2016.

111. Eisen, Inside Private Prisons, 123.

112. Eisen, Inside Private Prisons, 73–75; Center for Media Justice, "#PhoneJustice in Prison, Jail & Detention: Fact Sheet," October 2015.

113. Wagner and Rabuy, "Following the Money of Mass Incarceration"; Eisen, Inside Private Prisons, 76.

114. Wagner and Rabuy, "Following the Money of Mass Incarceration."

115. Eisen, Inside Private Prisons, 75; Wagner and Rabuy, "Following the Money of Mass Incarceration."

116. Wagner and Rabuy, "Following the Money of Mass Incarceration."

117. American Friends Service Committee, "Supervision and Surveillance Equipment," accessed March 20, 2018, http://investigate.afsc.org/screens/supervisionandsurveillance.

118. Eisen, Inside Private Prisons, 72.

119. Eisen, Inside Private Prisons, 73–75, 71.

120. Eisen, Inside Private Prisons, 215–17; American Friends Service Committee, "Community Corrections," accessed March 20, 2018, http://investigate.afsc.org/screens/communityservices.

121. David Robinson and Logan Koepke, Stuck in a Pattern: Early Evidence on "Predictive Policing" and Civil Rights, Upturn, August 2016, 2.

122. American Friends Service Committee, "Supervision and Surveillance Equipment"; Davis, Are Prisons Obsolete?, 86–87.

123. Similar dynamics can be seen around the impact of "low-skill" immigrant labor. Economist Editors, "Wage War: Who Are the Main Economic Losers from Low-Skilled Immigration?," Economist, August 25, 2016.

124. Wacquant, Prisons of Poverty, 81; Autumn Spanne, "Can Hiring Ex-offenders Make Business More Profitable?," Guardian, February 4, 2016.

125. Heather Long, "His Best Employee Is an Inmate from a Prison He Didn't Want Built," *Washington Post*, January 26, 2018; Monique Judge, "ACLU Makes the Case for Giving Formerly Incarcerated a Fair Chance at Employment," Root, June 9, 2017; Spanne, "Can Hiring Ex-offenders Make Business More Profitable?"

126. 70 Million Jobs, "For Employers, It's Not Just Morality and Second Chances. It's a Very Smart HR Decision," accessed March 20, 2018, https://www.70millionjobs.com/page/Its-Good-Business.

127. Prison Policy Initiative, "Section III: The Prison Economy," accessed March 20, 2018, https://www.prisonpolicy.org/prisonindex/prisonlabor.html; Whitney Benns, "American Slavery, Reinvented," *Atlantic*, September 21, 2015; Elk and Sloan, "Hidden History of ALEC and Prison Labor"; see also Pride Enterprises, accessed March 20, 2018, https://www.pride-enterprises.org. Laurel Wamsley, "Bloomberg Campaign Vendor Used Prison Labor to Make Presidential Campaign Calls," NPR, December 24, 2019; American Friends Service Committee, "Prison Labor," accessed March 20, 2018, http://investigate.afsc.org/screens/prisonlabor.

128. Jamilah King, "There's a Pretty Good Chance Your American Flag Was Made by a Prisoner," *Mother Jones*, October 4, 2017.

129. American Friends Service Committee, "Prison Labor"; Prison Policy Initiative, "Section III: The Prison Economy."

130. Elk and Sloan, "Hidden History of ALEC and Prison Labor"; Ethan Huff, "Left-Leaning Microsoft and Nike Both Rely on Prison Labor Camps to Produce High-Profit Products," Glitch.News, March 1, 2017; Christoph Sherrer and Anil Shah, "The Return of Commercial Prison Labor," MR Online, April 18, 2017.

131. Alex S. Vitale, *The End of Policing* (New York: Verso, 2017), 201–15.

132. Angela Allan, "40 Years Ago, *Norma Rae* Understood How Corporations Weaponize Race," *Atlantic*, March 2, 2019.

133. Sentencing Project, *Trends in U.S. Corrections*, 7 (noting that "6.1 million Americans are unable to vote due to state felony disenfranchisement policies").

134. Vitale, *End of Policing*, 48–50, 201–3; Eduardo Bonilla-Silva, *Racism without Racists: Color-Blind Racism and the Persistence of Racial Inequality in America* (Lanham, MD: Rowman & Littlefield, 2017), 42–43.

135. Vitale, *End of Policing*, 49; Gene Demby, "Why Have So Many People Never Heard of the MOVE Bombing?," NPR, May 18, 2015.

136. American Presidency Project, "Political Party Platforms," "Parties Receiving Electoral Votes, 1840–2016," accessed March 20, 2018, http://www.presidency.ucsb.edu/platforms.php.

137. Bruce Shapiro, "Nothing about the 1994 Crime Bill Was Unintentional," *Nation*, April 11, 2016.

138. Jake Miller, "An Unlikely Alliance Forms between Koch Brothers and Liberal Groups," CBS News, February 19, 2015; Ed Pilkington, "Koch Brothers Join Up with Liberals to Tackle Rising Prison Numbers," *Guardian*, February 19, 2015; Kerry A. Dolan, "Billionaire Charles Koch on Partnering with the Left in Congress and on Poverty Alleviation," *Forbes*, April 4, 2019.

139. Michelle Chen, "Beware of Big Philanthropy's New Enthusiasm for Criminal Justice Reform," *Nation*, March 16, 2018; see also PR Watch Editors, "Koch Criminal Justice Reform Trojan Horse: Special Report on Reentry and Following the Money," Center for Media and Democracy's PR Watch, June 16, 2016.

140. For examples see the attempts by Newt Gingrich and a representative from ALEC to deflect responsibility in Ava Duvernay's movie *13th*.

141. Katie Reilly, "Sesame Street Reaches Out to 2.7 Million American Children with an Incarcerated Parent," Pew Research Center, June 21, 2013.

142. Justin Jouvenal, "Raising Babies behind Bars," *Washington Post*, May 11, 2018.

143. Examples include: Communities United et al., *$3.4 Trillion Mistake*; Center for Popular Democracy et al., *Freedom to Thrive*; Freedom Cities, http://freedomcities.org; Movement for Black Lives, "Platform," accessed March 20, 2018, https://policy.m4bl. org/platform/; Ella Baker Center for Human Rights, "Our Work," accessed March 20, 2018, https://ellabakercenter.org/our-work; Justice L.A., http://justicelanow.org; Natelegé Whaley, "The Justice Teams Network Is Mobilizing to End Police Violence in California," Mic, May 4, 2018; Black Organizing Project, *The People's Plan for Police-Free Schools*, 2019.

144. Safiya Charles, "'Please Give Us Justice': New California Law Aims to Hold Police Accountable," *Nation*, May 2, 2018.

145. Advancement Project and Alliance for Educational Justice, *We Came to Learn*.

146. Youth First Initiative, http://www.youthfirstinitiative.org/.

147. PolicyLink and Center for Popular Democracy, *Justice in Policing Toolkit, Policy 5: Racial Impact Tool for All Criminal Justice Legislation*.

148. Movement for Black Lives, "Platform."

149. Justice L.A., Center for Popular Democracy, and Law 4 Black Lives, *Reclaim, Reimagine and Reinvest*; Communities United et al., *$3.4 Trillion Mistake*, 17.

150. Urban Institute Justice Policy Center, "What the Public Says," accessed March 20, 2018, https://www.urban.org/policy-centers/justice-policy-center/projects/community-public-safety-investment/what-public-says; American Civil Liberties Union, *Smart Justice Campaign Polling on Americans' Attitudes on Criminal Justice: Topline Memo*, November 13, 2017; Alliance for Safety and Justice, *Crime Survivors Speak: The First-Ever National Survey of Victims' Views on Safety and Justice*; Sered, *Accounting for Violence*, 12–16.

151. Phillip Atiba Goff, "A Better Solution for Starbucks," *New York Times*, May 30, 2018.

152. Sered, *Accounting for Violence*, 23–24; Common Justice, "Common Justice Model," accessed March 20, 2018, https://www.commonjustice.org/common_justice_model; PolicyLink and Center for Popular Democracy, *Alternatives to Policing*; Fair and Just Prosecution, *Building Community Trust: Restorative Justice Strategies, Principles and Promising Practices*, December 2017; Prison Culture, "Transformative Justice," accessed March 20, 2018, http://www.usprisonculture.com/blog/transformative-justice/.

153. Fair and Just Prosecution, *Promising Practices in Prosecutor-Led Diversion*, September 26, 2017; see also Intercept Editors, "Philadelphia DA Larry Krasner's Revolutionary Memo," March 20, 2018.

154. Colorado Department of Human Services, "Co-responder Programs," accessed March 20, 2018, https://www.colorado.gov/pacific/cdhs/co-responder-programs; Chris McKee, "Mayor Keller Announces New Albuquerque Community Safety Department," *KRQE*, June 15, 2020; Olga R. Rodriguez, "San Francisco Police Won't Respond to Non-Criminal Calls," Associated Press, June 11, 2020.

155. PolicyLink and Center for Popular Democracy, *Alternatives to Policing*; Center for NU Leadership on Urban Solutions, *The Promise of Cure Violence*, May 2016; Barry Carter, "Newark Street Team Builds Trust with Youth to Prevent Violence," NJ.com, March 28, 2017.

156. PolicyLink, "Promise Neighborhoods Institute," accessed March 20, 2018, http:// www.policylink.org/our-work/community/promise-neighborhoods-institute; Alliance for Safety and Justice, "Trauma Recovery Centers," accessed March 20, 2018, https://www. traumarecoverycentermodel.org.

157. US Department of Justice Bureau of Justice Assistance, "Justice Reinvestment Initiative," accessed March 20, 2018, https://www.bja.gov/Programs/jri_background.html.

158. UCLA School of Law Criminal Justice Program, *What Happens After We Defund Police? A Brief Exploration of Alternatives to Law Enforcement*, June 2020; Nicole Chavez, "A Movement to Push Police Out of Schools is Growing Nationwide. Here Is Why," CNN, June 28, 2020.

159. Communities United et al., *$3.4 Trillion Mistake*, 19.

160. Communities United et al., *$3.4 Trillion Mistake*, 15; National Center for Education Statistics, "Table Generator," accessed March 20, 2018, https://nces.ed.gov/ccd/elsi/tableGenerator.aspx; National Center for Education Statistics, "Fast Facts," accessed March 20, 2018, https://nces.ed.gov/fastfacts/display.asp?id=372.

161. Josie Duffy Rice, "Prosecutors Aren't Just Enforcing the Law—They're Making It," In Justice Today, April 20, 2018; Ana Zamora, Jessica Brand, and Rob Smith, *Meet California's District Attorneys: When It Comes to Justice Reform, They Say No Even When Voters Say Yes*, ACLU of California and Fair Punishment Project, August 2017.

162. Movement for Black Lives, "Platform."

4. FROM JIM CROW TO JUAN CROW

1. Box Office Mojo, accessed July 27, 2020, https://www.boxofficemojo.com/franchises/chart/?id=hungergames.htm.

2. US Citizenship and Immigration Services, "Refugees," accessed April 10, 2018, https://www.uscis.gov/humanitarian/refugees-asylum/refugees.

3. Jens Manuel Krogstad, Jeffrey S. Passel, and D'vera Cohn, "5 Facts about Illegal Immigration in the U.S.," Pew Research Center, April 27, 2017.

4. Samantha Raphelson, "Border Patrol Crackdown Shines Light on Rising Number of Migrant Deaths," NPR, January 26, 2018.

5. Aviva Chomsky, *Undocumented: How Immigration Became Illegal* (Boston: Beacon, 2014), x.

6. Catherine Reagor, "Arizona Draws More Baby Boomers Than Every State but Florida," AZ Central, August 13, 2017.

7. Ananda Rose, "Death in the Desert," *New York Times*, June 21, 2012.

8. Erin Siegal McIntyre, "Death in the Desert: The Dangerous Trek between Mexico and Arizona," Al Jazeera America, March 11, 2014.

9. Griselda Nevarez, "Arizona's Undocumented Immigrant Population Inches Up While Nation's Holds Steady," *Phoenix New Times*, September 22, 2016.

10. Population Reference Bureau, "Latinos, Whites, and the Shifting Demography of America," August 11, 2010.

11. Detention Watch Network, "Immigration Detention 101," accessed April 10, 2018, https://www.detentionwatchnetwork.org/issues/detention-101; Detention Watch Network, "Mandatory Detention," accessed April 10, 2018, https://www.detentionwatch network.org/issues/mandatory-detention; Human Rights Watch, *Turning Migrants into Criminals: The Harmful Impact of U.S. Border Prosecutions*, May 22, 2013; Matthew Lowen, "Immigrant Criminalization at the Border," American Friends Service Committee, August 16, 2016, https://www.afsc.org/blogs/news-and-commentary/immigrant-criminalization-border; Grassroots Leadership & Justice Strategies, *Indefensible: A Decade of Mass Incarceration of Migrants Prosecuted for Crossing the Border*, July 2016; American Friends Service Committee, *On the Borderline: Abuses at the United States–Mexico Border*, 2017; American Civil Liberties Union, "ACLU Reports on Immigration Detention," accessed April 10, 2018, https://www.aclu.org/other/aclu-reports-immigration-detention; American Civil Liberties Union, "Defending Civil Liberties at the Border," accessed April 10, 2018, https://www.aclu.org/issues/immigrants-rights/ice-and-border-patrol-abuses/defending-civil-liberties-border.

12. Adam Hunter and Angelo Mathay, "Driver's Licenses for Unauthorized Immigrants: 2016 Highlights," Pew Charitable Trusts, November 22, 2016.

13. Ballotpedia, "Arizona English Language Education for Children in Public Schools, Proposition 203 (2000)," accessed April 10, 2018, https://ballotpedia.org/Arizona_English_Language_Education_for_Children_in_Public_Schools,_Proposition_203_(2000).

14. Ballotpedia, "Arizona Taxpayer and Citizen Protection, Proposition 200 (2004)," accessed April 10, 2018, https://ballotpedia.org/Arizona_Taxpayer_and_Citizen_Protection,_Proposition_200_(2004).

15. Ballotpedia, "Arizona English as the Official Language, Proposition 103 (2006)," accessed April 10, 2018, https://ballotpedia.org/Arizona_English_as_the_Official_Language,_Proposition_103_(2006); Ballotpedia, "Arizona Public Program Eligibility, Proposition 300 (2006)," accessed April 10, 2018, https://ballotpedia.org/Arizona_Public_Program_Eligibility,_Proposition_300_(2006); Ballotpedia, "Arizona Bailable Offenses, Proposition 100 (2006)," accessed April 10, 2018, https://ballotpedia.org/Arizona_Bailable_Offenses,_Proposition_100_(2006); Ballotpedia, "Arizona Standing in Civil Actions, Proposition 102 (2006)," accessed April 10, 2018, https://ballotpedia.org/Arizona_Standing_in_Civil_Actions,_Proposition_102_(2006).

16. State of Arizona Senate, 49th Legislature, 2nd Regular Session, 2010, Senate Bill 1070, accessed April 10, 2018, https://www.azleg.gov/legtext/49leg/2r/bills/sb1070s.pdf.

17. National Council of State Legislatures, *Arizona's Immigration Enforcement Laws*, accessed April 10, 2018, http://www.ncsl.org/research/immigration/analysis-of-arizonas-immigration-law.aspx; Ballotpedia, "Arizona SB 1070," https://ballotpedia.org/Arizona_SB_1070.

18. Andy Barr, "Arizona Bans 'Ethnic Studies,'" Politico, May 12, 2010.

19. US Department of Justice Civil Rights Division, "United States' Investigation of the Maricopa County Sheriff's Office," December 15, 2011.

20. KTAR.com, "Last Inmates Leave Phoenix's Tent City, Jail Formally Closes," KTAR News, October 10, 2017; Valeria Fernández, "Arizona's 'Concentration Camp': Why Was Tent City Kept Open for 24 Years?," *Guardian*, August 21, 2017; Paul Mason, "Joe Arpaio's Prison Was a Circus of Cruelty—Now His Values Are Spreading," *Guardian*, August 28, 2017; Catherine Lizette Gonzalez, "A History of Violence: Joe Arpaio's Racist Crusade against Latinxs," Colorlines, August 28, 2017; Janine Jackson, "Before Trump Pardoned Him, Arpaio Was Promoted by Media," Fairness & Accuracy in Reporting, September 1, 2017; Gonzalez, "History of Violence."

21. Joseph Flaherty, "Seven Jaw-Dropping Moments Provided by Joe Arpaio's Posses," *Arizona New Times*, September 11, 2017.

22. To protect these individuals' identities, I am not including their last names and once again have changed the names of their children.

23. Corey Mitchell, "Latino Enrollment Shrank Where Police Worked with Federal Immigration Authorities," *Education Week*, October 30, 2018.

24. David Becerra et al., "Immigration Policies and Mental Health: Examining the Relationship between Immigration Enforcement and Depression, Anxiety, and Stress among Latino Immigrants," *Journal of Ethnic & Cultural Diversity in Social Work* 29, no. 1–3 (2020): 43–59; Patricia Gándara and Jongyeon Ee, *U.S. Immigration Enforcement Policy and Its Impact on Teaching and Learning in the Nation's Schools*, Civil Rights Project, February 28, 2018; Omar Martinez et al., "Evaluating the Impact of Immigration Policies on Health Status among Undocumented Immigrants: A Systematic Review," *Journal of Immigrant Minor Health* 17, no. 3 (June 2015): 947–70; Wendy Cervantes, Rebecca Ullrich, and Hannah Matthews, *Our Children's Fear: Immigration Policy's Effects on Young Children*, CLASP, March 2018; Maggie Fox, "Trump Immigration Policies Stress Out Parents and Kids Alike," NBC News, March 1, 2018; Elisabeth Poorman, "Houston Lesson: Anti-Immigrant Moves Put Public Health at Greater Risk," WBUR, September 7, 2017; Joel Rose, "Doctors Concerned about 'Irreparable Harm' to Separated Migrant Children," NPR, June 18, 2018.

25. Southern Poverty Law Center, *Under Siege: Life for Low-Income Latinos in the South*, March 31, 2009; Georgia Latino Alliance for Human Rights and National Immigration

Project of the National Lawyers Guild, *The Luchadoras of Georgia: Stories of Immigrant Women and Families Fighting Trump's Deportation Force*, 2017; Human Rights Watch, *No Way to Live: Alabama's Immigrant Law*, December 14, 2011; Southern Poverty Law Center, *Families in Fear: The Atlanta Immigration Raids*, January 28, 2016; Human Rights Watch, *"I Still Need You": The Detention and Deportation of Californian Parents*, May 15, 2017; Human Rights Watch, *The Deported: Immigrants Uprooted From the Country They Call Home*, December 5, 2017; Southern Poverty Law Center, *Injustice on Our Plates*, November 7, 2010.

26. American Civil Liberties Union, "SB 1070 at the Supreme Court: What's at Stake?"

27. Ian Gordon and Tasneem Raja, "164 Anti-Immigration Laws Passed since 2010? A MoJo Analysis," *Mother Jones*, March/April 2012; Reid Wilson, "Trump Spurs Wave of State Immigration Laws," The Hill, August 8, 2017.

28. American Civil Liberties Union, "Lozano v. City of Hazelton," accessed April 10, 2018, https://www.aclupa.org/our-work/legal/legaldocket/lozano-v-city-hazelton.

29. Migra Watch, "MigraMap," accessed April 10, 2018, https://migrawatch.wordpress.com/migra-map-uwd/; Samantha Schmidt, "'Utter Chaos': ICE Arrests 114 Workers in Immigration Raid at Ohio Gardening Company," *Washington Post*, June 6, 2018; Kristine Phillips, "ICE Arrests Nearly 150 Meat Plant Workers in Latest Immigration Raid in Ohio," *Washington Post*, June 20, 2018.

30. Editorial Board, "Arresting Immigrants at Schools, Hospitals and Courthouses Isn't Just Cold-Hearted, It's Counterproductive," *Los Angeles Times*, March 16, 2017.

31. Jynnah Radford, "Key Findings about U.S. Immigrants," Pew Research Center, June 17, 2019.

32. US Immigration and Customs Enforcement, "Delegation of Immigration Authority 287(g) Immigration and Nationality Act," accessed April 2, 2020, https://www.ice.gov/287g.

33. US Immigration and Customs Enforcement, "Secure Communities," accessed April 10, 2018, https://www.ice.gov/secure-communities.

34. Black Alliance for Just Immigration, https://baji.org/; see also Department of Homeland Security, *Immigration Enforcement Actions: 2016*, accessed April 10, 2018, https://www.dhs.gov/sites/default/files/publications/Enforcement_Actions_2016.pdf.

35. Detention Watch Network, "Immigration Detention 101"; US Immigration and Customs Enforcement, *Fiscal Year 2019 Enforcement and Removal Operations Report*, 4–5.

36. Department of Homeland Security, *FY 2021 Budget in Brief*, 25, 31, accessed April 2, 2020, https://www.dhs.gov/sites/default/files/publications/fy_2021_dhs_bib_0.pdf (combining the funds allocated to Immigration & Customs Enforcement [ICE] and Customs & Border Protection [CBP]).

37. Department of Justice, *Immigration & Naturalization Service Budget: 1975–2003*, http://www.justice.gov/archive/jmd/1975_2002/2002/html/page104-108.htm (for 1982–2002 immigration enforcement spending); Department of Homeland Security, *Annual Budgets*, at http://www.dhs.gov/dhs-budget (using actual expenditures on Immigration & Customs Enforcement, Customs & Border Protection, and US-VISIT programs). The figures were adjusted to 2017 dollars using the CPI conversion tables produced by Professor Robert Sahr, Oregon State University, College of Liberal Arts–School of Public Policy, "Individual Year Conversion Factor Tables," accessed April 2, 2020, http://liberalarts.oregonstate.edu/spp/polisci/faculty-staff/robert-sahr/inflation-conversion-factors-years-1774-estimated-2024-dollars-recent-years/individual-year-conversion-factor-table-0.

38. Human Rights Watch, *Turning Migrants into Criminals*; President Donald Trump, Executive Order 13768, "Enhancing Public Safety in the Interior of the United States," January 25, 2017 (describing how one need not have been convicted or even charged with

a criminal offense to be subjected to immigration consequences; merely committing an act that constitutes a "chargeable criminal offense" will suffice).

39. See also US Immigration and Customs Enforcement, "Criminal Alien Program," accessed April 2, 2020, https://www.ice.gov/criminal-alien-program.

40. Gustavo López and Kristen Bialik, "Key Findings about U.S. Immigrants," Pew Research Center, May 3, 2017.

41. Drug Policy Alliance, "Race and the Drug War," accessed April 10, 2018, http://www.drugpolicy.org/issues/race-and-drug-war.

42. Chomsky, *Undocumented*, 186.

43. Bernie Sanders, *Our Revolution* (New York: Thomas Dunne Books / St. Martin's, 2017), 396; Monica Campbell and Tyche Hendricks, "Mexico's Corn Farmers See Their Livelihoods Wither Away / Cheap U.S. Produce Pushes Down Prices under Free-Trade Pact," SF Gate.

44. Chomsky, *Undocumented*, 186–87; see also Telesur Editors, "John Bolton Admits U.S.-Backed Coup in Venezuela Is about Oil, Not Democracy," Telesur, January 30, 2019.

45. Greg Grandin, "Guatemalan Slaughter Was Part of Reagan's Hard Line," *New York Times*, May 21, 2013; Douglas Farah, "Papers Show U.S. Role in Guatemalan Abuses," *Washington Post*, March 11, 1999; Paul Wright, "An Interview with Noam Chomsky on Criminal Justice and Human Rights," *Prison Legal News*, April 15, 2014; Stephen Zunes, "The U.S. Role in the Honduras Coup and Subsequent Violence," Huffington Post, June 19, 2016.

46. Cole Kazdin, "The Violence Central American Migrants Are Fleeing Was Stoked by the US," Vice, June 27, 2018.

47. Lise Nelson, "Donald Trump's Wall Ignores the Economic Logic of Undocumented Immigrant Labor," UPI, October 26, 2016; Associated Press, "Many Illegal Immigrants Have Jobs in U.S. before Crossing Border," Fox News, April 16, 2016.

48. David Wickert, "How the Olympics Helped Lure Latinos to Atlanta," *Atlanta Journal-Constitution*, July 15, 2016; Alexia Fernández Campbell and Mauro Whiteman, "Is New Orleans Trying to Deport Undocumented Workers Now That the Rebuilding Is Over?," *Atlantic*, October 27, 2014; Vivian Yee, "'Please, God, Don't Let Me Get Stopped': Around Atlanta, No Sanctuary for Immigrants," *New York Times*, November 25, 2017; Southern Poverty Law Center, *Families in Fear*.

49. Paul Krugman, "Return of the Blood Libel," *New York Times*, June 21, 2018.

50. Ian Haney López, *Dog Whistle Politics: How Coded Racial Appeals Have Reinvested Racism and Wrecked the Middle Class* (New York: Oxford, 2014), 121.

51. Dartunorro Clark, "Trump Holds White House Event Focused on 'American Victims of Illegal Immigration,'" NBC News, June 22, 2018.

52. Jackson, "Before Trump Pardoned Him"; Eunji Kim, "Immigrants Missing from Immigration Debate," Fairness & Accuracy in Reporting, May 2013.

53. Adam Johnson, "Media Are Literally Copy-and-Pasting ICE Press Releases," Fairness & Accuracy in Reporting, May 12, 2017.

54. Consider, for example, some of the arguments that were commonly, and effectively, used in support of Jim Crow segregation and are still used regularly today to thwart racial justice efforts, such as the importance of "states' rights" in opposition to "federal tyranny," the need for "local control" over policy decisions, and the absolute respect that must be shown for the "rule of law" no matter how unjust a law may be.

55. The US Code of Federal Regulations defines terrorism as "the unlawful use of force and violence against persons or property to intimidate or coerce a government, the civilian population, or any segment thereof, in furtherance of political or social objectives": 28 C.F.R. Section 0.85.

56. Isabel Macdonald, "Marketing the Media's 'Toughest Sheriff,'" Fairness & Accuracy in Reporting, June 2009; Jackson, "Before Trump Pardoned Him."

57. Aura Bogado, "Arpaio v. Immigrants," Fairness & Accuracy in Reporting, June 2009.

58. Zachary Pleat, "How Fox Promoted Convicted Criminal Joe Arpaio, Who May Be Pardoned by Trump," MediaMatters for America, August 22, 2017.

59. Brendan Fischer, "Profit Motive Underlies Outbreak of Immigration Bills," Center for Media and Democracy's PRWatch, August 24, 2011; Beau Hodai, "Brownskins and Greenbacks: ALEC, the For-Profit Prison Industry and Arizona's SB 1070," Center for Media and Democracy's PRWatch, August 22, 2011; Laura Sullivan, "Prison Economics Help Drive Ariz. Immigration Law," NPR, October 28, 2010; Center for Media and Democracy, "ALEC Exposed: Guns, Prisons, Crime, and Immigration," accessed April 10, 2018, https://www.alecexposed.org/wiki/Guns,_Prisons,_Crime,_and_Immigration.

60. Center for Media and Democracy, "ALEC Exposed: Bills Related to Guns, Prisons, Crime, and Immigration," accessed April 10, 2018, https://www.alecexposed.org/wiki/Bills_related_to_Guns,_Prisons,_Crime,_and_Immigration.

61. Katie Lorenze, "Scaife-Funded Network Works Hard to Kill Immigration Reform," PRWatch, May 31, 2013.

62. Heritage Action for America, "Issue Toolkit: Immigration," accessed April 10, 2018, https://heritageaction.com/toolkit/immigration-toolkit.

63. Lorenze, "Scaife-Funded Network Works Hard to Kill Immigration Reform."

64. Reclaim Democracy!, "The Powell Memo (Also Known as the Powell Manifesto)," accessed April 10, 2018, http://reclaimdemocracy.org/powell_memo_lewis/.

65. American Presidency Project, "National Political Party Platforms," "Parties Receiving Electoral Votes, 1840–2016," http://www.presidency.ucsb.edu/platforms.php.

66. American Presidency Project, "National Political Party Platforms."

67. Will Weissert, "Ted Cruz on Immigration: How His Views Have Shifted," *Christian Science Monitor*, February 13, 2016; Rich Lowry, "Cruz Goes Full Jeff Sessions—and It's Great," *National Review*, January 5, 2016; Brian Snyder, "Billionaire Donors Aided Ted Cruz's Rise in 2016 Race," CBS News, January 25, 2016; Center for Responsive Politics, "OpenSecrets.org: Sen. Ted Cruz—Texas," accessed April 10, 2018, https://www.opensecrets.org/members-of-congress/summary?cid=N00033085&cycle=2018.

68. Martin Gilens and Benjamin I. Page, "Testing Theories of American Politics: Elites, Interest Groups, and Average Citizens," *Perspectives on Politics* 12, no. 3 (September 2014): 564–81.

69. Sharita Gruberg, *How For-Profit Companies Are Driving Immigration Detention Policies*, Center for American Progress, December 18, 2015.

70. Samantha Michaels and Madison Pauly, "Private Prison Companies Are About to Cash In on Trump's Deportation Regime," *Mother Jones*, December 29, 2017.

71. Detention Watch Network, "Alternatives to Detention," accessed April 10, 2018, https://www.detentionwatchnetwork.org/issues/alternatives; American Friends Service Committee, "Investigate: Supervision and Surveillance Equipment," accessed April 10, 2018, http://investigate.afsc.org/screens/supervisionandsurveillance; Jason Fernandes, "Alternatives to Detention and the For-Profit Immigration System," Center for American Progress, June 9, 2017.

72. Michelle Chen, "Wall Street's Ties to the Private Immigrant-Detention Network," *Nation*, July 24, 2018.

73. Partnership for Working Families et al., *Wall Street's Border Wall: How 5 Firms Stand to Benefit Financially from Anti-immigrant Policy*, November 2017.

74. Ben Collins and Meghan Sullivan, "Tech Companies Quietly Work with ICE as Border Crisis Persists," NBC News, June 20, 2018; Michelle Chen, "How Tech Workers Are Fighting Back against Collusion with ICE and the Department of Defense," *Nation*, June 27, 2018.

75. Chomsky, *Undocumented*, 49.

76. Chomsky, *Undocumented*, 55.

77. Jacqueline Stevens, "When Migrants Are Treated Like Slaves," *New York Times*, April 4, 2018; Michelle Chen, "ICE's Captive Immigrant Labor Force," *Nation*, October 11, 2017.

78. Catherine E. Shoichet, "Lawsuit Alleges 'Forced Labor' in Immigrant Detention," CNN, April 17, 2018.

79. Southern Poverty Law Center, National Immigration Project of the National Lawyers Guild, and Adelante Alabama Workers Center, *Shadow Prisons: Immigrant Detention in the South*, November 2016.

80. Howard Zinn, *A People's History of the United States* (New York: Harper & Row, 1980).

81. Josh Bivens and Heidi Shierholz, "Year One of the Trump Administration: Normalizing Itself by Working for the Top 1 Percent," Economic Policy Institute, January 29, 2018, https://www.epi.org/blog/year-one-of-the-trump-administration/.

82. Andrea Diaz, "He's Campaigning for Governor of Georgia on a 'Deportation Bus,'" CNN, May 17, 2018.

83. López, *Dog Whistle Politics*, 123; Erin Carlson, "White House Memos Reveal Emanuel's Agenda on Immigration, Crime," NBC5 Chicago, June 20, 2014.

84. Christianna Silva, "Trump Revives His False Campaign Claim about Mexicans Being Rapists," Vice, April 5, 2018.

85. Some of the organizations that have been most helpful have been Puente Human Rights Movement, Padres & Jóvenes Unidos (CO), Make the Road–New York, Mijente, Detention Watch Network, Communities United (IL), Desis Rising Up and Moving (DRUM), and the Black Alliance for Just Immigration.

86. Black Alliance for Just Immigration, "Top 5 Priorities for a Black Migrant Justice Agenda," accessed April 10, 2018, https://baji.org/top-5-priorities-for-a-black-migrant-justice-agenda/.

87. For examples of more detailed policy proposals that overlap in significant part with what is proposed here see Mijente, *Free Our Future: An Immigration Policy Platform for Beyond the Trump Era*, June 2018; Black Alliance for Just Immigration, "Top 5 Priorities for a Black Migrant Justice Agenda"; Sanders, *Our Revolution*, 400–403; American Friends Service Committee, *A New Path: Toward a Humane Immigration Policy*, 2013; American Civil Liberties Union, *ACLU Framework for Immigration Reform*, May 2013; American Civil Liberties Union, *Shutting Down the Profiteers: How and Why the Department of Homeland Security Should Stop Using Private Prisons*, September 2016.

88. For example, the European Union has largely open borders, as does South America and many other regions of the world.

89. Danny Glover and Rep. Ro Khanna, "Real Border Security Comes from a Moral Foreign Policy," *Nation*, July 6, 2018; Fair Immigration Reform Movement, "About Us," accessed April 10, 2018, https://fairimmigration.org/about; American Friends Service Committee, *New Path*, 7–8; Brendan Fischer, "America's Inefficient and Ineffective Approach to Border Security," Center for Media and Democracy's PRWatch, December 23, 2010.

5. DEFEATING GOLIATH

1. Center for Media and Democracy, "ALEC Exposed: ALEC Bills," accessed April 30, 2018, https://www.alecexposed.org/wiki/ALEC_Bills.

2. Philip Bump, "Here's How Much of Your Life the United States Has Been at War," *Washington Post*, August 22, 2017.

3. Alice Slater, "The U.S. Has Military Bases in 80 Countries. All of Them Must Close," *Nation*, January 24, 2018; National Priorities Project, "Federal Budget Tipsheet: Pentagon Spending," accessed April 30, 2018, https://www.nationalpriorities.org/guides/tipsheet-pentagon-spending/.

4. Meredith Bennett-Smith, "Womp! This Country Was Named the Greatest Threat to World Peace," Huffington Post, January 23, 2014; Eric Zuesse, "Polls: US Is 'the Greatest Threat to Peace in the World Today,'" Strategic Culture Foundation, July 8, 2017.

5. Martin Luther King Jr., "Beyond Vietnam," April 4, 1967, Martin Luther King, Jr. Research and Education Institute, Stanford University, transcript and audio, https://kin ginstitute.stanford.edu/king-papers/documents/beyond-vietnam.

6. White House Office of Management and Budget, "Historical Tables: Table 3.2— Outlays by Function and Sub-function, 1962–2025," accessed April 8, 2020, https://www. whitehouse.gov/omb/historical-tables/; Robert Sahr, "Individual Year Conversion Factor Tables," Oregon State University, accessed April 30, 2018, http://liberalarts.oregonstate. edu/spp/polisci/faculty-staff/robert-sahr/inflation-conversion-factors-years-1774-estimated-2024-dollars-recent-years/individual-year-conversion-factor-table-0.

7. Institute for Policy Studies, *The Souls of Poor Folk: A Preliminary Report*, December 2017, 14–15.

8. Noam Chomsky, *Hegemony or Survival: America's Quest for Global Dominance* (New York: Holt, 2003); Noam Chomsky, *How the World Works* (New York: Soft Skull, 2011).

9. Rachel Maddow, *Drift: The Unmooring of American Military Power* (New York: Broadway, 2012).

10. Maddow, *Drift*; Movement for Black Lives, "Invest-Divest," accessed April 30, 2018, https://policy.m4bl.org/invest-divest/; Chomsky, *Hegemony or Survival*; Jane Mayer, *Dark Money: The Hidden History of the Billionaires behind the Rise of the Radical Right* (New York: Anchor Books, 2016), 6; Lauren-Brooke Eisen, *Inside Private Prisons: An American Dilemma in the Age of Mass Incarceration* (New York: Columbia University Press, 2018), 43; Samuel Weigley, "10 Companies Profiting the Most from War," *USA Today*, March 10, 2013; Pam Vogel, "Here Are the Corporations and Right-Wing Funders Backing the Education Reform Movement," Media Matters for America, April 27, 2016 (showing that the Bradley Foundation's fortune was amassed through defense contracts).

11. Center for Media and Democracy, SourceWatch, "ALEC Corporations," accessed April 30, 2018, https://www.sourcewatch.org/index.php/ALEC_Corporations#R.

12. Common Cause, "More Than 200 Organizations Oppose Calls for New Constitutional Convention, Warn of Dangers," April 14, 2017; Common Cause, *A Dangerous Path: Big Money's Plan to Shred the Constitution*, May 2016.

13. Balanced Budget Amendment Task Force, "2019 Campaign Report," accessed April 8, 2020, http://bba4usa.org/report/.

14. Common Cause, *Dangerous Path*; Alex Kotch, "Kochs Bankroll Move to Rewrite the Constitution," Center for Media and Democracy's PRWatch, March 23, 2017.

15. Convention of States Action, "Progress Map: States That Have Passed the Convention of States Article V Application," accessed April 8, 2020, https://www.conventionof states.com/nu.

16. Jay Riestenberg, "U.S. Constitution Threatened as Article V Convention Movement Nears Success," Common Cause, March 21, 2018; Kotch, "Kochs Bankroll Move to Rewrite the Constitution."

17. Center for Media and Democracy, "ALEC Exposed: ALEC Bills"; Mayer, *Dark Money*; Nancy MacLean, *Democracy in Chains: The Deep History of the Radical Right's Stealth Plan for America* (New York: Viking, 2017).

18. Mayer, *Dark Money*, preface.

19. Noam Chomsky, *Requiem for the American Dream: The 10 Principles of Concentration of Wealth & Power* (New York: Seven Stories, 2017), 2.

20. Malcolm X, "If You Stick a Knife in My Back," YouTube video, uploaded by fini-finito, November 5, 2011, https://www.youtube.com/watch?v=XiSiHRNQlQo.

21. This was largely formulated through collaboration with my colleagues Purvi Shah, Jeena Shah, Amna Akbar, Marbre Stahly-Butts, and Krystina François during our joint facilitation of a Movement Lawyering Bootcamp in 2017.

22. Alexi Freeman and Jim Freeman, "It's about Power, Not Policy: Movement Lawyering for Large-Scale Social Change," *Clinical Law Review* 23, no. 1 (Fall 2016): 147–66.

23. Lani Guinier and Gerald Torres, *Miner's Canary: Enlisting Race, Resisting Power, Transforming Democracy* (Cambridge, MA: Harvard University Press, 2002).

24. Padres & Jóvenes Unidos and Advancement Project, *Lessons in Racial Justice and Movement Building: Dismantling the School-to-Prison Pipeline in Colorado and Nationally*, 37.

25. Matea Gold, "An Amazing Map of the Koch Brothers Massive Political Network," *Washington Post*, January 6, 2014.

26. Ashley Parker and Maggie Haberman, "With Koch Brothers Academy, Conservatives Settle in for Long War," *New York Times*, September 6, 2016; Peter Overby, "Koch Political Network Expanding 'Grass-Roots' Organizing," NPR, October 12, 2015; Peter Overby, "Koch Political Network Takes a Deep Dive into Community Organizing," NPR, October 12, 2015.

27. "Astroturfing," *Last Week Tonight with John Oliver*, August 12, 2018.

28. American Legislative Exchange Council, https://www.alec.org/; Americans for Prosperity, https://www.americansforprosperity.org/; State Policy Network, https://spn.org/.

29. Please don't try to interpret this as any kind of pro-life/anti-abortion statement. That's not at all what I'm getting at.

30. Center for Popular Democracy et al., *Freedom to Thrive: Reimagining Safety & Security in Our Communities*; see also Schott Foundation for Public Education, *Loving Cities Index: Creating Loving Systems across Communities to Provide All Students an Opportunity to Learn*, February 2018; Advancement Project California, "Healthy City," http://www.healthycity.org; Haas Institute for a Fair and Inclusive Society, https://haasinstitute.berkeley.edu.

31. Atossa Araxia Abrahamian, "The Rock-Star Appeal of Modern Monetary Theory," *Nation*, May 8, 2017; Stephanie Kelton, Andres Bernal, and Greg Carlock, "We Can Pay for a Green New Deal," Huffington Post, November 30, 2018.

32. Bernie Sanders, "Options to Finance Medicare for All," accessed April 9, 2020, https://www.sanders.senate.gov/download/options-to-finance-medicare-for-all?inline=file; Elizabeth Warren, "Ultra-Millionaire Tax," accessed April 9, 2020, https://elizabethwarren.com/plans/ultra-millionaire-tax. These documents refer to revenue projections over ten years, so what is included in the table is the average annual amount. All other figures were referenced earlier in the book.

33. Communities United et al., *The $3.4 Trillion Mistake: The Cost of Mass Incarceration and Criminalization, and How Justice Reinvestment Can Build a Better Future for All*, 2016, 15; National Center for Education Statistics, "Fast Facts: Back to School Statistics," accessed April 30, 2018, https://nces.ed.gov/fastfacts/display.asp?id=372; Solutions Project, "100% Wind, Water, and Solar (WWS) All-Sector Energy Roadmaps for Countries and States, Cities, and Towns," accessed April 30, 2018, http://stanford.edu/group/efmh/jacobson/Articles/I/WWS-50-USState-plans.html.

34. For example, it's estimated that the investments in clean and renewable energy sources alone would create more than five million "green jobs," far more than would be needed to meet the needs of those who would be displaced as a result of the cutbacks in military, criminal justice, and immigration enforcement spending. Solutions Project, "100% Wind, Water, and Solar."

35. Communities United et al., *$3.4 Trillion Mistake*, 17.

36. Common Cause, "More Than 200 Organizations Oppose Calls."

37. Lawrence Hurley, "Supreme Court Restricts Police on Cellphone Location Data," Reuters, June 22, 2018.

38. Constitute Project, accessed April 9, 2020, https://www.constituteproject.org/.

39. Constitute Project.

Index

Page numbers in *italics* indicate figures, tables, and charts.